Vindicating Socio-Economic Rights

Notwithstanding the widespread and persistent affirmation of the indivisibility and equal worth of all human rights, socio-economic rights continue to be treated as the 'Cinderella' of the human rights corpus. At a domestic level this has resulted in little appetite for the explicit recognition and judicial enforcement of such rights in constitutional democracies. The primary reason for this is the prevalent apprehension that the judicial enforcement of socio-economic rights is fundamentally at variance with the doctrine of the separation of powers.

This study, drawing on comparative experiences in a number of jurisdictions which have addressed (in some cases more explicitly than others) the issue of socio-economic rights, seeks to counter this argument by showing that courts can play a substantial role in the vindication of socio-economic rights, while still respecting the relative institutional prerogatives of the elected branches of government. Drawing lessons from experiences in South Africa, India, Canada and Ireland, this study seeks to articulate a 'model adjudicative framework' for the protection of socio-economic rights. In this context the overarching concern is to find some role for the courts in vindicating socio-economic rights, while also recognising the importance of the separation of powers and the primary role that the elected branches of government must play in protecting and vindicating such rights. The text incorporates discussion of the likely impact and significance of the Optional Protocol to the International Covenant on Economic, Social and Cultural Rights, and looks at the implications of the *Mazibuko* decision for the development of South Africa's socio-economic rights jurisprudence.

Paul O'Connell is a Lecturer in Law at the University of Leicester. He has published widely on socio-economic rights, and the impact of globalisation on human rights.

Routledge Research in Human Rights Law

Vindicating Socio-Economic Rights

International Standards and Comparative Experiences

Paul O'Connell

Routledge
Taylor & Francis Group

LONDON AND NEW YORK

First published 2012
by Routledge
2 Park Square, Milton Park, Abingdon, Oxon OX14 4RN

Simultaneously published in the USA and Canada
by Routledge
711 Third Avenue, New York, NY 10017

Routledge is an imprint of the Taylor & Francis Group, an informa business

British Library Cataloguing in Publication Data
A catalogue record for this book is available from the British Library

Library of Congress Cataloguing in Publication Data
O'Connell, Paul.
    Vindicating socio-economic rights: international standards and
    comparative experiences / Paul O'Connell.
        p. cm.
    Based on the author's thesis (doctoral)—National University of Ireland,
    Galway, 2010.
    1. Social rights. 2. Law—Economic aspects. 3. Basic needs—Law and
    legislation. 4. Economic policy. I. Title.
    K1700.O36 2012
    330—dc23   2011035389

ISBN 978-0-415-60988-3 (hbk)
ISBN 978-0-203-12665-3 (ebk)

Typeset in Garamond
by Keystroke, Station Road, Codsall, Wolverhampton

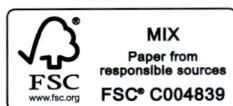

MIX
Paper from
responsible sources
FSC
www.fsc.org   FSC® C004839

Printed and bound in Great Britain by
CPI Antony Rowe, Chippenham, Wiltshire

To Cliona Hannon and all the staff (past and present) at the Trinity Access Programmes, for all they do to make education a right, not a privilege.

Contents

Preface

Over the last three or four years, in the context of the great financial crisis which began in late 2008,[1] socio-economic rights have gained a degree of prominence and urgency, as their systematic denial is implemented through numerous austerity programmes. This book, however, was written (or at least begun) at a time when derivatives, credit default swaps and myriad other products of financial alchemy, appeared to be fuelling a never-ending economic boom that, we were told, would gradually 'lift all boats'. However, even in the middle of plenty, opposition to socio-economic rights was well entrenched. Indeed, the impetus for this study was the trenchant rejection of judicial enforcement of socio-economic rights by the Supreme Court in so-called 'Celtic Tiger' Ireland. In 2001 the Irish Supreme Court held, in effect, that the separation of powers erected a near impenetrable barrier, precluding Irish courts from enforcing socio-economic rights. This study, then, was born of dissatisfaction with the Irish Supreme Court's reasoning, and represents an attempt to answer the question: how can courts play a meaningful role in the vindication of socio-economic rights, while at the same time respecting the separation of powers?

To answer this question I have sought guidance from both the normative standards established at the international level, and, more importantly, from the practical experiences of a number of jurisdictions. In terms of the comparative study undertaken here, it is by no means exhaustive. However, as is explained in Chapter 1, the jurisdictions studied here are pertinent. The lesson that can be drawn from these experiences, in South Africa, India, Canada and Ireland, is that if courts are to play a meaningful role in the vindication of socio-economic rights, then we need to break from static, zero-sum conceptions of the separation of powers. Instead, we need to recognise that all branches of government have a role to play in the protection of all rights, and that in any society with pretensions to democracy it is essential that each branch of government plays its respective role.

While I am satisfied that experience shows, and I hope that it becomes clear throughout this study also, that courts can play a meaningful role in the

---

1 On which, see John Bellamy Foster and Harry Magdoff, *The Great Financial Crisis* (New York: Monthly Review Press, 2009).

protection of socio-economic rights, the unfortunate reality is that current political and economic conditions do not promise much for socio-economic rights. This study, it is hoped, provides a coherent and defensible alternative to the canard that the separation of powers simply precludes judicial enforcement of socio-economic rights, by providing a positive account of an alternative conception of the separation of powers that allows for such judicial enforcement. However, the real battle for those concerned with the protection of socio-economic rights, as discussed in Chapter 8, is in challenging the political and economic orthodoxies that now prevail on a global scale, and are fundamentally inimical to the protection of socio-economic rights.[2]

This study has been a long time in the making, as a consequence of which I have incurred innumerable intellectual and personal debts. In the first instance I would like to thank Gerry Whyte for initially piquing my interest in the subject of socio-economic rights, while I was an undergraduate at Trinity College, Dublin. I would also like to thank Oran Doyle for nurturing that interest while supervising my final-year dissertation. My Ph.D. supervisor, Gerard Quinn, deepened and broadened my understanding of the intricacies of the subject and provided excellent guidance and support throughout the course of my studies. Over time various other people kindly read and commented on one or more of the chapters, including: Danie Brand, Cosmo Graham, Sandy Liebenberg, Aoife Nolan, Colm O'Cinneide, Andreas Rahmatian and Margot Young. I would like to express my thanks to them all. Shivaun Quinlivan read all of the chapters, and provided helpful and insightful comments on each, for which I am most grateful. Needless to say I also owe a great thanks to my parents, family and friends for all of their support and encouragement throughout the researching and writing of this book. Finally, words are a paltry currency through which to express my thanks to my wife Geraldine, but as they are all I have at my disposal here, I wish to express my deepest and profoundest thanks to her for all of the support, help and love she has given me over the years – *'buti na meron ka*.

---

2 See Paul O'Connell, 'The Death of Socio-Economic Rights' (2011) 74 *Modern Law Review* 532.

Table of cases

Canadian

Indian

Irish

South African

United Nations Human Rights Committee

1 Introduction

While the rhetoric of international human rights law maintains that all human rights are indivisible, interdependent, interrelated and consequently deserving of equal respect,[1] the reality is that socio-economic rights have traditionally been viewed and treated as 'the Cinderella of the international human rights corpus',[2] honoured more in 'the breach than the observance'.[3] This second-class status has, among other things, had 'a negative impact on the possibilities to claim effective implementation of these rights, both at the international and domestic level'.[4] And notwithstanding a degree of optimism generated in recent years by an emergent international, regional and domestic jurisprudence dealing with socio-economic rights,[5] a combination of global political developments,[6]

1 Articulated most famously in the Vienna Declaration and Programme of Action, adopted by the World Conference on Human Rights on 25 June 1993 (UN Doc. A/CONF.157/23), which stated, at para. 5, that: 'All human rights are universal, indivisible and interdependent and interrelated. The international community must treat human rights globally in a fair and equal manner, on the same footing, and with the same emphasis. While the significance of national and regional particularities and various historical, cultural and religious backgrounds must be borne in mind, it is the duty of States, regardless of their political, economic and cultural systems, to promote and protect all human rights and fundamental freedoms'. See also Manfred Nowak, 'Indivisibility of Human Rights' in Smith and van den Anker (eds.), *The Essentials of Human Rights* (New York: Hodder Arnold, 2005) 178.
2 Sandra Fredman, *Human Rights Transformed: Positive Rights and Positive Duties* (Oxford: Oxford University Press, 2008) at p. 2.
3 David Bilchitz, *Poverty and Fundamental Rights: The Justification and Enforcement of Socio-Economic Rights* (Oxford: Oxford University Press, 2007) at p. 2.
4 Fons Coomans, 'Some Introductory Remarks on the Justiciability of Economic and Social Rights in a Comparative Constitutional Context' in Coomans (ed.), *Justiciability of Economic and Social Rights* (Antwerp: Intersentia, 2006) 1 at p. 2.
5 Such optimism is exemplified by Langford's claim that 'It is arguable that one debate has been resolved, namely whether economic, social and cultural rights can be denied the status of human rights on the basis that they are not judicially enforceable' (Malcolm Langford, 'The Justiciability of Social Rights' in Langford (ed.), *Social Rights Jurisprudence: Emerging Trends in International and Comparative Law* (Cambridge: Cambridge University Press, 2008) 3 at p. 4).
6 See David Beetham, 'What Future for Economic and Social Rights?' in Beetham (ed.), *Politics and Human Rights* (Oxford: Blackwell, 1995) 41 at p. 43; and Paul O'Connell, 'On Reconciling Irreconcilables: Neo-liberal Globalisation and Human Rights' (2007) 7(3) *Human Rights Law Review* 483.

and continued hostility to the protection of such rights by domestic courts, has insured that socio-economic rights very much retain this second-class status.[7] The arguments against socio-economic rights are something of a hodgepodge, spanning arguments grounded in abstract moral philosophy to more focused, practical arguments about the competence of courts to adequately address cases involving the assertion of such rights, with a lot of blurring of the lines in between.[8] Over the last number of years these arguments have found favour in Ireland and other jurisdictions, and have emerged as a veritable orthodoxy in constitutional jurisprudence,[9] and it is the ultimate object of this study to critically engage with this incipient orthodoxy.

As will become clear in the pages and chapters that follow, the ultimate concern with the protection of socio-economic rights is the fear that providing constitutional protection for such rights will result in undermining the separation of powers by transferring too much authority to the courts, at the expense of elected branches of government. What this study aims to do is show, through a comparative survey of a number of jurisdictions which have grappled with the issue of socio-economic rights, that it is possible for the courts to play a meaningful role in the protection, realisation and vindication of such rights, without undermining the separation of powers. Through an assessment of the experience of other jurisdictions, noting both best practice and potential pitfalls, the ultimate aim will be to articulate a model, or ideal, framework for courts in general to play a role in vindicating socio-economic rights. The rest of this introductory chapter clarifies the terms of the debate, specifying the focus of the study, the main arguments to be addressed and addressing some issues of comparative methodology, before the subsequent chapters embark in earnest on the comparative exercise.

1.1 Socio-economic rights

A preliminary point which needs to be addressed, and which will be dealt with here, is what exactly is the subject matter of this study? The seemingly self-evident answer to this question may very well be intuitively obvious, but we nonetheless profit significantly from taking the time to spell out precisely what this study is about, to avoid, or at least reduce, confusion. To begin with, then,

---

7   As Barak-Erez and Gross note, 'despite the renewed consensus regarding the interdependence of rights, the debates over the similarities and differences between the two sets of rights, and the frequent relegation of social rights to second-class status, persist' (Daphne Barak-Erez and Aeyal Gross, 'Introduction: Do We Need Social Rights' in Barak-Erez and Gross (eds.), *Exploring Social Rights* (Oxford: Hart Publishing, 2007) 1 at p. 6).

8   See Herman Schwartz, 'Do Economic and Social Rights Belong in a Constitution?' (1995) 10 *American University Journal of International Law and Policy* 1233 at pp. 1234–1235.

9   See the Irish Supreme Court judgments in *Sinnott* v. *Minister for Education* [2001] 2 IR 545 and *TD* v. *Minister for Education* [2001] 4 IR 259, in particular the judgments of Hardiman J.; and Gerard Hogan, 'Directive Principles, Socio-Economic Rights and the Constitution' (2001) 36 *Irish Jurist* (n.s.) 174.

the focus of this study is the constitutional protection of socio-economic rights (or to put it slightly differently: the focus of this study is the separation-of-powers argument against the constitutionalisation of socio-economic rights). Now, this preliminary clarification requires the further explanation of the following three sub-matters: (i) what are 'socio-economic rights', or at least what is the understanding of the term as it is used here?; (ii) why the focus on constitutional, as opposed to legislative, protection of such rights?; and (iii) why the insistence on the judiciary playing a part in the enforcement and vindication of such rights? Each of these issues will now be addressed in turn, so that we can then move onto the substantive enterprise with the terms of reference, as it were, clarified.

1.1.1 *Defining socio-economic rights*

As to the first point, there is significant diversity in the ways in which different commentators refer to the rights which are the subject of this study. Commentators refer, variously, to: social rights, welfare rights, economic, social and cultural rights and, somewhat misleadingly, positive rights.[10] There is little or no explicit basis for choosing one nomenclature over the others, and preference tends to be conditioned by either geographical or disciplinary background; with US commentators generally preferring the term welfare rights,[11] British commentators, and social philosophers in general, preferring social rights,[12] and those most au fait with international human rights law opting for the more expansive economic, social and cultural rights.[13] They all refer to the same thing(s), namely 'rights to the meeting of needs, amongst which the most important are the right to a minimum income, the right to housing, the right to health care, and the right to education',[14] but do so in different ways. And while very little turns on the differing terminologies, I will,

---

10 Antonio Carlos Pereira-Menaut, 'Against Positive Rights' (1988) 22 *Valparaiso University Law Review* 359. I say 'somewhat misleadingly' because, as will become clear in section 1.2. of this chapter, the emergent consensus is that all rights have both positive and negative elements, and thus seeking to classify socio-economic rights alone as positive, is something of a misnomer.

11 See Amy Wax, 'Rethinking Welfare Rights: Reciprocity Norms, Reactive Attitudes and the Political Economy of Welfare Reform' (2000) 63 *Law and Contemporary Problems* 257; and Frank Michelman, 'Welfare Rights in a Constitutional Democracy' (1979) *Washington University Law Quarterly* 659.

12 See Cécile Fabre, *Social Rights Under the Constitution* (Oxford: Oxford University Press, 2000); and T. H. Marshall and Tom Bottomore, *Citizenship and Social Class* (London: Pluto, 1992).

13 This rather all-encompassing way of referring to socio-economic rights derives, perhaps unsurprisingly, from the primary international treaty for the protection of such rights: the International Covenant on Economic, Social and Cultural Rights (ICESCR), 1966. See Asbjorn Eide and Allan Rosas, 'Economic, Social and Cultural Rights: A Universal Challenge' in Eide, Krause and Rosas (eds.), *Economic, Social and Cultural Rights: A Textbook* (2nd edn, The Hague: Martinus Nijhoff, 2001) 3.

14 Fabre (n. 12) at p. 3.

for the sake of completeness, explain why the term socio-economic rights is preferred here.

On a very base level, one of the reasons for preferring the term socio-economic rights to the other terms on offer is to make clear that cultural rights, although immensely important in their own right, are not the concern of this study. At a higher level, the term socio-economic rights is preferred here because it 'reflects the inextricable link between the economic and social policy fields' and the law,[15] and therefore brings to the fore the relevance of socio-economic rights to the social and economic status of rights claimants, and the implications that the assertion of such rights has for power relations within societies. Furthermore, the term is understood, both by the myself and others, to have myriad, context-sensitive, dimensions to it. As Ellie Palmer notes:

> Thus, in human rights discourse it is a normative construct that conveys the idea that within a framework of fundamental human rights values, the repositories of collective power have corresponding moral obligations to protect the social and economic welfare of individuals in their jurisdictions. Secondly, it connotes a set of legal rights, for example rights enshrined in treaties such as the ICESCR . . . which impose corresponding legal obligations on states for their realisation. Thirdly, the term socio-economic rights may be used to connote legally enforceable individual entitlements . . . to public welfare provision.[16]

It is because it captures these different dimensions of the rights under consideration, and because it more readily signals the implications which these rights have for social and economic policy, that the term socio-economic rights is preferred here.

As understood here, socio-economic rights are those rights which are concerned 'with the material bases of human well being and include the rights to shelter, to a job under decent working conditions and to subsistence'.[17] More expansively they are 'those human rights that aim to secure for all members of a particular society a basic quality of life in terms of food, water, shelter, education, health care and housing'.[18] Regardless of how one catalogues such rights, they are concerned with the substance of human life, with the very basics necessary for human well-being. Such 'substantive or material' rights serve two important functions,[19] as Keith Ewing puts it:

15 Ellie Palmer, *Judicial Review, Socio-Economic Rights and the Human Rights Act* (Oxford: Hart Publishing, 2007) at p. 8.
16 *Ibid.* at p. 9.
17 Mark Tushnet, 'Civil Rights and Social Rights: The Future of the Reconstruction Amendments' (1992) 25 *Loyola of Los Angeles Law Review* 1207 at p. 1207.
18 Gerhard Erasmus, 'Socio-economic Rights and Their Implementation: The Impact of Domestic and International Instruments' (2004) 32 *International Journal of Legal Information* 243 at p. 243.
19 K. D. Ewing, 'Social Rights and Constitutional Law' (1999) *Public Law* 104 at p. 105.

[Socio-economic] rights of a substantive or material nature are of two types, serving two related goals of equality of opportunity and social justice. So far as the former is concerned this is a question which invites measures of several different kinds, including those designed to eliminate irrational discrimination in terms of access to or participation in civil society, whether in the public or private sphere. But it also invites measures to secure the removal of barriers (based on disability, religion, race or parental status) which impede access to social benefits, and to ensure access to educational, training and employment opportunities to facilitate participation by the individual in civil society to the limits and extent of his or her ability . . . So far as the goal of social justice is concerned, as already indicated this relates to these matters which are designed to ensure that people's basic needs are met, at a level which is appropriate for the community in which they live, that is to say at a level which in some objective way relates to the standards enjoyed by others. As a minimum this means either imposing on the State an obligation to guarantee, or conferring on individuals a right to (i) a minimum level of income while unemployed or incapable of work, and while retired from work; (ii) measures which ensure that people's health needs are met and that they have access to health care facilities; (iii) the provision of adequate housing for citizens and their families; and (iv) the availability of a broad range of cultural, recreational and leisure facilities for those who feel the need to use them.[20]

Socio-economic rights are therefore concerned with the material well-being of individuals and communities, and are, arguably, the necessary corollary of civil and political rights in a morally defensible political regime.[21]

While such rights, needless to say, are enjoyed by every member of society equally, they are of 'particular relevance to marginalised and disadvantaged groups'.[22] This is so for a number of reasons. First, because socially excluded individuals lack the very basics for the maintenance of a decent standard of living, the entrenchment of such rights, assuming that they are acted upon, results in their most pressing material needs being addressed. Furthermore, because such individuals tend to feel excluded from the political and democratic process, and thus tend not to participate in it, they are likely to lack a significant political voice to influence the formulation of governmental policy, which in turn leads to their further marginalisation and exclusion.[23] Ideally, the constitutional entrenchment of socio-economic rights would go some way towards mitigating this disparity, as the fact of such rights would 'become part of the

---

20 *Ibid.* at pp. 105–106.
21 Frank Michelman, 'The Constitution, Social Rights and Liberal Political Justification' (2003) 1 *International Journal of Constitutional Law* 13.
22 Geraldine Van Bueren, 'Including the Excluded: The Case for an Economic, Social and Cultural Human Rights Act' (2002) *Public Law* 456 at p. 457.
23 Michelman (n. 21).

constitutional culture guiding policy-makers and administrators',[24] thereby insuring equal regard for the interests of all sections of society in economic and social policy making. This, of course, is the ideal outcome following the recognition and entrenchment of socio-economic rights; it is by no means guaranteed. And this brings us on to the other sub-issues to be addressed in this section: why constitutionalise such rights and why insist on judicial enforcement of them?

1.1.2 Socio-economic rights as constitutional rights

As has already been said, the focus of this study is on constitutionally protected socio-economic rights, or rather judicial enforcement of constitutionally entrenched socio-economic rights. Consequently, legislative protection of social benefits is not considered. The reason for this is that the concern here is socio-economic rights as *fundamental* rights, whether constitutional or human, not necessarily as Dworkinian trumps, but as being in some sense deserving of special protection, as distinct from legislative benefits conferred on a discretionary basis, and consequently subject to revocation. Such constitutional socio-economic rights impose substantive, binding obligations on states to provide for the social and economic needs of the people whom they govern, as opposed to simply imposing a moral obligation on the state to do so,[25] and should be distinguished from mere legislative welfare entitlements, which are essentially discretionary in nature.[26] There are two primary reasons why socio-economic rights should be protected at the constitutional as opposed to the legislative level. In the first instance enshrining such rights in legislation, subject to repeal, carries with it the notion of a discretionary sop to the ragged masses, and the implicit morality of the old concepts of charity to the deserving poor.[27] While on the other hand the entrenchment of socio-economic rights at a constitutional level represents an affirmation of the needs of people within society, and enshrines them as rights enjoyed by equal members in a community, and not as *ex gratia* hand me downs.

Secondly, and in a more purely legal sense, statutory rights, at least in constitutional democracies with entrenched bills of rights, are of a lower order in the rights catalogue, and are treated as such. Thus, when expedience requires

---

24 Van Bueren (n. 22) at p. 462.
25 In this regard Alon Harel notes, of rights generally, that 'To say that one has a right is different from saying that it would be good, nice, or noble that one is provided with the good in question or with what one desires to have. More particularly, stating that one has a right implies an imperative, nondiscretionary requirement' ('Theories of Rights' in Golding and Edmundson (eds.), *The Blackwell Guide to the Philosophy of Law and Legal Theory* (Oxford: Blackwell, 2005) 191 at p. 191).
26 Palmer (n. 15) at p. 9.
27 In relation to this, see Lucy Williams, 'Welfare and Legal Entitlements: The Social Roots of Poverty' in Kairys (ed.), *The Politics of Law: A Progressive Critique* (3rd edn, New York: Basic Books, 1998) 569.

statutory rights granted in one fiscal year can be diminished, or completely abolished, in the following year. This reduces the value of any such guarantees and, as Asbjorn Eide and Allan Rosas have argued, such fundamental interests as those protected by socio-economic rights 'should not be at the mercy of changing governmental policies and programmes, but should be defined as entitlements'.[28] Indeed, this distinction in the value of statutory rights, vis-à-vis constitutional guarantees, has been acknowledged in Irish constitutional jurisprudence. In *The People (DPP)* v. *Healy*,[29] Finlay CJ for the majority of the Supreme Court held that an accused person's right of access to a legal adviser must be considered to be constitutional in character. He went on to say that 'to classify it as *merely legal would be to undermine its importance and the completeness of the protection of it which the courts are obliged to give'*.[30] For these reasons it is essential that socio-economic rights be entrenched at a constitutional level, so that they are given the fundamental respect which they warrant.

1.1.3 *Judicial enforcement of socio-economic rights*

I turn now to the final issue to be addressed in this section, namely why insist on judicial enforcement of socio-economic rights. There are two important points to make in this regard; the first is that empirical research supports the view that those countries with both constitutionally entrenched socio-economic rights and strong powers of judicial review have been shown to devote more of their national wealth towards the realisation of socio-economic rights. For example, Amy Makinen conducted a study of a selection of 22 OECD (Organisation for Economic Co-operation and Development) countries over time, some of which enshrined constitutionally protected socio-economic rights and/or had strong institutions for judicial review, others which had neither, which showed that countries with entrenched socio-economic rights and strong judicial review tended to devote the highest proportion of their gross domestic product (GDP) to social spending, and the relative percentage of GDP devoted to social spending fluctuated very little over time.[31] In contrast, countries lacking judicial review, or 'unconstrained' systems, experienced lower levels of spending on social programs and greater fluctuation over time in the amount of GDP devoted to social spending and from this Makinen concluded that the constitutional entrenchment of socio-economic rights 'raises the priority of [social] programs in the eyes of legislators, and may encourage groups to lobby for increased benefits. At the same time, judicial review provides an additional veto point on laws that might cut social programs', thus resulting in the overall greater protection of the interests associated with socio-economic rights.[32] A

28 Eide and Rosas (n. 13) at p. 6.
29 [1990] 2 IR 73.
30 *Healy* at p. 81 (emphasis added).
31 Amy Makinen, 'Rights, Review and Spending: Policy Outcomes With Judicially Enforceable Rights' (2001) 39 *European Journal of Political Research* 23 at p. 43.

more recent, albeit smaller-scale, study by Lanse Minkler reaches similar con-clusions, and therefore there is a very strong functional case for the courts playing a positive role in the vindication of socio-economic rights.[33]

The second argument for judicial involvement in the vindication of socio-economic rights is, ironically, related to one of the many arguments against the entrenchment of socio-economic rights, namely that such rights are too vague, imprecise or unsettled to be subject to judicial determination. The fundamental problem with this argument is its circularity: if socio-economic rights are indeed vague and imprecise, and in many respects they are, then this is because most domestic courts have refused to engage with them over the years, and generate jurisprudence clarifying the contours of specific socio-economic rights. As Fons Coomans notes 'it is primarily the failure of national courts to give judicial consideration to economic and social rights, which has meant that those rights have remained largely meaningless in practice'.[34] It is rather a case of putting the cart before the horse to argue that courts cannot adjudicate on rights that are vague because courts have not adjudicated on them. Rather, the fact that courts have historically neglected socio-economic rights is another positive argument as to why courts should play a role in their enforcement. If the lan-guage of indivisibility of human rights is to be anything more than rhetoric, it will require, among other things, courts to play a role in developing and clarifying our understanding of these rights so as to assist in their vindication.

These, then, are the broad terms of reference for the discussion that will follow in the rest of this study. The focus is the judicial enforcement of con-stitutionally entrenched socio-economic rights, and it is this specific category which is the focus for the reasons set out above. In the next section of this chapter we will consider the various arguments against the protection of socio-economic rights, and, more specifically, will try to show how, in truth, the hodgepodge of arguments against the protections of socio-economic rights can, reasonably, be reduced to one overarching concern which sees the judicial enforcement of socio-economic rights as fundamentally at variance with the separation of powers. The penultimate section of this chapter clarifies certain issues of com-parative constitutional methodology, before some final prefatory remarks bring this chapter to a close.

1.2 The 'problem' with socio-economic rights

There is a significant degree of confusion, and a certain muddying of the waters, with respect to the composite arguments made against socio-economic rights. Such arguments tend to be articulated in two distinct, albeit interrelated, forms:

32 *Ibid.*; see also Kim Lane Scheppele, 'A Realpolitik Defense of Social Rights' (2004) 82 *Texas Law Review* 1921.
33 Lanse Minkler, 'Economic Rights and Political Decision Making' (2009) 31 *Human Rights Quarterly* 368.
34 Coomans (n. 4) at p. 3.

philosophical arguments of principle and more limited arguments of practicality.[35] There are two standout arguments of principle against the protection of socio-economic rights. The first is that socio-economic rights are simply not real rights, in any meaningful sense.[36] The second noteworthy argument of principle is that the judicial enforcement of socio-economic rights is, fundamentally, at variance with a democratic form of government and should therefore not be undertaken.[37] Now, while the functional distinction between arguments of principle and practicality has its uses, it is also limited, as certain of the arguments against socio-economic rights straddle the border of these two categories. For example a more nuanced account of the democracy argument is that judicial enforcement of socio-economic rights 'saps at the sinews' of democracy by undermining the constitutionally mandated separation of powers;[38] this seems, at least implicitly, to be less an absolute, principled rejection of socio-economic rights, and more a practical argument which invites an inquiry into the appropriate balance to be struck between the courts and the elected branches of government.

Leaving aside these somewhat straightforward arguments of principle, we then confront a hodgepodge of arguments against the protection of socio-economic rights, which seek to differentiate them from civil and political rights, and thereby exclude them from constitutional protection and judicial enforcement, on the basis of a number of supposedly inherent dichotomies between the two sets of rights, which masquerade under the rather nebulous, umbrella concept of non-justiciability. These arguments include, but are not limited to:[39] the assertion that socio-economic rights, unlike civil and political rights, are by their nature resource intensive, and consequently unrealisable in practice;[40] the claim that courts cannot adjudicate on socio-economic rights because of the positive obligations they impose, whereas civil and political rights are said to impose only negative obligations;[41] the claim that the courts, because of their procedural setup and the skill set available to the average judge, are institutionally ill-suited to adjudicate on matters with potentially significant economic and social policy implications;[42] and the rather nebulous claim, which is both

---

35 Schwartz (n. 8) at pp. 1234–1235; and Ida Elisabeth Koch, 'The Justiciability of Indivisible Human Rights' (2003) 2 *Nordic Journal of International Law* 3 at p. 5.

36 Aryeh Neier, 'Social and Economic Rights: A Critique' (2006) 13(2) *Human Rights Brief* 1; and Erich Weede, 'Human Rights, Limited Government and Capitalism' (2008) 28 *Cato Journal* 35.

37 Neier and Weede (n. 36).

38 See Gerard Hogan, 'Judicial Review and Socio-Economic Rights' in Sarkin and Binchy (eds.), *Human Rights, the Citizen and the State: South African and Irish Perspectives* (Dublin: Round Hall Sweet and Maxwell, 2001) 1 at p. 12.

39 This, non-exhaustive list is drawn from the useful summary provided by Koch (n. 35) at p. 5.

40 Neier (n. 36) at p. 1; and Hogan (n. 9) at p. 189.

41 See Timothy Macklem, 'Entrenching Bills of Rights' (2006) 26 *Oxford Journal of Legal Studies* 107 at pp. 115–120.

42 Captured famously in Fuller's concept of polycentric disputes: Lon Fuller, 'The Forms and Limits of Adjudication' (1978) 92 *Harvard Law Review* 353.

an argument in its own right and an umbrella term for all of the arguments against socio-economic rights, that they are non-justiciable.[43]

Each of these arguments has been rehearsed, refuted and reasserted by a multitude of commentators over the last 40 years or more, and it is not my objective here to simply retrace their steps along these well-worn tracks. Nor is it my intention in this study to adopt the classically defensive position which supporters of socio-economic rights tend to, and exhaust myself refuting the myriad arguments against socio-economic rights. Rather, the object of this study is to articulate a positive argument for the judicial enforcement of socio-economic rights, with a focus on the practical objections to socio-economic rights; specifically it will be argued that the various arguments of practicality are best understood as being intimately related aspects of one central objection, namely a concern about how to strike the balance between the judiciary and the other branches of government in the context of vindicating socio-economic rights. However, in the interests of completeness, I will very briefly address the two primary arguments of principle against socio-economic rights, before taking more time to spell out the ultimate practical argument against socio-economic rights.

1.2.1 *Principled objections to socio-economic rights*

The first substantive argument of principle is that the term socio-economic rights is a misnomer, as the interests associated with this category of claims are not real rights, in the way in which civil and political rights are; but instead are merely aspirational goals to be realised over time.[44] According to Daphne Barak-Erez and Aeyal Gross, this type of argument is grounded, ultimately, on an 'ideological bias'.[45] And this ideological bias, in turn, rests either on the Lockean premise that atomistic, rational and atavistic individuals require only certain, limited civil liberties in order to flourish in a community;[46] or, at a baser level, on the self-serving rhetoric of neo-liberalism which justifies a limited set of 'market friendly' rights, small government and 'market solutions' ostensibly to enhance and improve human welfare, but which in fact serves the material interests of global economic elites.[47] To say that this argument is ultimately one of ideology is not to be pejorative or dismissive; rather it is simply to allow us to say that this is not the place to address this present argument.

---

43   Michael Dennis and David Stewart, 'Justiciability of Economic, Social and Cultural Rights: Should There Be an International Complaints Mechanism to Adjudicate the Rights to Food, Water, Housing and Health?' (2004) 98 *American Journal of International Law* 462.

44   Dennis and Stewart (n. 43); Neier (n. 36); and Weede (n. 36).

45   Barak-Erez and Gross (n. 7) at p. 7.

46   See Jeanne M. Woods, 'Justiciable Social Rights as a Critique of the Liberal Paradigm' (2003) 38 *Texas International Law Journal* 763.

47   See O'Connell (n. 6).

Instead, this study operates on the (admittedly contestable) positivist assumption that, because they are enshrined in various international treaties and a limited number of domestic constitutions, socio-economic rights are real rights. What is more, I accept the coherence and veracity of a number of philosophical arguments which have been advanced to justify socio-economic rights as rights,[48] and do not intend to simply reproduce or rehash these arguments here. Ultimately, ideological arguments such as these, while central, will only be resolved in the political arena, and as the focus of this study is limited to identifying the extent to which institutional arrangements can be put in place which allow the courts to play a meaningful role in the vindication of socio-economic rights while upholding the separation of powers, it is best to say that there are strong and persuasive arguments against this one, and leave it at that for the time being.

The second major argument of principle, that judicial enforcement of socio-economic rights is fundamentally at variance with democracy, is, in truth, a rehashed version of the old chestnut, and perennial obsession of constitutional lawyers the world over, namely the concern that judicial enforcement of constitutional rights, regardless of whether they are socio-economic or civil and political in nature, is democratically suspect.[49] However, if this line of argument is to be dispositive, it must be followed through to its logical conclusion; that is to say that if one opposes judicial enforcement of socio-economic rights on the basis that the realisation of such rights is quintessentially a political matter, which should be left to the elected branches of government, then one cannot logically distinguish between this and judicial enforcement of core civil and political rights. For example, if a government is elected primarily, or at least in large part, on the basis that it promises to both imprison for life and chemically castrate convicted paedophiles, why should courts be allowed to overturn legislation providing for such punishment as a breach of the right not to be subject to inhuman and degrading treatment, for example, when this is clearly a direct and temporally proximate manifestation of the popular will, but not be allowed to find a violation of the right to education where the government refuses, for example, to fund education for children with special educational needs? Both cases, assuming the respective rights are constitutionally entrenched, involve the assertion and judicial determination of whether or not a breach of rights has occurred, and if opponents of socio-economic rights argue that the latter example is democratically suspect, then surely they must say the same about

---

48 See, for example, Fredman (n. 2); Bilchitz (n. 3); Fabre (n. 12); and James Nickel, 'Poverty and Rights' (2005) 55 *Philosophical Quarterly* 385.

49 Otherwise known as the 'counter-majoritarian problem', see Barry Friedman, 'The Counter-Majoritarian Problem and the Pathology of Constitutional Scholarship' (2001) 95 *North-Western University Law Review* 933; and the recent exchange between Waldron and Fallon: Jeremy Waldron, 'The Core of the Case Against Judicial Review' (2006) 115 *Yale Law Journal* 1346; and Richard Fallon, 'The Core of an Uneasy Case for Judicial Review' (2008) 121 *Harvard Law Review* 1693.

the former case. This, however, is not the case, as many of the most fervent opponents of socio-economic rights are also advocates of judicial enforcement 'of very strong civil and political rights' protections.[50] In the absence of consistency, it is submitted that this argument is unsustainable, and therefore we can now turn our attention to the collection of practical arguments against the judicial enforcement of socio-economic rights which, it will be shown, really come down to the one central issue.

1.2.2 Untangling the knot: the ultimate objection to socio-economic rights

With the contested questions of principle put to one side, we can now focus on the hodgepodge of practical arguments against the protection of socio-economic rights. The arguments in question are: the issue of resources, the positive–negative dichotomy, the courts' limited institutional capacity and the nebulous idea of non-justiciability. It will be shown here that all of these arguments, in truth, fold into one overarching argument, which is that the judicial enforcement of socio-economic rights undermines the separation of powers. The American constitutional scholar Richard Fallon provides us with a useful framework for understanding the interrelationship between the seemingly distinct arguments against the judicial enforcement of socio-economic rights, and the way in which they all, ultimately, can be reduced to the one fundamental concern, namely that of the appropriate role for the courts in the vindication of such rights. Fallon begins by dismissing the conventional, neat distinction between different stages of the judicial process; admissibility or justiciability, merits and remedy. He argues that these various stages are not as rigid and static as they are often presented, but instead that courts 'view justiciability, substantive, and remedial doctrines as components of an integrated package and . . . seek an optimal balance among them rather than viewing each in isolation'.[51] He argues that consequently when 'determining which claims to uphold on the merits, courts will almost irresistibly tend to peek ahead at the remedial consequences and weigh their acceptability',[52] and similarly that '[implicit] judgments about appropriate judicial remedies exert an important, almost pervasive influence on justiciability doctrines'.[53] The ultimate conclusion to be drawn from this interconnectedness is that 'judicial apprehensions about practically necessary and acceptable remedies influence rulings concerning substantive rights. In crude terms, when courts are troubled about the remedial implications of upholding a substantive claim, they can and sometimes

---

50 Neier (n. 36) at p. 2; and Macklem (n. 41).
51 Richard Fallon, 'The Linkage Between Justiciability and Remedies – and Their Connection to Substantive Rights' (2006) 92 *Virginia Law Review* 633 at p. 705.
52 *Ibid.* at p. 642.
53 *Ibid.* at p. 643.

do respond by declining to recognize the substantive right at all'.[54] Bearing Fallon's insight in mind we can now look at each of the arguments, and the way in which they ultimately collapse back into the overarching concern about the role of the courts.

To look first at the question of resources, it can be said, on the substantive side, that it is inaccurate to say that civil and political rights are free and socio-economic rights are resource intensive. The first response to this argument is that it is common cause that certain civil and political rights, the right to legal representation or the right to participate in elections, will involve considerable costs, whereas the socio-economic rights to join trade unions, or to the peaceful enjoyment of one's home, are cost free, and therefore the argument is more hyperbolic than substantive.[55] Even more to the point, empirical research demonstrates that 'there is no evidence that enforceable [socio-economic rights] means that the government must spend itself into the poorhouse'.[56] All of this is somewhat beside the point, but nonetheless illustrates the weakness of the argument. With respect to the central argument of this chapter it can be shown that the resource argument makes two assumptions about socio-economic rights which implicate, and problematise, the role of the courts in the enforcement of such rights. The first assumption is that socio-economic rights are in some sense absolute or unqualified, and the second is that the only role the courts can play with respect to socio-economic rights is to issue demanding mandatory orders. Both of these assumptions, as the discussions in the chapters which follow will show, are unfounded; but it can nonetheless be seen how they could ground an ultimate concern about the role of the courts in the enforcement of socio-economic rights, and how the concern can be addressed by articulating an appropriate role for the courts.

The next argument then is that the courts are institutionally ill-suited or ill-equipped to deal with the sort of issues implicated in cases involving the assertion of socio-economic rights. This argument builds on Lon Fuller's concept of polycentric disputes.[57] Fuller defined polycentric disputes in a general sense as being cases which 'involve many affected parties and a somewhat fluid state of affairs'.[58] As an archetypal example Fuller noted any case which would concern the distribution or otherwise of public funds, and concluded that such cases 'present too strong a polycentric aspect to be suitable for adjudication'.[59] On a substantive level this argument can be criticised for incoherence, for if it justifies excluding the courts from addressing socio-economic rights cases on the basis of their resource implications, then surely it should also exclude courts

---

54 *Ibid.* at pp. 684–685.
55 See Paul Hunt, *Reclaiming Social Rights: International and Comparative Perspectives* (Aldershot: Dartmouth, 1996) at pp. 55–57.
56 Makinen (n. 31) at p. 43.
57 Jeff King, 'The Pervasiveness of Polycentricity' (2008) *Public Law* 101.
58 Fuller (n. 42) at p. 397.
59 *Ibid.* at p. 400.

from adjudicating on issues such as tax appeals, which patently have resource implications, but are nonetheless routinely dealt with by the courts.[60] Alternatively, and being somewhat flippant, we could adopt Paul Hunt's approach of saying that if the institutional and procedural status quo is a barrier to adjudicating on socio-economic rights, and we wish to adjudicate on such rights, then change the structures.[61] Again, leaving aside the substantive flaws in this argument, we can see that it too makes certain assumptions about the judicial role in the enforcement of socio-economic rights, namely that the courts will be obliged to take sole responsibility for remedying any apprehended violations of constitutionally entrenched socio-economic rights, thus implicating the role of the courts as the central concern.

We turn now to the positive–negative dichotomy. This argument posits an inherent difference between positive socio-economic rights and negative civil and political rights, with the latter being appropriate for judicial enforcement, and the former being wholly unsuited.[62] The most that can be said for this argument is that it wears its separation-of-powers concerns on its sleeve; it unfortunately also overstates the problem. In many respects this argument has been obviated by the development, initially by Henry Shue, of a tripartite typology which acknowledges that all human rights impose three levels of obligation on states: the obligation to respect, protect and fulfil.[63] This taxonomy thus reveals that all human rights, both socio-economic and civil and political, impose a bundle of both positive and negative obligations on states. Following the articulation and popularisation of this typology, most commentators, excluding the most ideologically obstinate, have come around to the view, expressed by Sandra Fredman, that 'rights cannot coherently be distinguished by the kind of duty to which they give rise'.[64] Indeed, it was accepted by the Joint Human Rights Committee of the UK Parliament that '[no] clear line of demarcation can be drawn between the substance of rights classified as civil and political and those classified as economic, social and cultural' on the basis of the obligation they purportedly give rise to.[65]

The articulation of the tripartite typology of states' obligations with respect to all human rights therefore goes a long way towards negating the positive–negative dichotomy posited by opponents of socio-economic rights; it does not, however, address the ultimate concern raised about socio-economic rights. And the mere invocation of the typology cannot be assumed to have addressed the

60 King (n. 57).
61 Hunt (n. 55) at p. 26.
62 Dennis and Stewart (n. 43).
63 See Asbjorn Eide, 'Economic, Social and Cultural Rights as Human Rights' in Eide, Krause and Rosas (eds.), *Economic, Social and Cultural Rights: A Textbook* (2nd edn, The Hague: Martinus Nijhoff, 2001) 9 at p. 23.
64 Fredman (n. 2) at p. 67.
65 House of Lords/House of Commons Joint Committee on Human Rights, *The International Covenant on Economic, Social and Cultural Rights* (Twenty-First Report of Session 2003-04, HL Paper 183, HC 1188, Published 2 November 2004) at p. 11.

legitimate concerns about the judicial enforcement of positive duties, regardless of whether they arise from civil and political or socio-economic rights. As Matthew Craven notes, the tripartite classification of obligations:

> suggest[s], in the main, that there is no reason not to regard economic, social and cultural rights as giving rise to the same types of claims as those encountered by courts dealing with civil and political rights. By the same token, however, they do not deal with the obvious objection that fully realising [socio-economic] rights *does* require significant resources, and that the involvement of judicial, or quasi-judicial, supervisory bodies in their implementation would place constraints on the liberty of governments to determine their own spending priorities and expose the political underbelly of judicial decision-making in a painfully obvious way. Such problems cannot be wished away either by pointing to the fact that these are not the only type of obligations imposed, or that civil and political rights also incur resource expenditure on a similar scale.[66]

Consequently, it can be said that the positive–negative dichotomy contains a grain of truth, but it is not one which goes to the essence of the rights concerned, but rather, as with the other objections, it is a concern that embraces and is ultimately centred on the judicial enforcement of positive duties; hence, the separation of powers.

The final practical argument we consider here is the purported non-justiciability of socio-economic rights. The first point to note in this context is, as Michael Dennis and David Stewart rightly note, the term justiciable/non-justiciable is used fairly haphazardly by both opponents and advocates of entrenched socio-economic rights;[67] indeed it is for this reason that the justiciability argument is often presumed to embrace all of the other arguments against socio-economic rights. The first problem in this context is that the concept of justiciability is a multifaceted one, precluding the courts from entertaining cases on the basis, *inter alia*, that the plaintiff lacks standing, that the point being argued is moot, and that the issue concerned is a 'political question' for determination by the elected branches of government or any number of other, jurisdiction-specific, prohibitions all of which come under the umbrella of the justiciability doctrine.[68] In order to fruitfully engage with this concern we need, therefore, to be quite explicit and definite about what we mean by justiciability. Martin Scheinin argues that at the level of domestic constitutional law justiciability is concerned with 'the search [for] a proper procedure that is capable of providing an adequate remedy' in response to the

---

66 Matthew Craven, 'Assessment of Progress on Adjudication of Economic, Social and Cultural Rights' in Squires, Langford and Thiele (eds.), *The Road to a Remedy: Current Issues in the Litigation of Economic, Social and Cultural Rights* (Sydney: University of New South Wales Press, 2005) 27 at p. 32.

67 Dennis and Stewart (n. 43) at p. 473.

68 Jonathon Siegel, 'A Theory of Justiciability' (2007) 86 *Texas Law Review* 73 at pp. 76–77.

violation of socio-economic rights.[69] In similar terms Coomans notes that justiciability refers to 'the extent to which an alleged violation of an economic or social subjective right invoked in a particular case is suitable for judicial or quasi-judicial review'.[70]

We can say then that in so far as justiciability is concerned with identifying and securing a judicial role in the enforcement and vindication of socio-economic rights, the argument of non-justiciability, retrieved from the amorphous ether, is ultimately an assertion that the courts cannot play a role in adjudicating on such rights. However, if we bear in mind the insight provided by Fallon, and Jonathon Siegel's observation that justiciability quite often operates as a 'discretionary judicial avoidance mechanism',[71] we might question the apparently neutral assertion that the courts cannot adjudicate on such rights and surmise that underlying this assertion is, again, certain assumptions about the judicial role in the vindication of socio-economic rights. If, for example, those who genuinely apprehend that judicial enforcement of socio-economic rights would require the courts to, for example, make extensive mandatory orders which sap the public finances and inhibit the functioning of government, or, alternatively, that the enforcement of socio-economic rights will put the courts in a position where they have to make extensive and expansive orders which are simply ignored by the elected branches of government, it might be thought better to simply avoid these undesirable vistas by denying socio-economic rights claims audience in the first instance.

Viewed in this light, 'justiciability' ceases to be an abstract account of what the courts *can* do, and is shown to be a normative view of what courts *should* do. The claim of non-justiciability is thus absorbed into the broader account which sees judicial enforcement of socio-economic rights as inherently inimical to the maintenance of the separation of powers. As Craven notes, the 'main argument [against judicial enforcement of socio-economic rights] . . . is not that courts are unable to deal with particular subject-matters, but that they should not involve themselves in distributive decision-making: that function is one assigned to governments or legislatures'.[72] This view is echoed by Cécile Fabre, who notes that:

> Generally, most people oppose constitutional [socio-economic] rights on the grounds that they give unacceptable powers of interference to the judiciary. Judges, it is thought, should not get involved in making policy and in allocating resources to individuals, first, because they would be encroaching upon the prerogative of the elected representatives of the

---

69   Martin Scheinin, 'Justiciability and the Indivisibility of Human Rights' in Squires, Langford and Thiele (eds.), *The Road to a Remedy: Current Issues in the Litigation of Economic, Social and Cultural Rights* (Sydney: University of New South Wales Press, 2005) 17 at p. 20.

70   Coomans (n. 4) at p. 4.

71   Siegel (n. 68) at p. 109.

72   Craven (n. 66) at p. 41.

people, and secondly, because even if one does not think that democracy should have pre-eminence over social justice, judges are not the best placed, institutionally, to make those kinds of decisions.[73]

Similarly David Beatty argues that:

> the judicial definition and enforcement of social and economic rights [is seen to constitute] a serious derogation of the principle of separation of powers. Investing judges with the authority to tell the elected branches of government what services and benefits they are under a constitutional duty to provide allows them to take over final responsibility for the budget and the financial affairs of the state.[74]

This, then, is the ultimate concern – or problem – with the judicial enforcement of constitutionally entrenched socio-economic rights, or at least this is the most coherent and defensible objection. The concern that the judicial enforcement of socio-economic rights will undermine the principle of the separation of powers is the golden thread which runs through the garish tapestry woven by the manifold arguments made by the opponents of socio-economic rights, and it is to this concern that the rest of this study is devoted.

1.3 The comparative approach

Before we embark in earnest on the comparative assessment of jurisdictions which have addressed the issues around the judicial enforcement of socio-economic rights, it is necessary in the penultimate section of this chapter to make a few points about the comparative approach taken in this study. The use of comparative analysis, in one form or another, has long been viewed as intrinsically valuable in the study of law.[75] And while in the past it was thought that its use in the context of comparative constitutional law was limited,[76] the last 25 years have seen a bourgeoning of comparative constitutional scholarship.[77] Such comparative study provides a framework for 'self-reflection through analogy, distinction, and contrast' thus allowing us to gain a better understanding of, or at least an alternative perspective on, our own constitutional conventions through comparing and contrasting them with the practices of other, broadly similar, jurisdictions.[78] For the purposes of the issues addressed in this study the main value of the comparative method is to allow us to assess the veracity

---

73 Fabre (n. 12) at p. 2.
74 David Beatty, *The Ultimate Rule of Law* (Oxford: Oxford University Press, 2004) at p. 125.
75 Otto Kahn-Freund, 'On Uses and Misuses of Comparative Law' (1974) 37 *Modern Law Review* 1.
76 *Ibid.* at p. 17.
77 Ran Hirschl, 'The Rise of Comparative Constitutional Law: Thoughts on Substance and Method' (2008) 2 *Indian Journal of Constitutional Law* 11 at pp. 11–12.
78 *Ibid.* at p. 12.

of the separation-of-powers arguments against socio-economic rights, which
have been accepted as canonical in a number of jurisdictions, with Ireland
providing the archetypal example, through an examination of the different ways
in which a variety of countries have dealt with this issue. In order to ensure that
the comparative exercise undertaken in this study is exploited to its utmost,
this section briefly addresses some methodological questions of comparative
constitutional study, potential pitfalls and shortcomings, and also sets out the
reasons for choosing the jurisdictions which form the basis of the comparative
element of this study.

1.3.1 *Comparative constitutional methodology*

With respect to methodology, Mark Tushnet identifies three broad approaches,
or 'ways of doing', comparative constitutional law, which he calls: normative
universalism, functionalism and contextualism, the latter being further subdi-
vided into simple contextualism and expressivism.[79] There appears, in truth,
to be very little difference between the first two approaches; they both seek to
look at the way in which a variety of jurisdictions engage with the same constitutional issue, in order to improve the approach of the comparatist's own
country. For Tushnet, however, these two approaches are flawed, because they
'operate on too high a level of abstraction', that is to say that they engage in the
analysis of abstract concepts devoid of context.[80] This is where contextualism,
in both its forms, improves on the other two approaches, because contextualism
'emphasizes the fact that constitutional law is deeply embedded in the institutional, doctrinal, social, and cultural contexts of each nation' and that failing
to appreciate this seriously undermines the comparative exercise.[81] While this
simple contextualism requires us to be cognisant of the broader context, expressivism goes even further and insists that we view the constitutional system of
a given country as both derivative and expressive of the people of that country's
sense of self.[82]

   We might refine Tushnet's typology somewhat and say that, in truth, there
are two broad approaches that we may term: the emulative and the sensitive.
These approaches should not, however, be viewed as mutually exclusive, but
rather should be seen as essential component parts of any fruitful comparative
exercise. In the first instance a comparatist employing the emulative approach
studies the way in which different jurisdictions have addressed the same
problem, in order to articulate 'best practice' for the benefit or improvement of
their own jurisdiction. The problem with this is, as Tushnet noted, one cannot
simply look at the legal developments in one country and, if one deems them

---

79 Mark Tushnet, *Weak Courts, Strong Rights* (New Jersey: Princeton University Press, 2008) at
    p. 5.
80 *Ibid.* at p. 9.
81 *Ibid.* at p. 10.
82 *Ibid.* at p. 12.

admirable, transplant them into another jurisdiction. Because different countries develop solutions and institutional arrangements which meet their needs and are consonant with the 'culture' of the polity which gives rise to them, such solutions and arrangements cannot be fully appreciated in the abstract and certainly cannot be blithely transposed into another legal system, without significant modification. This then highlights the importance of context sensitivity, as Otto Kahn-Freund puts it, 'the comparative method . . . requires knowledge not only of the foreign law, but also of its social, and above all its political, context. The use of comparative law for practical purposes becomes an abuse only if it is informed by a legalistic spirit which ignores this context of the law'.[83] The simple emulative approach is, therefore, refined, nuanced and improved through the concurrent use of the sensitive approach, which requires the comparatist to be at all times cognisant of the economic, social and political maelstrom which gives rise to particular legal solutions in a given jurisdiction.

It is clear, then, that one can conduct a fruitful comparative inquiry into the different approaches taken by broadly similar jurisdictions to the same problem, with a view to articulating an ideal or model framework to address this problem, so long as one is conscious of the specific circumstances which gave rise to the respective approaches and equally conscious of the limits of transplantation. There is, however, one slight caveat that should be added to this, according to Ran Hirschl 'the more universal and widespread certain norms and practices become . . . the less effective or significant the contextualist concern becomes'.[84] A similar argument is made by Philip Alston, who acknowledges the importance of recognising the specificity of each individual constitutional regime, and warns that 'any recipes [for solving contested constitutional issues] which might emerge from . . . individual case studies are unlikely to be capable of easy application' in other jurisdictions, but also goes on to note that the development of the international human rights regime, particularly with respect to 'new' human rights challenges, is generating pressure for a degree of convergence with respect to certain issues confronted by constitutional regimes with entrenched bills of rights.[85] It is fair to say that, given their historical neglect,

83 Khan-Freund (n. 75) at p. 27; and see Andrew Harding and Peter Leyland, 'Comparative Law in Constitutional Contexts' in Örücü and Nelken (eds.), *Comparative Law: A Handbook* (Oxford: Hart Publishing, 2007) 313, who note, at p. 331, that 'it is impossible to understand the law, the constitution, and the institutions of any nation without understanding the context in which they come into being'.

84 Hirschl (n. 77) at p. 27.

85 Philip Alston, 'A Framework for the Comparative Analysis of Bills of Rights' in Alston (ed.), *Promoting Human Rights Through Bills of Rights: Comparative Perspectives* (Oxford: Oxford University Press, 1999) 1 at p. 6. Cf. Harding and Leyland (n. 83) at p. 333, who argue 'that while certain contemporary global trends do in fact encourage elements of convergence, and there is plenty of evidence of this taking place, it does not follow that constitutions will all eventually look the same or that they should look the same. And of course, when it comes to constitutional practice strong divergences do remain in the implementation of human rights principles and other constitutional features'.

socio-economic rights can be considered as coming within the ambit of these 'new' human rights challenges being faced by countries throughout the world. Therefore, seeking to articulate a model framework for the judicial enforcement of such rights is a legitimate, or at least defensible, exercise.

1.3.2 Selection of comparators

The substantive chapters of this study look at the protection of socio-economic rights at the level of international human rights law, as a normative ideal, and in a number of comparable jurisdictions, namely: South Africa, India, Canada and Ireland. These comparators have been chosen because they are all countries in the broad common law tradition,[86] which have entrenched bills of rights and judiciaries empowered to enforce them and they have all had a number of noteworthy cases dealing with socio-economic rights, what Malcolm Langford calls a 'reasonably mature jurisprudence' on socio-economic rights, thus making them noteworthy in this regard.[87] However, notwithstanding these similarities, another important reason for choosing the jurisdictions studied here is that each has its own idiosyncrasies, and each has dealt with the question of socio-economic rights in a distinct manner, conditioned by its own historical development. They therefore provide illustrative examples of the different paradigms through which socio-economic rights can be protected in domestic constitutional law, which, broadly speaking, are: (i) through direct constitutional entrenchment of socio-economic rights; (ii) protection in the form of non-justiciable 'directive principles' of state policy; (iii) protection of socio-economic rights as essential corollaries of civil and political rights – what Ida Elisabeth Koch and others refer to as the 'integrated approach';[88] and (iv) protection of socio-economic rights through the expansive application of equality or non-discrimination provisions.[89]

The focus of each of the chapters dealing with comparative domestic experiences is, as might be expected, on the relevant constitutional provisions and the leading cases in each jurisdiction. However, bearing in mind the importance of context sensitivity, and Hirschl's warning that 'the traditional focus on legal provisions and court rulings' alone is bound to 'yield an incomplete picture concerning the realization of rights',[90] each of the chapters also consciously seeks to situate the relevant domestic jurisprudence in the countries' historical, political, social and economic context, as well as being sensitive to relevant

86 Although Canada does have the element of the civil law tradition in Quebec, and South Africa has, historically, involved a mix of the common law and Roman–Dutch law.
87 Langford (n. 5) at p. 4.
88 Ida Elisabeth Koch, 'Economic, Social and Cultural Rights as Components in Civil and Political Rights: A Hermeneutic Perspective' (2006) 10 *International Journal of Human Rights* 405 at p. 408.
89 Jeanne M. Woods, 'Emerging Paradigms of Protection for "Second-Generation" Human Rights' (2005) 6 *Loyola Journal of Public Interest Law* 103.
90 Hirschl (n. 77) at p. 35.

political currents which impacted significantly on the shaping of constitutional provisions and on evolving jurisprudence. The important point being that while analysing the experiences superior courts have had adjudicating on socio-economic rights in other jurisdictions has obvious benefits, as noted above, it must always be borne in mind that 'each domestic system of protection of economic and social rights . . . has its own special features',[91] and for a comparative analysis to be truly beneficial these idiosyncrasies have to be taken into account. Attempting to blithely apply the principles developed in one jurisdiction directly to another undermines the benefits of the comparative exercise, and such a pedantic approach must be quite consciously avoided. There is, of course, the Hirschl/Alston caveat to this general concern with normative model building; namely that certain issues, and it is submitted that the judicial enforcement of socio-economic rights qualifies, lend themselves to the articulation of transcendent solutions.

1.4 Conclusion

The ultimate question addressed in this study is: how can socio-economic rights be meaningfully protected at the constitutional level, while at the same time maintaining the integrity of the separation of powers. Assistance in answering this question is sought from both normative, ideal international standards and from an analysis of comparative, practical experiences of superior courts grappling with the issue in a number of jurisdictions. One concern at the outset is, as Bruce Porter has argued, that the 'project of elaborating an over-arching framework for the adjudication of [socio-economic] rights claims is too often marginal, tentative and incoherent'.[92] It is hoped that this study will at least avoid the last two of these shortcomings, although the extent to which the analysis presented here will become central is dependent on factors beyond the control of the present author, but which will nonetheless be considered in the final chapter. The next chapter looks first at the international standards for the protection of socio-economic rights as normative ideals which may, and arguably should, shape any incipient national jurisprudence on the protection of socio-economic rights. Chapters 3 to 6 then contain a series of case studies, showing how the issue of socio-economic rights has been dealt with in South Africa, India, Canada and Ireland; before Chapter 7, drawing on the experiences in the jurisdictions considered, seeks to articulate an ideal or model framework for the judicial role in the vindication of socio-economic rights. The final chapter of the study then re-situates the doctrinal discussion undertaken here in its broader political context.

---

91 Coomans (n. 4) at p. 8.
92 Bruce Porter, 'The Crisis of Economic, Social and Cultural Rights and Strategies for Addressing It' in Squires, Langford and Thiele (eds.), *The Road to a Remedy: Current Issues in the Litigation of Economic, Social and Cultural Rights* (Sydney: University of New South Wales Press, 2005) 43 at p. 44.

2 International standards on socio-economic rights

The focus of this chapter is on the standards developed for the protection of socio-economic rights at the international level. Specifically, the focus here is on what is commonly called the International Bill of Rights,[1] comprising the Universal Declaration of Human Rights (UDHR),[2] the International Covenant on Economic, Social and Cultural Rights (ICESCR) and the International Covenant on Civil and Political Rights (ICCPR),[3] in so far as these instruments, and with respect to the latter two their respective monitoring bodies, have articulated norms pertaining to the protection of socio-economic rights. The bulk of the discussion centres on the ICESCR, particularly the work of the Committee on Economic, Social and Cultural Rights (CESCR, or 'the Committee'), the body established to monitor the implementation of the ICESCR, and the various ways in which the Committee has elaborated on the nature of States' obligations with respect to socio-economic rights. Aside from the ICESCR this chapter also considers, albeit somewhat briefly, the more general evolution of the International Bill of Rights and the fracturing of the human rights catalogue following the initial optimism of the unified Bill of Rights contained in the UDHR. Penultimately, this chapter will look at the ways in which the ICCPR has been extended to provide a form of protection, albeit limited, for socio-economic rights, principally, although not exclusively, through the application of its freestanding non-discrimination provision.

2.1 The value of international human rights norms

However, before proceeding to consider in detail the doctrinal developments under the various international instruments, I digress somewhat in this opening

---

1 Described by Freeman and Van Ert as the 'primary source' of human rights at the international level, and by Weir as the 'foundation stone' of international human rights protection: Mark Freeman and Gibran Van Ert, *International Human Rights Law* (Ontario: Irwin Law Inc., 2004) at p. 69; and Stuart Weir, *Unequal Britain: Human Rights as a Route to Social Justice* (London: Politico's, 2006) at p. 25.
2 General Assembly Resolution 217 A (III), 10 December 1948; for a useful introductory discussion of the UDHR, see: Mary Ann Glendon, 'Knowing the Universal Declaration of Human Rights' (1998) 73 *Notre Dame Law Review* 1153.
3 General Assembly Resolution 2200 A (XXI), 16 December 1966.

section to make a general, normative argument for the value of international human rights norms in domestic legal systems. To some, the value of such norms may very well seem self-evident, but as the discussion which follows will show it is far from uncontroversial. The problem is illustrated by the authors of the leading textbook on international human rights law, who characterise the practice of most States with respect to the protection of socio-economic rights in the following terms:

> [Support] for the equal status and importance of [socio-economic rights] . . . together with . . . failure to take any steps to entrench those rights constitutionally, to adopt legislative or administrative provisions based explicitly on the recognition of specific [socio-economic rights] as international human rights, or to provide effective means of redress to individuals or groups alleging violations of those rights.[4]

While it may be that this disjuncture, official recognition coupled with non-implementation, is particularly blatant with respect to socio-economic rights, it is arguably no more than a pronounced symptom of a more generalised crisis in the implementation of international human rights norms at the domestic level.[5] This vista is troubling, because ultimately if human rights are to be meaningful and effective they must be so at the domestic level.[6] Consequently, international human rights norms (for present purposes norms with respect to socio-economic rights) are of value only in so far as they are reflected at the domestic level. Therefore, before going on to consider the various principles developed under the International Bill of Rights, this section will first set out a normative argument for the use of such international human rights norms in the domestic context, in particular by domestic courts.

The argument advanced here has, obviously, far greater relevance for those States which adopt the classically British dualist approach to international law.[7]

---

4 Henry Steiner, Philip Alston and Ryan Goodman, *International Human Rights in Context: Law, Politics, Morals* (3rd edn, Oxford: Oxford University Press, 2008) at pp. 263–264. In a similar vein, Olowu has noted 'an asymmetry between the formal commitment of states to [the ICESCR], and the very scanty attempts at prioritizing the contents of this treaty in their most fundamental laws' (Dejo Olowu, 'Human Rights and the Avoidance of Domestic Implementation: The Phenomenon of Non-Justiciable Constitutional Guarantees' (2006) 69 *Saskatchewan Law Review* 39 at p. 41).

5 See Ann Bayefsky, 'The UN Human Rights Treaties: Facing the Implementation Crisis' (1996) *Windsor Yearbook of Access to Justice* 189.

6 As Steiner, Alston and Goodman put it, 'Human rights violations occur within a state, rather than on the high seas or in outer space outside of the jurisdiction of any one state. Ultimately, effective protection must come from within the state' (n. 4) at p. 1087.

7 Contrasted, routinely, with so-called 'monist' legal systems; in the latter international legal norms to which a State has subscribed are automatically part of the municipal law of the State and can trump domestic legislation and, in some cases, domestic constitutional provisions. Whereas in dualist systems international legal norms have to be 'transformed' into domestic law before they can play any meaningful part in the municipal legal system. See generally Malcolm Shaw, *International Law* (6th edn, Cambridge: Cambridge University Press, 2008)

That is, those States in which international law, save in limited circumstances customary international law, plays little or no part until such time as it is transposed into domestic law, usually by an act of the legislative organ of State. The argument developed here relates to the attitude which domestic courts should adopt in relation to international human rights norms in both the context where international human rights instruments have been transposed into domestic law and, crucially, situations in which international human rights instruments to which the State is a party have not been so transposed. The argument defended here, in a nutshell, is that domestic courts should look to international human rights standards as persuasive, normative ideals which should guide, but not in a binding, rigid all-or-nothing sense, their deliberations in cases concerning fundamental human rights.[8] This argument, of course, is not uncontroversial, and I want to briefly outline some of the arguments against this sort of approach, before returning to my own positive argument and defending it against the various objections.

The context for the discussion is set by Mr Justice Michael Kirby of the Australian High Court, who recently noted that 'the interaction of international and national law constitutes one of the largest challenges for the law in the century ahead'.[9] Indeed, the relationship between international law and domestic law, in the context of human rights the relationship between 'two positive legal systems for the articulation and protection of the fundamental rights of individuals',[10] is very much a live issue. While it is true to say that the status which international law enjoys in domestic legal systems varies significantly from country to country,[11] there has been a discernible trend over the last number of years in traditionally dualist countries such as Australia,[12] Canada,[13] the

at pp. 129–194; and David Feldman, 'Monism, Dualism and Constitutional Legitimacy' (1999) 20 *Australian Yearbook of International Law* 105.

8 In this respect, the argument for international human rights norms advanced here adopts, in large part, an approach to international human rights norms advocated by Karen Knop, in which such norms are viewed and used by domestic courts as persuasive authority, which in turn obviates the traditional binding–non-binding dichotomy ('Here and There: International Law in Domestic Courts' (2000) 32 *New York University Journal of International Law and Politics* 501).

9 Michael Kirby, 'International Law – The Impact on Domestic Constitutions' (2006) 21 *American University International Law Review* 327 at p. 363.

10 Gerald Neuman, 'The Use of International Law in Constitutional Interpretation' (2004) 98 *American Journal of International Law* 82 at p. 84.

11 M. Shah Alam, 'Enforcement of International Human Rights Law by Domestic Courts: A Theoretical and Practical Study' (2006) 53 *Netherlands International Law Review* 399 at pp. 400–401.

12 Although it should be said that in the Australian context the precise position of international law remains somewhat uncertain, see Kristen Walker, 'International Law as a Tool of Constitutional Interpretation' (2002) 28 *Monash University Law Review* 85; and Ernst Willheim, 'Globalisation, State Sovereignty and Domestic Law: The Australian High Court Rejects International Law as a Proper Influence on Constitutional Interpretation' (2005) 1–2 *Asia-Pacific Journal of Human Rights and the Law* 38.

13 See Knop (n. 8); and Gerald V. La Forest, 'The Expanding Role of the Supreme Court of Canada in International Law Issues' (1996) 34 *Canadian Yearbook of International Law* 89.

United Kingdom[14] and the United States,[15] of national courts having greater 'recourse to international instruments, particularly in the context of applying international human rights norms'.[16]

However, this increased judicial regard for international norms has provoked significant opposition. Among the main arguments advanced against judicial reliance on international law in the domestic setting are the following: (i) what may be termed the 'uniqueness' argument, that is that each domestic constitution and legal system is designed to govern a specific polity, with all of the idiosyncrasies which that entails, and consequently recourse should not be had to, for want of a better term, foreign influences in interpreting and applying domestic law; (ii) the sovereignty argument, that reference to and reliance on international law will lead to a loss in national sovereignty; (iii) the separation-of-powers argument, that treaty making and transposition into domestic law is, appropriately, the role of the executive in the first instance and parliament subsequently; therefore domestic courts should not subvert the powers of the other branches of government by seeking to introduce international law through the proverbial backdoor;[17] and (iv) the indeterminacy argument, that international law is usually ambiguous and therefore unhelpful.[18]

While Gerald Neuman argues that these various objections play on 'exaggerated fears . . . of foreign domination, fear of judicial activism, fear of the unknown',[19] they are nonetheless symptomatic of legitimate concerns about the role which international law does, and should, play in domestic legal systems. However, with that said the veracity of these various arguments only

14 See Charles Banner and Richard Moules, 'Public Law in the House of Lords: Emerging Trends and Guidance on Petitions for Leave to Appeal' (2007) 12 *Judicial Review* 24; and Katherine Reece Thomas, 'The Changing Status of International Law in English Domestic Law' (2006) 53 *Netherlands International Law Review* 371.

15 See Ruth Bader Ginsburg, '"A Decent Respect to the Opinions of [Human]Kind": The Value of a Comparative Perspective in Constitutional Adjudication' (2005) 64 *Cambridge Law Journal* 575.

16 Daphne Barak-Erez, 'The International Law of Human Rights and Constitutional Law: A Case Study of an Expanding Dialogue' (2004) 2 *International Journal of Constitutional Law* 611 at p. 611. In her article Barak-Erez details the growing influence of international human rights norms on the Israeli Supreme Court; thus Israel might fairly be added to the list of countries given above.

17 This is related to another, barely distinct argument, about the judicial invocation of international law in the domestic setting. Specifically, the claim is that the principles developed, either at the international level or in another jurisdiction, have no democratic legitimacy within another domestic legal system. Consequently, judicial reliance on such norms or principles is, *ipso facto*, democratically suspect.

18 Kirby (n. 9) at pp. 347–356. For a trenchant defence of the uniqueness, democracy and indeterminacy arguments, see A. Mark Weisburd, 'Using International Law to Interpret Domestic Constitutions – Conceptual Problems: Reflections on Justice Kirby's Advocacy of International Law in Domestic Constitutional Jurisprudence' (2006) 21 *American University International Law Review* 365.

19 Neuman (n. 10) at p. 82; similarly M. Shah Alam (n. 11) argues, at p. 414, that such concerns are 'more imaginary than real'.

really holds if we confine ourselves to one paradigmatic approach to the relationship between international and domestic law, namely the classic approach which poses a binding–non-binding dichotomy between international and domestic legal norms. This approach is summed up by Karen Knop in the following terms:

> The traditional model of international law in domestic courts asks when a state's international legal obligations are binding in its domestic law. Whether that occurs automatically, through legislation, via some interpretative presumption, or otherwise depends on the state. Whatever the particular mode of incorporation, the general interest of this model is the hard-wiring of international law into domestic law, the existence of vertical connections that require the courts of a state to enforce the state's international legal obligations. In the traditional model, the court's inquiry is structured by a set of binary choices. Under the rules of reception, the binding/non-binding distinction corresponds to the all-or-nothing application of an international legal norm domestically . . . The process is thus modelled as dichotomous: binding/non-binding, all or nothing, particular or universal.[20]

Within the confines of this polarised paradigm lies the strength of the various arguments against judicial reliance on international human rights norms. When the contest is perceived to be one of winner takes all, national versus international law, binding or non-binding, the various concerns raised about the trampling of domestic values and municipal democracy sound a chord.

However, while the binding–non-binding approach has traditionally been the dominant optic through which the relationship between national and international law has been viewed,[21] it is not the only one on offer. In contrast to this approach, Knop advocates what she terms 'transjudicialism', which involves 'the blurring of international law into comparative law'.[22] From this perspective international law is approached as persuasive authority, which may aid domestic courts in their deliberations, but which does not mandate or command a given result. Within this paradigm 'the authority of international law is persuasive rather than binding';[23] it is thus authority which 'attracts adherence as opposed to obliging it'.[24] If we adopt this perspective on the nature of international law, and its role in the domestic legal system, we then see that the various arguments against judicial reliance on international human rights norms are based on a number of core presuppositions, which do not necessarily correlate with reality.

---

20 Knop (n. 8) at p. 515.
21 See H. Patrick Glenn, 'Persuasive Authority' (1987) 33 *McGill Law Journal* 261.
22 Knop (n. 8) at p. 525.
23 *Ibid.* at p. 535.
24 Glenn (n. 21) at p. 263.

So, the arguments that judicial reliance on international norms would undermine national sovereignty or the domestic separation of powers both presuppose the courts being obliged to reach a particular result on the basis of international norms, whereas the transjudicial approach furnishes the courts with a potential site of persuasive authority, without mandating any given solution to the case in hand, and thus obviates the sovereignty and separation-of-powers concerns.

Similarly, the uniqueness and ambiguity objections both presuppose that the domestic courts will be obliged to take authoritative direction from international norms in the adjudication of domestic disputes, thereby diminishing the importance of the national genius or otherwise proving unworkable in practice. This apprehension again is obviated by Knop's typology, which understands that 'the domestic interpretation of international law is not merely the transmission of the international, but a process of translation from international to national'.[25] Consequently, domestic courts can, within reason, augment general international principles to give practical effect to them in the specific domestic context, so long as the net result is the tangible and practical improvement or advancement of the right in question. Furthermore, the vagueness argument can be turned somewhat on its head, by arguing that when domestic courts are confronted with novel rights claims or cases, international norms can assist them in resolving any ambiguities or uncertainties in domestic law; in other words the work of international bodies 'provides a welcome and helpful tool not only for Governments but also for domestic judges, whether they are interpreting and applying the [international instrument] itself or other forms of legislation'.[26] As Neuman notes, international norms developed by treaty monitoring bodies represent 'a relevant source of insight on the human rights issues they address',[27] and domestic courts should '[examine] the reasoning in international elaborations of human rights for the functional and normative insight which they contain', particularly with respect to cases presenting novel issues before the domestic court.[28] Similarly, Rosalyn Higgins argues that 'even in the absence of incorporation the findings of [treaty monitoring bodies] . . . are part of the source material of international human rights law that might assist a domestic court when it seeks to determine issues of domestic law in a way compatible with international obligations'.[29]

---

25 Knop (n. 8) at p. 506.
26 Office of the United Nations High Commissioner for Human Rights (OHCHR), *Human Rights in the Administration of Justice: A Manual on Human Rights for Judges, Prosecutors and Lawyers* (New York: United Nations, 2003) at p. 748.
27 Gerald Neuman, 'Human Rights and Constitutional Rights: Harmony and Dissonance' (2003) 55 *Stanford Law Review* 1863 at p. 1890.
28 *Ibid.* at p. 1899.
29 Rosalyn Higgins, 'The Relationship Between International and Regional Human Rights Norms and Domestic Law' (1992) 18 *Commonwealth Law Bulletin* 1268 at p. 1274; see also the International Commission of Jurists (ICJ), *Courts and the Legal Enforcement of Economic, Social and Cultural Rights: Comparative Experiences of Justiciability* (Geneva: ICJ, 2008) at p. 101.

Notwithstanding, then, the sincere and cogently argued objections to judicial reliance on or regard for international human rights norms in domestic courts, it can be argued that if we reconceptualise our understanding of the relationship between international human rights law and domestic law, these arguments hold little water. Domestic courts can, quite legitimately, look to the principles developed by international treaty-monitoring bodies, with a view to helping them articulate domestic solutions to problems implicating the relevant international norm or principle. What is more, there is a pragmatic argument for courts to have recourse to such material, again as persuasive authority, when they are confronted with a novel case or rights claim on which there are established international principles. It is submitted that this latter argument has particular resonance with respect to socio-economic rights, which, due to their historical neglect, will present novel claims in many jurisdictions. The principles developed at the international level for the protection of socio-economic rights therefore have both a pragmatic and normative value to domestic courts, and it is to these principles that we now turn.

2.2 The Universal Declaration of Human Rights

The UDHR, adopted by the UN General Assembly in December 1948, was the progenitor of, and subsequently a central element in, what has come to be known as the International Bill of Rights. It is, as one commentator has noted, 'the single most important reference point for cross-cultural discussion of human freedom and dignity in the world today';[30] thus the UDHR, notwithstanding the fact that it is not legally binding, represents the international normative standard for the protection of human rights. The Declaration was drafted in the aftermath of the atrocities of the Second World War and was committed to the 'advent of a world in which human beings shall enjoy freedom of speech and belief and freedom from fear and want'.[31] As such, the rights set out in the UDHR were to be a 'common standard of achievement' towards which all peoples and nations should strive.[32] In adumbrating a set of fundamental rights that would lead to the development of a more just and humane world, the authors of the UDHR drew no distinction between civil, political and socio-economic rights.[33] Thus, one can find in the Declaration commitments to the right to life,[34] equality before the law,[35] freedom of thought and conscience[36] and freedom of expression,[37] alongside rights to work,[38] to a decent

---

30 Glendon (n. 2) at p. 1153.
31 Preamble UDHR.
32 *Ibid*.
33 Craig Scott, 'Reaching Beyond (Without Abandoning) the Category of "Economic, Social and Cultural Rights"' (1999) 21 *Human Rights Quarterly* 633.
34 Article 3 UDHR.
35 Article 7 UDHR.
36 Article 18 UDHR.
37 Article 19 UDHR.
38 Article 23 UDHR.

standard of living[39] – including food, clothing, housing and medical care – and to education.[40] Within the paradigm of the UDHR these various individual human rights are 'interrelated and mutually reinforcing'.[41]

When the time came to transpose the ideals set out in the UDHR into binding legal norms the original intention of the UN, according to Arambulo, 'was clearly to draft one Covenant, a legally binding document that was to contain both sets [socio-economic and civil and political] of rights'.[42] Indeed, the UN General Assembly initially resolved to do just this, but subsequently resiled from this position and, instead, opted to draft two instruments, with qualitatively different levels of State obligations and different monitoring mechanisms, one guaranteeing civil and political and the other socio-economic rights.[43] This volte-face by the UN is an important turning point in the development of international human rights, and of socio-economic rights in particular, and contributed significantly to the subsequent marginalisation of socio-economic rights at both the international and domestic levels. Therefore, the reasons for this turnaround merit some consideration, as they shed light on the persistent canard that socio-economic rights, for some intrinsic reason or other, are not real rights.

This standard narrative, discussed in Chapter 1, is maintained by commentators such as Michael Dennis and David Stewart, who argue that the decision to draft two covenants was as a result of the 'appreciation of practical differences between the two sets of rights',[44] and that it had nothing to do with ideological differences over the respective categories of rights.[45] In contrast Abdullahi An-Na'im argues that:

> The relegation of [socio-economic rights] to a lower class of human rights goes back to the division of the human rights proclaimed in the UDHR into two groups during a particularly 'hot' phase of the Cold War in the early 1950s. That clearly ideological and political classification of human rights was initially expressed in the adoption of two separate Covenants, with different formulations and enforcement mechanisms for each set of rights. The dichotomy between the two sets of rights was also re-enforced by mounting Western–Soviet rivalry in the cooptation of newly emerging

---

39 Article 25 UDHR.
40 Article 26 UDHR.
41 Asbjorn Eide, 'Economic, Social and Cultural Rights as Human Rights' in Eide, Krause and Rosas (eds.), *Economic, Social and Cultural Rights: A Textbook* (2nd edn, The Hague: Martinus Nijhoff, 2001) 9 at p. 15.
42 Kitty Arambulo, *Strengthening the Supervision of the International Covenant on Economic, Social and Cultural Rights: Theoretical and Procedural Aspects* (Antwerp: Intersentia, 2000) at p. 15.
43 *Ibid.* at p. 16. See also OHCHR (n. 26) at pp. 681–685.
44 Michael Dennis and David Stewart, 'Justiciability of Economic, Social and Cultural Rights: Should There Be an International Complaints Mechanism to Adjudicate the Rights to Food, Water, Housing and Health?' (2004) 98 *American Journal of International Law* 462 at p. 477.
45 *Ibid.*

states in Africa and Asia to their respective camps. Since West European and North American governments and their allies emphasised civil and political rights, while the Soviet Bloc and some developing countries favoured [socio-economic rights], the division of human rights became entrenched in a global power struggle.[46]

And notwithstanding the fact that Daniel Whelan and Jack Donnelly characterise this sort of explanation as 'revisionist history of the worst kind, not simply false but an almost complete inversion of the truth',[47] the reality is that their views are marginal and the consensus among most human rights scholars is that the fracturing of the unified human rights catalogue was indeed as a result of the great political and ideological conflict which dominated the second half of the twentieth century: the Cold War.[48]

The significance of this, then, is that the initial relegation of socio-economic rights to their second-class status was not as a result of any intrinsic deficiency with the rights themselves, but rather as a result of power politics and ideological disagreement. This, of course, is not to denigrate either power politics or ideological disagreement, but simply to make the point that the history of socio-economic rights in the twentieth and twenty-first centuries has been one of neglect and underdevelopment not because of the rights per se, but rather because of the opposition from certain powerful interests to the protection of such rights. Notwithstanding this marginalisation, the initial idealism of the UDHR still provides a strong moral claim for the centrality of socio-economic rights, thereby reinforcing the argument for their domestic protection.[49] Furthermore, the sister covenants born of the UDHR, the ICESCR and the ICCPR, have both facilitated the development and articulation of an extensive body of principles for the protection of socio-economic rights in spite of the formal relegation of socio-economic rights to the second tier, and it is to a consideration of these various principles that the rest of this chapter is devoted.

2.3 The sister covenants and socio-economic rights

The ICESCR was drafted along with the ICCPR in 1966 in order to transform the aspirations of the UDHR into binding legal norms and constitutes the

---

46 Abdullahi A. An-Na'im, 'To Affirm the Full Human Rights Standing of Economic, Social and Cultural Rights' in Ghai and Cottrell (eds), *Economic, Social and Cultural Rights in Practice* (London: INTERIGHTS, 2004) 7 at p. 12.

47 Daniel Whelan and Jack Donnelly, 'The West, Economic and Social Rights, and the Global Human Rights Regime: Setting the Record Straight' (2007) 29 *Human Rights Quarterly* 908 at p. 910.

48 See, for example, Arambulo (n. 42) at pp. 15–16; Freeman and Van Ert (n. 1) at p. 74; Steiner, Alston and Goodman (n. 4) at p. 139; Weir (n. 1) at pp. 26–27; and Manfred Nowak, 'The International Covenants on Civil and Political Rights and on Economic, Social and Cultural Rights' in Smith and van den Anker (eds), *The Essentials of Human Rights* (New York: Hodder Arnold, 2005) 193 at p. 194.

49 See Arambulo (n. 42) at p. 14; and Eide (n. 41) at p. 22.

'principal instrument for the protection of economic, social and cultural rights within the United Nations human rights system'.[50] The Covenant entered into force on 3 January 1976 and enshrined, *inter alia*, the rights to work,[51] form and join trade unions,[52] social security,[53] an adequate standard of living, including adequate food, clothing and housing,[54] the right to the highest attainable level of mental and physical health[55] and the right to education.[56] The 'linchpin of the ICESCR'[57] can be found in Article 2(1) of the Covenant, which sets out in broad outline the nature of the obligations of the States who are party to the Covenant. Article 2(1) provides that:

> Each State Party to the present Covenant undertakes to take steps, individually and through international assistance and co-operation, especially economic and technical, to the maximum of its available resources, with a view to achieving progressively the full realisation of the rights recognized in the present Covenant by all appropriate means, including particularly the adoption of legislative measures.[58]

The 'obscure and imprecise nature'[59] of the language in Article 2(1) – in particular the resource qualification and the idea of progressive realisation – created much uncertainty, particularly given trenchant opposition to the protection of economic and social rights from certain quarters,[60] and the absence of international and domestic jurisprudence on the protection of such rights.[61] There were serious concerns that the ideas of progressive realisation and resource limitation would allow signatories to the Covenant to shirk their obligations under it and render the guarantees contained therein nugatory.[62] In these circumstances, it was essential that substantive meaning be given to the terms of Article 2(1), so that the rights protected by the ICESCR would become a tangible reality for those whom it was designed to benefit. Following a decade

---

50 Allan Rosas and Martin Scheinin, 'Implementation Mechanisms and Remedies' in Eide, Krause and Rosas (eds.), *Economic, Social and Cultural Rights: A Textbook* (2nd edn, The Hague: Martinus Nijhoff, 2001) 425 at p. 426.
51 Article 6 ICESCR.
52 Article 8 ICESCR.
53 Article 9 ICESCR.
54 Article 11 ICESCR.
55 Article 12 ICESCR.
56 Article 13 ICESCR.
57 Matthew Craven, *The International Covenant on Economic, Social and Cultural Rights: A Perspective on its Development* (Oxford: Clarendon Press, 1995) at p. 106.
58 Article 2(1) ICESCR.
59 Craven (n. 57) at p. 3.
60 Philip Alston and Gerard Quinn, 'The Nature and Scope of States Parties' Obligations under the International Covenant on Economic, Social and Cultural Rights' (1987) 9 *Human Rights Quarterly* 156 at pp. 159–160.
61 Craven (n. 57) at p. 4.
62 Alston and Quinn (n. 60) at pp. 172–177.

of stagnation after its entering into force, the ICESCR was reinvigorated in the late 1980s through, in the first instance, the work of a number of international experts committed to the development of the rights protected by the Covenant and subsequently through the work of the newly established CESCR. In the following pages we will see how the obligations of the States party to the ICESCR were clarified and substantiated.

2.3.1 *The Limburg Principles*

In 1986 a group of international experts was convened to consider the nature and scope of States' obligations under the ICESCR. What emerged from this meeting was the 'Limburg Principles on the Implementation of the ICESCR'.[63] The purpose of these principles was to '(1) emphasize the rightful place of economic, social and cultural rights in international human rights law, (2) aid the development of the Covenant as a whole, and (3) indicate how the object and purpose of the Covenant may be achieved'.[64] In this way the Limburg Principles represent the first authoritative statement on the nature of States' obligations under the ICESCR. The Limburg Principles are also important because many of the positions which were first articulated therein, vis-à-vis States' obligations in relation to the ICESCR, were subsequently adopted by the CESCR.

The Limburg Principles begin by reiterating that socio-economic rights are 'an integral part' of the international human rights regime, and by restating the indivisible and interdependent nature of all human rights, as a consequence of which 'equal attention and urgent consideration should be given to the implementation, promotion and protection of both civil and political, and economic, social and cultural rights'. Limburg Principle 8 makes the point that while Article 2(1) of the ICESCR accepts that full realisation of the rights contained therein can only be attained progressively and over time, certain of the rights in the Covenant can be 'made justiciable immediately', while others can become justiciable over time. The point about the need for the State to adopt immediate measures towards the realisation of the Covenant rights, although such rights can only be fully realised progressively, is reiterated in Principle 16.

Principles 17 and 18 address the nature of the steps that States should take towards the realisation of socio-economic rights, with legislation singled out as a particularly important means of realising such rights. However, it is stressed that, by itself, legislation will rarely be sufficient and should therefore be augmented by appropriate administrative, judicial, economic, social and educational measures and that States party to the ICESCR are obliged to make provision for adequate remedies at a domestic level, including judicial remedies, where a violation of a Covenant right occurs. Principle 21 stresses again the

---

63   UN doc. E/CN.4/1987/17, Annex.
64   E. V. O. Dankwa and Cees Flinterman, 'Commentary by the Rapporteurs on the Nature and Scope of States Parties' Obligations' (1987) 9 *Human Rights Quarterly* 136 at p. 136.

nature of the obligation to progressively realise the rights contained in the covenant, and notes that this requires:

> [States] parties to move as expeditiously as possible towards the realisation of the rights. Under no circumstances shall this be interpreted as implying for States the right to defer indefinitely efforts to ensure full realization. On the contrary all States parties have the obligation to begin immediately to take steps to fulfil their obligations under the Covenant.

In this way the Limburg Principles reject the idea that the requirement of progressive realisation, placed on States by Article 2(1) ICESCR, limits in any way the efficacy and value of the rights protected by the Covenant. As if to emphasise this point, Principle 22 provides that some of the obligations under the Covenant, for example the requirement of non-discrimination in Article 2(2), require immediate implementation.

The issue of resources is addressed in Principles 23 and 24; they provide that the States' obligation to take steps towards the progressive realisation of the Covenant rights is not contingent on the level of resources available, instead it requires the effective use of whatever resources are available. Principle 25 establishes a very important point. It provides that regardless of the level of economic development in a given State, all States are obliged to ensure respect for certain 'minimum subsistence rights'. Principles 35 to 41 deal with the prohibition on discrimination contained in Article 2(2) of the Covenant, which is held to be of immediate domestic application, and which should immediately be made amenable to judicial supervision. Finally, for present purposes at least, Principles 70 to 73 set out some examples of what will constitute a violation of the Covenant, which include: (i) a failure to take a step required by the Covenant; (ii) failure to promptly remove barriers inhibiting the full enjoyment of Covenant rights; and (iii) deliberately retarding or halting the progressive realisation of a Covenant right.

2.3.2 *General Comments*

The CESCR was created by the Economic and Social Council (ECOSOC) in 1987,[65] and is the body with principal responsibility for the monitoring and implementation of the ICESCR. The Committee is primarily concerned with assessing the reports submitted by States under the Covenant and producing concluding comments in relation to such reports. However, from an early point in its existence the Committee has also developed the practice of adopting General Comments in relation to the ICESCR and the rights protected therein.

---

65 See, generally, Malcolm Langford and Jeff King, 'Committee on Economic, Social and Cultural Rights: Past, Present at Future' in Langford (ed.), *Social Rights Jurisprudence: Emerging Trends in International and Comparative Law* (Cambridge: Cambridge University Press, 2008) 477; and Craven (n. 57) at pp. 42–105.

To date the Committee has adopted 20 such comments,[66] dealing with both procedural and substantive aspects of the Covenant. These General Comments represent an 'important mechanism for developing the jurisprudence of the Committee',[67] and through these comments the Committee establishes normative standards with respect to the Covenant's various provisions.[68] However, we shall concern ourselves here with only those General Comments that touch most directly on the question of States' obligations under the Covenant.

The first of these is General Comment No. 3 which contains the Committee's assessment of the obligations imposed on States by Article 2(1) of the Covenant. For the Committee Article 2(1) imposes both obligations of conduct and result, that is it obliges States to act in a certain manner, but also to meet certain mandated goals. The Committee picks up on the Limburg Principles in holding that while Article 2(1) 'provides for progressive realisation and acknowledges the constraints due to the limits of available resources, it also imposes various obligations which are of immediate effect'.[69] The Committee gives the example of the non-discrimination provision in Article 2(2), but also holds that the term 'to take steps' in Article 2(1) of the Covenant imposes a duty on States, notwithstanding the fact the Covenant rights can only be fully realised progressively, to take 'steps towards that goal . . . within a reasonably short time after the Covenants entry into force for the State concerned', such steps should be 'deliberate, concrete and targeted as clearly as possible towards meeting the obligations recognized in the Covenant'.[70]

---

66 They are: General Comment No. 1 – Reporting by States Parties (1989); General Comment No. 2 – International Technical Assistance Measures (1990); General Comment No. 3 – The Nature of States Parties' Obligations (1990); General Comment No. 4 – The Right to Adequate Housing (1991); General Comment No. 5 – Persons With Disabilities (1994); General Comment No. 6 – The Economic, Social and Cultural Rights of Older Persons (1995); General Comment No. 7 – The Right to Adequate Housing: Forced Evictions (1997); General Comment No. 8 – The Relation Between Economic Sanctions and Economic, Social and Cultural Rights (1997); General Comment No. 9 – Domestic Application of the Covenant (1998); General Comment No. 10 – The Role of National Human Rights Institutions in Protecting Economic, Social and Cultural Rights (1998); General Comment No. 11 – Plans of Action for Primary Education (1999); General Comment No. 12 – The Right to Adequate Food (1999); General Comment No. 13 – The Right to Education (1999); General Comment No. 14 – The Right to the Highest Attainable Standard of Health (2000); General Comment No. 15 – The Right to Water (2002); General Comment No. 16 – Article 3, The Equal Right of Men and Women to the Enjoyment of Economic, Social and Cultural Rights (2005); General Comment No. 17 – The Right of Everyone to Benefit From the Protection of the Moral and Material Interests Resulting From Any Scientific, Literary or Artistic Production of Which he is the Author (2005); General Comment No. 18 – The Right to Work (2005); General Comment No. 19 – The Right to Social Security (2008); and General Comment No. 20 – Non-Discrimination in Economic, Social and Cultural Rights (2009).
67 Craven (n. 57) at p. 90.
68 *Ibid.* at p. 91.
69 General Comment No. 3 – The Nature of States Parties' Obligations, UN doc. E/1991/23 at para. 1.
70 *Ibid.* at para. 2.

As regards the measures to be taken towards the realisation of the Covenant rights, the Committee's thinking is again concurrent with the Limburg Principles. In General Comment No. 3 the Committee notes that in many instances the adoption of legislative measures will be highly desirable, and in certain cases indispensable, for the satisfaction of the States' obligations.[71] However, the Committee is quick to point out that 'the adoption of legislative measures . . . is by no means exhaustive of the obligations of States parties'.[72] States should therefore be open to the adoption of a wide variety of measures, in particular the provision of judicial remedies for Covenant rights which are consonant with the States' domestic legal order.[73] In this regard the Committee points out that a number of the rights contained in the Covenant would seem to be 'capable of immediate application by judicial or other organs in many national legal systems'.[74] The Committee also notes that the adoption of appropriate administrative, financial, educational and social measures might be sufficient,[75] but the ultimate arbiter of the appropriateness or otherwise of a State's actions will be the Committee.[76]

The Committee considers the significance and the nature of the idea of progressive realisation contained in Article 2(1) and holds that:

> The concept of progressive realisation constitutes a recognition of the fact that full realisation of all economic, social and cultural rights will generally not be able to be achieved in a short period of time . . . Nevertheless, the fact that realisation over time, or in other words progressively, is foreseen under the Covenant should not be misinterpreted as depriving the obligation of all meaningful content. It is on the one hand a necessary flexibility device, reflecting the realities of the real world and the difficulties involved for any country in ensuring full realisation of economic, social and cultural rights. On the other hand, the phrase must be read in the light of the overall objective, indeed the *raison d'être*, of the Covenant which is to establish clear obligations for States parties in respect of the full realisation of the rights in question. It thus imposes an obligation to move as expeditiously and effectively as possible towards that goal. Moreover, any deliberately retrogressive measures in that regard would require the most careful consideration and would need to be fully justified by reference to the totality of the rights provided for in the Covenant and in the context of the full use of the maximum available resources.[77]

71 *Ibid.* at para. 3.
72 *Ibid.* at para. 4.
73 *Ibid.* at para. 5.
74 *Ibid.*
75 *Ibid.* at para. 7.
76 *Ibid.* at para. 4.
77 *Ibid.* at para. 9.

Consequently, the Committee rejects the idea that the rights guaranteed by the ICESCR are, by virtue of the concept of progressive realisation, mere paper tigers. Instead the Committee makes the point that Article 2(1) of the Covenant imposes tangible obligations on States to introduce measures targeted towards the realisation of the substantive Covenant rights. What is more, the Committee also introduced here what might be referred to as the principle of non-retrogression, according to which any back-pedalling, as it were, with regard to the progressive realisation of socio-economic rights, will be presumptively invalid.

The Committee also introduced another important principle in General Comments No. 3, one which had also been intimated in the Limburg Principles, the idea of 'minimum core obligations'. According to the Committee:

> [A] minimum core obligation to ensure the satisfaction of, at the very least, minimum essential levels of each of the rights is incumbent upon every State party. Thus, for example, a State party in which any significant number of individuals is deprived of essential foodstuffs, of essential primary health care, of basic shelter and housing, or of the most basic forms of education is, *prima facie*, failing to discharge its obligations under the Covenant. If the Covenant were to be read in such a way as not to establish such a minimum core obligation, it would be largely deprived of its *raison d'être*.[78]

This obligation, however, is somewhat qualified by the Committee noting that it would have cognisance of the available resources in a given State when deciding whether or not its failure to secure certain minimum core obligations was so egregious as to constitute a violation of the Covenant. However, the Committee again stressed the importance of such minimum core obligations by noting that a heavy burden of proof will rest on the State to demonstrate that 'every effort has been made to use all resources that are at its disposition in an effort to satisfy, as a matter of priority, those minimum obligations'.[79]

General Comment No. 9 also addresses a number of important issues with regard to States' obligations under the ICESCR. The Committee begins this comment by asserting that the central, overarching obligation of States in relation to the ICESCR is to 'give effect to the rights recognized therein'.[80] The Covenant, however, adopts an intentionally flexible and eclectic approach as regards the manner in which such rights are effectuated within the domestic legal order.[81] Notwithstanding this flexibility, the Covenant places an obligation on States to ensure that appropriate means of redress and remedies are

---

78 *Ibid.* at para. 10.
79 *Ibid.*
80 General Comment No. 9 – The Domestic Application of the Covenant, UN doc. E/1999/22 at para. 1.
81 *Ibid.*

available for the violation of Covenant rights.[82] In particular the Committee believes there must be some form of domestic judicial remedy available for infringements of socio-economic rights.[83] The central point, however, of General Comment No. 9 is the Committee's desire to emphasise the interdependence and interrelatedness of the rights enshrined in the ICESCR, as well as their justiciability. In this regard, the Committee leaves to the discretion of individual States the manner in which they implement the Covenant within their domestic legal order.[84] However, the Committee insists that the means through which this is done should be on a par with the way in which the State provides protection for other rights, for example civil and political rights, and where a State fails to do this it will have to provide a compelling justification for its failure.[85] As regards the issue of judicial remedies for the protection of Covenant rights, the Committee expresses the view that such remedies will not always be necessary; in certain circumstances administrative remedies will suffice, the guiding principle in this regard should be that 'whenever a Covenant right cannot be made fully effective without some role for the judiciary, judicial remedies are necessary' and should be provided.[86]

Finally in General Comment No. 9 the Committee rejects the commonly held view that economic, social and cultural rights are not amenable to judicial enforcement and protection; are not justiciable. The Committee notes that while the Covenant provides a degree of flexibility to States in relation to the means to be used in realising Covenant rights, it would be difficult to show that, for example, legislative and administrative means are effective where they 'are not reinforced or complemented by judicial remedies'. Thus, the Committee implicitly rejects the idea that Covenant rights are non-justiciable, by holding that their effective realisation is unlikely to be achieved in the absence of avenues of judicial recourse. The Committee then addresses, in a more explicit manner, the question of justiciability, and its comments in this regard merit quotation at some length:

> In relation to civil and political rights, it is generally taken for granted that judicial remedies for violations are essential. Regrettably, the contrary assumption is too often made in relation to economic, social and cultural rights. This discrepancy is not warranted either by the nature of the rights or by the relevant Covenant provisions. The Committee has already made clear that it considers many of the provisions in the Covenant to be capable of immediate implementation. Thus, in General Comment No. 3 (1990) it cited, by way of example, articles 3; 7, paragraph (a) (i); 8; 10, paragraph 3; 13, paragraph 2 (a); 13, paragraph 3; 13, paragraph 4; and 15, paragraph

82 *Ibid.* at para. 2.
83 *Ibid.* at para. 3.
84 *Ibid.* at paras. 4–8.
85 *Ibid.* at para. 7.
86 *Ibid.* at para. 9.

3. It is important in this regard to distinguish between justiciability (which refers to those matters which are appropriately resolved by the courts) and norms which are self-executing (capable of being applied by courts without further elaboration). While the general approach of each legal system needs to be taken into account, *there is no Covenant right which could not, in the great majority of systems, be considered to possess at least some significant justiciable dimensions.* It is sometimes suggested that matters involving the allocation of resources should be left to the political authorities rather than the courts. While the respective competences of the various branches of government must be respected, it is appropriate to acknowledge that courts are generally already involved in a considerable range of matters which have important resource implications. *The adoption of a rigid classification of economic, social and cultural rights which puts them, by definition, beyond the reach of the courts would thus be arbitrary and incompatible with the principle that the two sets of human rights are indivisible and interdependent.* It would also drastically curtail the capacity of the courts to protect the rights of the most vulnerable and disadvantaged groups in society.[87]

The Committee therefore refutes the idea that socio-economic rights are qualitatively different to civil and political rights, as many of their detractors claim, and instead reasserts their justiciability within the paradigm of the interdependence and indivisibility of all international human rights standards.

2.3.3 The Maastricht Guidelines

Ten years after the adoption of the Limburg Principles the International Committee of Jurists again convened a gathering of international experts on socio-economic rights with a view to addressing the issue of violations of such rights. What emerged from this meeting were the: 'Maastricht Guidelines on Violations of Economic, Social and Cultural Rights',[88] which represent an important summing up, as it were, a sort of codification of the principles which had been developed, in the ten years since the Limburg Principles, through the General Comments and other practices of the CESCR and other relevant bodies and therefore represent another important element in the normative development of the ICESCR.

The Guidelines begin by restating the relevance and importance of socio-economic rights in the present era of globalisation,[89] as well as reaffirming the indivisibility and interdependence of all human rights.[90] The emergent multi-layered typology of States' obligations in relation to human rights, under which

87 *Ibid.* at para. 10 (emphasis added).
88 'The Maastricht Guidelines on Violations of Economic, Social and Cultural Rights' (1998) 20 *Human Rights Quarterly* 691.
89 *Ibid.* at paras. 1–3.
90 *Ibid.* at para. 4.

States are understood to have the related obligations to respect, protect and fulfil all human rights is introduced and affirmed.[91] Each of these layers of obligation is understood to create a corresponding State duty at that level. The Maastricht Guidelines also restate a number of important principles, which had already been developed in the Limburg Principles and the various General Comments of the CESCR, including the importance of the protection of a 'minimum core' level of certain Covenant rights.[92] The Guidelines then set out a non-exhaustive list of potential violations of the Covenant rights in the following terms:

> A violation of economic, social and cultural rights occurs when a State pursues, by action or omission, a policy or practice which deliberately contravenes or ignores obligations of the Covenant, or fails to achieve the required standard of conduct or result. Furthermore, any discrimination on grounds of race, colour, sex, language, religion, political or other opinion, national or social origin, property, birth or other status with the purpose or effect of nullifying or impairing the equal enjoyment or exercise of economic, social and cultural rights constitutes a violation of the Covenant.[93]

More specific violations of Covenant rights are also indicated in the Guidelines.[94] Finally the Guidelines restate the point that the State is the primary duty bearer in relation to ensuring the realisation of economic, social and cultural rights.[95]

2.3.4 Concluding observations on states' reports

Under the terms of Article 16(1) ICESCR, States are obliged to submit reports 'on the measures which they have adopted and the progress made in achieving the observance of the rights' recognised in the Covenant. Failure on behalf of a State to submit such reports constitutes a violation of the Covenant.[96] Commenting on States' obligations with respect to reporting under the Covenant the CESCR has noted that such obligations are principally intended to assist that State in fulfilling its obligations under the Covenant and to assist the Committee in monitoring State compliance with the terms of the Covenant.[97] The Committee rejects the view that the States' obligations to report under the Covenant are merely of a formal nature to satisfy the States' international obligations, rather the Committee views the process of preparing

91 *Ibid.* at para. 6.
92 *Ibid.* at paras. 9 and 10.
93 *Ibid.* at para. 11.
94 *Ibid.* at paras.14 and 15.
95 *Ibid.* at paras. 18–23.
96 Craven (n. 57) at p. 57.
97 CESCR General Comment No. 1, UN doc.E/1989/22 at para. 1.

and submitting reports under the Covenant as being conducive to certain substantive objectives.[98] The substantive objectives which the States' reporting obligations are conducive to include are: (i) to ensure that States are aware of the actual extent to which the rights protected by the Covenant are, or are not, being enjoyed within the State;[99] (ii) to provide the State with a framework within which it can formulate clearly stated and targeted policies to effect the progressive realisation of the rights recognised in the Covenant;[100] (iii) to facilitate public scrutiny of government policies with respect to economic, social and cultural rights;[101] (iv) to provide a concrete basis on which the State, and the Committee, can evaluate the progress which has been made towards realisation of States' obligations under the Covenant;[102] and (v) to allow States to recognise the difficulties and obstacle impeding the progressive realisation of economic, social and cultural rights.[103]

Article 17(1) provides that the periodicity of States reporting shall be set by the ECOSOC, in consultation with States and specialised agencies; however, since the establishment of the CESCR it has been that body which has set standards and procedures for the production of States reports. The current practice is that States are expected to issue an initial report within two years of the Covenant's entry into force and thereafter at five-yearly intervals.[104] The Committee has also established guidelines for the content of States' reports, which includes the obligation that reports are required to cover all of the rights in the Covenant on the same basis and that reports should include all the information necessary for the Committee to make a proper evaluation of the extent to which the State is in compliance with its obligations under the Covenant.[105] Having considered a State's report the Committee will then issue concluding observations and recommendations in relation to the report and the State's compliance with the Covenant.[106] Given the historical lack of a complaints mechanism within the context of the ICESCR, the examination of States' reports, and the concluding observations with respect to such reports provide an insight, of sorts, into what practical, real-world steps the CESCR would consider appropriate for the realisation of socio-economic rights.

While these recommendations are by no means legally binding,[107] they nonetheless enjoy a special status when they purport to authoritatively interpret the Treaty,[108] and are particularly noteworthy when they discuss violations

---

98 *Ibid.*
99 *Ibid.* at para. 3.
100 *Ibid.* at para. 4.
101 *Ibid.* at para. 5.
102 *Ibid.* at para. 6.
103 *Ibid.* at para. 8.
104 Craven (n. 57) at p. 62.
105 *Ibid.* at p. 63.
106 *Ibid.* at pp. 87–89.
107 Michael O'Flaherty, 'The Concluding Observations of the United Nations Human Rights Treaty Bodies' (2006) 6(1) *Human Rights Law Review* 27 at p. 33.
108 *Ibid.* at p. 34.

of the Treaty.[109] In this section we will very briefly look at some of the recommendations which the Committee has made with respect to Ireland's implementation of the ICESCR. To date, Ireland has submitted two reports under the ICESCR; the initial report was dealt with in May 1999 and the second one in May 2002. In response to Ireland's first report the main areas of concern identified by the Committee included the fact that the Covenant had not been fully incorporated or reflected in domestic legislation,[110] and that the National Anti-Poverty Strategy did not adopt a human rights approach to tackling the issues related to poverty.[111] In its suggestions and recommendations in relation to the protection of Covenant rights within the Irish legal order the Committee urged the State, *inter alia*, to incorporate justiciable socio-economic rights through an amendment to the Constitution.[112] In dealing with Ireland's second report the Committee again highlighted the continued failure to take steps to transpose the Covenant's provisions into domestic law as a matter of concern.[113] In its conclusions and recommendations the Committee again 'strongly [recommended] that the State party incorporate economic, social and cultural rights in . . . the Constitution, as well as in other domestic legislation'.[114] The Committee went on to make the point that regardless of the State's constitutional approach to international law (monism or dualism), the State, following ratification of an international instrument, was under an obligation to comply with and give full effect to the terms of that instrument in the domestic legal order.[115]

Its concluding observations, in particular the matters of concern and the recommendations, albeit directed at one country, nonetheless give further insight into the Committee's view, articulated also in its General Comments, that socio-economic rights can and should be made judicially enforceable at the level of domestic law.[116] Even more notable is the fact that the Committee in its recommendations on both of Ireland's reports recommends that socio-economic rights be added to the Constitution by way of amendment; this, again, goes to illustrate the Committee's firmly held, and often articulated, view that most socio-economic rights are amenable to judicial enforcement at the level of domestic constitutional law, and should be so enforced. Before concluding this section on the ICESCR, the next sub-section looks briefly at the recent

---

109 *Ibid.* at p. 36.
110 Concluding Observations of the Committee on Economic, Social and Cultural Rights: Ireland E/C.12/1/Add.35 (15/05/1999) at para. 9.
111 *Ibid.* at para. 12.
112 *Ibid.* at para. 22.
113 Concluding Observations of the Committee on Economic, Social and Cultural Rights: Ireland E/C.12/1/Add.77 (05/06/02) at para. 12.
114 *Ibid.* at para. 23.
115 *Ibid.*
116 See also Leila Choukroune, 'Justiciability of Economic, Social and Cultural Rights: The UN Committee on Economic, Social and Cultural Rights' Review of China's First Periodic Report on the Implementation of the International Covenant on Economic, Social and Cultural Rights' (2005) 19 *Columbia Journal of Asian Law* 30 at p. 32.

adoption by the UN General Assembly of an Optional Protocol to the ICESCR allowing for individual complaints to be made to the CESCR against States for alleged violations of the rights protected by the ICESCR.

2.3.5 The Optional Protocol to the ICESCR

In December 2008, following a long series of 'advances and setbacks',[117] the UN General Assembly approved the text of an Optional Protocol to the ICESCR,[118] which, once it enters into force, will allow for both groups and individuals to lodge complaints about violations of socio-economic rights with the CESCR.[119] Advocates of socio-economic rights have, since at least the early 1990s, called for the adoption of an Optional Protocol to the ICESCR, and over the last number of years the continued absence of such a mechanism had increasingly come to look 'like an historical hangover'.[120] Those who argued for the adoption of an Optional Protocol had long maintained that such an instrument 'might prompt states to ensure the availability of more effective remedies at the national level'.[121] More broadly, advocates of the Optional Protocol argue that it 'will offer victims of socio-economic rights violations a new avenue for claiming these rights at the international level',[122] and furthermore that the fear of international censure will induce States to pay greater attention to the realisation of socio-economic rights.[123]

The extent to which the Optional Protocol is likely to live up to these expectations may be doubted.[124] However, before considering its likely impact and, more pertinently, its significance for the arguments at the centre of this study, I will set out the operative provisions of the Optional Protocol. The Optional Protocol provides that complaints can be made to the Committee either by individuals or groups of individuals who claim that their rights under the ICESCR have been violated;[125] it provides that the Committee shall only consider a communication when it is shown that all domestic remedies have been

---

117 Arambulo (n. 42) at p. 49; for a useful summary of the various stages leading up to the ultimate drafting and adoption of the Optional Protocol, see Lilian Chenwi, 'Towards the Adoption of the International Complaints Mechanism for Enforcing Socio-Economic Rights Under the ICESCR' (2008) 9(2) *ESR Review* 20 at p. 22.
118 General Assembly Resolution 832, UN GAOR, 63rd Session, UN Doc A/RES/63/117 (2008).
119 Article 2 OP–ICESCR.
120 Langford and King (n. 65) at p. 514.
121 Arambulo (n. 42) at p. 49.
122 Chenwi (n. 117) at p. 22.
123 See Jan Kratochvil, 'Realizing a Promise: A Case for Ratification of the Optional Protocol to the Covenant on Economic, Social and Cultural Rights' (2009) 16(3) *Human Rights Brief* 30 at p. 33; and Pius Langa, 'Taking Dignity Seriously – Judicial Reflections on the Optional Protocol to the ICESCR' (2009) 27 *Nordisk Tidsskrift For Menneskerettigheter* 29 at p. 31.
124 Clare Mahon, 'Progress at the Front: The Draft Optional Protocol to the International Covenant on Economic, Social and Cultural Rights' (2008) 8 *Human Rights Law Review* 617 at p. 620.
125 Article 2 OP–ICESCR.

exhausted;[126] furthermore it provides, somewhat unusually, that the Committee may decline to consider a communication 'where it does not reveal that the author has suffered a clear disadvantage' unless the Committee considers the communication raises a serious issue of general importance.[127] Perhaps the most significant provision of the Optional Protocol provides that in the substantive assessment of the merits of a communication the Committee:

> shall consider the reasonableness of the steps taken by the State Party in accordance with Part II of the Covenant. In doing so, the Committee shall bear in mind that the State Party may adopt a range of possible policy measures for the implementation of the rights set forth in the Covenant.[128]

It also provides for the Committee to request the State which is the subject of a communication, without prejudice to the finding on the merits of the complaint, to adopt interim measures in exceptional circumstances in order to avoid irreparable harm to the victims of the alleged violation;[129] for friendly settlement of complaints,[130] and for interstate communications.[131] The main provisions, though, are those contained in Articles 2, 3, 4 and 8 noted above.

While it is far too soon to speculate on the likely impact of the Optional Protocol, its supporters have, perhaps unsurprisingly, enthusiastically welcomed its adoption and are confident that it will make a substantial contribution to the realisations of socio-economic rights. As Jan Kratochvil argues:

> it is fair to say that the Protocol is a major success in terms of its coherence and integrity. It does not compromise or undermine any of the rights in the Covenant or any aspects of the rights. On the contrary, it establishes the first comprehensive and universal procedure for individual complaints regarding violations of all aspects of [socio-economic] rights.[132]

In similarly optimistic terms Lilian Chenwi argues that '[in] a nutshell, it will promote the better implementation of socio-economic rights',[133] while Pius Langa is also confident that the adoption of the Optional Protocol will result in greater State efforts towards the realisation of socio-economic rights.[134] However, there are grounds to be cautious, or at least less optimistic, about the potential impact of the Optional Protocol. In particular, Claire Mahon wonders

126 Article 3(1) OP–ICESCR.
127 Article 4 OP–ICESCR.
128 Article 8(4) OP–ICESCR.
129 Article 5(1) OP–ICESCR.
130 Article 7 OP–ICESCR.
131 Article 10 OP–ICESCR.
132 Kratochvil (n. 123) at p. 31.
133 Chenwi (n. 117) at p. 22.
134 Langa (n. 123) at p. 31.

if the 'government-friendly' language in Article 8 may serve to 'water down the Committee's power to intervene' and rigorously assess States' compliance with the Covenant, and thereby undermine the entire enterprise.[135] Only time will tell what the significance of the Optional Protocol will be for the protection of socio-economic rights. At this stage we may say that, in a general sense, it is a welcome development (as it represents another step towards the genuine parity of all human rights), but that ultimately we must wait to see how the Committee's jurisprudence develops before we can fully assess the significance of the complaints procedure.

With respect to the central focus of this study the adoption of the Optional Protocol also merits a cautious welcome. On the one hand, the adoption of an individual complaints mechanism for the protection of socio-economic rights reinforces the point made by the CESCR time and time again in its General Comments, and concluding observations on State reports, that socio-economic rights can and should be made amendable to adjudication. However, because the CESCR will, upon the coming into force of the Optional Protocol, adjudicate on alleged violations of socio-economic rights in an institutional context which is qualitatively different to that which domestic supreme and constitutional courts operate in, the extent to which its case law will assist in answering the question of the appropriate balance to be struck between the courts and the elected branches of government may be doubted. On the other hand, the Committee's case law will no doubt serve to further clarify the normative content and limitations of various socio-economic rights, and if this ultimately filters down to domestic jurisprudence it will be a most welcome addition.

This, then, represents the general nature of the States' obligations under the ICESCR with respect to the protection of socio-economic rights. For present purposes, the key, normative point running through the Limburg Principles, the Maastricht Guidelines and all of the work of the CESCR, is that socio-economic rights can and should be adjudicated on, preferably in court and on a par with civil and political rights. This general point is further reinforced by the recent adoption of the Optional Protocol to the ICESCR. These various principles also admit to the potential difficulties in realising socio-economic rights, but nonetheless stress that this cannot be a justification for denying them adjudicative space within the domestic legal order. Before concluding this chapter, the next section considers briefly the ways in which the ICCPR has been interpreted to provide protection for certain socio-economic rights.

2.3.6 *International Covenant on Civil and Political Rights*

The ICCPR is the sister covenant to the ICESCR and was adopted on the same date, but the two instruments differ significantly in the obligations they impose on States with respect to the rights protected in the respective instruments.

---

135 Mahon (n. 124) at p. 634.

Furthermore, since its inception the ICCPR has had a more expansive and effective monitoring mechanism in place, with the First Optional Protocol to the ICCPR allowing for individual complaints to be made to the Human Rights Committee (HRC), the body established to monitor the implementation of the ICCPR, with respect to alleged violations of the rights protected in the ICCPR.[136] While the focus of the ICCPR is, as the name suggests, civil and political rights, the HRC has, through its determination of individual complaints, extended the ICCPR to provide a degree of protection for socio-economic rights.

The main way in which the HRC has extended the ICCPR to encompass protection of socio-economic rights is through Article 26 of the Covenant, which provides that:

> All persons are equal before the law and are entitled without any discrimination to the equal protection of the law. In this respect, the law shall prohibit any discrimination and guarantee to all persons equal and effective protection against discrimination on any grounds such as race, colour, sex, language, religion, political or other opinion, national or social origin, property, birth or other status.

Because this non-discrimination provision is not qualified, in so far as it does not prohibit discrimination with respect to the enjoyment of the rights protected in the Covenant, but rather discrimination per se, it 'opens up possibilities for claims related to social security' and many other socio-economic rights.[137] And the HRC has not been slow to realise these possibilities. The first case in which the HRC extended the scope of the ICCPR to rights which may more properly be considered the concern of the ICESCR was *Zwaan-de Vries* v. *the Netherlands*.[138]

The complainant in this case sought to challenge a Dutch law which provided that a married woman could only receive unemployment benefits if she could demonstrate that she was the primary breadwinner for her family; no such condition applied to unmarried women, or men, regardless of their marital status, seeking such benefits. The HRC held that the legislation violated the non-discrimination provision in Article 26 ICCPR, but stressed that while the ICCPR did not impose positive obligations on States to provide for social welfare, Article 26 required that where such welfare was provided it was available on a non-discriminatory basis.[139] In the subsequent case of *Gueye et al*

---

136 See Nowak (n. 48) at p. 194.
137 Martin Scheinin, 'Human Rights Committee: Not Only a Committee on Civil and Political Rights' in Langford (ed.), *Social Rights Jurisprudence: Emerging Trends in International and Comparative Law* (Cambridge: Cambridge University Press, 2008) 540 at p. 540.
138 Communication No. 182/1984 (09/04/1987); see also *Broeks* v. *the Netherlands*, Communication No. 172/1984 (09/04/1987).
139 *Zwaan-de Vries* (n. 138) at para. 12.4.

v. *France*,[140] the HRC found a violation of Article 26, where France provided different levels of pension benefit to retired soldiers depending on whether or not they were French citizens. These cases demonstrate that 'it is possible to claim access to social and economic benefits in the absence of legal protection for socio-economic rights, by relying on general prohibitions on discrimination'.[141]

As well as providing protection for certain aspects of socio-economic rights through the application of Article 26, the HRC has extended certain substantive rights contained in the ICCPR to encompass the protection of socio-economic rights by necessary implication. The most noteworthy case being *Lantsova* v. *the Russian Federation*,[142] in which a mother claimed that the failure of the Russian authorities to provide her son with adequate medical treatment while he was in pre-trial detention, resulting in his death from pneumonia after one month in detention, constituted a violation of his right to life under Article 6 ICCPR.[143] The case, therefore, established the intrinsic relationship between civil and political rights and socio-economic rights, an example of what Ida Elisabeth Koch and others refer to as the 'integrated approach',[144] and showed how rights protected under the ICCPR can be interpreted to impose positive obligations on the State for their protection.

The main point to be taken, both from the HRC's Article 26 jurisprudence and the cases which identified positive obligations arising from Covenant rights, is that '[despite] its name, the ICCPR is not a treaty merely concerned with civil and political rights'. More to the point, the cases decided under the ICCPR which extend protection to socio-economic rights serve to reinforce: (i) the general claim of the indivisibility of all human rights; and (ii) the point made consistently by the CESCR, namely that socio-economic rights are amenable to adjudication. However, as with the newly adopted Optional Protocol to the ICESCR, the individual complaints heard by the HRC are dealt with in an institutional context which is markedly different to that of a domestic supreme or constitutional court, and therefore the otherwise commendable work of the HRC in providing protection for socio-economic rights is of limited assistance in terms of addressing the ultimate concern of this study.

---

140 Communication No. 196/1985 (03/04/1989).
141 Denise Meyerson, 'Equality Guarantees and Distributive Inequity' (2008) 19 *Public Law Review* 32 at p. 36.
142 Communication No. 763/1997 (26/03/2002); and see *Pauger* v. *Austria*, Communication No. 716/1996 (25/03/1999), which found an Austrian law which provided higher levels of State pension payments to widows as opposed to widowers as contrary to Article 26.
143 *Ibid.* at para. 9.2.
144 Ida Elisabeth Koch, 'Economic, Social and Cultural Rights as Components in Civil and Political Rights: A Hermeneutic Perspective' (2006) 10 *International Journal of Human Rights* 405 at p. 408.

2.4 Conclusion

From this extensive, albeit not quite exhaustive, examination of the principles developed for the protection of socio-economic rights at the international level we can draw a number of conclusions. The first is that under the International Bill of Rights socio-economic rights are recognised as an integral and equal part of the human rights protection enterprise. Furthermore, the practices of both the CESCR and the HRC, under the ICESCR and the ICCPR respectively, attest to the firmly held view, stated in numerous contexts, that socio-economic rights can and should be subject to adjudicative enforcement, at both the international and domestic levels. However, it is also recognised that the full realisation of socio-economic rights is no mean feat, and that adjudicating on the implementation of socio-economic rights at the domestic level requires careful balancing and respect for the various organs of State. All of these considerations, however, do not justify a blanket prohibition on the judicial enforcement of socio-economic rights.

As was noted a number of times throughout this chapter, while the principles developed at the international level are of value, they cannot simply be transposed into a given domestic context without significant modification. They are, in a sense, normative ideals which set out in broad outline the overarching principles which should govern the way in which human rights are implemented. However, due to the relative institutional autonomy of treaty-monitoring bodies, much of what is established as the aspirational ideals at the international level, is not easily translated into the domestic arena of constitutional adjudication. Therefore, the focus in the next four chapters is on the practical experiences which a variety of countries have had in adjudicating on socio-economic rights. In one sense, then, the international standards discussed here provide the foundations of an evaluative framework for assessing the extent to which domestic practices with respect to socio-economic rights live up to the normative ideal. At the same time the domestic experiences discussed show, in some respects, the limits of the aspirational international norms. Ultimately, the aim is to find a synthesis between the two which contributes to the tangible vindication of socio-economic rights.

3   The South African experience

Towards the end of the twentieth century, South Africa was transformed from a 'racist autocracy',[1] in which institutionalised prejudice and systematic discrimination, buttressed by an 'intricate network' of repressive security laws,[2] defined every aspect of the state's organisation;[3] into a 'society based on democratic values, social justice and fundamental rights . . . in which government is based on the will of the people and every citizen is equally protected by the law'.[4] This radical political transformation was accompanied by an 'equally dramatic legal revolution',[5] which saw apartheid-South Africa's 'unrestrained conception of parliamentary sovereignty',[6] replaced by 'one of the most advanced constitutions in history'.[7] One of the 'truly radical' constitutional developments accompanying this transition[8] was the inclusion of justiciable socio-economic rights in the new South African Constitution, as a result of which the most well-developed and extensive domestic jurisprudence on socio-

---

1   Matthew Chaskalson and Dennis Davis, 'Constitutionalism, the Rule of Law and the *First Certification* Judgment' (1997) 13 *South African Journal on Human Rights* 430 at p. 430.
2   Arthur Chaskalson, 'From Wickedness to Equality: The Moral Transformation of South African Law' (2003) 1 *International Journal of Constitutional Law* 590 at p. 591.
3   For discussions of apartheid-era South Africa and the, relatively, peaceful transition to democratic-constitutionalism see: Nigel Worden, *The Making of Modern South Africa* (2nd edn, Oxford: Blackwell, 1995) at pp. 65–120, 121–146; Heinz Klug, *Constituting Democracy: Law, Globalism and South Africa's Political Reconstruction* (Cambridge: Cambridge University Press, 2000) at pp. 69–177; Pius Langa, 'Social Justice and Rights: The South African Model' (1998) 16 *Windsor Yearbook of Access to Justice* 149; Arthur Chaskalson, 'The Transition to Democracy in South Africa' (1997) 29 *New York University Journal of International Law and Politics* 285; and Chaskalson (n. 2).
4   Preamble to the Constitution of the Republic of South Africa, 1996 (hereinafter 'South African Constitution'].
5   Klug (n. 3) at p. 1.
6   *Ibid.* at p. 35.
7   Cyrus Dugger, 'Rights Waiting for Change: Socio-Economic Rights in the New South Africa' (2007) 19 *Florida Journal of International Law* 195 at p. 195.
8   Pierre de Vos, 'Pious Wishes or Directly Enforceable Human Rights? Social and Economic Rights in South Africa's 1996 Constitution' (1997) 13 *South African Journal on Human Rights* 67 at p. 67.

economic rights to date is provided by the South African Constitutional Court.[9] Consequently, any attempt to understand the appropriate role of courts in enforcing socio-economic rights must include an examination of the South African experience. This chapter begins with an overview of the historical background to the adoption of the new South African Constitution and a description of its key provisions. The core of the chapter then involves an exposition and evaluation of the South African Constitutional Court's socio-economic rights jurisprudence, with a view to identifying the approach adopted by the Court and the way in which it seeks to strike the appropriate balance between respect for the elected branches of government and vindicating socio-economic rights.

3.1 Post-apartheid and the New South African Constitution

The process leading up to the adoption of the new South African Constitution unfolded as follows: multiparty negotiations for a political settlement, which began in earnest in 1991, led to the adoption of a transitional constitution in 1993; the first democratic elections in South Africa were held on the basis of this constitution in 1994; significantly this transitional constitution contained 34 constitutional principles to which the final constitution would have to conform in order for it to be validly enacted. The 1996 Constitution was drafted by a Constitutional Assembly comprising the two houses of parliament elected in 1994. The Constitutional Court was required to certify the draft constitution devised by the Constitutional Assembly, but refused to do so at the first time of asking, as it found that certain aspects conflicted with the constitutional principles contained in the transitional constitution.[10] The Constitutional Assembly reconvened to remedy the constitutional infirmities identified by the Constitutional Court and the Court subsequently approved the revised constitution, which then came into force on the 4 February 1997.[11]

---

9 For useful introductory discussions of the South African Constitutional Court's socio-economic rights jurisprudence, see Danie Brand, 'Socio-Economic Rights and the Courts in South Africa: Justiciability on a Sliding Scale' in Coomans (ed.), *Justiciability of Economic and Social Rights* (Antwerp: Intersentia, 2006) 207; Dennis Davis, 'Socio-Economic Rights: The Promise and Limitation – The South African Experience' in Barak-Erez and Gross (eds.), *Exploring Social Rights* (Oxford: Hart Publishing, 2007) 193; and Sandra Liebenberg, 'South Africa: Adjudicating Social Rights Under a Transformative Constitution' in Langford (ed.), *Social Rights Jurisprudence: Emerging Trends in International and Comparative Law* (Cambridge: Cambridge University Press, 2008) 75.

10 *Ex parte Chairperson of the Constitutional Assembly: In re Certification of the Constitution of the Republic of South Africa 1996* 1996 (10) BCLR 1253 (CC) ['*First Certification* judgment']; for a summary discussion of this judgment see Chaskalson and Davis (n. 1).

11 See Liebenberg (n. 9) at p. 75; Chaskalson (n. 3) at pp. 289–292; and Worden (n. 3) at pp. 121–145.

3.1.1 *The debate over the Constitution*

During the negotiations on the drafting of the new Constitution 'most political parties supported the entrenchment of at least some socio-economic rights'.[12] There was nonetheless a spirited academic debate about the inclusion of such rights,[13] with commentators such as Dennis Davis (who subsequently went on to become a trenchant defender of socio-economic rights), arguing that 'introducing a battery of specific social and economic demands in a constitution is to place far too much power in the hands of the judiciary, which . . . is never as accountable to the population as is the legislature or an executive'.[14] In response Etienne Mureinik, quite presciently given the Constitutional Court's subsequent socio-economic rights jurisprudence, argued that the courts could play a meaningful role in vindicating socio-economic rights, without trampling on the separation of powers, by confining themselves to a deferential analysis of whether or not the elected branches of government were seeking to implement socio-economic rights in a sincere and rational manner.[15] In the end the argument was won by those in favour of including socio-economic rights, primarily because the majority of the people involved in the debate, indeed the majority of South Africans, recognised apartheid's legacy of gross material inequality, thus making 'the argument for socio-economic rights irresistible, in large part because [they] seemed an indispensable way of expressing a commitment to overcome the legacy of apartheid'.[16]

Nonetheless some of the concerns about the constitutional entrenchment of socio-economic rights filtered into the Constitutional Court's deliberations in the *First Certification* judgment. During the certification process objections were raised to the inclusion of socio-economic rights in the new Constitution, the main argument against their inclusion being that they would breach the doctrine of the separation of powers. In reply to this the Constitutional Court held that:

> It is true that the inclusion of socio-economic rights may result in courts making orders which have direct implications for budgetary matters. However, even when a court enforces civil and political rights such as equality, freedom of speech and the right to a fair trial, the order it makes

12 Liebenberg (n. 9) at p. 76.
13 See for example: Nicholas Haysom, 'Constitutionalism, Majoritarian Democracy and Socio-economic Rights' (1992) 8 *South African Journal on Human Rights* 451; Etienne Mureinik, 'Beyond a Charter of Luxuries: Economic Rights in the Constitution' (1992) 8 *South African Journal on Human Rights* 464; and 'The Case Against the Inclusion of Socio-economic Demands in a Bill of Rights Except as Directive Principles' (1992) 8 *South African Journal on Human Rights* 475.
14 Davis (n. 13) at p. 489.
15 Mureinik (n. 13) at p. 474.
16 Cass Sunstein, *Designing Democracy: What Constitutions Do* (Oxford: Oxford University Press, 2001) at p. 224.

will often have such implications. A court may require the provision of legal aid, or the extension of state benefits to a class of people who formerly were not beneficiaries of such benefits. In our view it cannot be said that by including socio-economic rights within a bill of rights, a task is conferred upon the courts so different from that ordinarily conferred upon them by a bill of rights that it results in a breach of the separation of powers.[17]

The Court also rejected the idea that socio-economic rights were in some essential respect non-justiciable, by arguing that socio-economic rights were 'at least to some extent justiciable' and, in the main, imposed similar obligations on the state (and therefore required the exercise of a similar judicial function) as did civil and political rights.[18] The Court thereby affirmed the legitimacy of constitutionalising socio-economic rights, and cleared the way for their inclusion in the new South African Constitution.

3.1.2 *The New South African Constitution*

As enacted the new South African Constitution contains a number of noteworthy provisions. Here we will look briefly at those provisions that are the most immediately relevant to our discussion of the Constitutional Court's socio-economic rights jurisprudence. From the opening lines of the Preamble the centrality of social justice and human rights is evident; the Constitution, in an effort to stress its distinctness from the apartheid era and to mark the new departure, also emphasises that the 'Constitution is the supreme law' and that any 'law or conduct inconsistent with it is invalid' and, interestingly with respect to socio-economic rights, that 'the obligations imposed by it must be fulfilled'.[19] The centrepiece of the Constitution is the Bill of Rights, which is described as 'a cornerstone of democracy in South Africa'. With respect to all of the rights protected in the Bill of Rights a general provision of the Constitution provides that, reflecting international human rights standards, the 'state must respect, protect, promote and fulfil the rights in the Bill of Rights'.[20]

The specific socio-economic rights guarantees are provided in sections 26–29 and in section 35.[21] Section 26 provides that:

---

17 *First Certification* judgment at para. 77.
18 *First Certification* judgment at para. 78.
19 South African Constitution s. 2.
20 South African Constitution s. 7.
21 Section 35(2)(e) of the South African Constitution provides that detained persons, including sentenced prisoners, are entitled, *inter alia*, to 'conditions of detention that are consistent with human dignity, including at least exercise and the provision, at state expense, of adequate accommodation, nutrition, reading material and medical treatment'; however this provision has not, as of yet, been of central concern in the Constitutional Court's socio-economic rights jurisprudence, and will therefore not be considered any further in this chapter. Although see *B* v. *Minister of Correctional Services* 1997 (6) BCLR 789 (CC), in which the Court considers the extent of the entitlement to adequate medical treatment for HIV infected prisoners.

1.   Everyone has the right to have access to adequate housing.
2.   The state must take reasonable legislative and other measures, within its available resources, to achieve the progressive realisation of this right.
3.   No one may be evicted from their home, or have their home demolished, without an order of court made after considering all the relevant circumstances. No legislation may permit arbitrary evictions.

And section 27 provides that:

1.   Everyone has the right to have access to:

     a.   health care services, including reproductive health care;
     b.   sufficient food and water; and
     c.   social security, including, if they are unable to support themselves and their dependants, appropriate social assistance.

2.   The state must take reasonable legislative and other measures, within its available resources, to achieve the progressive realisation of each of these rights.
3.   No one may be refused emergency medical treatment.

Patently these provisions render socio-economic rights 'explicitly . . . justiciable' and, as will be shown presently, the Constitution also 'gives the courts the power to interpret these rights and to resolve disputes on their basis' in respect of which 'South African courts possess an impressive array of powers'.[22] However, the rights are by no means absolute and all encompassing, as the second sub-section of both provisions contain explicit 'internal limitations' clauses, which, according to Pierre de Vos, were included as 'an acknowledgment that not all rights can be immediately and completely fulfilled by the state'.[23]

   Unlike the clearly circumscribed obligations contained in sections 26 and 27, section 28 imposes a seemingly absolute, i.e. not limited by available resources, obligation on the state to provide children with 'basic nutrition, shelter, basic health care services and social services'.[24] As will be seen below, the Constitutional Court has shown considerable unease when presented with claims grounded on this provision, and has yet to articulate an entirely satisfactory position on it.[25] Along with the explicitly guaranteed socio-

---

22   Brand (n. 9) at p. 208.
23   de Vos (n. 8) at p. 93.
24   South African Constitution s. 28(1)(c); the opening line of s. 28 provides that 'Every child has the right' to, *inter alia*, the socio-economic services listed above, and this general entitlement is not qualified within the text of the provision, leading to the legitimate, admittedly literal, interpretation that this section imposes an absolute obligation with respect to socio-economic rights, albeit of a limited and specified class of persons.
25   See Davis (n. 9) at p. 206; and Sunstein (n. 16) at pp. 228–229.

economic rights, the new Constitution also, as mentioned above, entrusts the Constitutional Court with an 'important institutional role' in the new constitutional dispensation,[26] manifested in the extensive powers of judicial review,[27] and broad remedial powers in constitutional matters conferred on the Court.[28] It can therefore be seen that the new South African Constitution contains a significant catalogue of judicially enforceable socio-economic rights. In the next substantive section we will look at how the Constitutional Court has performed its role in adjudicating on these rights. However, before proceeding to this survey, the next sub-section briefly notes another significant aspect of the new South African Constitution.

3.1.3 A transformative constitution

Before moving on to consider the jurisprudence of the Constitutional Court under the new South African Constitution, it is important to highlight one other significant feature of the new Constitution, one which is arguably as significant as the explicit inclusion of socio-economic rights. It is the fact that the 'South African Constitution is the world's leading example of a transformative constitution'.[29] By 'transformative constitutionalism' it is meant that the new Constitution enjoins the South African polity, and all of the institutions established under the Constitution, to pursue:

> a long-term project of constitutional enactment, interpretation and enforcement committed . . . to transforming [the] country's political and social institutions and power relationships in a democratic, participatory, and egalitarian direction . . . [which] connotes an enterprise of inducing social change through nonviolent political processes grounded in law.[30]

Commenting on this transformative vision, Davis goes so far as to argue that taken together the various provisions of the Constitution 'provide support for the contention that, read as a whole, the text should be read as a social democratic narrative in which, in the words of the preamble, the Constitution seeks to heal the divisions of our past and lay the foundations for a democratic and

---

26 Jonathan Klaaren, 'Structures of Government in the 1996 South African Constitution: Putting Democracy Back into Human Rights' (1997) 13 *South African Journal on Human Rights* 3 at p. 11.

27 See South African Constitution ss. 167 and 173.

28 Section 172(1) provides that 'When deciding a constitutional matter within its power, a court . . . may make any order that is just and equitable'; and see the decision of the Constitutional Court in *Fose* v. *Minister of Safety and Security* 1997 (7) BCLR 851 (CC).

29 Sunstein (n. 16) at p. 224.

30 Karl Klare, 'Legal Culture and Transformative Constitutionalism' (1998) 14 *South African Journal on Human Rights* 146 at p. 150.

open society'.[31] Whether or not the Constitution is, or was intended to be, the manifesto Davis claims it to be,[32] it is indisputably imbued with *a* transformative vision which places great store on, among other things, the value of socio-economic rights and the role of the courts with respect to them.

Consequently, the transformative vision of the new South African Constitution places a particular onus on the judiciary, long implicated in the maintenance of apartheid, to take an active part in the transformation of South African society.[33] In particular the new constitutional dispensation accords the courts an 'important role' in achieving the transformative potential of socio-economic rights.[34] As Pius Langa notes, the '[preamble] to our Constitution records our commitment to attaining social justice and a better quality of life for everyone . . . Courts must strive to achieve substantive equality, dignity and freedom' and these concepts must infuse 'the court's approach to the application of [socio-economic] rights and in giving meaning to their content'.[35] Similarly Dikgang Moseneke argues that the:

> constitutional design of conferring vast powers of judicial review to the courts becomes optimal only if the courts are true to the constitutional mandate . . . in their work, courts should search for substantive justice, which is to be inferred from the foundational values of the Constitution. After all, that is the injunction of the Constitution – transformation.[36]

Therefore, as distinct from many other constitutional or superior courts, the South African Constitutional Court arguably enjoys greater latitude in its dealings with the other branches of government. The transformative vision and

31 Davis (n. 9) at p. 196; cf. Klare (n. 30) who argues, at p. 151, that none of the traditional political or ideological categories, such as social, democratic or liberal, sufficiently capture the *sui generis* nature of the South African constitutional project.
32 For an incisive discussion of the competing normative characterisations of the South African constitutional project, in particular the Bill of Rights project, see Martin Chanock, 'A Post-Calvinist Catechism or a Post-Communist Manifesto? Intersecting Narratives in the South African Bill of Rights Debate' in Alston (ed.), *Promoting Human Rights Through Bills of Rights: Comparative Perspectives* (Oxford: Oxford University Press, 1999) 392.
33 See Pius Langa, 'The Vision of the Constitution' (2003) 120 *South African Law Journal* 670 at pp. 671–672.
34 Geoff Budlender, 'The Role of the Courts in Achieving the Transformative Potential of Socio-Economic Rights' (2007) 8(1) *ESR Review* 9 at p. 9; as Craig Scott puts it 'The 1996 Constitution has given a meta-democratic mandate to the judiciary to interpret and enforce socio-economic rights' (Craig Scott, 'Towards a Principled, Pragmatic Judicial Role' (1999) 1(4) *ESR Review* 4 at p. 4).
35 Pius Langa, 'Taking Dignity Seriously – Judicial Reflections on the Optional Protocol to the ICESCR' (2009) 27 *Nordisk Tidsskrift For Menneskerettigheter* 29 at p. 34. Indeed, s. 39 of the South African Constitution obliges the courts, when interpreting the Bill of Rights, to 'promote the values that underlie an open and democratic society based on human dignity, equality and freedom'.
36 Dikgang Moseneke, 'Transformative Adjudication' (2002) 18 *South African Journal on Human Rights* 309 at p. 316.

commitment of the new South African Constitution as evidenced, *inter alia*, in the Preamble and the socio-economic rights provisions empowers, or more to the point obliges, the courts to take a proactive role in the vindication of constitutional rights.

3.2 The socio-economic rights jurisprudence of the Constitutional Court

This section outlines the socio-economic rights jurisprudence of the South African Constitutional Court. In particular, the focus here is on a trilogy of cases, *Soobramoney*, *Grootboom* and *Treatment Action Campaign*, which 'laid the foundation for socio-economic rights jurisprudence' in South Africa,[37] and also on two more recent cases which, arguably, intimate a qualitative shift in the Court's jurisprudence. The emphasis is on the problems which confronted the Court in these cases, the analytical framework which the Court developed and the ways in which the judgments reveal, both explicitly and by necessary implication, the Court's approach to the overarching issue of the separation of powers and the appropriate role of the courts in enforcing socio-economic rights. This section also considers some more recent cases, which may or may not represent a further evolution of the Court's jurisprudence in the direction of, arguably, a more exacting and less deferential standard of review. The focus here is on elucidation rather than evaluation of the pros and cons of the approach developed by the Constitutional Court, which is left to the next substantive section of this chapter; although, at times, first-blush impressions of how the relevant decision was perceived may be noted.

3.2.1 *Soobramoney*

Following the enactment of the new Constitution, the Constitutional Court's socio-economic rights jurisprudence got off to a somewhat inauspicious, or at the very least anti-climactic, start with the case of *Soobramoney* v. *Minister for Health, KwaZulu-Natal*.[38] The applicant in this case was an unemployed man who suffered from a number of serious medical conditions, including irreversible kidney failure. He had applied to his local public hospital to be admitted to their dialysis programme. However, the hospital notified him that he did not qualify for admission to their programme as places on the programme were reserved for individuals who could either be cured within a relatively short period of time, or those suffering from chronic renal failure who qualified for a liver transplant. Due to the applicant's other medical conditions he did not qualify under the terms of the hospital's policy. The applicant applied to

---

37 Davis (n. 9) at p. 195; similarly Liebenberg (n. 9) at p. 81, notes that these three are the 'landmark cases that have established the foundations of the Constitutional Court's jurisprudence on socio-economic rights'.

38 1997 (12) BCLR 1696 (CC).

the High Court seeking an order compelling the hospital to admit him to the programme, on the basis that a refusal to do so constituted a breach of his constitutional rights; specifically the right to life under section 11 and the right not to be refused emergency medical treatment under section 27(3). His application was dismissed and he appealed, ultimately, to the Constitutional Court and presented it with its first substantive socio-economic rights case.

The lead judgment for the Court was delivered by Chaskalson P., who began his judgment by noting that one of the defining characteristics of the socio-economic rights enshrined in the Constitution was that they were 'dependent upon the resources available for such purposes, and that the corresponding rights themselves are limited by reason of the lack of resources'.[39] With respect to the applicant's case the Court held that his interpretation of section 27(3) was too far reaching, and did not accord with the proper meaning of the provision, and furthermore that as the Constitution explicitly provided for socio-economic rights it was both unnecessary and inappropriate to invoke the right to life as a basis for claiming medical treatment; the Court thus held that the applicant's case fell to be determined in accordance with the right to health provided for in section 27(1) and 27(2).[40] As to the substance of the claim, the Court held that, taking into account the resource-limited nature of the socio-economic rights guaranteed in the Constitution and the limited resources of the hospital, the admissions policy of the hospital could not be said to be arbitrary or discriminatory, and therefore was not in breach of the applicant's limited right of access to medical services.[41]

With respect to the broader issue of the separation of powers, the Court in *Soobramoney* appeared to back-pedal somewhat from the robust role it intimated the courts could play with respect to resource allocation in socio-economic rights cases,[42] to a more restrained and deferential approach. Chaskalson P. argued that:

> decisions about the funding that should be made available for health care and how such funds should be spent . . . involve difficult decisions *to be taken at the political level* in fixing the health budget, and at the functional level in deciding upon the priorities to be met. A court will be slow to interfere with the rational decisions taken in good faith by the political organs and the medical authorities whose responsibility it is to deal with such matters.[43]

39 *Soobramoney* at para. 11.
40 *Soobramoney* at paras. 13–22; and at para. 57 per Sachs J.
41 *Soobramoney* at paras. 25–28.
42 See the *First Certification* judgment (n. 10) at paras. 77–78.
43 *Soobramoney* at para. 29 (emphasis added); note how the judicial role articulated here correlates with the role advocated by Mureinik (n. 13) at p. 474, during the drafting of the new Constitution.

In similar terms Sachs J. argued that as important as the Court's constitutional review function was 'there are areas where *institutional incapacity and
appropriate constitutional modesty require us to be especially cautious*'.[44] On a generous
reading, Sandra Liebenberg argues that in this case the 'Court signalled a
deferential review standard in matters of social and economic policy'.[45] Jeanne
Woods goes somewhat further and argues that it represented an 'overly-
deferential standard of review',[46] and that the Court's approach was tantamount
to 'a retreat from the challenge of justiciable social rights'.[47] Similarly, Darrell
Moellendorf argues that the decision signalled a 'disturbing possibility for the
basis of future decisions about socio-economic rights claims',[48] which might
'foreshadow a downgrading of the status of socio-economic rights'.[49] Though
cognisant of such misgivings and concerns about the decision in *Soobramoney*,
Craig Scott and Philip Alston argued that this was 'too quick a judgment' and
that the appropriate way to understand *Soobramoney* was as the first, tentative
steps of the Court into the terrain of socio-economic rights jurisprudence, which
should by no means be read as limiting the horizons of future jurisprudence.[50]

3.2.2 Grootboom

As the Court's jurisprudence subsequently developed, it would seem that Scott
and Alston had the right of it, as in the next noteworthy case the Constitutional
Court 'largely abandoned' the approach articulated in *Soobramoney*, with its
reliance on 'simple rationality',[51] and began to lay the foundations of an arguably
more nuanced model of socio-economic rights adjudication.[52] This shift took
place in the case of *Government of the Republic of South Africa* v. *Grootboom*,[53] and
it was the first case in which the Court articulated its now well-established reasonableness standard of review. This case concerned the plight of a community
of 800 adults and children who were living in conditions of severe deprivation
and vulnerability on a disused sports ground. The applicants claimed an
entitlement to be provided with emergency accommodation by the state on the

---

44 *Soobramoney* at para. 58 (emphasis added).
45 Liebenberg (n. 9) at p. 81.
46 Jeanne M. Woods, 'Justiciable Social Rights as a Critique of the Liberal Paradigm' (2003)
   38 *Texas International Law Journal* 763 at p. 781.
47 *Ibid.* at p. 783.
48 Darrell Moellendorf, 'Reasoning About Resources: *Soobramoney* and the Future of Socio-
   Economic Rights Claims' (1998) 14 *South African Journal on Human Rights* 327 at p. 327.
49 *Ibid.* at p. 329.
50 Craig Scott and Philip Alston, 'Adjudicating Constitutional Priorities in a Transnational
   Context: A Comment on *Soobramooney's* Legacy and *Grootboom's* Promise' (2000) 16 *South
   African Journal on Human Rights* 206 at pp. 241 and 268.
51 Brand (n. 9) at p. 227.
52 Murray Wesson, '*Grootboom* and Beyond: Reassessing the Socio-Economic Rights
   Jurisprudence of the South African Constitutional Court' (2004) 20 *South African Journal on
   Human Rights* 284 at p. 285.
53 2000 (11) BCLR 257 (CC).

basis of the right of access to adequate housing under section 26 of the Constitution, and also asserted a right to be provided with shelter, on behalf of the children in the group, grounded on section 28(1)(c) of the Constitution. In the High Court Davis J. held that the children affected were entitled to immediate shelter under section 28(1)(c), and that their parents were, by extension, also so entitled, and ordered the relevant authorities to immediately provide them with tents, latrines and a regular supply of water to meet their entitlement to minimal shelter, and it was this order that formed the basis of the appeal to the Constitutional Court.

The decision of the Court was delivered by Yacoob J., who began his decision by noting that while the High Court judge had purported to articulate a minimum core right to which the applicants were immediately entitled, such an approach posed 'difficult questions' for the courts, and the more constitutionally appropriate question for the courts to address was 'whether the measures taken by the state to realise the right afforded by section 26 are reasonable'.[54] Yacoob J. rejected the approach of the High Court judge with respect to section 28(1)(c) on the basis, *inter alia*, that it would produce 'anomalous results' whereby people with children would have a direct and enforceable right to housing not enjoyed by people with no children. Furthermore, the judge held that if the approach of the High Court judge were to be followed the 'carefully constructed constitutional scheme for the progressive realisation of socio-economic rights would make little sense' as it could be trumped in every case by the rights of children to shelter on demand.[55] The issue for the Constitutional Court then became whether or not the policies of the state which were geared towards the progressive realisation of the resource-bounded right of access to adequate housing were reasonable having regard to all the circumstances of the case.

Yacoob J. gives a number of, non-exhaustive, examples of what a reasonable policy would look like; for example it must be supported by adequate financial and human resources, must be reasonably conceived and implemented, balanced, flexible and responsive and transparent. However, in the instant case the judge, although acknowledging the strengths of the government's housing plan which aimed to progressively provide more people with adequate housing, found that the overall policy was unreasonable because it failed to make any provision for the short-term housing needs of the most desperate people.[56] Although in this case the Court found the state to be in breach of its obligations under section 26 of the Constitution, Yacoob J. nonetheless continued the deferential tone first sounded in *Soobramoney* by noting that:

> The precise contours and content of the measures to be adopted are primarily a matter for the legislature and the executive. They must, however,

54 *Grootboom* at para. 33.
55 *Grootboom* at para. 71.
56 *Grootboom* at para. 66.

ensure that the measures they adopt are reasonable. In any challenge based on section 26 in which it is argued that the state has failed to meet the positive obligations imposed upon it by section 26(2), the question will be whether the legislative and other measures taken by the state are reasonable. A court considering reasonableness will not enquire whether other more desirable or favourable measures could have been adopted, or whether public money could have been better spent. The question would be whether the measures that have been adopted are reasonable. It is necessary to recognise that a wide range of possible measures could be adopted by the state to meet its obligations. Many of these would meet the requirement of reasonableness. Once it is shown that the measures do so, this requirement is met.[57]

This standard of review clearly gives the elected branches of government considerable latitude, and to further emphasise the Court's limited role. Yacoob J., notwithstanding the finding of a violation of the applicants' constitutional rights and the dire conditions they were in, confined himself to issuing a declaratory order requiring the state 'to act to meet the obligations' placed on it by section 26, including the obligation to devise, fund, implement and supervise measures to provide relief for those in desperate need of accommodation.[58]

Notwithstanding this clear deferential tone, commentators such as David Beatty argue that *Grootboom* 'is a landmark case in part because the horrible history of homelessness in South Africa is so evocative and in part because the Court was able to help people whose situation was truly desperate in a way that respected the traditional roles of the judiciary and the elected branches of government'.[59] Although *Grootboom* was undoubtedly a landmark case, the extent to which it merits the other plaudits proffered by Beatty is contested by a number of authors, who are critical of the entire concept of reasonableness review and of, what they deem, the Court's timid and ineffectual remedial approach in *Grootboom*, and indeed in subsequent cases.[60] We shall return to all of these criticisms is section 3.3. below, but before that we will consider the next major case in which the Constitutional Court's reasonableness review approach was further refined and crystallised, before considering two more recent cases which seem to break with the deferential approach of reasonableness review.

---

57 *Grootboom* at para. 41.
58 *Grootboom* at para. 96.
59 David Beatty, *The Ultimate Rule of Law* (Oxford: Oxford University Press, 2004) at p. 129.
60 See for example David Bilchitz, *Poverty and Fundamental Rights: The Justification and Enforcement of Socio-Economic Rights* (Oxford: Oxford University Press, 2007); and Marius Pieterse, 'Resuscitating Socio-Economic Rights: Constitutional Entitlements to Health Care Services' (2006) 22 *South African Journal on Human Rights* 473.

3.2.3 *Treatment Action Campaign (TAC)*

The next noteworthy case was *Minister of Health* v. *Treatment Action Campaign (TAC)*,[61] which involved one of the most, if not the most, pressing issues in South Africa today, namely the spread of the HIV/AIDS pandemics. In particular the case centred on the government's policy to prevent mother-to-child transmission of HIV. With respect to this the government had introduced a pilot programme of the making antiretroviral drug Nevirapine available at a limited number of test sites throughout the country. The net result was that only two test sites per province were authorised to provide Nevirapine, and doctors in other public hospitals were precluded from doing so, meaning that only 10 per cent of all births in public hospitals benefited from the policy. The applicants challenged the government's policy as being in breach of the right to have access to medical treatment under section 27 of the Constitution, on the basis that it unreasonably confined availability of the potentially life-saving drug to the limited number of test sites, and on the basis that thereby meant that the government's policy was not comprehensive.

The Court found that the policy of the government in confining the availability of Nevirapine to the designated test sites was an overly rigid and inflexible policy, and therefore constituted a breach of section 27.[62] No doubt a consideration for the Court in this regard was that the manufacturer of Nevirapine had committed to providing the government of South Africa with the drug free of charge for a number of years, which meant that the extent to which scarce resources were implicated by the Court's judgment was limited. The Court therefore ordered the government to lift the restrictions on the availability of Nevirapine, and facilitate the use of Nevirapine in all public hospitals where it was deemed medically necessary. In the context of granting this relief, and in the judgment more broadly, the Court sent out mixed messages with respect to the separation of powers and its understanding of the appropriate balance between the courts and the elected branches of government. On the one hand, in the context of rejecting the notion of the minimum core entitlement (to which we return shortly) the Court held that:

> It should be borne in mind that in dealing with such matters the courts are not institutionally equipped to make the wide-ranging factual and political enquiries necessary for determining what the minimum-core standards call for . . . nor for deciding how public revenues should most effectively be spent . . . Courts are ill-suited to adjudicate upon issues where court orders could have multiple social and economic consequences for the community. The Constitution contemplates rather a restrained and focused role for the courts, namely to require the state to take measures to meet its constitutional obligations and to subject the reasonableness of these measures to

---

61 2002 (10) BCLR 1075 (CC).
62 *TAC* at para. 80.

evaluation. Such determinations of reasonableness may in fact have budgetary implications but are not in themselves directed at rearranging budgets. In this way the judicial, legislative and executive functions achieve appropriate constitutional balance.[63]

Here the Court clearly maintains the deferential approach first articulated in *Soobramoney* and *Grootboom*.

However, a contrasting tenor is provided in response to an objection from the state that the case concerned issues of policy, which were within the prerogative of the executive and therefore beyond the remit of the courts and therefore the Court was confined to issuing a declaratory order should it find a breach of constitutional rights, to which Constitutional Court replied:

> This Court has made it clear on more than one occasion that although there are no bright lines that separate the roles of the legislature, the executive and the courts from one another, there are certain matters that are pre-eminently within the domain of one or other of the arms of government and not the others. All arms of government should be sensitive and respect this separation. This does not mean, however, that the courts cannot and should not make orders that have an impact on policy. Where State policy is challenged as inconsistent with the Constitution, Courts have to consider whether in formulating and implementing such policy the State has given effect to its constitutional obligations. If it should hold in any given case that the State has failed to do so, it is obliged by the Constitution to say so. Insofar as that constitutes an intrusion into the domain of the executive, that is an intrusion mandated by the Constitution itself.[64]

The Court thus rejected the government's argument, and asserted that not only was it empowered to grant mandatory orders in appropriate cases, but if it deemed it necessary the Court could also exercise supervisory jurisdiction over the implementation of any such mandatory orders.[65]

Many commentators see the Constitutional Court's judgment in *TAC* as the high watermark in the Court's reasonableness-centred, socio-economic rights jurisprudence. For example Jonathan Klaaren argues that the judgment 'demonstrated not only real scrutiny but also real judicial remedial action'.[66] While the significance of the mandatory order cannot be disputed, if for no other reason

---

63 *TAC* at paras. 37–38.
64 *TAC* at paras. 98–99.
65 *TAC* at para. 106. Although in the instant case the Court declined to exercise supervisory jurisdiction over the mandatory order granted on the basis that 'The government has always respected and executed orders of this Court. There is no reason to believe that it will not do so in the present case' (at para. 129); the veracity of this statement has been contradicted by a number of studies, which are considered in section 3.3.2. below.
66 Jonathan Klaaren, 'A Remedial Interpretation of the *Treatment Action Campaign* Decision' (2003) 19 *South African Journal on Human Rights* 455 at pp. 461.

than that it resulted in access to a potentially life-saving drug for a significant number of women and their new-born children who otherwise would not have had access to it, it is also possible to overstate it from the perspective of the evolution of the Court's jurisprudence. Throughout the judgment the Court maintained the reasonableness approach, with the deferential connotations that come with it, and continued to reject the minimum core approach, although arguably with good cause. Furthermore, the Court had a significantly freer hand in the context of this case, in so far as the medical treatment sought (the 'thorny' resource issue) was a drug that was freely available to the government. Therefore, while recognising that *TAC* was indeed an important decision, its significance in the context of the overall evolution of the Court's jurisprudence should not be overstated.

3.2.4 Departures from convention?

Arguably of more significance, in terms of the long-term evolution of the Court's socio-economic rights jurisprudence, are two somewhat more recent cases. The first is *Khosa* v. *Minister of Social Development*;[67] this was in fact two joint cases which raised similar issues, which concerned a number of Mozambican citizens who enjoyed permanent resident status in South Africa. They sought to challenge the constitutionality of certain sections of the South African social welfare code, which excluded non-South African citizens from certain social welfare grants.[68] All of the applicants in the case were shown to be destitute, and therefore would have qualified for the grants if not for the citizenship-based exclusion. The applicants grounded their case on section 27(1)(c) of the Constitution, which provides that 'Everyone has the right to have access to . . . social security, including, if they are unable to support themselves and their dependants, appropriate social assistance', and on the guarantee of non-discrimination in section 9 of the Constitution.[69] In the High Court the respondents failed to file replies, and the respective judges therefore found for the applicants and struck down the offending provision. The High Court judges also issued orders requiring the state to, *inter alia*, pay the applicant's arrears for the benefits they did not receive but were otherwise entitled to, and to extend the benefits to all similarly situated individuals. These decisions were appealed to the Constitutional Court.

---

67 2004 (6) BCLR 569 (CC).
68 Specifically ss. 3(c), 4(b)(ii) and 4B(b)(ii) of the Social Assistance Act 59 of 1992, as amended by the Welfare Laws Amendment Act 106 of 1997.
69 Section 9 of the Constitution provides, in relevant part, that '1. Everyone is equal before the law and has the right to equal protection and benefit of the law . . . 3. The state may not unfairly discriminate directly or indirectly against anyone on one or more grounds, including race, gender, sex, pregnancy, marital status, ethnic or social origin, colour, sexual orientation, age, disability, religion, conscience, belief, culture, language and birth . . . 5. Discrimination on one or more of the grounds listed in subsection (3) is unfair unless it is established that the discrimination is fair'.

The majority judgment was delivered by Mokgoro J., who began the substantive part of her judgment by noting that the 'socio-economic rights in our Constitution are closely related to the founding values of human dignity, equality and freedom'.[70] Emphasising in particular the issue of equality, Mokgoro J. stressed that, unlike the other leading socio-economic rights cases the Court had decided, this one directly implicated the prohibition on discrimination in the context of social provision.[71] In assessing the state's decision to exclude non-citizens from certain social benefits Mokgoro J. introduced, in effect, a test of proportionality to determine whether or not the distinction passed constitutional muster; she stated that there 'must be a rational connection' between the impugned law, and the legitimate purpose pursued by the government and the means used to achieve that purpose.[72] The judge then considered a number of justifications put forward by the government for the impugned provision, including, *inter alia*, the claim that requiring the state to extend access of the various welfare grants to all permanent residents would place an impermissible burden on the state,[73] but rejected the various arguments by arguing that 'the importance of providing access to social assistance to all who live permanently in South Africa and the impact upon life and dignity that a denial of such access has, far outweighs the financial and immigration considerations on which the state relies'.[74]

Based on this, and on the Court's prior acceptance that the guarantee of social security in the Constitution was not limited to citizens,[75] Mokgoro J. concluded that:

> The Constitution vests the right to social security in 'everyone'. By excluding permanent residents from the scheme for social security, the legislation limits their rights in a manner that affects their dignity and equality in material respects. Dignity and equality are founding values of the Constitution and lie at the heart of the Bill of Rights. Sufficient reason for such invasive treatment of the rights of permanent residents has not been established. The exclusion of permanent residents is therefore inconsistent with section 27 of the Constitution.[76]

By way of remedy the Court ordered that the words 'or permanent resident . . . or permanent residents' be read in to the offending sections of the relevant legislation, thereby maintaining the existing welfare scheme, but also immediately extending it to qualifying permanent residents.[77] The Court's decision

70 *Khosa* (n. 67) at para. 40.
71 *Khosa* at paras. 41–44 and para. 49.
72 *Khosa* at para. 53.
73 *Khosa* at paras. 54–67.
74 *Khosa* at para. 82.
75 *Khosa* at paras. 46–47.
76 *Khosa* at para. 85.
77 *Khosa* at para. 89.

in *Khosa* is significant in a number of respects. On the one hand the inter-mingling of the overarching concepts of dignity and equality with the socio-economic guarantees in a sense liberates the Court from the inherent limitations of the socio-economic rights provisions, and allows them to engage in a more exacting review of the government's policy. Also, the order granted by the Court, with its concomitant resource implications and the Court's attendant rejection of the government's bald 'resource defence', evinces a significantly less deferential tone from the Court. For these reasons *Khosa* is 'regarded as a positive portent for expanding access to socio-economic rights through constitutional litigation in the future'.[78] With that said, it must be borne in mind that the impugned provision provided for explicit discrimination on the basis of nationality, thereby, in the words of the Court, stigmatising a vulnerable minority,[79] in a country that had only relatively recently emerged from an institutionalised system of discrimination and stigmatisation and the fact that the Court determined that any increased costs would be very modest;[80] both of these factors strengthened the Court's hand, and may have made it feel more institutionally secure in delivering such a judgment and granting the order it did.[81]

A more recent case, and the final one we consider in detail here, is that of *Rail Commuters Action Group* v. *Transnet Ltd*.[82] This case concerned an application by a pressure group established by individuals who had been victims of crime and violence, or the family members of such victims, or were otherwise concerned about such crime on the rail network in the Western Cape. In this case they sought to oblige the rail operators and the state more generally, to provide greater security for passengers on the relevant rail service. The instant case is interesting because it sought to rely on positive obligations arising other than from the socio-economic guarantees in the Constitution; in particular the applicants based their claim on the rights to dignity,[83] life[84] and security of the person.[85] In the High Court the applicants were successful and the court issued, *inter alia*, a mandatory order requiring the respondents to take steps to improve security on their train services, and a structural interdict requiring the respondents to report back to the court on the steps being taken to improve security. This judgment was appealed to the Supreme Court of Appeal, where it was overturned and subsequently appealed to the Constitutional Court.

---

78 Julia Sloth-Nielsen, 'Extending Access to Social Assistance to Permanent Residents' (2004) 5(3) *ESR Review* 9 at p. 11; see also Liebenberg (n. 9) at p. 87.
79 *Khosa* at para. 74.
80 *Khosa* at paras. 61–62.
81 See Liebenberg (n. 9) at p. 89.
82 2005 (4) BCLR 301 (CC).
83 Section 10 of the South African Constitution, which provides 'Everyone has inherent dignity and the right to have their dignity respected and protected'.
84 Section 11 of the South African Constitution, which provides 'Everyone has the right to life'.
85 Section 12 of the South African Constitution, which, in relevant part, provides '1. Everyone has the right to freedom and security of the person, which includes the right . . . (c). to be free from all forms of violence from either public or private sources'.

The judgment of the majority was delivered by O'Regan J. In respect of the applicant's substantive claim the learned judge accepted that 'rights other than the social and economic rights in the Constitution do at times impose positive obligations'.[86] The learned judge then accepted that the respondent service providers, because of the nature of the functions they performed and their statutory framework read in light of the constitutional guarantees contained in sections 10, 11 and 12 of the Constitution, were under a positive obligation to take reasonable measures to insure the safety of commuters using their services.[87] She went on to hold that the respondents had heretofore acted under the erroneous assumption that they were not under any positive obligation to protect the Constitutional rights of the commuters using their services, and had therefore acted unconstitutionally. In the instant case she determined that the appropriate response was for the Court to issue a declaratory order, clarifying the obligations of the respondents and requiring them to take steps, as expeditiously as possible, to improve the overall safety of commuters using their services.[88]

The judgment of O'Regan J. in the *Rail Commuters* case oscillates between the marked deference of *Grootboom* and the more exacting review standards of *Khosa*. For example, she is at pains to defend the reasonableness standard of review on the basis that it 'strikes an appropriate balance between the need to ensure that constitutional obligations are met, on the one hand, and recognition for the fact that bearers of those obligations should be given appropriate leeway to determine the best way to meet the obligations';[89] similarly it could be argued that confining the relief granted to a declaratory order is equally reminiscent of *Grootboom*-esque deference. In contrast O'Regan J., arguably building on the *Khosa* decision, is far less deferential to the respondent's assertion of resource scarcity, this being an issue the Court was strongly criticised for in the past. For example in *Soobramoney* the court simply accepted, without inquiring any further, the state's claim of limited resources;[90] in the *Rail Commuters* case O'Regan J. argues that 'an organ of state will not be held to have reasonably performed a duty simply on the basis of a bald assertion of resource constraints. Details of the precise character of the resource constraints, whether human or financial, in the context of the overall resourcing of the organ of state will need to be provided'.[91]

The judgment in this case thus straddles the borders of the traditional, deferential approach and the more exacting model intimated in *Khosa*. For

---

86 *Rail Commuters* (n. 82) at para. 70.
87 *Rail Commuters* at paras. 83–84.
88 *Rail Commuters* at para. 109.
89 *Rail Commuters* at para. 87.
90 Brand (n. 9) at p. 223; for other critiques of the Court for failing to adequately interrogate the State when presented with assertions of resource scarcity, see Dugger (n. 7); and Sandra Liebenberg, 'Needs, Rights and Transformation: Adjudicating Social Rights in South Africa' (2005) 6(4) *ESR Review* 3 at p. 5.
91 *Rail Commuters* at para. 88.

Davis, in particular, the *Rail Commuters* case is extremely significant, as he puts it 'if *Khosa* represented a hint towards a more progressive approach, the Court pointed expressly to a more fruitful route towards a judicial implementation of the social democratic character of the constitutional text' in the *Rail Commuters* case.[92] For him the case is important because it was 'the first decision where the Court made no reference to the express socio-economic rights provisions in the Constitution, but rather employed the rights of dignity, life and freedom and security of the person to impose a positive obligation upon the rail company, thereby for the first time affirming the concept of a positive right of an individual litigant to claim improved public resources'.[93] It therefore clearly represents a significant development, if not necessarily a revolutionary one, in the Court's jurisprudence.

3.3 Debating the Court's jurisprudence

The South African Constitutional Court has, thus, crafted an extensive body of precedent on the judicial enforcement of socio-economic rights and while, in a general sense, the Court's jurisprudence has been welcomed, it has not been welcomed uncritically. On the one hand commentators such as Cass Sunstein laud the Constitutional Court's jurisprudence as representing 'a novel and highly promising approach to judicial protection of socio-economic rights',[94] which 'is respectful of democratic prerogatives and of the limited nature of public resources, while also requiring special deliberative attention to those whose minimal needs are not being met'.[95] While on the other hand a number of commentators, as we will see presently, are highly critical of the Court's jurisprudence for being, among other things, overly deferential, unprincipled, theoretically unsound and, ultimately, ineffectual. We shall consider the arguments on either side of these various charges here, before drawing some conclusions about the Court's jurisprudence.

3.3.1 *Reasonableness and the minimum core*

The most conspicuous aspect of the Constitutional Court's socio-economic rights jurisprudence, and the most significant contribution to the protection of socio-economic rights on a global scale,[96] is its articulation of the reasonableness review standard for assessing state compliance with socio-economic

---

92   Davis (n. 9) at p. 208.
93   Davis (n. 9) at p. 209.
94   Sunstein (n. 16) at p. 236.
95   *Ibid.* at pp. 221–222.
96   See for example the way in which the language of reasonableness has migrated from South African socio-economic rights jurisprudence, into the realm of international human rights law with its inclusion in Article 8(4) of the Optional Protocol to the International Covenant on Economic, Social and Cultural Rights, General Assembly Resolution 832, UN GAOR, 63rd Session, UN Doc A/RES/63/117 (2008).

rights. Perhaps unsurprisingly, then, this is also the aspect of the Court's jurisprudence which has come in for the greatest criticism. Two prominent features of the critique of the reasonableness approach are that it is unprincipled and theoretically incoherent, and that it results in the Court being excessively deferential to the elected branches of government. But, the approach also has its defenders; Danie Brand, for example, while acknowledging that the Court's use of reasonableness is somewhat unprincipled,[97] nonetheless characterises the approach as being commendably flexible: 'the Court varies the intensity of its review and the intrusiveness of its remedies from case to case based on its perception of how acutely or not its institutional capacity and democratic illegitimacy constrain it'.[98] Liebenberg similarly defends the reasonableness standard of review on the basis that it:

> gives the Court [a] flexible and context-sensitive tool for adjudicating socio-economic rights claims. It allows government the space to design and formulate appropriate policies to meet its socio-economic rights obligations. At the same time, it subjects government's choices to the requirements of reasonableness, inclusiveness and . . . the threshold requirement that all programmes must provide short-term measures of relief for those whose circumstances are urgent and intolerable. Government has the latitude to demonstrate that the measures it has adopted are reasonable in light of its resources and capacity constraints and the overall claims on its resources'.[99]

She does, however, acknowledge that the reasonableness standard has its shortcomings and thus calls for a 'substantively interpreted and applied' model of reasonableness which would, *inter alia*, place a stringent burden on the state to justify its failure to adopt policies to allow disadvantaged groups to gain access to basic social services and resources, placing the burden on proving reasonableness on the state, and incorporating an element of proportionality analysis.[100]

Where commentators such as Brand and Liebenberg see sensible, flexible adjudicative tools, others see unprincipled groping in the dark.[101] One of the leading critics of the Court's jurisprudence is David Bilchitz, the Court's use of reasonableness review, with its origins in administrative law notions of curial deference, does not accord with the purpose behind empowering the Constitutional Court to enforce entrenched socio-economic rights.[102] Bilchitz further argues the vague and unprincipled manner in which the Court employs

---

97 Brand (n. 9) at pp. 230–236.
98 *Ibid.* at p. 227.
99 Liebenberg (n. 9) at p. 89.
100 *Ibid.* at p. 91.
101 Bilchitz (n. 60) at p. 161.
102 *Ibid.* at p. 160.

the concept of reasonableness and the Court's unwillingness to engage with the minimum content of socio-economic rights, which we will return to presently, renders the Court's socio-economic rights jurisprudence 'theoretically weak' and functionally inadequate.[103] In more expansive terms Bilchitz argues that the reasonableness approach is deficient because:

> reasonableness alone lacks the content necessary to make determinations on matters concerning socio-economic rights. Secondly, it deflects the focus of the constitutional enquiry from the interests at stake in these cases and allows these to be overshadowed by a general balancing of multiple considerations. Thirdly, the contextual nature of a determination of reasonableness requires certain a-contextual standards or principles to determine how it is to be applied in particular cases . . . *Fourthly, the vagueness of the notion does not help provide any certainty as to the nature of the government's obligations in terms of the Constitution. That leaves other branches of government without clear guidance as to the nature of their obligations to realize socio-economic rights . . . Fifthly, reasonableness does not provide a principled criterion to determine the circumstances in which it is legitimate for judges to interfere with the decisions of other branches of government.*[104]

While all of these criticisms are significant, it is the latter two which are the most immediately relevant for the purposes of this study. Because it is essential that any approach to adjudicating on socio-economic rights provides, among other things, clarity about the respective roles of the court and the elected branches of government, and concrete guidance to the elected branches as to the nature of their obligations with respect to constitutionally entrenched socio-economic rights. To the extent, then, that Bilchitz's criticism of the Court's reasonableness review approach holds true in this respect, it is a significant shortcoming in the model of review.

On the issue of the overly deferential nature of reasonableness review, Davis, rather scathingly, argues that:

> it is doubtful whether a court will ever conceive of reasonableness in any other way other than to defer to the decision of a democratically elected legislature and executive. Reasonableness is a standard that judges understand within the context of administrative law, in which deference to the competence and democratic pedigree of the executive authority or the legislature is well established.[105]

---

103 *Ibid.* at p. 139.
104 *Ibid.* at p. 176 (emphasis added). It is also interesting to note that the suitability of reasonableness as a standard of reviewing state action, or indeed inaction, has been called into question, at least where fundamental rights are implicated, in its intellectual and jurisprudential birthplace; see for example *R* v. *Secretary of the State for the Home Department ex parte Daly* [2001] 2 AC 532 and *R (ABCIFER)* v. *Secretary of State for Defence* [2003] QB 1397.
105 Davis (n. 9) at p. 210.

Marius Pieterse echoes this criticism when he notes that the Constitutional Court has thus far failed to develop 'an appropriately deferent but also appropriately transformative judicial role within a reconceptualised, uniquely South African, separation of powers' doctrine.[106] Instead the Court, daunted by 'a lingering sense of institutional unease . . . with engaging with the explicit prioritization of social interests' as mandated by the Constitution, has retreated into the comfort zone of pre-constitutional era, administrative law deference,[107] and consequently exercises its constitutional review functions in a 'remarkably tentative manner'.[108] This would appear to be a fair assessment, and while the *Khosa* and *Rail Commuters* cases seemed to signal a departure from this deferential approach, more recent cases, in particular *Mazibuko*,[109] seem to confirm that the Constitutional Court's jurisprudence is indeed overly deferential and therefore it can be doubted whether or not it strikes the appropriate balance between the courts and the elected branches in the area of socio-economic rights enforcement.

The primary alternative to the Court's established reasonableness review standard, posited by Bilchitz and others, is for the Court to adopt a 'minimum core approach' to adjudicating on socio-economic rights claims. This approach, drawn from international human rights standards, is based, in the South African context, on the premise that the Constitutional Court has heretofore inverted the relationship between the respective subsections of sections 26 and 27 of the Constitution. As Bilchitz puts it:

> The Court has approached socio-economic rights cases by claiming that the test in terms of the Constitution is whether the measures adopted by the government were reasonable. This approach is guilty of failing to integrate sections 27(2) and 27(1): it focuses the whole enquiry on section 27(2) without providing a role for section 27(1). Yet, section 27(1) is in fact the right, and the Constitution directs us to evaluate the reasonableness of government policy in relation to an understanding of what the rights in question demand of the government.[110]

---

106 Marius Pieterse, 'Coming to Terms with Judicial Enforcement of Socio-Economic Rights' (2004) 20 *South African Journal on Human Rights* 383 at p. 385.

107 Marius Pieterse, 'Possibilities and Pitfalls in the Domestic Enforcement of Social Rights: Contemplating the South African Experience' (2004) 26 *Human Rights Quarterly* 882 at p. 902.

108 Pieterse (n. 107) at p. 406.

109 *Mazibuko* v. *City of Johannesburg* [2009] ZACC 28 (8 October 2009).

110 Bilchitz (n. 60) at p. 159, this of course applies to the Court's approach to s. 26 also. Similarly Davis (n. 9) at p. 201, notes that in *TAC* and other cases the Constitutional Court can be criticised for 'failing to integrate sub-sections 27(2) and 27(1); it focuses the whole enquiry on sub-section 27(2) without providing a role for sub-section 27(1); that is, the Court failed to give any meaning to the right to health care services and based the "right" on the obligation of the State to take measures to ensure by way of incremental steps the realisation of a right enshrined in sub-section 27(1) but never defined by the Court'.

Davis is also critical of the Constitutional Court for this approach, and argues that in order to remedy it 'the Court's analysis in each case needs to involve an extra step: first, it should attempt to understand the content of the right, and only then should it engage in the enquiry of determining whether the measures adopted by the government were reasonable measures of progressively realising the right'.[111] That is to say that the first step in the Court's deliberations should be to identify a minimum core element of the right in question, to which individuals are entitled as a matter of priority, and then judge the extent to which the government's actions are reasonably likely to deliver, in the first instance, this minimum core and subsequently and progressively a more substantive enjoyment of the right in question.[112]

However, the Court has to date steadfastly refused to recognise the minimum core concept as integral to its socio-economic rights jurisprudence. The Court is weary of the minimum core approach because, *inter alia*, it imposes what the Court deems to be unrealistic obligations on the state in so far as it is 'impossible to give everyone access even to a "core" service immediately',[113] and because enforcing a minimum core is incompatible with the institutional role of the courts.[114] The Constitutional Court had shied away from the concept of immediately enforceable, individual minimum core entitlements in both *Soobramoney*[115] and *Grootboom*,[116] but most clearly spelled out its rejection of the idea in *TAC*, where it held that:

> section 27(1) of the Constitution does not give rise to a self-standing and independent positive right enforceable irrespective of the considerations mentioned in s. 27(2). Sections 27(1) and 27(2) must be read together as defining the scope of the positive right that everyone has and the corresponding obligations on the State to 'respect, protect, promote and fulfil' such rights. The rights conferred by ss. 26(1) and 27(1) are to have 'access' to the services that the State is obliged to provide in terms of ss. 26(2) and 27(2).[117]

Notwithstanding this explicit rejection, a former chief justice of the Constitutional Court has argued, extra-judicially, that adopting the reasonableness standard of review does not *ipso facto* preclude judicial reference to minimum core rights, as he puts it the 'standard of reasonableness may still allow a court to recognize a minimum core in assessing the reasonableness of government action: it allows courts to recognize which services are urgent for

---

111 Davis (n. 9) at p. 201.
112 Bilchitz (n. 60) at pp. 183–196.
113 *TAC* at para. 35.
114 *TAC* at paras. 37–38.
115 *Soobramoney* at paras. 11 and 19.
116 *Grootboom* at paras. 33–35.
117 *TAC* at para. 39.

the survival of vulnerable groups and places a strong duty of justification on state officials for a failure to act accordingly'.[118]

In spite of the chief justice's comments, the reality is that the Court has shown itself to be uneasy with the minimum core concept, and unwilling to adopt it. It is, however, difficult to argue with Bilchitz's reasoning, drawing on the text of the Constitution, for the inclusion of the minimum core. As he puts it:

> in understanding the role of reasonableness, it is crucial to recognize that the word 'reasonable' qualifies the word *measures* in section 26 and not the right itself. In other words, the right is not just the right to have the government act reasonably when it comes to socio-economic provision in society. Deference is not owed to the government in defining the content of the right to have access to adequate housing, but only in allowing it a 'margin of appreciation' to decide which *measures* it will adopt in fulfilling its obligations. In giving effect to the right, the *measures* the government adopts must be reasonable in relation to the objective it seeks to achieve, which is to realize the right of access to adequate housing. This enquiry requires the specification of some content to the right, independently of the notion of reasonableness'.[119]

It could therefore be argued that the Constitutional Court, perhaps too acutely aware of the institutional tightrope which it was walking, has gone too far in the direction of deference to the elected branches of government. Therefore it has, arguably, abdicated its responsibility to define and elaborate more concretely the content of socio-economic rights, and this has neutered the efficacy or transformative potential of the Court's judgments.[120] Furthermore, as Pieterse argues, the 'point blank' refusal of the Constitutional Court to recognise the minimum core concept 'makes a mockery of the justiciability and rights-status of socio-economic rights'.[121]

While Bilchitz certainly makes a compelling case for the recognition of the minimum core in the South African context, there are a number of other commentators who stoutly defend the Court's decision to eschew the minimum core approach on the basis that it demands 'too much', and is unfeasible.[122] Furthermore, they argue that because the Constitutional Court is on relatively new ground, from a comparative constitutional perspective, 'the Court's circumspection avoids an [unnecessary] escalation of separation of powers and other

---

118 Langa (n. 35) at p. 34; and see *Grootboom* at para. 33 and *TAC* at para. 34.
119 Bilchitz (n. 60) at p. 143 (emphasis original).
120 Bilchitz (n. 60) at p. 139.
121 Pieterse (n. 60) at p. 474.
122 Mark Kende, 'The South African Constitutional Court's Construction of Socio-Economic Rights: A Response to Critics' (2004) 19 *Connecticut Journal of International Law* 617 at pp. 622–623.

tensions'.[123] Others argue further that while the concept of the minimum core may be useful at the level of international human rights law for evaluating national health programmes, for example, it is 'singularly unhelpful' as a tool for courts and decision makers confronted with concrete cases,[124] and its adoption 'could lead to outcomes that exacerbate rather than alleviate poverty as spending is shifted from one type of social spending to another'.[125] From a pragmatic perspective, Klaaren, while not rejecting the minimum core, argues that while the Constitutional Court in *TAC* and, to a lesser extent *Grootboom*, may have 'deflated' the transformative potential of the Constitution by rejecting the concept of the minimum core, this might be a fair, short-term price to pay 'to ensure that socio-economic rights are taken seriously and afforded judicial enforcement'.[126]

In contrast to these commentators, Pieterse disputes the extent to which recognition of the minimum core would threaten the institutional integrity of the Constitutional Court; for him:

> a finding that a minimum core obligation had been breached would merely require the Court to insist that respondents justify the non-satisfaction of core needs, and to pronounce on the constitutional acceptability of such justification, in exactly the same manner as it decides and pronounces on the justifiability of apparent infringements of civil and political rights.[127]

This is a fair point, and indeed it echoes the argument articulated by the Constitutional Court itself in the *First Certification* judgment when rejecting the arguments that socio-economic rights would undermine the separation of powers.[128] It would therefore seem that Bilchitz's interpretative and normative case for the recognition of the minimum core is compelling, while the institutional–legitimacy concerns of supporters of the Court's *Grootboom*-reasonableness standard are, at least, somewhat overstated. There is therefore a strong case for inclusion of the minimum core concept in the Court's jurisprudence. Notwithstanding this, the Court's recent judgment in the *Mazibuko* case appears to firmly set the Court against any such minimum core approach, and to entrench a narrow reading of the Court's reasonableness approach.[129]

---

123 *Ibid.* at p. 616; see also Paul Nolette, 'Lessons Learned From the South African Constitutional Court: Toward a Third Way of Judicial Enforcement of Socio-Economic Rights' (2003) 12 *Michigan State Journal of International Law* 91 at pp. 117–118.

124 Karin Lehmann, 'In Defence of the Constitutional Court: Litigating Socio-Economic Rights and the Myth of the Minimum Core' (2006) 22 *American University International Law Review* 163 at pp. 185–187.

125 *Ibid.* at p. 197.

126 Klaaren (n. 66) at pp. 467–468.

127 Pieterse (n. 60) at p. 486.

128 *First Certification* judgment at paras. 77–78.

129 In *Mazibuko* the Constitutional Court overturned a High Court order which, *inter alia*, required the respondent body to provide residents of a poor Soweto community with 50

3.3.2 *The approach to remedies*

Alongside, indeed intimately related to, criticism of the Court's reasonableness review standard, the Court has also been criticised for its remedial approach, in particular its overreliance on declaratory orders. The criticisms in this regard are, again, twofold; on the one hand it is argued that the Court has, by and large, been far too deferential when granting remedies; secondly, and possibly somewhat more significantly, it is argued that the Court's orders are fundamentally ineffectual. As to the deference side of the argument, Brand makes the point that we really should not be surprised, as the Court's remedial practice is merely 'an extension of its reasonableness test – just as the Court tries as far as possible "only" to determine that the state's conduct is unconstitutional, without prescribing how it must rectify that conduct, the court through its remedies tries to avoid prescribing specific policy options to the state'.[130]

Similarly, Davis identifies the Court's approach to remedies as the logical extension of its overall deferential approach to adjudicating on socio-economic rights claims; for him the shortcomings in the Court's jurisprudence are explained by 'an unstated, inarticulate premise' on which the reasoning is based:

> namely a concept of deference to the political autonomy of the legislature and the executive. The Court has developed a framework for dealing with socio-economic rights which seeks to maximise the autonomy of the other branches of the state, employing a concept of rationality sourced in international law, fashioned in domestic administrative law and packaged as reasonableness. So long as the government is shown to have put in place a plan which is rationally connected to dealing with the least privileged in society as a matter of priority, the Court will not intervene.[131]

This, for Davis, also explains why the Court is unwilling to provide supervision of the implementation of orders made in socio-economic rights cases, and instead confines itself, with the main exception being the mandatory order issued in the *TAC* case, to issuing declaratory orders.[132]

The Constitutional Court's preference for, and almost exclusive reliance on, declaratory orders where it has found breaches of socio-economic rights leads

litres of free water a day (changed to 44 litres by the Supreme Court of Appeal), as the minimum core entitlement conferred on them by section 27(2) of the Constitution. The Constitutional Court's decision showed a reversion back to *Grootboom*-deferential form and a rejection of the minimum core as outside the bounds of the appropriate judicial role; it would therefore seem to have reined in the continued development of the more exacting and progressive approaches to judicial review of State action found in cases such as *Khosa* and *Rail Commuters*. For discussion of the case see: Sandra Liebenberg, *Socio-Economic Rights: Adjudication Under a Transformative Constitution* (Juta, Claremont 2010) at pp. 466–480.

130 Brand (n. 9) at p. 229.
131 Davis (n. 9) at pp. 205–206.
132 Davis (n. 9) p. 205.

on to the second major criticism of the Court's approach to remedies; namely the concern that the Court's orders are simply not being implemented. While some commentators argue that '[all] indications are that the government is serious about speeding up delivery and working towards the progressive realisation of socio-economic rights',[133] significant empirical and anecdotal evidence suggests that non-implementation of the Constitutional Court's orders in socio-economic rights cases is endemic.[134] As Liebenberg notes, five years after their successful action, the applicants in the *Grootboom* case were 'still located in crowded, unsanitary conditions . . . with highly inadequate services'.[135] And eight years after this landmark case, Mrs Irene Grootboom, the woman who gave the case its name, died 'while still waiting for formal housing'.[136] According to Christopher Mbazira the example of the non-implementation of the *Grootboom* order is 'just the tip of the iceberg' of a far greater problem concerning a lack of 'political commitment to implementing socio-economic rights . . . [and] compliance with court orders'.[137]

Without straying too far from the point at hand, it can be said that a large contributing factor to non-compliance with or non-implementation of Court orders stems from the State's commitment to a particular vision of economic development, and is therefore unlikely to self-correct in the short term.[138] So significant is the issue of non-implementation that Murray Wesson goes so far as to argue that it:

> suggests that the approach of the Constitutional Court is ultimately ineffective, and will do little to promote the interests of the vulnerable sectors of society, or further the transformative vision of the Constitution . . . [and] the most effective means of remedying this difficulty would . . . be for the Court to, in certain cases, exercise supervisory jurisdiction.[139]

133   Edgar Pieterse and Mirjam van Donk, 'The Politics of Socio-Economic Rights in South Africa' (2004) 5(5) *ESR Review* 12 at p. 12.
134   See Christopher Mbazira, 'Non-Implementation of Court Orders in Socio-Economic Rights Litigation in South Africa: Is the Cancer Here to Stay?' (2008) 9(4) *ESR Review* 2.
135   Liebenberg (n. 9) at p. 99.
136   Mbazira (n. 134) at p. 3.
137   *Ibid.* at p. 5.
138   As Davis (n. 9) at pp. 202–203, puts it: 'Since the introduction of the South African Constitution in 1996, tensions have arisen between its transformative vision and the macro-economic policy adopted by the South African government in which economic growth has been preferred over social reconstruction as the key policy objective . . . Accordingly, a dichotomy has begun to be created between this growth via the market-orientated policy adopted by the government and the constitutional vision of a democratic society based on a set of social democratic'; see also Ashwin Desai, 'Neoliberalism and Resistance in South Africa' (2003) 54(8) *Monthly Review* 16; and Patrick Bond, 'From Racial to Class Apartheid: South Africa's Frustrating Decade of Freedom' (2004) 55(10) *Monthly Review* 45.
139   Wesson (n. 52) at p. 306.

Similarly Davis argues that 'the evidence points strongly in the direction of the need for a form of supervisory jurisdiction'.[140] Because of the gravity and extent of the non-implementation problem the:

> Court should overcome its reluctance to grant supervisory remedies in order to facilitate the long-term structural reforms required to realise socio-economic rights. Supervisory orders have a rich potential not only for the courts to monitor the implementation of such orders, but also to enhance the participation of both civil society and the state institutions . . . in the implementation of socio-economic rights judgments.[141]

However, it should be noted that the Constitutional Court has exercised a limited form of supervisory jurisdiction in the context of eviction cases, where it has ordered public bodies to engage with communities affected by proposed evictions, to arrange for appropriate alternative accommodation etc, before proceeding with the eviction.[142]

However, such an excursion into a limited form of supervisory jurisdiction represents the exception that proves the general rule. The South African Constitutional Court has, for the most part, contented itself with an assumption that the elected branches of government would respond appropriately to court orders declaring breaches of socio-economic rights, and has therefore been extremely tentative in exercising the full array of remedial options available to it. Indeed, even the one significant case where the Court did issue a mandatory order (*TAC*) was, in a sense, a free pass for the Court, so to speak, in so far as it had limited resource implications as the drug sought by the applicants was available free of charge to the state. In light of the evidence of non-implementation of Court orders, and taking into account the well-publicised macro-economic policy preferences of the government, it would appear that such a deferential approach by the Court, and the attendant presumption of a positive state response, is ill-placed and further undermines the Court's overall approach as being excessively deferential.

3.4 Conclusion

Any assessment of the South African Constitutional Court's socio-economic rights jurisprudence will necessarily be somewhat paradoxical. Pilar Domingo offers a

---

140 Davis (n. 9) at p. 205; Davis also notes that the courts of first instance in both *Grootboom* and *TAC* granted such orders, but the Constitutional Court declined to follow. Although in different contexts, not implicating socio-economic rights, the Constitutional Court has granted structural interdicts, see: *August* v. *Electoral Commission* 1999 (4) BCLR 363 (CC) and *Sibiya* v. *Director of Public Prosecutions (Sibiya 1)* 2005 (8) BCLR 812 (CC).

141 Liebenberg (n. 9) at p. 100.

142 See *Occupiers of 51 Olivia Road* v. *City of Johannesburg* 2008 (5) BCLR 475 (CC); and Brian Ray, '*Occupiers of 51 Olivia Road* v. *City of Johannesburg*: Enforcing the Right to Adequate Housing through Engagement' (2008) 8 *Human Rights Law Review* 703.

nuanced and considered assessment, when she notes that the Constitutional Court's:

> social rights jurisprudence illustrates that the arguments made against the judicialisation of these rights remain relevant to understanding courts' capacity to enforce them. In particular, limits on the Court's democratic credentials and dispute-resolution methods mean that its social rights orders have rarely conferred direct benefits on poor litigants. Rather, the role of the Court has been to intervene in the policy arena, by forcing re-assessment of the reasonableness of legislative and executive action. Still, the South African experience indicates that social rights can be successfully enforced by a judicious court, and that they may play an important role in defending progressive social and economic reforms against constitutional attack by elite groups.[143]

At an absolute minimum, then, the experience of the South African Constitutional Court in adjudicating on socio-economic rights has served to dispel the notion that the entrenchment and judicial enforcement of such rights will inevitably undermine the constitutional separation of powers.[144] On the other hand the endemic problem of non-implementation of Court orders, and the Court's marked deference to the elected branches of government, means that '[despite] South Africa's remarkable constitutionalization of justiciable [socio-economic rights], meaningful access to these rights remains, for many, a distant dream'.[145] And while, of course, the continued and widespread denial of socio-economic rights that characterises South African society cannot be laid squarely at the door of the Constitutional Court, it can be said that the Court's timid approach to vindicating socio-economic rights has, at least to some extent, facilitated the broader economic and political decisions which results in the continued, systemic denial of socio-economic rights in South Africa.

Alongside the shortcomings of the Court's approach in assuring the efficacy of the entrenched socio-economic rights in practice, the Court can also be

---

143 Pilar Domingo, 'Introduction', in Gargarella, Domingo and Roux (eds.), *Courts and Social Transformation in New Democracies: An Institutional Voice for the Poor?* (Hampshire: Ashgate, 2006) 1 at p. 5.

144 As Liebenberg (n. 9) at p. 100, puts it 'the caution of sceptics that social rights adjudication would cast the courts in an inappropriate and unmanageable role has proven to be unfounded. The courts have proved themselves quite capable of developing a sophisticated and nuanced model of review for adjudicating social rights claims. This has enabled the courts to respect the institutional competencies and roles of the other branches of government while playing a meaningful role in enforcing constitutionally guaranteed socio-economic rights'; similarly Jeanne Woods (n. 46) at p. 791, argues that the Court's developing jurisprudence 'demonstrates that there are no institutional obstacles' to the adjudication and vindication of socio-economic rights; and see Sunstein (n. 16).

145 Mitra Ebadolahi, 'Using Structural Interdicts and the South African Human Rights Commission to Achieve Judicial Enforcement of Economic and Social Rights in South Africa' (2008) 83 *New York University Law Review* 1565 at p. 1590.

criticised for failing to live up to the transformative role assigned to it under the Constitution. As Karl Klare argued, the transformative vision of the new South African Constitution, and the role it accorded the courts, required them to 'address the problems concerning the democratic legitimacy of judicial power by honesty about and critical understanding of the plasticity of legal interpretation and of how interpretative practices are a medium for articulating social visions';[146] furthermore he urged South African lawyers to 'reexamine their analytical and argumentative methods and to attend to the burden their legal culture imposes on their work . . . [and] to harmonize judicial method and legal interpretation with the Constitution's substantively progressive aspirations'.[147] It appears, however, that this was just a bridge too far for the courts and the South African legal establishment more generally.[148] Instead of embracing its role in the transformative enterprise the Constitutional Court has sought to 'limit the appearance of its own agency in the interpretive project' and retreated into limited, formalist and overly deferential models of judicial reasoning.[149] Indeed, Davis goes so far as to argue that the Court's jurisprudence is testament to the fact that 'even when armed with progressive texts, judges retreat into models of adjudication which are based on earlier traditions of legal practice and which reduce the potential promise of the text'.[150]

This may, indeed, be the ultimate irony of the Constitutional Court's jurisprudence; in one sense the Court has fashioned an extensive and much admired body of jurisprudence around the judicial enforcement of socio-economic rights, but in doing so the Court may very well be said to have abdicated the transformative role conferred on it by South Africa's transformative Constitution.[151] So while the Court has articulated an approach to adjudicating on socio-economic rights which is, at the very least, defensible from the perspective of a-contextual institutional analysis, its approach might also be said to be too deferential in the context of the institutional and normative arrangements in place in South Africa

---

146 Klare (n. 30) at p. 188.
147 Klare (n. 30) at pp. 188–189.
148 As Pieterse (n. 60) at p. 416, puts it: 'the remains of South Africa's pre-constitutional legal culture (with its peculiar mix of classical liberalism, positivism and extreme judicial deference) continues to blind South African legal scholars and judges alike to the transformative possibilities inherent in the institution of judicial review. Its traces are evident even in the judgments of the Constitutional Court which, despite unequivocally affirming the justiciability of socio-economic rights and the judiciary's competence to enforce them, remain peculiarly hesitant to showcase the full extent of this competence'.
149 Pierre de Vos, 'South Africa's Constitutional Court: Starry-Eyed in the Face of History?' (2002) 26 *Vermont Law Review* 837 at p. 845.
150 Davis (n. 9) at p. 212.
151 This view is strengthened, in particular, by recent decisions such as *Mazibuko* (n. 109) and *Nokotyana* v. *Ekurhuleni Metropolitan Municipality* [2009] ZACC 33 (19 November 2009).

4 Developing social rights in India

Prior to the adoption of the South African Constitution in 1996, the most advanced domestic jurisprudence on the protection of socio-economic rights was that of the Indian Supreme Court.[1] Therefore, an examination of the Indian jurisprudence on this issue can be 'especially instructive' for the wider discussion of the appropriate judicial role in protecting socio-economic rights.[2] At the outset two points should be made: the first is that the Indian Constitution, at least as enacted, does not contain specifically enumerated and enforceable socio-economic rights. Rather, as will be discussed in more detail below, the Constitution contains a catalogue of justiciable civil and political rights along-

---

Due to significant difficulties in accessing original, true copies of all of the relevant Indian Supreme Court cases referred to here, the decision was taken to adopt, for the most part, the neutral citation for the relevant cases, so as to maintain a degree of uniformity. The neutral citations adopted here are taken from the database of Indian Supreme Court judgments maintained at: www.commonlii.org/in/cases/INSC. However, exceptions have had to be made in relation to some cases which are not reported on this database, and some unreported cases which are similarly absent from the database. Again, in the interests of maintaining some degree of uniformity, the decision was also taken not to attribute page numbers to the quotes from the relevant cases, as they were only available for some judgments and not others. This is, of course, far from ideal, but at present the most that can be done is for me to apologise for any confusion or inconvenience this causes the reader.

1 Paul Hunt, *Reclaiming Social Rights: International and Comparative Perspectives* (Aldershot: Dartmouth, 1996) at p. 153. For useful introductory discussions of the Indian experience with socio-economic rights see: Jayna Kothari, 'Social Rights Litigation in India: Developments of the Last Decade' in Barak-Erez and Gross (eds.), *Exploring Social Rights* (Oxford: Hart Publishing, 2007) 171; S. Muralidhar, 'India: The Expectations and Challenges of Judicial Enforcement of Social Rights' in Langford (ed.), *Social Rights Jurisprudence: Emerging Trends in International and Comparative Law* (Cambridge: Cambridge University Press, 2008) 102; Jeanne M. Woods and Hope Lewis, *Human Rights in the Global Marketplace: Economic, Social and Cultural Dimensions* (New York: Transnational, 2005) at pp. 653–713; Sandra Fredman, *Human Rights Transformed: Positive Rights and Positive Duties* (Oxford: Oxford University Press, 2008) at pp. 124–149; and Colin Gonsalves, 'Reflections on the Indian Experience' in Squires, Langford and Thiele (eds.), *The Road to a Remedy: Current Issues in the Litigation of Economic, Social and Cultural Rights* (Sydney: University of New South Wales Press, 2005) 177.
2 Hunt (n. 1) at p. 153.

side a chapter of the Constitution which sets out Directive Principles of State Policy (DPSP), in many respects these DPSP exhort the state to work towards the realisation of, in essence, certain socio-economic rights. Consequently, in crafting a socio-economic rights jurisprudence the Indian Supreme Court has had to rely on creative interpretations of civil and political rights, in particular a substantive and expansive interpretation of the right to life, read in light of the DPSP. The second point, which arguably flows from the first, is that the Indian Supreme Court's socio-economic rights jurisprudence has been, to put it mildly, somewhat incoherent.[3] It is therefore inappropriate, when it comes to discussing the Court's socio-economic rights jurisprudence, to attempt a strictly linear narrative. So, instead, the approach taken here is to focus on certain key rights and themes which emerge from the Court's jurisprudence, and the way in which the Court has dealt with them on the whole.

This chapter will begin by setting out the basic history and framework of the Indian Constitution, before then going on to look at the activist era of the Indian Supreme Court, when, through the concept of public interest litigation, the Court developed innovative ways of protecting the rights of the poor and excluded, including their socio-economic rights. The chapter will then go on to consider whether or not the Indian Supreme Court can be said to have retreated from this activist stance, and if so what the implications of such a move may be for socio-economic rights in India. As with other chapters, this one will conclude with a preliminary assessment of the implications of the Indian experience for the protection of socio-economic rights globally. However, as a point of departure, we begin by sketching the key provisions, for present purposes, of the Indian Constitution and the animating ideals of the Indian constitutional order.

4.1 The Indian Constitution

The long struggle for Indian independence came to a stuttering close in the years following the end of Second World War,[4] with the final acknowledgement of Indian independence, and the partition of India and Pakistan, arriving in the

---

3 Commenting specifically on the right to housing Kothari (n. 1) at p. 183, notes that 'the development of the right to housing in India has not followed a coherent, chronological or principled pattern'; and, with respect, the same can fairly be said about the Indian Supreme Court's socio-economic rights jurisprudence more generally. In somewhat less diplomatic tones Gobind Das argues, in relation to the Court's jurisprudence in general, that 'In reality the decisions of the Court are the choices of the particular elderly persons chosen from time to time, and appear to be mere preferences . . . One notices that the decisions are often inconsistent, the pendulum of the court sometimes swinging from one side to the other. Its orders are likened by some to a throw of dice' ('The Supreme Court: An Overview' in Kirpal, Desai, Subramanium, Dhavan and Ramachandran (eds.), *Supreme But Not Infallible: Essays in Honour of the Supreme Court of India* (New Delhi: Oxford University Press, 2004) 16 at pp. 44–45).

4 For a very helpful chronology of the key events, political and legal, leading up to the achievement of Indian independence and adoption of the Constitution, see Brij Kishore

form of the Indian Independence Act 1947. Towards the culmination of the struggle, and the final establishment of an independent India, a Constituent Assembly was established to draft a Constitution for a free India. The Assembly began its work in December 1946 and completed it in November 1949; the proposed Constitution was approved by the majority of the eligible electorate and came into force on the 26 January 1950. The Constitution approved by the (limited) electorate was a substantial document, containing no fewer than 395 Articles and 8 Schedules. The drafters of the Constitution were influenced by a variety of sources: [5] for the administrative structure of the state they decided against re-inventing the wheel, and instead drew heavily on the Government of India Act 1935 in crafting the constitutional provisions setting out the Federal Scheme for the country, issues relating to state governors and the question of emergency powers, along with most of the functional administration of the nation. Also from the British the drafters of the Constitution adopted the system of parliamentary government, although the new Constitution departed significantly from the British tradition of parliamentary sovereignty by adopting, from the US constitutional experience, entrenched fundamental rights, with a Supreme Court empowered to enforce them through the exercise of extensive powers of judicial review.[6] Here, we look first at the key constitutional provisions, at least for present purposes, then at the overarching character of the Indian Constitution, before going on to look at the way in which the Supreme Court has addressed the issue of socio-economic rights.

4.1.1 Key constitutional provisions

As was mentioned above the Indian Constitution is a substantial document, setting out in great detail the relationship between the central and state governments that make up the federal Union of India, along with detailed provisions on virtually every aspect of the administrative structure of the state. For present purposes, we can confine ourselves to a consideration of the key provisions of

Sharma, *Introduction to the Constitution of India* (2nd edn, New Delhi: Prentice-Hall of India, 2004) at pp. 11–25.

5 See Sharma (n. 4) at p. 32; Saberwal is somewhat critical of this extensive constitutional 'borrowing'; for him the forms adopted in the drafting of the new constitution, drawn as they were primarily from Western examples, presume certain forms of social ordering and praxis which were not necessarily consonant with those that predominated in India either at the time of drafting the constitution or since (Satish Saberwal, 'Introduction: Civilization, Constitution, Democracy' in Hasan, Sridharan and Sudarshan (eds.), *India's Living Constitution* (London: Anthem, 2005) 1 at pp. 10–11).

6 The decision to include both a catalogue of entrenched fundamental rights and extensive powers of judicial review in the Constitution stemmed from the significant denials of basic rights which had occurred in India under British colonial rule; see Sharma (n. 4) at p. 57 and Atul Setalvad, 'The Supreme Court on Human Rights and Social Justice: Changing Perspectives' in Kirpal, Desai, Subramanium, Dhavan and Ramachandran (eds.), *Supreme But Not Infallible: Essays in Honour of the Supreme Court of India* (New Delhi: Oxford University Press, 2004) 232 at p. 232.

the Constitution which touch on the related issues of fundamental rights, socio-economic rights and judicial power. The fundamental rights are set out in Part III of the Constitution, and include a familiar catalogue of civil and political rights such as the right to life,[7] the right to equality,[8] a general prohibition on arbitrary discrimination,[9] freedom of speech, expression and the right to protest[10] and freedom of religion.[11] Added to these familiar rights, Part III of the Constitution also enshrines peculiarly Indian provisions, such as those abolishing 'untouchability',[12] abolition of '*begar*' and forced labour,[13] and provisions allowing the state to positively discriminate in favour of historically disadvantaged tribes and castes.[14]

With respect to the issue of judicial power, Part III of the Constitution also contains certain significant provisions; Article 13(2) for example provides that the state 'shall make no law which takes away or abridges the rights conferred' by the Constitution, and that any such law shall to the extent of such contravention be void. In this way the Constitution banishes the ghost of parliamentary supremacy, and establishes instead the supremacy of the written Constitution. Perhaps of more significance, Article 32 provides that:

(1) The right to move the Supreme Court by appropriate proceedings for the enforcement of the rights conferred by this Part is guaranteed.

(2) The Supreme Court shall have power to issue directions or orders or writs, including writs in the nature of habeas corpus, mandamus, prohibition, quo warranto and certiorari, whichever may be appropriate, for the enforcement of any of the rights conferred by this Part.[15]

According to Sharma this provision reflects the sentiment that a 'right without a remedy is but a worthless declaration. A right becomes valuable when there is an effective means to implement it'.[16] And it not only establishes the original jurisdiction of the Supreme Court to judicially review the actions of the other branches of government, but also makes it a right of individuals to compel the Court to review governmental action, or indeed inaction, where a breach of the rights contained in Part III is implicated. The Supreme Court is also conferred with extensive remedial powers in this regard and on numerous

7 Constitution of India, Article 21.
8 Constitution of India, Article 14.
9 Constitution of India, Article 15.
10 Constitution of India, Article 19.
11 Constitution of India, Article 25.
12 Constitution of India, Article 17.
13 Constitution of India, Article 23.
14 Constitution of India, Article 15(4) and 15(5).
15 Article 142 of the Constitution further enhances the Supreme Court's remedial powers, granting it significant discretion to craft remedies so that it can do 'full justice' in any case before it.
16 Sharma (n. 4) at p. 105.

occasions has, drawing on these provisions, asserted the centrality of judicial review, deeming it to be part of the 'basic structure' of the Indian Constitution that cannot be removed, even by way of amendment to the Constitution.[17]

In so far as socio-economic rights were directly implicated in the Indian Constitution, as enacted,[18] it was in Part IV of the Constitution which contains the DPSP. These Directive Principles are explicitly rendered non-justiciable by the courts, but instead are held to be 'fundamental in the governance of the country' and are deemed to impose 'a duty on the State' to apply these principles in making laws, and one would imagine by implication policies, for the country.[19] Among the various obligations placed on the state by the DPSP, which correspond broadly with our understanding of socio-economic rights, is the duty to ensure all citizens have the 'right to an adequate means of livelihood',[20] to work towards 'raising the level of nutrition and the standard of living' of the people and improve public health,[21] and to provide, within ten years of the commencement of the Constitution, for free and compulsory education for all children up to the age of 14.[22]

According to Jayna Kothari the reason for including these DPSP 'was . . . to establish a new social order based on social, economic and political justice' and to make explicit the socialist and social revolutionary content of the Constitution,[23] although Muralidhar argues that at the time of drafting the Constitution a compromise had to be struck 'between those who felt that the DPSP could not possibly be enforced as rights and those who insisted that the Constitution should reflect a strong social agenda'.[24] Notwithstanding these divisions, the DPSP were adopted and provide the most explicit commitment to what we consider socio-economic rights in the Constitution, as it was enacted. They therefore 'suggest a more active role for government in securing citizens needs';[25] and Sudarshan argues that even though they are explicitly rendered non-justiciable they are not merely 'an assortment of second-class rights that

---

17 See *Kesavananda Bharati* v. *State of Kerala* (1973) 4 SCC 225 (hereinafter the '*Fundamental Rights* case') and *Minerva Mills* v. *Union of India* [1980] INSC 141 (31 July 1980).

18 As we will see when we come to discuss the right to education cases below, a number of Supreme Court judgments prompted the Eighty-sixth Amendment to the Constitution (2002), which enshrined the right to free and compulsory education for all children between the ages of 6 and 14 in Article 21A of the Constitution, where it had originally been recognised as a DPSP in Article 45 of the Constitution, as enacted.

19 Constitution of India, Article 37.

20 Constitution of India, Article 39(a).

21 Constitution of India, Article 47.

22 Constitution of India, Article 45; as we will see when we come to discuss the education cases below, this provision has, for all intents and purposes, been moved to Article 21A of the Constitution and has been replaced with a DPSP requiring the state to provide 'early childhood care and education' to children up to the age of 6.

23 Kothari (n. 1) at pp. 173–174.

24 Muralidhar (n. 1) at pp. 103–104.

25 Jeanne M. Woods, 'Emerging Paradigms of Protection for "Second-Generation" Human Rights' (2005) 6 *Loyola Journal of Public Interest Law* 103 at p. 106.

cannot be enforced in a court of law. These principles were meant to represent basic values of the political community with reference to which power and authority should be exercised'.[26]

A contentious issue, at least in the early years of the Supreme Court's jurisprudence, was the precise relationship between the fundamental rights in Part III of the Constitution and the DPSP in Part IV. In the *Fundamental Rights* case,[27] the Supreme Court departed from the earlier view which saw the DPSP as inferior and secondary to the explicitly justiciable fundamental rights contained in Part III of the Constitution,[28] and moved to a position which saw both the DPSP and the fundamental rights as mutually reinforcing and complementary. Also in the *Fundamental Rights* case, the Supreme Court stressed the organic and evolving nature of the rights guaranteed by the Constitution, and stressed the value of the DPSP in crafting and developing understandings of fundamental rights guaranteed by the Constitution:

> Fundamental rights have themselves no fixed content; most of them are empty vessels into which each generation must pour its content in the light of its experience. Restrictions, abridgments, curtailment and even abrogation of these rights in circumstances not visualised by the constitution makers might become necessary; their claim to supremacy or priority is liable to be overborne at particular stages in the history of the nation by the moral claims embodied in Part IV.[29]

Therefore the accepted view, since at least this judgment, is that the DPSP provide a useful interpretive tool for the courts in determining the scope of the rights contained in Part III of the Constitution, particularly, as we shall see, with respect to the right to life under Article 21. With the key constitutional provisions in hand, we can now turn to consider the overall 'nature' or vision of the Indian Constitution, as this necessarily bears on the evolution of the Supreme Court's constitutional jurisprudence.

---

26 R. Sudarshan, '"Stateness" and Democracy in India's Constitution' in Hasan, Sridharan and Sudarshan (eds.), *India's Living Constitution* (London: Anthem, 2005) 159 at p. 163.

27 *Fundamental Rights* case (n. 17).

28 Exemplified in early cases such as *State of Madras* v. *Srimathi Champakam Dorairajan* [1951] INSC 25 (9 April 1951), where Das J. held that 'The directive principles of the State policy, which by article 37 are expressly made unenforceable by a Court, cannot override the provisions found in Part III which, notwithstanding other provisions, are expressly made enforceable by appropriate Writs, Orders or directions under article 32. The chapter of Fundamental Rights is sacrosanct and not liable to be abridged by any Legislative or Executive Act or order, except to the extent provided in the appropriate article in Part III. The directive principles of State policy have to conform to and run as subsidiary to the Chapter of Fundamental Rights. In our opinion, that is the correct way in which the provisions found in Parts III and IV have to be understood'.

29 *Fundamental Rights* case (n. 17).

4.1.2 The nature of the Indian Constitution

In his magisterial work on the development of the Indian Constitution Granville Austin notes that, as enacted, the Indian Constitution was infused with a commitment to three overarching themes: 'protecting and enhancing national unity and integrity; establishing the institutions and spirit of democracy; and fostering a social revolution to better the lot of the mass of Indians'.[30] Flowing, in particular, from this last point it can be said that the Indian Constitution, much like the South African Constitution adopted more than forty years later, was infused with a transformative vision. This much is clear from the Preamble, which, as amended, commits the people of India to transform the country into a 'Sovereign Socialist Secular Democratic Republic', and further commits the state to ensure to all citizens 'Justice, social, economic and political . . . [and] Equality of status and of opportunity'.[31] Austin argues that the 'essence of the democracy and social reform strands is to be found throughout the Constitution: in the democratic political institutions and processes of the parliamentary system, in adult suffrage, and in the independent judiciary; and in Parts III and IV of the Constitution, which lay down the "Fundamental Rights" and the "Directive Principles of State Policy"'.[32] One commentator goes so far as to say that 'the central feature of the Indian Constitution is the state's commitment to the welfare of the Indian people and the attainment of social justice'.[33]

Similarly Upendra Baxi argues that the Constitution, in particular the DPSP, commits the state to 'the progressive implementation of policies, programmes and measures that disproportionately benefit and empower the impoverished masses of India'.[34] Baxi further argues that, at the time it was enacted, no 'previous constitutional model envisaged such an explicit and comprehensive

---

30 Granville Austin, *Working a Democratic Constitution: The Indian Experience* (New Delhi: Oxford University Press, 1999) at p. 6; what he refers to as the 'seamless web' of Indian constitutionalism.

31 Indian Constitution, first, second and fourth Preambular paragraphs. The terms 'Socialist' and 'Secular' were not in the Constitution as initially drafted, but were added by way of the 42nd Amendment to the Constitution in 1976; Sharma (n. 4) at p. 43, criticises the decision to add these terms as it makes 'the Constitution look like a party manifesto', rather than the fundamental law of a democratic society. In contrast Bhagwati J., as he then was, argued that 'The Preamble contains the profound declaration pregnant with meaning and hope for millions of peasants and workers that India shall be a socialist democratic republic where social and economic justice will inform all institutions of national life and there will be equality of status and opportunity for all and every endeavour shall be made to promote fraternity ensuring the dignity of the individual' (*National Textile Workers' Union* v. *P.R. Ramkrishnan* [1982] INSC 94 (10 December 1982)).

32 Austin (n. 30) at p. 7.

33 Sheetal Shah, 'Illuminating the Possible in the Developing World: Guaranteeing the Human Right to Health in India' (1999) 32 *Vanderbilt Journal of Transnational Law* 435 at p. 464.

34 Upendra Baxi, 'The (Im)possibility of Constitutional Justice: Seismographic Notes on Indian Constitutionalism' in Hasan, Sridharan and Sudarshan (eds.), *India's Living Constitution* (London: Anthem, 2005) 31 at p. 38.

transformation of a "traditional" society and installed a description of a consti-tutionally desired social order and good life'.[35] However, it can reasonably be doubted that part of the transformative vision of the Indian Constitution was to confer significant powers on the courts with respect to the enforcement of socio-economic rights. Rather, it would seem that the drafters of the Indian Constitution, while supportive of the idea of an independent judiciary, envi-sioned a rather restrained role for the courts and little or no role for the courts with respect to issues of social and economic policy.[36] As one of the chief architects of the Constitution, and a founding father of modern India, Jawaharlal Nehru put it, it was not for the judiciary to 'decide about high political, social or economic or other questions. It is for Parliament to decide the laws we have'.[37] Indeed, the first decades in the life of the Indian Constitution involved an incessant struggle between the elected branches of government and the newly empowered courts, in particular the Supreme Court, for what Austin calls 'custody of the Constitution'.[38]

This tussle began in the first year of the operation of the Constitution, with Nehru and his contemporaries dissatisfied with the way in which judicial enforcement of the fundamental rights provisions of the Constitution, in particular the right to property before it was removed from Part III of the Constitution, was frustrating and delaying the government's project of social transformation. This led the government to amend the Constitution so as to make certain laws immune to constitutional challenge; this set a dangerous precedent which, ultimately, allowed for the expansion of Indira Gandhi's authoritarian government and the now infamous 'internal emergency' which she imposed from 1975–1977. During Mrs Ghandi's time in power the cumulative effect of a number of constitutional amendments which she pushed through Parliament was that 'the legislative and executive branches of government had triumphed over the judiciary for custody of the constitution' with the concomi-tant result that the judiciary was 'no longer a co-equal branch of government'.[39] The Supreme Court went some way towards overturning Mrs Ghandi's

---

35 *Ibid.* at p. 55; while Baxi is very likely correct that no previous constitution had so explicitly articulated a transformative vision in the way in which the Indian Constitution did, it is arguable that the second part of this claim is somewhat misplaced as, ultimately, all constitutions contain, in one way or another, a vision of a desirable social order, albeit not all necessarily consonant with what Baxi might consider 'progressive'.

36 S. P. Sathe argues that 'The debates in the Constitutional Assembly show that the makers of the Constitution wanted a limited [role for] judicial review' (*Judicial Activism in India* (2nd edn, New Delhi: Oxford University Press, 2002) at p. 3).

37 Quoted in Granville Austin, 'The Supreme Court and the Struggle for Custody of the Constitution' in Kirpal, Desai, Subramanium, Dhavan and Ramachandran (eds.), *Supreme But Not Infallible: Essays in Honour of the Supreme Court of India* (New Delhi: Oxford University Press, 2004) 1 at p. 2.

38 For a general narrative of this protracted contest see Austin (n. 30); and Granville Austin, 'The Expected and the Unintended in Working a Democratic Constitution' in Hasan, Sridharan and Sudarshan (eds.), *India's Living Constitution* (London: Anthem, 2005) 319.

39 Austin (n. 38) at p. 325.

neutering of the courts in the *Fundamental Rights* case, when, among other things, it reasserted the centrality of the power of judicial review and held it to be part of the 'basic structure' of the Constitution, which could not be removed even by way of constitutional amendment.[40] Pratap Mehta argues that the assertion of judicial power in the *Fundamental Rights* case brought the tussle full circle, and 'seemed to relocate power between the various branches of government' and 'appears to have replaced parliamentary sovereignty and the separation of powers with judicial supremacy'.[41]

It would be fair to say that Mehta's perspective is a little hyperbolic; it nonetheless does reflect the significance of the *Fundamental Rights* case in asserting the centrality of judicial review within the Indian constitutional order. In truth the relationship between the courts and the elected branches of government, as we shall see, has continued to fluctuate even after this strong assertion of judicial power. We can say, then, that the Indian Constitution is a document committed to a substantive vision of democracy and social justice, which includes within it empowering provisions for an independent judiciary to enforce the fundamental rights protected by the Constitution, although it seems highly unlikely that the drafters of the Constitution envisioned an expansive role for the courts in the area of social and economic policy, or in relation to what we might refer to as the enforcement of socio-economic rights.[42] However, constitutions, and the Indian Constitution has been no exception, are living instruments which both impact on and are impacted by changing social and political conditions, and we will now look at the way in which the Supreme Court of India has reconceived its own role under the Constitution, principally through the development of what has come to be known as public interest litigation (PIL),[43] and the way in which this innovation provided a vehicle for the Supreme Court to incrementally develop protection for socio-economic rights under the Indian Constitution.

40 For a general discussion of the 'basic structure' doctrine, see Raju Ramachandran, 'The Supreme Court and the Basic Structure Doctrine' in Kirpal, Desai, Subramanium, Dhavan and Ramachandran (eds.), *Supreme But Not Infallible: Essays in Honour of the Supreme Court of India* (New Delhi: Oxford University Press, 2004) 107.

41 Pratap Bhanu Mehta, 'The Inner Conflict of Constitutionalism: Judicial Review and the "Basic Structure"' in Hasan, Sridharan and Sudarshan (eds.), *India's Living Constitution* (London: Anthem, 2005) 179 at p. 180.

42 Although VanderMay argues that the drafters of the Indian Constitution had a 'narrow view' of the role which the judiciary should play in the transformation of Indian society, the Court's subsequent abrogation of an expansive role for itself in this regard can nonetheless be justified, as it may contribute to the realisation of the substantive vision to which the drafters of the Constitution were committed (Maureen Callahan VanderMay, 'The Role of the Judiciary in India's Constitutional Democracy' (1996) 20 *Hastings International and Comparative Law Review* 103 at p. 105).

43 Or Social Action Litigation (SAL); Baxi, for one, prefers the term SAL and views the use of PIL as an unjustified borrowing from US experience, which pays insufficient attention to the *sui generis* nature of the enterprise undertaken in India (Upendra Baxi, 'Taking Suffering Seriously: Social Action Litigation in the Supreme Court of India' (1985) *Third World Legal Studies* 107 at pp. 110–111).

4.2 Public interest litigation and socio-economic rights

A watershed, both in the development of India in general and of Indian Constitutional jurisprudence, was the period referred to as the 'internal emergency', which lasted from June 1975 to March 1977.[44] The emergency was engineered by the then Prime Minister, Indira Gandhi, in a last desperate effort to hold on to political power in the face of mounting opposition and charges of electoral fraud. Mrs Gandhi convinced the then president to declare a state of emergency under Article 352 of the Constitution, under the colour of which elections and civil liberties were suspended. Commenting on this period Austin notes that for twenty months between 1975 and 1977 'democracy was extinguished, personal liberty and fundamental rights suspended, legitimate political opponents kept under preventative detention, and the opportunity taken further to subvert democracy by amending the Constitution'.[45] During the emergency the Supreme Court was highly criticised for 'acquiescing in the subversion of the Constitution and flagrant violations of civil liberties by the Executive'.[46] At the height of the emergency the Supreme Court, in the now infamous case of *ADM Jabalpur* v. *Shiv Kant Shukla* embraced a form of hyper-positivism in holding that once a state of emergency had been declared, and the rights in the Constitution (in the instant case in Article 21) had been suspended, individuals no longer enjoyed the protection of such rights.[47] Following this decision, and indeed based on the Court's general timidity throughout the emergency, the commonly held perception emerged that 'the Court had in the hour of need betrayed the nation'.[48] The Court therefore was completely devoid of legitimacy in the popular consciousness.

In the wake of the emergency, then, the Court was faced with the need to rehabilitate its image in the public's mind. This led the Court to embark on a 'series of unprecedented and electrifying initiatives',[49] which cumulatively have come to be known as PIL. This new development 'sought to use judicial power to protect excluded and powerless groups . . . and to secure entitlements that were going unredeemed'.[50] Austin notes that in this period the Supreme Court went 'from handing down many conservative/technical rulings to judicial activism, using as its instrument public interest litigation'.[51] One of the things, therefore, that marks the Indian experience of PIL out is that it was 'primarily

44 On the internal emergency, in general, see Austin (n. 30) at pp. 278–391.
45 *Ibid.* at p. 9.
46 Vijayashri Sripati, 'Towards Fifty Years of Constitutionalism and Fundamental Rights in India: Looking Back to See Ahead' (1998) 14 *American University International Law Review* 413 at p. 440.
47 [1976] INSC 129 (28 April 1976); and see the cognate judgment in the case of *Union of India* v. *Bhanudas Krishna Gawde* [1977] INSC 29 (25 January 1977).
48 Sharma (n. 4) at p. 229.
49 Marc Galanter and Jayanth Krishnan, '"Bread for the Poor": Access to Justice and the Rights of the Needy in India' (2004) 55 *Hastings Law Journal* 789 at p. 795.
50 *Ibid.*
51 Austin (n. 38) at p. 340.

judge-led and even judge-induced'.[52] Baxi argues that the emergence of this, what he terms 'judicial populism', was 'partly an aspect of post-Emergency catharsis. Partly it was an attempt to refurbish the image of the Court tarnished by a few emergency decisions and also an attempt to seek new, historical bases of legitimation of judicial power'.[53] Against this backdrop, and in pursuit of these various goals, the Court, led in particular by Justices Bhagwati and Krishna Iyer, embarked on a truly original process of redefining the judicial role.

4.2.1 The emergence of public interest litigation

In one of the earliest PIL cases, in which the Court among other things significantly relaxed the rules with respect to standing, Bhagwati J. held that the driving force behind PIL was the judicial recognition that:

> it is necessary to democratise judicial remedies, remove technical barriers against easy accessibility to justice and promote public interest litigation so that the large masses of people belonging to the deprived and exploited sections of humanity may be able to realise and enjoy the socioeconomic rights granted to them and these rights may become meaningful for them instead of remaining mere empty hopes.[54]

PIL, therefore, was marked out first and foremost by the innovative procedural reforms introduced by the Court. In particular the Court significantly relaxed the rules around standing; broadened the manner in which a writ petition could be filed, extending it to encompass Bhagwati J.'s 'epistolary jurisdiction', whereby a PIL case could be commenced by simply addressing a complaint in the form of a letter, or indeed a postcard, to the Supreme Court; and introduced the practice of appointing expert commissions to both help the Court in the fact-finding aspect of a substantive hearing, and to monitor implementation of court orders, where appropriate, to name but the most prominent.[55]

Also in the context of PIL, the Court showed a 'willingness to experiment with remedial strategies that require continuous supervision'.[56] As Colin Gonsalves notes, an 'interesting innovation' took place 'after the judiciary noticed that orders of even the superior courts were routinely disobeyed in

---

52 Baxi (n. 43) at p. 111.
53 *Ibid.* at p. 113.
54 *S. P. Gupta* v. *Union of India* (1981) Supp SCC 83.
55 See generally Ashok Desai and S. Muralidhar, 'Public Interest Litigation: Potential and Problems' in Kirpal, Desai, Subramanium, Dhavan and Ramachandran (eds.), *Supreme But Not Infallible: Essays in Honour of the Supreme Court of India* (New Delhi: Oxford University Press, 2004) 159 at p. 159; similar views are expressed by Baxi (1985) at p. 111; Sathe (n. 36) at pp. 162–168; and Jamie Cassels, 'Judicial Activism and Public Interest Litigation in India: Attempting the Impossible?' (1989) 37 *American Journal of Comparative Law* 495 at pp. 496–507.
56 Cassels (n. 55) at p. 506.

India'. In response the 'court developed the practice of issuing the "continuing mandamus", whereby after the orders are issued, courts continued to retain jurisdiction over the matter and periodically review the progress of the implementation of the respective court order';[57] while Jamie Cassels expresses some trepidation with this development because it 'appear[s] significantly to shift the line between adjudication and administration'.[58] Others, such as Sathe, argue that it is justified in the context of the Supreme Court's drive to transform the traditional, inherited conventions of judicial procedure into 'a new paradigm that was polycentric and even legislative'.[59]

Similarly, Desai and Muralidhar note that as a result of PIL the 'Court is now seen as an institution not only reaching out to provide relief to citizens but even venturing into formulating policy which the State must follow', and that this is considered a positive development.[60] They also acknowledge that in practice PIL tends to narrow the divide between the role of the various organs of government, and has invited controversy principally for this reason. It is remarkable, though, that notwithstanding the candid acknowledgement by both observers and judges that PIL does involve a reordering of the relationship between the courts and the elected branches of government, it nonetheless flourished for at least twenty years; during which time the Supreme Court began to work out the contours of a distinctively Indian socio-economic rights jurisprudence, and it is to this which we now turn.

4.2.2 A life worth living

While PIL is notable first and foremost for the institutional innovations which it introduced, more broadly the PIL movement generally emboldened the Supreme Court, and encouraged, some would say compelled, them to be more expansive in their interpretation of constitutional provisions and more exacting in the demands it placed on public bodies. This no doubt contributed to and facilitated what Pilar Domingo refers to as a 'sudden and unexpected explosion of social-rights litigation . . . in India'.[61] The Supreme Court's emergent socio-economic rights jurisprudence was built, first and foremost, around the guarantee of the right to life in Article 21 of the Constitution, read in light of the DPSP. As Sharma notes:

> Article 21 is one article which has been so transformed by the Supreme Court that it now encompasses all conceivable human rights within its

57 Gonsalves (n. 1) at p. 179.
58 Cassels (n. 55) at p. 506.
59 Sathe (n. 36) at p. 17.
60 Desai and Muralidhar (n. 55) at p. 159.
61 Pilar Domingo, 'Introduction' in Gargarella, Domingo and Roux (eds.), *Courts and Social Transformation in New Democracies: An Institutional Voice for the Poor?* (Hampshire: Ashgate, 2006) 1 at p. 2.

ambit. On a plain reading it is a directive to the State to refrain from infringing the right to life or personable liberty of a person. The courts have taken a very liberal view and transformed the negative injunction to a positive mandate to do all things which will make life worth living.[62]

In effect the Supreme Court transformed Article 21 into 'a canvass for various other human rights'.[63]

A precursor for this development was the Court rejecting the formalism of its earlier case law, in which it had held that all Article 21 required was that any limitations placed on the rights to life and liberty was that any such infringement be grounded on a validly enacted law.[64] In the post-emergency era the Supreme Court, in the *Maneka Gandhi* case,[65] departed from the excessive formalism of its earlier case law and began the process of imbuing Article 21 with a concept of due process; henceforth the Supreme Court would not only inquire into whether the limitation or interference with a fundamental right was valid, but whether or not it was reasonable, fair and just and not arbitrary or fanciful. In this way the Court introduced the concept of due process into Indian constitutional law, and ushered in a new era of a more activist and demanding Supreme Court.[66] As Balakrishnan Rajagopal put it, in this case 'the Court turned away from formalism and positivism entirely . . . and launched Article 21 in a new, expansive direction'.[67]

The extent of this 'new, expansive direction' was sketched out in the subsequent case of *Francis Coralie Mullin* v. *The Administrator, Union Territory of Delhi*;[68] this case concerned the right of an individual held under preventative detention to, *inter alia*, have access to legal advisers. However, flush with the new life breathed into Article 21 by the *Maneka Ghandi* case, Bhagwati J. took the opportunity to spell out the expansive, indeed near imperialist, nature of the right to life. The judge set the scene by holding that in:

> arriving at the proper meaning and content of the right to life, the attempt of the court should always be to expand the reach and ambit of the fundamental right rather than to attenuate its meaning and content. A constitutional provision must be construed, not in a narrow and constricted sense, but in a wide and liberal manner so as to anticipate and take account of changing conditions and purposes so that the constitutional provision does not get atrophied or fossilized but remains flexible enough to meet the

---

62 Sharma (n. 4) at p. 87.
63 Sathe (n. 36) at p. 116.
64 *A. K. Gopalan* v. *State of Madras* [1950] INSC 14 (19 May 1950).
65 *Maneka Gandhi* v. *Union of India* [1978] INSC 16 (25 January 1978).
66 Sharma (n. 4) at p. 88.
67 Balakrishnan Rajagopal, 'Pro-Human Rights But Anti-Poor? A Critical Evaluation of the Indian Supreme Court From a Social Movement Perspective' (2007) 8 *Human Rights Review* 157 at p. 165.
68 [1981] INSC 12 (13 January 1981).

newly emerging problems and challenges. This principle applies with greater force in relation to a fundamental right enacted by the Constitution. The fundamental right to life which is the most precious human right and which forms the arc of all other rights must therefore be interpreted in a broad and expansive spirit so as to invest it with significance and vitality which may endure for years to come and enhance the dignity of the individual and the worth of the human person.[69]

He then went on to hold that the right to life under Article 21 was not 'restricted to mere animal existence', but instead meant much more. In particular, Bhagwati J. held that:

> the right to life includes the right to live with human dignity and all that goes along with it, namely, the bare necessaries of life such as adequate nutrition, clothing and shelter and facilities for reading, writing and expressing one-self in diverse forms . . . Of course, the magnitude and content of the components of this right would depend upon the extent of the economic development of the country, but it must, in any view of the matter, include the right to the basic necessities of life and also the right to carry on such functions and activities as constitute the bare minimum expression of the human-self. Every act which offends against or impairs human dignity would constitute deprivation *pro tanto* of this right to live and it would have to be in accordance with reasonable, fair and just procedure established by law which stands the test of other fundamental rights.[70]

This holding by the Court provided the bedrock for the further expansion of the Court's socio-economic rights jurisprudence, extending, as we will see shortly, to encompass the explicit recognition of the rights to health care, food, education and shelter.

With respect to the right to health, the Supreme Court held in a case concerning workers exposed to asbestos that, read in light of the DPSP, 'it must be held that the right to life and medical care is a fundamental right under Article 21'. The Court then went so far as to mandate compulsory health insurance for all workers in the instant industry where they were at a high risk of contracting asbestosis.[71] In a subsequent case, which concerned an individual who had fallen from a train in Calcutta and suffered extensive head injuries, but had been refused access to several public medical facilities on the basis that they were either ill-equipped to treat his condition or did not have free beds, the Court held that:

69 *Ibid.*
70 *Ibid.*
71 *Consumer Education and Research Centre* v. *Union of India* [1995] INSC 91 (27 January 1995).

The Constitution envisages the establishment of a welfare State at the federal level as well as at the State level. In a welfare State the primary duty of the Government is to secure the welfare of the people. Providing adequate medical facilities for the people is an essential part of the obligation undertaken by the Government in a welfare state. The Government discharges this obligation by running hospitals and health centres which provide medical care to the person seeking to avail of those facilities. Article 21 imposes an obligation on the State to safeguard the right to life of every person. Preservation of human life is thus of paramount importance. The Government hospitals run by the State and the medical officers employed therein are duty bound to extend medical assistance for preserving human life. Failure on the part of a Government hospital to provide timely medical treatment to a person in need of such treatment results in [a] violation of his right to life guaranteed under Article 21.[72]

The Court, thus, read timely access to emergency medical treatment as a minimum core of the right to health derived from Article 21 of the Constitution. As well as awarding the applicant damages, the Court also issued a declaration requiring the state to implement a comprehensive plan to improve availability of and access to emergency medical treatment. In response to a query about the resource implications of its finding and order, the Court held that while the judgment did implicate resource expenditure 'it cannot be ignored that it is a constitutional obligation of the State to provide adequate medical services to people. Whatever is necessary for this purpose has to be done'.[73]

The right to education is arguably the real success story of the Indian Supreme Court's PIL–socio-economic rights jurisprudence. In *Mohini Jain's* case,[74] the Supreme Court recognised for the first time that Article 21, again read in light of the DPSP and the Preamble, encompassed a guarantee of a right to education. As Kuldip Singh J. put it, the:

'Right to life' is the compendious expression for all those rights which the Courts must enforce because they are basic to the dignified enjoyment of life. It extends to the full range of conduct which the individual is free to pursue. The right to education flows directly from right to life. The right to life under Article 21 and the dignity of an individual cannot be assured unless it is accompanied by the right to education. The State Government is under an obligation to make endeavour to provide educational facilities at all levels to its citizens. The fundamental rights guaranteed under Part III of the Constitution of India including the right to freedom of speech and expression and other rights under Article 19 cannot be appreciated

---

72 *Paschim Banga Khet Mazdoor Samity* v. *State of West Bengal* [1996] INSC 659 (6 May 1996).
73 *Ibid.*
74 *Miss Mohini Jain* v. *State of Karnataka* [1992] INSC 184 (30 July 1992).

and fully enjoyed unless a citizen is educated and is conscious of his indi-
vidualistic dignity. The 'right to education', therefore, is concomitant to
the fundamental rights enshrined under Part III of the Constitution. The
State is under a constitutional-mandate to provide educational institutions
at all levels for the benefit of the citizens. The educational institutions must
function to the best advantage of the citizens.[75]

This extensive holding had potentially limitless financial implications for the
government; consequently Sathe argues that in the next education case
the Supreme Court reined in somewhat the finding in *Mohini Jain*, to limit to
right to free and compulsory education to children between the ages of 6 and
14.[76]

The Court did this in the case of *Unni Krishnan* v. *State of Andhra Pradesh*,[77]
although this case concerned an unsuccessful challenge by private medical and
engineering colleges to legislation limiting the capitation fees they could charge
students seeking admission, the Court used the case for the broader purpose of
delineating the nature of the right to education under the Constitution, and,
for the first time, explicitly recognised free *primary* education as a fundamental
right. The Court held that:

> It is noteworthy that among several articles in Part IV, only Article 45
> speaks of a time-limit: no other article does . . . Does not the passage of 44
> years – more than four times the period stipulated in Article 45 – convert
> the obligation created by the article into an enforceable right? In this
> context, we feel constrained to say that the allocation of available funds to
> different sectors of education in India discloses an inversion of priorities
> indicated by the Constitution.[78]

The Court therefore held that the 'right to education is implicit in and flows
from the rights to life guaranteed under Article 21' and that every Indian child
'has a fundamental right to free education up to the age of fourteen years'. It is
also noteworthy that in this case Jeevan Reddy J. rejected the argument that
because of the budgetary implications of such a finding the Court was imper-
missibly straying into the realm of the elected branches of governments, by
holding that the Court was 'not seeking to lay down the priorities of the
Government – we are only emphasising the constitutional policy as disclosed
by Articles 45, 46 and 41'.[79]

The Court then sent out slightly mixed messages by stating that the:

75 *Ibid.*
76 Sathe (n. 36) at p. 138.
77 [1993] INSC 60 (4 February 1993).
78 *Ibid.*
79 *Ibid.*

right to education further means that a citizen has a right to call upon the State to provide educational facilities to him within the limits of its economic capacity and development. By saying so, we are not transferring Article 41 from Part IV to Part III, we are merely relying upon Article 41 to illustrate the content of the right to education flowing from Article 21. We cannot believe that any State would say that it need not provide education to its people even within the limits of its economic capacity and development. It goes without saying that the limits of economic capacity are, ordinarily speaking, matters within the subjective satisfaction of the State.[80]

On the one hand this appears to imply that the Supreme Court will enforce the individual's right to education, through mandatory orders if necessary, but on the other hand it also seems to imply that the Court will defer, to some extent, to defences of limited resources. Notwithstanding this confusion, the net effect of both *Mohini Jain* and *Unni Krishnan* was to establish beyond doubt that every Indian child had a right to free and compulsory education, derived from the judicially enforceable right to life in Article 21 of the Constitution. In response to these judgments, the government enacted the Constitution (Eighty-sixth Amendment) Act, 2002 which inserted the right to primary education into Part III of the Constitution,[81] thereby explicitly making it judicially enforceable.

The right to food was held to be implicitly protected by the right to life in a number of the Supreme Court's judgments;[82] however the matter came up for concrete consideration in the case of *People's Union for Civil Liberties* v. *Union of India*.[83] This case arose as a result of a severe drought which was affecting a number of the poorest provinces in India, and as a consequence of which people in these provinces were starving in large numbers. Kothari notes that the drought and consequent food shortages in Orissa and other provinces caused an 'enormous public outcry', because it was openly acknowledged that the Food Corporation of India had granaries which were 'overflowing with food grains' and food was being allowed to rot and go to waste, while people in the provinces worst hit by the drought were being allowed to starve to death.[84] The applicants, relying explicitly on the right to food derived from Article 21, asked the Court to order, *inter alia*, that the unused national food stocks be made available to

---

80 *Ibid.*
81 Indian Constitution, Article 21A states that 'The State shall provide free and compulsory education to all children of the age of six to fourteen years in such manner as the State may, by law, determine'; this amendment also effected a change to Article 45 of the DPSP, replacing the original article dealing with the issue of primary education with a provision requiring that 'The State shall endeavour to provide early childhood care and education for all children until they complete the age of six years'.
82 See for example *Francis Coralie Mullin* (n. 68) and *Paschim Banga Khet* (n. 72).
83 Writ Petition (Civil) No.196/2001 (23 July 2001) Unreported ('*PUCL* case').
84 Kothari (n. 1) at p. 178.

those in dire need, and more generally the applicants asked the Court to mandate strict implementation of the existing anti-famine laws and policies.

In what Kothari has described as an 'unprecedented' interim order,[85] the Court ordered the central government and the states to effectively implement eight established food schemes for the poor. Chief among them was the mid-day meal scheme, and the Court ordered that all children in public schools be provided with a cooked mid-day meal by January 2002.[86] Also of significance, the Court appointed two commissioners to monitor the implementation of the court order and to report back on progress and continued violations. These reports have consistently highlighted failure on behalf of certain states to implement the order, and have provided important tools for groups to lobby the central government leading to major increases in budgetary allocations for the schemes.[87] The Court's intervention in this case was 'instrumental in ensuring the extension of the mid-day meal programme to most of the states in the country', and that sense will have contributed to improving the health, and possibly saving the lives, of countless poor and excluded children.[88]

Finally, we look at the right to shelter. As with the right to food, the Supreme Court had intimated in a number of its judgments that the right to life in Article 21 encompassed the right to shelter. On various occasions the Court has explicitly recognised the right to shelter, but has been quite tentative when it comes to enforcing it. In *Shantistar Builders* v. *Narayan Khimalal Totame*,[89] the Court was asked to intervene in a context were it was alleged that a builder was failing to build affordable housing on land specially designated under a scheme for that very purpose. In the course of the judgment it was held that the right to life included 'within its sweep the right to food, the right to clothing, the right to a decent environment *and reasonable accommodation to live in*'.[90] On the facts before it, the Court ordered the builders to construct and allocate reasonable accommodation for those of the respondents who qualified under the applicable scheme within a set time-frame.

In a subsequent case, which concerned the eviction of pavement dwellers and their claim that they were entitled to alternative accommodation if evicted,[91] the Supreme Court again held that the right to life 'in any civilised society implies the right to food, water, decent environment, education, medical care and shelter'. The Court further held that this implicit right to shelter meant that:

85 Kothari (n. 1) at p. 181.
86 Unreported Order, 28 November 2001: www.righttofoodindia.org/orders/nov28.html
87 Kothari (n. 1) at p. 181; the various reports of the two commissioners and the various interim orders of the Court issued in this case can all be accessed at: www.righttofoodindia.org
88 Muralidhar (n. 1) at p. 117.
89 (1990) 1 SCC 520.
90 *Ibid.* (emphasis added).
91 *Ahmadabad Municipal Corporation* v. *Nawab Khan* [1996] INSC 1300 (11 October 1996).

the State has the Constitutional duty to provide adequate facilities and
opportunities by distributing its wealth and resources for settlement of life
and erection of shelter over their heads to make the right to life meaningful,
effective and fruitful . . . It would, therefore, be the duty of the State to
provide a right to shelter to the poor and indigent weaker sections of the
society in fulfilment of the Constitutional objectives.[92]

Following this trenchant restatement of the fundamental nature of the right to
shelter, the Court held that certain of the applicants were entitled to be provided
with alternative accommodation by the relevant corporation if they were to be
evicted from their pavement dwellings. The Court, thus, has explicitly recognised the right to shelter, but has also been careful about balancing it against
the need not to encourage illegal encroachments on public property, and further
has been somewhat meek in the extent to which it is willing to enforce the
right.

   It is clear, from all of the foregoing, that the Supreme Court of India, using
the medium of PIL and through creative interpretations of the Indian
Constitution's provisions, has developed a substantial jurisprudence on socio-
economic rights. Particularly noteworthy are the Court's judgments in the
context of the right to education and right to food. Commenting on the Court's
socio-economic rights jurisprudence Kothari argues that it 'illustrates how the
absence of formal constitutional guarantees of social rights does not preclude
constitutional protection of certain interests associated with social citizenship
through expansive interpretations of civil and political rights';[93] furthermore
she argues that the Indian experience 'suggests a potential role for a creative and
sensitive judiciary to enforce constitutional social rights'.[94] While the Supreme
Court's socio-economic rights jurisprudence is certainly a feat of ingenuity, and
in certain respects laudable, particularly in the context of the *PUCL* case were
the Court's orders resulted in the delivery of food to people who otherwise might
have starved, it is not without its shortcomings. These shortcomings are intimately related to certain shortcomings in the Court's overall PIL jurisprudence.
In the next section we consider some of these shortcomings, and also take stock
of the overall nature of the Indian Supreme Court's socio-economic rights
jurisprudence.

4.3 Swings and roundabouts

While the Indian Supreme Court's PIL–socio-economic rights jurisprudence has
been widely acknowledged and on the whole well received,[95] there are certain

92 *Ibid.*
93 Kothari (n. 1) at p. 171.
94 Kothari (n. 1) at p. 191.
95 For example Desai and Muralidhar (n. 55) at p. 180, argue that 'The emergence of PIL over
    the last twenty years has been a salutary development towards providing the vast majority
    of citizens with access to justice and effective protection of their fundamental rights'.

shortcomings with the Court's overall approach to the question of socio-economic rights. Here we examine two of the more noteworthy concerns: the first, which was intimidated earlier, relates to the relative lack of principle underpinning the Court's jurisprudence, which has resulted in a number of inconsistent and contradictory judgments. The second problem is of a more recent vintage, and relates to an apparent shift in the orientation of the Supreme Court, arguably occasioned by acquiescence in a prevailing development paradigm that holds sway in the halls of power. This apparent shift sees the Supreme Court casting itself in a more deferential and less activist role, and in this context relinquishing its traditional pro-rights and interventionist role. Radha D'Souza notes that since the late 1990s the Supreme Court's acquiescence in government-sponsored neo-liberal reforms has 'raised concerns' about the role and future of PIL.[96]

Furthermore, Gobind Das notes that in the last decade or so PIL has moved from being a judge-led initiative to advance the rights of the poor and socially excluded, to being 'an instrument in the hands of the conscientious middle-class citizen' to enforce notions of good governance and otherwise advance the interests of India's rising middle class.[97] This, coupled with the hegemony of neo-liberal notions of development among India's ruling elites, has resulted in a discernible shift in the nature and tenor of the Supreme Court's PIL jurisprudence. As Rajagopal notes, 'the Court's activism increasingly manifests several biases – in favour of the state and development, in favour of the rich against workers, in favour of the urban middle-class against rural farmers, and in favour of a globalitarian class and against the distributive ethos of the Indian Constitution'.[98] We begin this penultimate section by looking at the ways in which this new Zeitgeist has contributed to the Supreme Court delivering judgments which show inconsistencies in its socio-economic rights jurisprudence, before then drawing some overall conclusions on the Court's experience with socio-economic rights.

4.3.1 *Conflicting judgments*

One of the Supreme Court's earliest PIL cases, and one which became very well known around the world, was the *Olga Tellis* case.[99] Essentially the case concerned a large number of pavement dwellers who sought to prevent their proposed eviction from their pavement dwellings on the basis that evicting them would deny them the right to pursue their livelihood, and thereby constitute a breach of the right to life under Article 21 of the Constitution. The Supreme Court, in a much celebrated *dictum*, held that the right to life did

96 Radha D'Souza, 'The "Third World" and Socio-Legal Studies: Neo-Liberalism and Lessons From India's Legal Innovations' (2005) 14 *Social and Legal Studies* 487 at p. 488.
97 Das (n. 3) at pp. 38–44.
98 Rajagopal (n. 67) at p. 158.
99 *Olga Tellis* v. *Bombay Municipal Corporation* [1985] INSC 155 (10 July 1985).

encompass the right to earn a livelihood; however the Court, essentially for public policy reasons, refused to validate the illegal occupation of public property by the applicants and other similarly situated individuals, and simply ordered a temporary delay before the eviction of the applicants could proceed. Gonsalves is highly critical of the 'partially ambiguous and recommendatory nature of the Court in the [*Olga Tellis* case]' and argues that because the Court refused to countenance the right to shelter of the applicants it 'resulted in mass evictions of pavement dwellers in 1985'.[100]

Related to this, Gonsalves notes that housing rights campaigners in India are concerned about 'the ease with which middle class groups have been able to secure eviction orders against poor urban and rural dwellers'.[101] This concern is borne out by some recent judgments of the Supreme Court, in particular in the case of *Almitra Patel* the Supreme Court, criticising the usurpation of public land 'for private use free of cost' and characterising slum dwellers as 'pickpockets', issued orders requiring the clearing of slum settlements in Delhi, without allowing those affected an opportunity to argue against the Court's determination, or in any other way taking their interests into account.[102] This case demonstrates how, enamoured with the newly ascendant concerns of the middle class, the Court has turned its back on the basic needs of the most deprived and marginalised people in Indian society. This judgment is also not entirely commensurate with the Supreme Court's trenchant assertions of the centrality of the right to shelter in securing human dignity and as a prerequisite of a decent life in any civilised nation in cases such as *Shantistar Builders* and *Nawah Khan* and in fact seems to be completely at variance with such pronouncements.

Inconsistencies in the Court's PIL–socio-economic rights jurisprudence are also evident in cases which raised the issue of the extent to which the Court would require redistribution of resources so as to vindicate constitutional rights. In one case, concerned with the failure of a municipal authority to provide slum dwellers with sufficient sanitary facilities, as they were statutorily obliged to do, Krishna Iyer J. for the Supreme Court, in upholding the order of a lower court requiring the municipal council to provide sanitary facilities within a set time-frame, held that the plea of limited resources would not absolve the state of its statutory or constitutional obligations, stating that 'human rights under Part III of the Constitution have to be respected by the State regardless of budgetary provision'.[103] He went on to say that a 'responsible municipal council constituted for the precise purpose of preserving public health and providing better finances cannot run away from its principal duty by pleading financial inability' and that 'affirmative action to make the remedy effective is of the essence of the right which otherwise becomes sterile'. He concluded his

100 Gonsalves (n. 1) at p. 180.
101 *Ibid.* at p. 181.
102 *Almitra H. Patel* v. *Union of India* [2000] INSC 54 (15 February 2000).
103 *Municipal Council, Ratlam* v. *Shri Vardichand* [1980] INSC 138 (29 July 1980).

judgment by sounding the warning that 'the plea of poor finance will be [a] poor alibi when people in misery cry for justice'.[104]

However, in a more recent case the Court struck a more deferential tone where public employees sought to challenge the government's decision to reduce the extent of their health care coverage.[105] In rejecting the applicant's case, Misra J. held that:

> No State of any country can have unlimited resources to spend on any of its project. That is why it only approves its projects to the extent it is feasible. The same holds good for providing medical facilities to its citizens including its employees. Provision of facilities cannot be unlimited. It has to be to the extent finance permits. If no scale or rate is fixed then in case private clinics or hospitals increase their rate to exorbitant scales, the State would be bound to reimburse the same. Hence we come to the conclusion that principle of fixation of rate and scale under this new policy is justified and cannot be held to be violative of Article 21 or Article 47 of the Constitution of India.[106]

While the acknowledgement of resource constraints in the context of fundamental rights adjudication is not objectionable per se, the contrast between the approach of the Court in this case and the assertion of the primacy of fundamental rights by Krishna Iyer J. in *Ratlam* could not be starker. It again illustrates the inconsistent nature of the Court's PIL–socio-economic rights jurisprudence, with all of the attendant problems that come with such inconsistency.

It will suffice to give one last example under this heading. In the case of *TMA Pai Foundation* v. *State of Karnataka*,[107] the Supreme Court essentially handed *carte blanche* to private, for-profit education providers. The case concerned a challenge to the quota system established in the wake of *Unni Krishnan*, whereby 50 per cent of the places in third-level institutions were reserved for members of scheduled castes and other disadvantage groups, and such students fees were subsidised by significantly higher fees being charged to the other students. The Court held that the right to establish and operate educational institutions was inherent in Articles 19(1)(g) and 26 of the Constitution, and such privately established institutions, if they eschewed state funding, should be entitled to near untrammelled freedom in determining the admissions policy of their institution, including the fees to be charged. This decision seems to completely contradict the sentiment in the Court's earlier education cases. For example in *Mohini Jain* Kuldip Singh J. held that for-profit educational institutions were 'contrary to the constitutional scheme and . . . wholly abhorrent

---

104 Ibid.
105 *State of Punjab* v. *Ram Lubhaya Bagga* [1998] INSC 131 (26 February 1998).
106 Ibid.
107 [2002] INSC 455 (31 October 2002); followed and further reiterated in the subsequent decision of *P. A. Inamdar* v. *State of Maharashtra* [2005] INSC 413 (12 August 2005).

to the Indian culture and heritage', he further held that 'education in India has never been a commodity for sale'.[108] Similarly in *Unni Krishnan* Jeevan Reddy J. held that while:

> we do not wish to express any opinion on the question whether the right to establish an educational institution can be said to be carrying on any 'occupation' within the meaning of Article 19(1)(g) . . . we are certainly of the opinion that such activity can neither be a trade or business nor can it be a profession within the meaning of Article 19(1)(g). Trade or business normally connotes an activity carried on with a profit motive. Education has never been commerce in this country.[109]

Consequently, the decision in the *Pai Foundation* case has led Sathe to ask '[how] does one reconcile the open advocacy of commercialization/marketization of education by judges [in *Pai*] with the social justice concerns reflected in the earlier [education] judgments of the Court'. Ultimately he concludes that 'the philosophy underlying the *Pai Foundation* decision that one who can afford alone would have the access to education is quite opposed to the philosophy of the Constitution of India and opposed to the settled law of the Supreme Court of India'.[110]

4.3.2 The 'heart of darkness' of Indian constitutionalism

Aside from the contradictory decisions which result from the fluid and some-what haphazard nature of PIL, the Supreme Court in recent years has also issued judgments that conflict with or undermine the rights of marginalised and excluded groups. Although in contrast to the contradictory cases discussed above, these judgments appear to be imbued with the tacit acceptance of a particular substantive morality. As Woods argues, the 'limits of judicial intervention are . . . evident in the Court's response to neo-liberal development schemes'.[111] Chief among these development schemes are the World Bank and IMF massive dam constructions, and according to Baxi the various dam project cases, or more particularly the massive social struggles, State repression and continued opposition surrounding them, reveal 'the 'heart of darkness' of the Indian practices of development as justice, proselytised as 'development' by the peddlers of Indian constitutionalism'.[112] One such case was the *Narmada* valley case, which concerned a challenge by an organisation representing the interests of a number of communities that would be adversely affected by the con-struction of a massive dam in the Narmada valley region.[113] In particular this

108　*Mohini Jain* (n. 74).
109　*Unni Krishnan* (n. 77).
110　Sathe (n. 36) at pp. vi–vii.
111　Woods (n. 25) at p. 110.
112　Baxi (n. 34) at p. 53.
113　*Narmada Bachao Andolan* v. *Union of India* [2000] INSC 518 (18 October 2000).

case sought to prevent the raising of the water level on the Sardar Sarovar Project, on the basis, *inter alia*, that forcibly removing the tribal and small farmer communities, comprising some 41,000 families, would result in a breach of their rights under Article 21 of the Constitution. On this substantive point, the Supreme Court majority rejected the applicant's case on the basis of a mix of paternalism and utilitarianism, noting that '[at] the rehabilitation sites they will have more and better amenities than which they enjoyed in their tribal hamlets. The gradual assimilation in the mainstream of the society will lead to betterment and progress' and that the displacement of these communities was 'necessary for the greater good'.[114]

However, of more significance, for present purposes at least, is the heavily deferential tone sounded by the Supreme Court majority in this case. Kirpal J. argued that:

> While protecting the rights of the people from being violated in any manner utmost care has to be taken that the court does not transgress its jurisdiction. There is, in our constitutional framework a fairly clear demarcation of powers. The court has come down heavily whenever the executive has sought to impinge upon the court's jurisdiction. At the same time, in exercise of its enormous power the court should not be called upon to undertake governmental duties or functions. The courts cannot run the Government nor can the administration indulge in abuse or non-use of power and get away with it. The essence of judicial review is a constitutional fundamental. The role of the higher judiciary under the Constitution casts on it a great obligation as the sentinel to defend the values of the Constitution and the rights of Indians. The courts must, therefore, act within their judicially permissible limitations to uphold the rule of law and harness their power in [the] public interest. It is precisely for this reason that it has been consistently held by this Court that in matters of policy the court will not interfere. . . . If a considered policy decision has been taken, which is not in conflict with any law or is not mala fide, it will not be in public interest to require the court to go into and investigate those areas which are the function of the executive. For any project which is approved after due deliberation the court should refrain from being asked to review the decision just because a petitioner in filing a PIL alleges that such a decision should not have been taken because an opposite view against the undertaking of the project, which view may have been considered by the Government, is possible. When two or more options or views are possible and after considering them the Government takes a policy decision it is then not the function of the court to go into the matter afresh and, in a way, sit in appeal over such a policy decision.

---

114 *Ibid.*

Rajagopal argues that 'the court examined the facts of the dispute through lenses which were themselves biased in ways that approved only one version of the facts' and consequently it 'was clear that completing the construction of the dam was more important to the court than the social and environmental costs it imposed'.[115] Ultimately, Rajagopal argues that the Court's acceptance of and commitment to a hybrid ideology, encompassing the prevailing neo-liberal development orthodoxy, made the Court's decision a foregone conclusion.[116] He also notes that in this case 'the Court put its seal of approval on the largest Court-sanctioned forced eviction in the world'.[117] Kothari is scathing in her criticism of the *Narmada* valley case, and argues that this 'single judgment contradicts all previous Supreme Court rulings that have upheld the right to housing and shelter as an integral part of the fundamental right to life' and represents a 'regressive' move on the part of the Supreme Court.[118]

Unfortunately the Supreme Court reiterated its stance in another case concerning dam projects, in rejecting the applicant's challenge to the decision to construct the Tehri Dam in the state of Uttaranchal, Rajendra Babu J. for a majority of the Supreme Court held that when 'the government or the authorities concerned after due consideration of all view points and full application of mind took a decision, then it is not appropriate for the court to interfere. Such matters must be left to the mature wisdom of the Government or the implementing agency. It is their forte'.[119] In a dissenting judgment Dharmadhikari J. noted that the 'displacement of economically weaker sections of the society and tribals is the most serious aspect of displacement from the point of view of uprooting them from their natural surroundings. Absence of these surroundings in the new settlement colonies shatters their social, cultural and physical links'. The judge further argued that when:

> social conflicts arise between the poor and more needy on the one side and the rich or affluent or less needy on the other, prior attention has to be paid to the former group which is both financially and politically weak. Such less-advantaged group is expected to be given prior attention in a welfare state like ours which is committed and obliged by the Constitution, particularly by its provisions contained in the preamble, fundamental rights, fundamental duties and directive principles, to take care of such deprived sections of people who are likely to lose their home and source of livelihood.[120]

---

115 Balakrishnan Rajagopal, 'Limits of Law in Counter-Hegemonic Globalization: The Indian Supreme Court and the Narmada Valley Struggle' in De Sousa Santos and Rodriguez-Garavito (eds.), *Law and Globalization from Below: Towards a Cosmopolitan Legality* (Cambridge: Cambridge University Press, 2005) 183 at pp. 202–203.
116 *Ibid.* at pp. 203–208.
117 Rajagopal (n. 67) at p. 162.
118 Kothari (n. 1) at p. 186.
119 *N. D. Jayal* v. *Union of India* (2004) 9 SCC 362 [hereinafter the '*Tehri Dam* case'].
120 *Ibid.*

It would not be too much of a stretch to say that of the differing approaches articulated, the approach of Dharmadhikari J. is in greater harmony with the attitude of the Supreme Court developed over the years in the exercise of its PIL jurisdiction.

In contrast the new-found modesty of Rajendra Babu J. and others looks rather more like a relic from the Court's pre-*Maneka Gandhi* jurisprudence. In both of these cases the Supreme Court, with the exception of Dharmadhikari J.'s impassioned dissent in the *Tehri Dam* case and to a lesser extent Bharucha J.'s dissent in *Narmada*, evidenced a marked disregard for the rights of vulnerable and marginalised groups, and also framed its own role in a hyper-deferential manner. But as Muralidhar notes, the 'purported major premise of the *Narmada* and *Tehri* decisions that it would be neither legitimate nor competent for courts to enter into the arena of policy decisions of the State concerning [socio-economic] rights is . . . belied in the decisions in certain other PIL cases that suggest otherwise'.[121] Similarly Rajagopal notes that the Supreme Court's retreat into deference and notions of the appropriate balance between the respective organs of state is somewhat Janus-faced, as 'the Court has rarely paid much attention to these issues in its impressive career of judicial activism'.[122]

One final case may be worth mentioning as further evidence of the way in which the Supreme Court, tempted by the siren call of acquiescence to neo-liberal policy implementation and the rediscovery of legal formalism, has edged towards divesting itself of its hard-won PIL jurisdiction. In a case in which employees of a public company sought to prevent the state from disinvesting in the company and privatising it, as this would result in a breach of their right to earn a livelihood, the Supreme Court explicitly sounded a note of caution about appeals to its PIL jurisdiction, when Kirpal J. held that:

> There is, in recent years, a feeling which is not without any foundation that Public Interest Litigation is now tending to become publicity interest litigation or private interest litigation and has a tendency to be counter-productive. PIL is not a pill or a panacea for all wrongs. It was essentially meant to protect basic human rights of the weak and the disadvantaged and was a procedure which was innovated where a public spirited person files a petition in effect on behalf of such persons who on account of poverty, helplessness or economic and social disabilities could not approach the Court for relief . . . It will be seen that whenever the Court has interfered and given directions while entertaining PIL it has mainly been where there has been an element of violation of Article 21 or of human rights or where the litigation has been initiated for the benefit of the poor and the under-privileged who are unable to come to Court due to some disadvantage. In those cases also it is the legal rights which are secured by the Courts. We

---

121 Muralidhar (n. 1) at p. 120.
122 Rajagopal (n. 67) at p. 164.

may, however, add that Public Interest Litigation was not meant to be a weapon to challenge the financial or economic decisions which are taken by the Government in exercise of their administrative power.[123]

Sathe is critical of this approach from the Court, and argues that it is 'rather too broad a proposition' which, if implemented 'would make PIL impotent'.[124] More broadly this judgment appears to reinforce what D'Souza refers to as an identifiable 'trend prominent since 1998 where the Supreme Court has upheld liberalization and privatization, but declined to intervene in matters of distributive justice'.[125]

All of the cases discussed under this heading expose weaknesses and shortcomings in the Court's PIL–socio-economic rights jurisprudence. Some of these shortcomings have been evident from the start; others have only come to prominence more recently. With respect to the contradictory holdings on the Court in socio-economic rights cases, it can be said that one of the key strengths of PIL, its flexibility, is also one of the weaknesses of the Supreme Court's socio-economic rights jurisprudence. Precisely because the Court had the freedom to read rights to health, education, food and shelter into Article 21 of the Constitution, it was similarly unconstrained, or perhaps more accurately lacked guidance, in actually deciding concrete cases on the basis of these newly discovered rights. Instead, the Court, and more to the point individual judges, had to rely on their own perception of what the appropriate balance was between the public policy or law and the rights of affected parties. For this reason Rajagopal is right to say that 'the Court's record is characterized by a serious measure of substantive ad hocism'.[126] The Indian example shows the very real danger when courts, without a solid textual basis, begin to adjudicate on socio-economic rights. The Supreme Court's jurisprudence, in the end, appears highly unprincipled and inconsistent.

In relation to the Court's recent shift of emphasis away from the basic rights of the most excluded and needy, to a position where the Court can sanction the mass eviction of more than 40,000 families, the clearest explanation appears to be that, confident of its institutional strength, the Court no longer feels the need to court the approval of the masses, and instead has opted to cast its lot in with India's economic and political elites. Das gets at this point in a roundabout way when he notes that:

> The current political mood of the country, the prevailing economic situation, the dominant ideas prevalent in the society at a particular time have governed the activities of the Court. The values that the Court seeks to uphold during any particular period are determined by such ideas and the

123 *BALCO Employees Union* v. *Union of India* [2001] INSC 646 (10 December 2001).
124 Sathe (n. 36) at p. xxv.
125 D'Souza (n. 96) at p. 506.
126 Rajagopal (n. 67) at p. 160.

Court's own appreciation of the needs of society. Assessment of such needs and requirements is often moulded by the philosophy and beliefs of individual judges.[127]

Similarly Sathe notes that the 'tides and currents which engulf the rest of the people, do not pass the judge by. Therefore, there have been decisions which showed that even the judges have not been left out of the influence of the prevailing climate of privatization and soft Hindutva'.[128] Thus, the Court's shift in emphasis, and the reasons for which it is willing to entertain PIL claims, is explicable by recognising that a new generation of judges no longer feels the need to reinforce their institutional legitimacy through what Baxi called 'judicial populism'; but instead feel institutionally secure enough to side with the interests of the ruling elites.

4.4 Conclusion

It would appear, then, that in India the Supreme Court's PIL–socio-economic rights jurisprudence is on the wane; as Sathe notes, the 'euphoria and thrust of judicial activism seems to be fading, and public interest litigation seems to be cosmetic and reducing to tokenism'.[129] Notwithstanding the apparent decline in PIL, the central inquiry of this study requires us to look also at the broader question of the balance which the Indian Supreme Court struck between the courts and elected branches of government. As Cassels notes, notwithstanding the popular support for PIL it has still been dogged by 'charges of judicial legislation, violation of separation of powers, encroachment on administration, and judicial despotism' which have all been levelled at the Court in exercising its PIL jurisdiction.[130] It appears fair to say, as Desai and Muralidhar do, that 'the Court has sometimes . . . obliterated the distinction between law and policy'.[131] Interestingly, however, even the Court's most invasive forays into the functional areas of the elected branches of government were viewed, other than by the affected body no doubt, as legitimate; and the reasons for this bring us somewhat into the realm of 'Indian exceptionalism'.

The key point in this regard is well made by Colin Gonsalves, when he writes that:

> There are some who criticise the activist nature of the courts and say that ultimately an activist judiciary encroaches on the executive branch of government. While this may be true, the situation in India must be

---

127   Das (n. 3) at p. 17.
128   Sathe (n. 36) at p. xxxix.
129   Sathe (n. 36) at p. xxxviii; cf. Kothari (n. 1) at p. 176, who argues that 'social rights litigation in India is . . . vibrant and dynamic'.
130   Cassels at p. 507.
131   Desai and Muralidhar (n. 55) at p. 177.

understood. The executive branch is riddled with corruption and has long ceased to function properly, particularly with respect to its duties towards the poor. Has the Supreme Court encroached upon this realm? Yes, it has. But it has done so on behalf of the poor, and to that extent people feel that the judiciary has done something good. In the long term, it is not a healthy trend to have the judiciary constantly pulling up the government. Accountability and responsibility of the government must be restored. Today in India, however, the situation is that the judiciary remains the only democratic institution whose integrity is to a substantial extent, intact.[132]

Similarly Mehta argues that the Court's interventions have been widely seen as legitimate, or at least tolerated, because the 'representative institutions are widely seen as being immobilized, self-serving, corrupt, and incapable of exercising their basic policy prerogatives or their powers of enforcement', this 'serious disaffection with majoritarian institutions of accountability makes the exercise of judicial power almost necessary.[133] While these perspectives go some way to explaining, and perhaps even justifying, the pervasiveness of judicial activism in India, at least historically, Granville Austin is also surely correct to sound a note of caution when he argues that 'if the courts supplant the legislatures and the executives as the principle engines of social reform, whether from their own pride . . . or from the other branches' irresponsibility, it will dangerously imbalance the relationship among . . . the three branches of government'.[134]

Ultimately, assessing the experience of the Indian Supreme Court in relation to adjudicating on socio-economic rights necessarily involves a combination of what Baxi refers to as *shehnai* and *matam*;[135] on the one hand the Supreme Court's PIL–socio-economic rights jurisprudence should be celebrated for the various institutional reforms which it introduced, broadening, in a general sense, access to justice and thereby coming face to face with the basic needs of the poorest in society, framed in the form of claims for socio-economic rights, and for imbuing the judiciary with the optimism to take these cases on. The Supreme Court's socio-economic rights jurisprudence was certainly imbued with an admirable sentiment, which was appropriate to the circumstances of India at that time. There is, however, also cause for lamentation. The near boundless freedom conferred on the Supreme Court by the inherent flexibility of PIL meant that the Court could read socio-economic rights into the fundamental rights provisions in the Constitution; this lack of constraint also meant that the Court could do so in a haphazard and unprincipled way, which would frustrate

---

132 Gonsalves (n. 1) at p. 182; see also Sathe at pp. 20–21.
133 Mehta (n. 41) at pp. 186–187.
134 Austin (n. 38) at p. 341.
135 Baxi (n. 34) at p. 41: celebration (*shehnai*) and lamentation (*matam*). Similarly Sathe (n. 36) at p. xxxviii, notes that as the Supreme Court's PIL jurisprudence has evolved 'Hope and disappointment have alternated'.

the expectations of many claimants, and this freedom also meant that when the ideological and normative winds shifted, the Court could gradually row back on the earlier pro-socio-economic rights jurisprudence of the Supreme Court. The Indian Supreme Court's socio-economic rights jurisprudence has been dynamic and notable, and certainly worthy of study; whether, on the whole, it is worthy of imitation, may be doubted.

5 The Canadian *Charter*, substantive equality and social rights

Canada's transition from a system of parliamentary supremacy, to a constitutional order in which the courts are empowered to curtail the exercise of governmental power through the enforcement of an entrenched Bill of Rights, was one of the first in a modern era which has seen the gradual abandonment of parliamentary sovereignty and the ascent of judicial power.[1] The shift, in the Canadian context, was brought about by what is referred to as the 'patriation' of the Canadian Constitution in the form of the Constitution Act 1982. The Constitution Act recognises a collection of documents as comprising the Canadian Constitution, and establishes the supremacy of the Constitution in Canadian law.[2] Among the most notable innovations contained in this new constitutional dispensation was the constitutional entrenchment of a judicially enforceable catalogue of fundamental rights in the form of the Canadian *Charter* of Rights and Freedoms (the *Charter*).[3] The adoption of the *Charter* 'brought about a fundamental change in Canadian law and politics',[4] and while it is primarily concerned with the protection of civil and political rights the Canadian Supreme Court has, nonetheless, had significant experience in dealing with the issue of socio-economic rights under the *Charter*, both directly and by implication.[5]

---

1 For general discussions of this phenomenon, see Ran Hirschl, *Towards Juristocracy* (Harvard: Harvard University Press, 2004); and John Ferejohn, 'Judicializing Politics, Politicizing Law' (2002) 65 *Law and Contemporary Problems* 41.
2 The Constitution Act 1982 was enacted as a schedule to the Canada Act 1982; which was an Act of the UK Parliament. Among the various documents recognised by section 52 of the Constitution Act as comprising the Canadian Constitution, the most important are: the Constitution Act 1867 (formerly the British North America Act 1867) and the Canadian *Charter of Rights and Freedoms*. For a valuable general introduction see: Patrick J. Monahan, *Constitutional Law* (3rd edn, Toronto: Irwin Law Inc., 2006).
3 On the *Charter*, generally, see Robert Sharpe and Kent Roach, *The Charter of Rights and Freedoms* (3rd edn, Toronto: Irwin Law Inc., 2005).
4 *Ibid.* at p. 1.
5 For useful introductory discussions of socio-economic rights in Canada, see David Wiseman, 'Methods of Protection of Social and Economic Rights in Canada' in Coomans (ed.), *Justiciability of Economic and Social Rights* (Antwerp: Intersentia, 2006) 173; Patrick Macklem, 'Social Rights in Canada' in Barak-Erez and Gross (eds.), *Exploring Social Rights* (Oxford: Hart

This chapter begins by setting out the general nature of the Canadian constitutional system, highlighting in particular the key provisions of the *Charter* and also noting the emergence in Canadian constitutional jurisprudence of the concept of 'constitutional dialogue' as a means of ameliorating the tensions between the elected branches of government and the judiciary.[6] We then go on to consider the decisions of the Canadian Supreme Court which have touched, in some instances more directly than others, on the issue of judicial enforcement of socio-economic rights. In this regard we focus, in particular, on section 15 of the *Charter* and the concept of substantive equality; and on section 7 of the *Charter* and attempts to encourage an expansive reading of the rights to life and security of the person contained therein so as to encompass the protection of certain socio-economic rights. Ultimately, then, this chapter concludes by assessing what lessons the Canadian experience may offer for the protection of socio-economic rights on a more global scale.

5.1 The Canadian Constitution

As was noted above, what is referred to as the 'Canadian Constitution' is a composite of a number of important documents; for the purposes of this study, the most important of which are the *Charter* of rights, and section 52 of the Constitution Act 1982 which establishes the supremacy of the Constitution and, by implication, empowers the courts to strike down legislation which is inconsistent with the terms of the Constitution. In this section we will focus on the central provisions of the *Charter*, namely those setting out fundamental rights, noting the absence of specific socio-economic rights.[7] We will also consider the provisions of the *Charter* that pertain to judicial power and the relevant sections of the Constitution Act which do likewise, as well as looking at other key institutional features such as the general limitations provision in section 1 of the *Charter* and the 'notwithstanding clause' in section 33. Finally under this heading we will discuss the concept of constitutional dialogue: an optic for viewing the relationship between courts and the elected branches of government in a constitutional democracy, which is particularly suited to the Canadian constitutional order, but which may also have important implications for other jurisdictions.

Publishing, 2007) 213; and Martha Jackman and Bruce Porter, 'Canada: Socio-Economic Rights Under the Canadian *Charter*' in Langford (ed.), *Social Rights Jurisprudence: Emerging Trends in International and Comparative Law* (Cambridge: Cambridge University Press, 2008) 209.

6 The seminal contribution to the concept of 'constitutional dialogue', at least in the Canadian context, is provided by Peter Hogg and Allison Bushell, 'The *Charter* Dialogue Between Courts and Legislatures (Or Perhaps the *Charter of Rights* Isn't Such a Bad Thing After All)' (1997) 35 *Osgoode Hall Law Journal* 75; the concept is considered in more detail below in section 5.1.2.

7 Detailed discussion of the provisions of the *Charter*, primarily sections 7 and 15, under which socio-economic rights claims have been advanced is left until sections 5.2 and 5.3 below.

5.1.1 The Charter of Rights and Freedoms

Peter Hogg notes that following the formation of Canada in 1867 there was little or no interest in the adoption of a Canadian Bill of Rights, and the absence of such an instrument was 'entirely uncontroversial' in Canadian society, and in Canada's legal culture with its inherited tradition of parliamentary sovereignty. This attitude changed however post-Second World War, particularly in the context of the 'human rights climate' engendered by the adoption of the Universal Declaration of Human Rights (UDHR), leading to the adoption of the Canadian Bill of Rights in 1960. This was an ordinary Act adopted by the Canadian Parliament, which was limited by the fact that it only applied to federal legislation. In large part because of this the Bill of Rights, during its operative period, made little or no impact on the functions of governments or on the protection of rights in general in Canada.[8] This resulted in continued pressure for the adoption of a more substantial rights-protecting instrument, which ultimately came in the form of the *Charter*, adopted in 1982. As enacted the *Charter* contained a familiar catalogue of civil and political rights, including the rights: to freedom of conscience, thought, expression and peaceful assembly, to vote, to be presumed innocent, to *habeas corpus* and not to be subject to cruel and unusual punishment.

The *Charter* does not, however, contain explicit recognition of socio-economic rights, and while it does include protection of minority language education rights David Wiseman argues that this is better understood as the protection of a cultural, as opposed to socio-economic, right.[9] The absence of explicit guarantees for socio-economic rights has led to persistent campaigns and calls, and even a failed attempt to adopt, a 'Canadian Social Charter'; this, however, has failed to gain headway.[10] Therefore in the continued absence of expressly guaranteed socio-economic rights in the *Charter*, it has long been argued that the guarantees of life and security of the person in section 7 and of equality in section 15, read in light of a perceived Canadian commitment to social justice and the welfare state, 'provide a solid basis' for asserting socio-economic rights.[11] The potential of these two sections of the *Charter* are summed up by Wiseman, who writes:

8   Peter Hogg, 'Canada's New *Charter* of Rights' (1984) 32 *American Journal of Comparative Law* 283 at pp. 286–287; see also Monahan (n. 2) at pp. 14–16 and 386.
9   Wiseman (n. 5) at p. 177.
10 See Martha Jackman, 'Constitutional Rhetoric and Social Justice: Reflections on the Justiciability Debate' in Bakan and Schneiderman (eds.), *Social Justice and the Constitution: Perspectives on a Social Union for Canada* (Carleton University Press, 1992) 17; Jennifer Nedelsky and Craig Scott, 'Constitutional Dialogue' in Bakan and Schneiderman (eds.), *Social Justice and the Constitution: Perspectives on a Social Union for Canada* (Carleton University Press, 1992) 59; and Noel Kinsella, 'Can Canada Afford a *Charter* of Social and Economic Rights? Toward a Canadian Social Charter' (2008) 71 *Saskatchewan Law Review* 7.
11 See Martha Jackman, 'From National Standards to Justiciable Rights: Enforcing International Social and Economic Guarantees Through *Charter of Rights* Review' (1999) 14 *Journal of Law and Social Policy* 69 at p. 79.

Lacking any express mention, protection of labour, housing, health and social assistance rights relies entirely upon judicial interpretation of the *Charter*'s guarantees of freedom of association . . . the right to life, liberty and security of the person . . . and the right to equality . . . The phrases used in these sections are sufficiently open-textured that there is at least the potential that they can be interpreted as protecting social and economic rights.[12]

While there has been some progress in advancing labour rights under section 2(d) of the *Charter*, the cases pertaining to those developments are not considered here.[13] Instead the focus of this chapter is on sections 7 and 15 and the potential which these provisions provide for the protection of socio-economic rights in Canada. Before going on to consider the relevant case law under these provisions, the rest of this section sets out some of the other key institutional innovations introduced by the *Charter*.

Alongside the entrenchment of a catalogue of fundamental rights the *Charter* and the Constitution Act also significantly enhanced the powers of the courts. While judicial review had been practised in Canada, in the context of policing the federal distribution of powers, the new constitutional dispensation introduced a new, firmer ground for judicial review in Canada. This is reflected in section 52(1) of the Constitution Act which provides an 'explicit basis for judicial review of legislation in Canada'.[14] Also of relevance in this context is section 24(1) of the *Charter* which confers the power on the courts, where they find a breach of the *Charter*, to grant 'such remedy as the court considers appropriate and just in the circumstances', thus conferring substantial remedial discretion on the courts in the context of breaches of *Charter* rights. These various provisions led Hogg, writing contemporaneously with the adoption of the *Charter*, to observe that 'Canadians have . . . taken an irrevocable step towards the judicialization of their politics and the politicization of their judiciary. It is the beginning of a new era in Canadian constitutional law'.[15]

These substantial changes in the Canadian constitutional landscape were not welcomed by all, and even prior to its adoption the *Charter* had its critics who claimed, among other things, that the *Charter* would 'transfer undue power from elected politicians and into the hands of unelected and unaccountable judges'.[16] Among the critics Christopher Manfredi was particularly critical of section 24(1) on the basis that it 'provides judges with an opportunity to shape

---

12 Wiseman (n. 5) at p. 186.

13 See, for example, *Dunmore* v. *Ontario (Attorney General)* [2001] 3 SCR 1016 and *Health Services and Support – Facilities Subsector Bargaining Association* v. *British Columbia* [2007] 2 SCR 391.

14 Hogg (n. 8) at p. 300; section 52(1) provides that: 'The Constitution of Canada is the supreme law of Canada, and any law that is inconsistent with the provisions of the Constitution is, to the extent of the inconsistency, of no force or effect'.

15 *Ibid.* at p. 305; see also Peter Russell, 'The Political Purposes of the Canadian *Charter* of Rights and Freedoms' (1983) 61 *Canadian Bar Review* 30 at pp. 51–52.

16 See Monahan (n. 2) at p. 387.

and administer social policy directly through positive and prospective remedies'.[17] Similarly Rainer Knopff expressed the concern that the *Charter* would take 'judicialization . . . [to] new heights',[18] and effect a substantial 'departure from the inherited tradition of British constitutionalism'.[19] Anticipating, and in an effort to assuage, the fears of such critics, the drafters of the *Charter* included a number of provisions which sought to maintain, in part, the inherited Canadian tradition of parliamentary sovereignty and the primacy of elected representatives in public policy. Chief among these provisions is section 1 which allows general limitations on the rights protected by the *Charter*, so that *Charter* rights can, where appropriate, yield to public policy requirements.[20]

Another significant feature of the *Charter* which seeks to reconcile the advent of entrenched rights and empowered courts with the tradition of parliamentary sovereignty is contained in section 33 of the *Charter*, otherwise known as the 'notwithstanding clause'. In essence this provision provides that legislatures may, subject to a five-year time limit, explicitly adopt legislation notwithstanding the fact that the legislation would be considered to be in breach of rights protected by the *Charter*.[21] According to Hogg section 33 of the *Charter* is 'a prudent concession to the democratic political process and the long Anglo-Canadian tradition of parliamentary supremacy',[22] although Patrick Monahan argues that in practice 'resort to the override is politically costly and has been infrequently used'.[23] In any event, Monahan and others argue that irrespective of sections 1 and 33, the advent of strong judicial review under the *Charter* is still democratically defensible; as he puts it:

> the *Charter* was itself the product of a democratic process, in which it was clearly contemplated and understood that the judiciary would be assigned a much more prominent role in reviewing the substance of legislation enacted by Parliament and the legislatures. The *Charter* was drafted with

---

17 Christopher Manfredi, '"Appropriate and Just in the Circumstances": Public Policy and the Enforcement of Rights Under the Canadian *Charter* of Rights and Freedoms' (1994) 27 *Canadian Journal of Political Science* 425 at p. 436.

18 Rainer Knopff, 'Populism and the Politics of Rights: The Dual Attack on Representative Democracy' (1998) 31 *Canadian Journal of Political Science* 683 at p. 683.

19 *Ibid.* at p. 694.

20 Section 1 provides that: 'The *Canadian Charter of Rights and Freedoms* guarantees the rights and freedoms set out in it subject only to such reasonable limits prescribed by law as can be demonstrably justified in a free and democratic society'. For discussion, see Martha Jackman, 'Protecting Rights and Promoting Democracy: Judicial Review Under Section 1 of the *Charter*' (1996) 34 *Osgoode Hall Law Journal* 661 and see the seminal Supreme Court case of *R.* v. *Oakes* [1986] 1 SCR 103.

21 Section 33(1) provides: 'Parliament or the legislature of a province may expressly declare in an Act of Parliament or of the legislature, as the case may be, that the Act or a provision thereof shall operate notwithstanding a provision included in section 2 or sections 7 to 15 of this *Charter*'.

22 Hogg (n. 8) at p. 298.

23 Monahan (n. 2) at p. 16.

the express purpose of avoiding the deferential and restrained interpretation that had been given to the *Canadian Bill of Rights*.[24]

Clearly then, and for some controversially, the *Charter* confers significant powers on Canadian courts in the enforcement of *Charter* rights. Before going on to consider the ways in which the Supreme Court has navigated this tricky new path, especially in the context of socio-economic rights claims, we will turn next to a discussion of one of the novel ways in which some Canadian constitutional scholars have sought to resolve the tensions between judicial enforcement of rights and the democratic legitimacy of elected officials.

5.1.2 *Constitutional dialogue*

The primary way in which supporters of the *Charter* have sought to square the circle of the 'counter-majoritarian problem' inherent in judicial enforcement of rights,[25] is through the concept of 'constitutional dialogue'. In their seminal article on the concept of constitutional dialogue Peter Hogg and Allison Bushell, relying on sections 1 and 33 of the *Charter*, argued that in a constitutional order such as Canada's:

> Where a judicial decision is open to legislative reversal, modification or avoidance, then it is meaningful to regard the relationship between the Court and the competent legislative body as a dialogue. In that case, the judicial decision causes a public debate in which *Charter* values play a more prominent role than they would if there had been no judicial decision. The legislative body is in a position to devise a response that is properly respectful of the *Charter* values that have been identified by the Court, but which accomplishes the social or economic objectives that the judicial decision has impeded.[26]

Viewed in this light, they argued, the *Charter* did inhibit the choices of the elected branches of government, but not in an absolutist sense. Rather, the *Charter* acted 'as a catalyst for a two-way exchange between the judiciary and the legislature' about human rights, without unduly hindering the democratic will.[27] They then went on to argue that not only was this a defensible and appealing theory, but that in practice the courts and elected branches in Canada had been engaging in such a dialogue since the adoption of the *Charter*. Because

---

24 *Ibid.* at p. 398; similarly Sharpe and Roach (n. 3) at p. 27, argue that 'the text of the constitution reflects the conscious political choice to grant judges extensive power to interfere with the decisions of the democratically elected representatives of the people'.

25 For the origins of this famous phrase see Alexander Bickel, *The Least Dangerous Branch: The Supreme Court at the Bar of Politics* (Indianapolis: Bobbs-Merrill, 1962) at p. 16.

26 Hogg and Bushell (n. 6) at pp. 79–80.

27 *Ibid.* at p. 81.

the majority of cases in which legislation was struck down for being in breach of the *Charter*, resulted in subsequent legislative enactments which took account of the *Charter* principles articulated by the courts, but nonetheless allowed the elected branches of government to achieve their substantive policy objective.[28] On the basis of this they concluded that 'the critique of the *Charter* based on democratic legitimacy cannot be sustained'.[29]

In a recent update on their original article, the authors have reiterated their defence of the notion of dialogue, and argued that it 'poses a serious challenge (although perhaps not a complete answer) to the anti-majoritarian critique of judicial review'.[30] They also argued that in the majority of cases since the original article was published judicial decisions to strike down legislation were followed by legislative enactments, thus evincing the continued vibrancy of the concept of dialogue. Furthermore, the authors argue that the concept of dialogue has generally influenced the courts, particularly in their remedial responses to findings of unconstitutionality. They pinpointed, in particular, the emergence of the 'suspended declaration of invalidity', whereby the courts do not immediately remedy the identified constitutional infirmity by striking the law down, but instead suspend the declaration in deference to the elected branch's greater knowledge of what the appropriate response should be.[31] The authors therefore maintain that the concept of dialogue, at least in the Canadian context, goes some way to obviating the tensions between the elected branches of government and the courts.

The concept of dialogue has certainly proved to be popular with the judiciary. In the seminal case of *Vriend* v. *Alberta*,[32] which will be discussed further below, Iacobucci J. noted that:

> the *Charter* has given rise to a more dynamic interaction among the branches of governance. This interaction has been aptly described as a 'dialogue' . . . To my mind, a great value of judicial review and this dialogue among the branches is that each of the branches is made somewhat accountable to the other. The work of the legislature is reviewed by the courts and the work of the court in its decisions can be reacted to by the legislature in the passing of new legislation . . . This dialogue between and accountability of each of the branches have the effect of enhancing the democratic process, not denying it.[33]

Similarly in the subsequent case of *M* v. *H* Bastarache J. noted that '[this] case, like all *Charter* challenges to legislation, represents another episode in the

---

28 *Ibid.* at pp. 96–105.
29 *Ibid.* at p. 105.
30 Peter Hogg, Allison Bushell-Thornton and Wade Wright, '*Charter* Dialogue Revisited – Or "Much Ado About Metaphors"' (2007) 45 *Osgoode Hall Law Journal* 1 at p. 7.
31 *Ibid.* at p. 18.
32 [1998] 1 SCR 493.
33 *Vriend* at paras. 138–139.

continuing dialogue between the branches of government'.[34] But while it has been influential, particularly with the higher judiciary, dialogue theory does have its critics.

Christopher Manfredi and James Kelly, for example, are critical of the Hogg–Bushell thesis and argue that while the 'dialogue metaphor undeniably constitutes a powerful account of judicial review as an instrument of democratic governance',[35] Hogg and Bushell's arguments are grounded on shaky empirical foundations.[36] They further argue that even if the statistics relied on by Hogg and Bushell are presumed to be sound, the dialogue metaphor still does not address the 'democratic critique' of *Charter*-based review as leaves the courts in a pre-eminent position to dislodge the policy preferences of the elected branches of government.[37] Andrew Petter is equally unimpressed with the notion of dialogue, and argues that it 'mitigates more than it legitimates' as it still, ultimately, involves the courts in making decisions which should properly be the prerogative of the elected branches of government.[38] Similarly Frederick DeCoste argues that the conception of the separation of powers embodied in the dialogue metaphor, which the Supreme Court embraced in *Vriend*, 'is unacceptable on grounds of democratic principle' as it elevates the judicial branch above the other branches of government.[39] He further criticises the concept of dialogue for being 'a discourse impoverished by clichés and disfigured by misinformation and misunderstanding'.[40]

For supporters of dialogue theory, such as Kent Roach, it occupies the sensible 'middle ground between those who are suspicious of courts and rights protection and those who are passionate defenders of courts and rights defenders',[41] because it both seeks to justify the role which courts play in rights protection, but at the same time seeks to respect the primacy of democratically elected decision makers. And writing with Robert Sharpe, Roach further argues that:

> One of the strengths of dialogue theory is its ability to account for the power of legislatures under the *Charter* to place explicit limits and overrides

---

34 [1999] 2 SCR 3 at para. 286 *per* Bastarache J.
35 Christopher Manfredi and James Kelly, 'Six Degrees of Dialogue: A Response to Hogg and Bushell' (1999) 37 *Osgoode Hall Law Journal* 513 at p. 515.
36 *Ibid.* at p. 521. Manfredi and Kelly argue that 'genuine *Charter* dialogue' only took place in 33 per cent of the cases where the Supreme Court nullified legislation, as opposed to Hogg and Bushell's claim (n. 6) at p. 96, that it took place in 'a majority' of cases in which legislation was stuck down.
37 *Ibid.* at p. 522.
38 Andrew Petter, 'Twenty Years of *Charter* Justification: From Liberal Legalism to Dubious Dialogue' (2003) 52 *University of New Brunswick Law Journal* 187 at p. 195.
39 Frederick DeCoste, 'The Separation of Powers in a Liberal Polity: *Vriend* v. *Alberta*' (1999) 44 *McGill Law Journal* 231 at p. 248.
40 *Ibid.* at p. 253.
41 Kent Roach, 'Sharpening the Dialogue Debate: The Next Decade of Scholarship' (2007) 45 *Osgoode Hall Law Journal* 169 at p. 177.

on rights as interpreted by the courts. Another strength of dialogue theory is its ability to account for the frequent interplay between courts and legislatures on matters affected by the *Charter* . . . the metaphor of dialogue and the recognition it accords to the distinct but related roles played by courts and legislatures reflects a fundamental aspect of the Canadian approach to judicial review under the *Charter*.[42]

Dialogue certainly is a concept particularly suited to the Canadian constitutional scheme, and as a meta-narrative it articulates a desirable vision of how the courts and the elected branches of government relate to one another. In practice, however, the extent to which the practice of dialogue lives up to its high aspirations may be doubted. As Monahan argues, experience to date suggests that most governments have restructured their policy process to *Charter*-proof legislative enactments and policies.[43] This lends some credence to the views of sceptics that what is involved is less a dialogue (a talking *with*) and more a talking *to*, with the courts articulating the rules of the game and the elected branches of government responding accordingly. In the next two sections we look at the socio-economic rights jurisprudence which has developed under the *Charter* and in this context will consider what extent, if any, the delicate balance between the branches of government embodied in the dialogue metaphor holds true.

5.2 Section 15 and the promise of substantive equality

One of the defining features of *Charter* jurisprudence, and of modern Canadian constitutionalism, is the guarantee of equality contained in section 15 of the *Charter* and the jurisprudence of 'substantive equality' which has emerged from it.[44] As Gwen Brodsky notes, section 15 of the *Charter* has given rise to:

> a uniquely Canadian substantive equality jurisprudence, that [is] both different from United States constitutional jurisprudence and distinct from Canada's own earlier jurisprudence under the Canadian Bill of Rights . . . an equality rights jurisprudence that is less hostile to group-based claims of disadvantage than it might have been. The [Supreme Court of Canada] purports to have adopted new purposive, contextual, effects orientated approaches to the interpretation of the *Charter*'s equality rights guarantees; to have repudiated the similarly situated test and extreme deference to the legislators that characterized decisions under the Bill of Rights; to have

42 Sharpe and Roach (n. 3) at pp. 38–40.
43 Monahan (n. 2) at p. 403.
44 Among the distinguishing characteristics of substantive equality – at least in the Canadian context – is the requirement, as Wiseman (n. 5) at p. 200 notes, that 'governments . . . respond to the unequal circumstances of disadvantage . . . experienced by such groups which . . . impedes them from equally realizing their rights and interests'.

accepted the insight that discrimination is a question of adverse effects; to have recognised that s 15 is not just an individual rights guarantee; and to have made a commitment to a theory of equality rights that is centrally concerned with the amelioration of group disadvantage.[45]

This expansive conception of equality carries with it the promise that section 15 of the *Charter* will extend beyond mere formal equality, which in Anatole France's caustic phrase forbids rich and poor alike from sleeping under bridges and begging in the streets, to embrace the protection of the substantive material needs of disadvantaged and excluded sections of society. Or, in other words, that the equality jurisprudence under the *Charter* would be 'geared towards the amelioration of economic and social disadvantage'.[46] In the remainder of this section we will consider the extent to which the Supreme Court's equality jurisprudence has lived up to this aspiration.

In an account of the genesis of section 15 of the *Charter*, Bruce Porter argues that the wording used in section 15(1) resulted from 'intense lobbying' by groups representing the interests of women, people with disabilities and other historically disadvantaged minorities,[47] who managed to effect some 'critical changes' to the language of section 15,[48] transforming it from 'a negatively oriented right to non-discrimination to a positively orientated right to equality'.[49] Porter further notes that the groups who were so influential in recrafting the wording and orientation of section 15 during the drafting of the *Charter*, believed that 'section 15 affirmed not only protection from discriminatory exclusion . . . but also, and more fundamentally, a positive right to appropriate and adequate governmental programs and positive measures to address socio-economic disadvantage'.[50] Thus, section 15 was thought to have established a 'unique Canadian paradigm of equality' which encompassed a 'broad . . . array of social rights and government obligations'.[51] While not necessarily going as far as Porter, Sharpe and Roach note that the language used in section 15 'was meant to signal to the courts that section 15 was intended to be a much more powerful instrument of protection than its predecessor' in the Canadian Bill of Rights.[52]

In its first major equality case, in keeping with the progressive promise of section 15, the Supreme Court rejected the notion of formal equality, and

45 Gwen Brodsky, 'Constitutional Equality Rights in Canada' (2001) *Acta Juridica* 241 at pp. 241–242.
46 Macklem (n. 5) at p. 238.
47 Bruce Porter, 'Expectations of Equality' (2006) 33 *Supreme Court Law Review* 23 at p. 23.
48 *Ibid.* at p. 25.
49 *Ibid.* at p. 27; section 15(1), as enacted, provides that: 'Every individual is equal before and under the law and has the right to the equal protection and equal benefit of the law without discrimination and, in particular, without discrimination based on race, national or ethnic origin, colour, religion, sex, age or mental or physical disability'.
50 *Ibid.* at p. 29.
51 *Ibid.* at p. 43.
52 Sharpe and Roach (n. 3) at p. 279.

asserted that section 15 was committed to a concept of substantive equality with a particular focus on addressing the needs of historically disadvantaged groups. [53] The Court, however, did not directly address the issue of positive obligations arising under section 15. In subsequent cases the Court sent mixed messages about the reach of section 15: in *Schachter*, for example, Lamer CJ was willing to contemplate that section 15 could impose positive obligations on the state to provide social benefits to excluded groups and individuals in certain cases.[54] However, in the subsequent case of *Egan* it was held that that under section 15 Parliament 'does not have any constitutional obligation to provide benefits. However, once the decision has been made to confer a benefit, it cannot be applied in a discriminatory manner'.[55] Subsequently in *Thibaudeau* L'Heureux-Dube J., although dissenting from the majority opinion, accepted that section 15 'does not impose upon governments the obligation to take positive actions to remedy the symptoms of systemic inequality'.[56] These judgments led Porter to observe that 'a consensus seemed to be emerging on the Court that positive measures beyond those required to remedy discriminatory underinclusion were beyond the ambit of section 15'.[57] Two cases in the late 1990s appeared to challenge this incipient consensus and give a degree of hope to campaigners for socio-economic rights in Canada.

5.2.1 *The cutting edge of substantive equality: Eldridge and Vriend*

The first of these cases was *Eldridge v. British Columbia*,[58] which involved a challenge by a deaf couple to the policy of the government of British Columbia not to fund the provision of sign-language interpreting services in the public health care system. The thrust of the applicants' claim was that the failure to fund such interpreting services constituted de facto discrimination against the deaf community, contrary to section 15(1) of the *Charter*. In the Supreme Court La Forest J. rejected the submission advanced by the government that section 15(1) did not require the state to take positive measures to alleviate disadvantage which was not caused by government action, and that once government provided facially neutral services to the public at large, responsibility for any pre-existing disadvantage suffered by specific groups could not be attributed to the government. According to La Forest J. the government's position articulated 'a thin and impoverished vision' of section 15 which was 'belied . . . by

53 *Andrews* v. *Law Society of British Columbia* [1989] 1 SCR 143.
54 *Schachter* v. *Canada* [1992] 2 SCR 679; see also *McKinney* v. *University of Guelph* [1990] 3 SCR 229 *per* Wilson J. and *Haig* v. *Canada* [1993] 2 SCR 995 *per* L'Heureux-Dube J.
55 *Egan* v. *Canada* [1995] 2 SCR 513 at p. 596 *per* Cory J.
56 *Thibaudeau* v. *Canada* [1995] 2 SCR 627 at p. 655.
57 Bruce Porter, 'Beyond *Andrews*: Substantive Equality and Positive Obligations After *Eldridge* and *Vriend*' (1998) 9(3) *Constitutional Forum* 71 at p. 74.
58 [1997] 3 SCR 624.

the thrust of this Court's equality jurisprudence' to date.[59] The judge went on to note that while it was not clear that section 15 necessarily imposed positive obligations on the state to take positive measures to ameliorate systemic disadvantage, 'once the state does provide a benefit, it is obliged to do so in a non-discriminatory manner . . . In many circumstances, this will require governments to take positive action, for example by extending the scope of a benefit to a previously excluded class of persons'.[60] Reiterating this point the learned judge held that '[if] we accept the concept of adverse effect discrimination, it seems inevitable . . . that the government will be required to take special measures to ensure that disadvantaged groups are able to benefit equally from government services'.[61]

In summing up for the majority La Forest J. concluded by noting that 'it is fair to say that the absence of a publicly funded sign language interpretation service discriminated against the appellants by denying them equal benefit of the British Columbia health care system . . . the quality of care received by the appellants was inferior to that available to hearing persons'.[62] The judge went on to address the issue of the deference owed by the courts to the elected branches of government in cases such as this – with resource implications – and held that:

> while financial considerations alone may not justify *Charter* infringements . . . governments must be afforded wide latitude to determine the proper distribution of resources in society . . . This is especially true where Parliament, in providing specific social benefits, has to choose between disadvantaged groups.[63]

However, Justice La Forest held that such latitude was not infinite, and governments would have to show that the infringement rights in any given case were no more than was reasonably necessary to achieve their goal. Given the small amount of money required for interpreter services in this case, $150,000 (or 0.0025 of the provincial health budget at the time), the government failed to show that the total denial of interpreting services constituted the minimum impairment of the rights of the deaf necessary to achieve the goal.

With respect to the remedy to be provided in the present case La Forest J. held that a declaration to the effect that the relevant health care legislation should be administered in a manner compatible with the *Charter*, in the instant case through providing deaf interpreting services, was the appropriate form of relief. The judge held that:

59 *Eldridge* at para. 73.
60 *Eldridge* at para. 73.
61 *Eldridge* at para. 77.
62 *Eldridge* at para. 83.
63 *Eldridge* at para. 85.

A declaration, as opposed to some kind of injunctive relief, is the appropriate remedy in this case because there are myriad options available to the government that may rectify the unconstitutionality of the current system. It is not this Court's role to dictate how this is to be accomplished. Although it is to be assumed that the government will move swiftly to correct the unconstitutionality of the present scheme and comply with this Court's directive, it is appropriate to suspend the effectiveness of the declaration for six months to enable the government to explore its options and formulate an appropriate response. In fashioning its response, the government should ensure that, after the expiration of six months or any other period of suspension granted by this Court, sign language interpreters will be provided where necessary for effective communication in the delivery of medical services. Moreover, it is presumed that the government will act in good faith.[64]

The decision of the Court in *Eldridge* is highly significant because it seemed, at first flush, to impose substantive, positive obligations on the state to provide certain services to disadvantage sections of society, although this aspect of the judgment was tempered, somewhat, by the Court's more circumspect approach to the question of remedies. The significance of *Eldridge*, however, can only be fully understood when viewed alongside the second of the two late-1990s substantive equality cases.

In the subsequent case of *Vriend* the Supreme Court further expanded the concept of substantive equality under section 15 of the *Charter* and the extent of positive obligations on the state. The applicant in this case had been dismissed from his employment in a private educational institution because of his sexual orientation. He had sought to challenge his dismissal under the applicable provincial human rights code – the Alberta Individual Rights Protection Act 1988 (IRPA) – but was unable to do so as the Act did not recognise sexual orientation as a prohibited ground of discrimination. The applicant then sought a declaration that the omission of sexual orientation as a ground of discrimination from the Alberta human rights code constituted a breach of section 15 of the *Charter*. A majority of the Supreme Court found in favour of the applicant. Building on the Court's earlier judgment in *Eldridge*, Cory J. held that there was no legal basis for drawing a distinction between positive state acts infringing on *Charter* rights, and governmental omissions which led to rights violations. Both scenarios were contemplated and addressed by the *Charter*.[65] The judge went on to note that while in the instant case:

---

64 *Eldridge* at para. 96.
65 *Vriend* (n. 32) at paras. 56–60. This echoes the views of Gwen Brodsky and Shelagh Day that 'the idea that *Charter* rights can be rigidly categorized as civil and political rather than social and economic, negative rather than positive, or legal rather than economic . . . is profoundly inconsistent with a substantive conception of equality'; Gwen Brodsky and Shelagh Day, 'Beyond the Social and Economic Rights Debate: Substantive Equality Speaks to Poverty' (2002) 14 *Canadian Journal of Women and the Law* 185 at p. 188.

there is, on the surface, a measure of formal equality: gay or lesbian individuals have the same access as heterosexual individuals to the protection of the *IRPA* in the sense that they could complain to the Commission about an incident of discrimination on the basis of any of the grounds currently included . . . the exclusion of the ground of sexual orientation, considered in the context of the social reality of discrimination against gays and lesbians, clearly has a disproportionate impact on them as opposed to heterosexuals. Therefore the *IRPA* in its underinclusive state denies substantive equality to the former group.[66]

Justice Cory therefore concluded that 'this Court has no choice but to conclude that the *IRPA*, by reason of the omission of sexual orientation as a protected ground, clearly violates s. 15 of the *Charter*'.[67]

Following on from the finding that the IRPA did breach section 15 of the *Charter*, it then fell to be decided whether or not this breach could be justified under section 1 of the *Charter*, and if not what remedy was appropriate to the violation. These issues were addressed by Iacobucci J. in a judgment which also made some important points about the broader issues of the relationship between the courts and the elected branches of government under the *Charter*. Iacobucci J. held that:

it should be emphasized again that our *Charter*'s introduction and the consequential remedial role of the courts were choices of the Canadian people through their elected representatives as part of a redefinition of our democracy. Our constitutional design was refashioned to state that henceforth the legislatures and executive must perform their roles in conformity with the newly conferred constitutional rights and freedoms. That the courts were the trustees of these rights insofar as disputes arose concerning their interpretation was a necessary part of this new design . . . So courts in their trustee or arbiter role must perforce scrutinize the work of the legislature and executive not in the name of the courts, but in the interests of the new social contract that was democratically chosen.[68]

On the facts Iacobucci J. held that the exclusion of sexual orientation as a ground of discrimination from the IRPA could not be justified under section 1 of the *Charter* and that the appropriate remedy was for the Court to 'read in' sexual orientation as a prohibited ground of discrimination under the Act, so as to remedy its *Charter* incompatibility. Viewed alongside *Eldridge* the Supreme Court decision in *Vriend* was highly significant, both for the strong assertion of judicial power in the enforcement of *Charter* rights and, of particular significance

66 *Vriend* at para. 82.
67 *Vriend* at para. 107.
68 *Vriend* at paras. 134–136.

for present purposes, because of the further assertion of the existence of positive state obligations under section 15 of the *Charter*.

Commenting on *Eldridge* and *Vriend* Martha Jackman argued that, viewed together, they established that 'state inaction which results from the discounting of, or wilful blindness to, the needs and rights of a disadvantaged group may be as offensive to equality rights principles as more overtly discriminatory government action'.[69] Bruce Porter argued that *Eldridge*, in particular, represented 'a high watermark, in the recognition of positive measures to ensure substantive equality'.[70] For other commentators it seemed inevitable that the recognition of positive obligations flowing from section 15 would lead, logically, to the recognition of substantive socio-economic rights. As Gwen Brodsky and Shelagh Day put it, '[once] we recognize the extent to which it has already been accepted that positive government obligations flow from *Charter* rights, the resistance to such obligations in the economic sphere should abate',[71] although it should be noted that in *Vriend* Cory J. simply left open the issue of whether or not section 15 would require the state to provide certain benefits where they completely failed to act to alleviate disadvantage, without explicitly addressing it.[72] In any event the Supreme Court declined to embrace this expansive reading of section 15 in its subsequent case law.

5.2.2 *Reining in expectations: Auton*

Even in the middle of the optimism and excitement generated by the Supreme Court's decisions in *Vriend* and *Eldridge*, there were cautious voices. Margot Young, for example, argued that 'despite the positive results in both of these cases, one ought to remain less than sanguine about the future of equality law and its potential for social change'.[73] Such hesitance proved to be well founded in light of the subsequent Supreme Court judgment in the *Auton* case.[74] The applicants in this case claimed that the failure of the government of British Columbia to fund a specific form of treatment for all autistic children – applied behavioural therapy (ABA) – constituted a breach of section 15 of the *Charter*. For the majority Chief Justice McLachlin framed the issue at the heart of the case in the following terms: 'the issue before us is not what the public health system should provide, which is a matter for Parliament and the legislature. The issue is rather whether the British Columbia Government's failure to fund these services under the health plan amounted to an unequal and discriminatory

---

69 Martha Jackman, '"Giving Real Effect to Equality": *Eldridge* v. *British Columbia (Attorney General)* and *Vriend* v. *Alberta*' (1998) 4(2) *Review of Constitutional Studies* 352 at pp. 365–366.
70 Porter (n. 47) at p. 36.
71 Brodsky and Day (n. 65) at p. 208.
72 *Vriend* at paras. 63–64.
73 Margot Young, 'Change at the Margins: *Eldridge* v. *British Columbia (AG)* and *Vriend* v. *Alberta*' (1998) 10 *Canadian Journal of Women and the Law* 244 at p. 245.
74 *Auton (Guardian ad litem of)* v. *British Columbia (Attorney General)* [2004] 3 SCR 657.

denial of benefits under that plan, contrary to s. 15 of the *Charter*.[75] For reasons that would follow, the Chief Justice stated that '[despite] their forceful argument, the petitioners fail to establish that the denial of benefits violated the *Charter*'.[76]

A key point in the case for the Chief Justice was that the positive benefit sought by the applicants in this case, provision of a specific 'ancillary' medical treatment, was distinct from the positive obligation imposed on the state in *Eldridge* and *Vriend*. As the Chief Justice put it: '*Eldridge* was concerned with unequal access to a benefit that the law conferred and with *applying* a benefit-granting law in a non-discriminatory fashion. By contrast, this case is concerned with access to a benefit that the law has not conferred. For this reason, *Eldridge* does not assist the petitioners'.[77] The Chief Justice then went on to state the general principle that under section 15 of the *Charter*:

> It is not open to Parliament or a legislature to enact a law whose policy objectives and provisions single out a disadvantaged group for inferior treatment . . . On the other hand, a legislative choice not to accord a particular benefit absent demonstration of discriminatory purpose, policy or effect does not offend this principle and does not give rise to s. 15(1) review. This Court has repeatedly held that the legislature is under no obligation to create a particular benefit. It is free to target the social programs it wishes to fund as a matter of public policy, provided the benefit itself is not conferred in a discriminatory manner.[78]

In light of this the Chief Justice concluded that 'the benefit claimed, no matter how it is viewed, is not a benefit provided by law'.[79] And that as section 15 does not require the state to establish programs or provide certain benefits, the fact that the law did not confer a general right to receive ABA or other cognate treatments, meant that the applicants had not been discriminated against; thus the government's failure to fund ABA was not contrary to section 15 of the *Charter*.

The Supreme Court judgment in *Auton* appears to confirm that section 15 will only be implicated in circumstances where government has acted in an underinclusive manner, and not where it has completely refrained from acting. In other words, section 15 by itself will not give rise to substantive benefits for marginalised and excluded groups and individuals. Commenting on *Auton*, Porter notes that in the decision 'we see worrying signs that the McLachlin Court may in fact wish to increase the divide between expectations and the Court's approach by closing the door on a positive rights approach to section

75 *Auton* at para. 2.
76 *Auton* at para. 2.
77 *Auton* at para. 38 (original emphasis).
78 *Auton* at para. 41.
79 *Auton* at para. 47.

15 that was quite explicitly left open in *Eldridge* and *Vriend*.[80] He further criticises the Court for reverting to 'the kind of non-discrimination analysis that had been rejected during the drafting of section 15',[81] and argues that the decision 'represents an unprecedented betrayal of the expectations of equality seekers that the right to equality ought to mean something to those who have unique and significant needs'.[82]

Without necessarily adopting the language of betrayal, it can be said that the Court's decision in *Auton* certainly appears at variance with the expansive reading of section 15 in cases such as *Vriend* and *Eldridge*, and does appear almost to approach the sort of 'thin and impoverished' conception of equality which La Forest J. criticised in the latter case. It certainly poses a serious challenge to the apparent commitment to substantive equality in section 15 of the *Charter*, as Gwen Brodsky puts it:

> Ultimately it will not be credible to have a rhetoric of substantive quality that stops at the point of engaging with real disadvantage. Unless our Court finds some capacity to speak to the injustice of poor women and men in Canada being homeless, hungry and unable to feed and clothe themselves and their children properly, the *Charter*, an important symbol of social justice, is in danger of falling into irrelevance. It is not necessarily the case that we need courts to take on the problem of social programme design, but we do need them to strongly remind governments in Canada of their human rights obligations.[83]

Certainly the Supreme Court's judgment has been greeted with dismay by those who saw section 15 as a potential 'launch pad' for socio-economic rights claims under the *Charter*;[84] while others argue that this narrow reading was always implicit in both the text of the *Charter* and the Court's earlier case law.[85] In seeking to rationalise, if not justify, the decision Sharpe and Roach argue that in *Auton* the Supreme Court's judgment was in part motivated by a judicial concern about 'becoming embroiled in a complex debate about difficult choices regarding medicare funding'.[86] They conclude by noting that while the 'Court's approach has disappointed those who saw section 15 as a charter of social rights capable of remedying injustice on a more general scale . . . it coincides with

---

80 Porter (n. 47) at p. 38.
81 *Ibid.* at p. 39.
82 *Ibid.* at p. 40.
83 Brodsky (n. 45) at p. 254.
84 See, for example, Margot Finley, 'Limiting Section 15(1) in the Health Care Context: The Impact of *Auton* v. *British Columbia*' (2005) 63 *University of Toronto Faculty of Law Review* 213 and Ellie Venhola, 'Goliath Arisen: Taking Aim at the Health Care Regime in *Auton*' (2005) 20 *Journal of Law and Social Policy* 67.
85 See Hirschl (n. 1) at p. 130; and Joel Bakan, *Just Words: Constitutional Rights and Social Wrongs* (Toronto: University of Toronto Press, 1997).
86 Sharpe and Roach (n. 3) at p. 314.

the Supreme Court's general inclination under the *Charter* to defer to legislative judgment on questions of distributive justice'.[87] In summary this may very well reflect the story of section 15's unfulfilled promise, but it is by no means the full story.

5.3 Section 7, penumbral rights and positive duties

While section 15 of the *Charter* has certainly not lived up to the expectations of those who saw it as a vehicle for advancing substantive, material equality, section 7 of the *Charter* has, at the very least, thrown up some interesting cases in which the Supreme Court has, on occasion, been far less deferential to the policy choices of elected officials than Sharpe and Roach's conclusions on section 15 would lead one to expect. The language used in section 7 consciously eschews the commitment to 'life, liberty and property' of the US model of consti-tutionalism; instead it provides that 'Everyone has the right to life, liberty and security of the person and the right not to be deprived thereof except in accordance with the principles of fundamental justice'. This language is, as Sharpe and Roach acknowledge, broad and 'the scope of the guarantee is potentially significant and far reaching'.[88] One of the potentially far-reaching and significant implications of section 7, and one explored by anti-poverty campaigners in Canada, is that section 7 encompasses the protection of certain socio-economic rights. In this section we will explore first the basis for holding out such a 'hope' as to the potential interpretation of section 7, before then going on to look at two high-profile cases in which the Supreme Court addressed the progressive potential of section 7.

5.3.1 The promise of section 7

While, for the most part, the lower courts in Canada have rejected socio-economic rights claims framed in light of section 7 as non-justiciable,[89] the Canadian Supreme Court has explicitly left open the possibility of section 7 giving rise to, in essence, entitlements similar to those arising from socio-economic rights. An early case in which the Supreme Court explicitly left open the possibility of section 7 being interpreted as extending to encompass rights to food, clothing, housing and medical care was *Singh* v. *Minister of Employment and Immigration*, where Wilson J. declined to rule out the possibility, articulated by the Canadian Law Reform Commission, that section 7 should be interpreted as entailing protection of the various subsistence rights set out in Article 25(1) of the UDHR.[90] Similarly in *Slaight Communications* the Supreme Court – in

87 *Ibid.* at p. 319.
88 *Ibid.* at p. 200.
89 See *Brown* v. *British Columbia (Minister of Health)* (1990) 66 DLR (4th) 444; *Fernandes* v. *Manitoba (Director of Social Services)* (1992) 93 DLR (4th) 402; and *Clark* v. *Peterborough Utilities Division* (1995) 24 OR (3d) 7 (Gen. Div).
90 [1985] 1 SCR 177 at paras. 46–47; Article 25(1) UDHR provides that 'Everyone has the

the context of discussing the general relationship between the *Charter* and Canada's international legal obligations – held that 'the *Charter* should generally be presumed to provide protection at least as great as that afforded by similar provisions in international human rights documents which Canada has ratified' including the International Covenant on Economic, Social and Cultural Rights.[91]

In the subsequent case of *Irwin Toy Ltd.* v. *Quebec*,[92] Dickson CJ held – in rejecting the applicant's claim that a provincial ban on advertising aimed at children breached their rights to liberty under section 7 of the *Charter* – that:

> What is immediately striking about this section is the inclusion of 'security of the person' as opposed to 'property' . . . The intentional exclusion of property from s.7, and the substitution therefore of 'security of the person' . . . leads to a general inference that economic rights as generally encompassed by the term 'property' are not within the perimeters of the s.7 guarantee. This is not to declare, however, that no right with an economic component can fall within 'security of the person'. Lower courts have found that the rubric of 'economic rights' embraces a broad spectrum of interests, ranging from such rights, included in various international covenants, as rights to social security, equal pay for equal work, adequate food, clothing and shelter, to traditional property – contract rights. To exclude all of these at this early moment in the history of *Charter* interpretation seems to us to be precipitous. We do not, at this moment, choose to pronounce upon whether those economic rights fundamental to human life or survival are to be treated as though they are of the same ilk as corporate-commercial economic rights.[93]

Significantly, in addition to these judicial pronouncements about the potential scope of section 7, the Canadian federal government, in its reports to the UN Committee on Economic, Social and Cultural Rights, has also encouraged the view that while the *Charter* does not explicitly provide for socio-economic rights, section 7 may be interpreted to provide protection to cognate interests.[94]

---

right to a standard of living adequate for the health and wellbeing of himself and of his family, including food, clothing, housing and medical care and necessary social services, and the right to security in the event of unemployment, sickness, disability, widowhood, old age, or other lack of livelihood in circumstances beyond his control'.

91 *Slaight Communications Inc.* v. *Davidson* [1989] 1 SCR 1038 at pp. 1056–1057.
92 [1989] 1 SCR 927.
93 *Irwin Toy* at 1003–1004.
94 See the UN Committee on Economic, Social and Cultural Rights, *Summary Record of the 5th Meeting: Canada*, UN Doc. E/C.12/1993/SR.5, 25 May 1992 at para. 21 where the Canadian government stated that 'While the guarantee of security of the person under section 7 of the *Charter* might not lead to a right to a certain type of social assistance, it ensured that persons were not deprived of the basic necessities of life'; see also Government of Canada, *Responses to the Supplementary Questions to Canada's Third Report on the International Covenant on Economic, Social and Cultural Rights*, UN Doc. HR/CESCR/NONE/98/8/, November 1998 at para. 53.

Further support for the view, or hope, that section 7 could give rise to positive state obligations to provide social benefits or other subsistence requirements was provided by the Supreme Court judgment in the case of *G. (J.)*, which concerned a claim by an indigent woman that the failure of the government to provide legal aid for child custody hearings breached her rights under section 7 of the *Charter*.[95] The Supreme Court held that, in certain circumstances, section 7 could require the state to provide and fund civil legal aid for indigent citizens, and that this was one such case. For the majority Chief Justice Larmer strongly stressed both the positive obligation on the state under section 7 to ensure a fair hearing for individuals, and power of the courts under section 24 to require the expenditure of public funds – through requiring state-funded legal counsel for those who could not afford it – to vindicate *Charter* rights. Cumulatively these judicial assertions of the positive nature of the rights protected by section 7, both actually and potentially, taken with the federal government's concessions at the level of the UN, fuelled the hope that section 7 would provide the guarantee for socio-economic rights which section 15 had heretofore failed to do. However, in two cases at the start of the new century the Supreme Court, guided by Chief Justice McLachlin, adopted an entirely different interpretation of section 7, one which would significantly dampen the hopes of those who viewed it, and the *Charter* more generally, as a progressive and emancipatory instrument.

5.3.2 Paradise lost: Gosselin and Chaoulli

The first of these was the *Gosselin* case,[96] which provided the 'first occasion for the Supreme Court of Canada to consider to what extent there is any adjudicative space for social rights and poverty issues within sections 7 and 15(1) of the *Charter*'.[97] The applicants in this case challenged the law and policy of the Quebec government, which set the amount of welfare payable to persons under the age of 30 at approximately one-third of that payable to the over thirties, in an effort to 'incentivise' younger welfare claimants into finding work or educational opportunities. The applicants alleged that this policy resulted in a breach of their rights under both sections 7 and 15 of the *Charter*; however for present purposes we are primarily concerned with the section 7 aspect of their claim. The opinion of the majority of the Court was delivered by Chief Justice McLachlin and in rejecting the applicants' claim the Chief Justice stressed the negative character of the rights protected by section 7 of the *Charter*, holding that:

---

95 *New Brunswick (Minister of Health and Community Services)* v. *G. (J.)* [1999] 3 SCR 46.

96 *Gosselin* v. *Quebec (Attorney General)* [2002] 4 SCR 429.

97 Bruce Porter, 'Claiming Adjudicative Space: Social Rights, Equality and Citizenship' in Young, Boyd, Brodsky and Day (eds.), *Poverty: Rights, Social Citizenship and Legal Activism* (Vancouver: UBC Press, 2007) 77 at p. 89.

Even if s.7 could be read to encompass economic rights, a further hurdle emerges. Section 7 speaks of the right *not to be deprived* of life, liberty and security of the person, except in accordance with the principles of fundamental justice. Nothing in the jurisprudence thus far suggests that s.7 places a positive obligation on the state to ensure that each person enjoys life, liberty or security of the person. Rather, s. 7 has been interpreted as restricting the state's ability to *deprive* people of these. Such a deprivation does not exist in the case at bar.[98]

The Chief Justice then left some room for future development by noting that 'One day s.7 may be interpreted to include positive obligations'.[99] However on the facts of the instant case the Chief Justice held there was no basis for such a 'novel application of s.7', because the applicants had failed to demonstrate that the policy actually caused them hardship sufficient to trigger the imposition derived from section 7 of a positive obligation to provide citizen support.[100]

In a powerful dissent Arbour J. held that the issues raised in the instant case fell squarely within the remit of section 7:

> Simply put, the rights at issue here are so intimately intertwined with considerations related to one's basic health (and hence 'security of the person') – and, at the limit, even of one's survival (and hence 'life') – that they can readily be accommodated under the s.7 rights of 'life, liberty and security of the person' without the need to constitutionalize 'property' rights or interests.[101]

In explicitly rejecting the reasoning of the majority Arbour J. held that '[as] a theory of the *Charter* as a whole, any claim that only negative rights are constitutionally recognized is of course patently defective'; she then listed a number of rights protected by the *Charter* – such as the rights to vote, to trial in due course and minority language rights – along with earlier Court judgments, such as *Vriend*, to illustrate that the *Charter* imposed a combination of both positive and negative obligations on the state.[102]

Accepting, then, that the *Charter* could impose positive obligations on the state, and that section 7 in particular did impose obligations with respect to the

---

98 *Gosselin* at para. 81 (original emphasis). Similarly Bastarache J. held, at para. 218, that 'in order for s. 7 to be engaged, the threat to the person's right itself must emanate from the state'.

99 *Gosselin* at para. 82.

100 *Gosselin* at paras. 82–83; this aspect of the Chief Justice's opinion is criticised by Porter (n. 97) at p. 81, who notes that 'the chief justice's determination that "evidence of actual hardship is wanting" was puzzling, given the wealth of evidence on the record of hunger, homelessness, and destitution among those affected by the impugned provision'.

101 *Gosselin* at para. 311.

102 *Gosselin* at para. 320; see also the views of Cory J., above (n. 65), in *Vriend*.

material wellbeing of indigent citizens,[103] Justice Arbour turned her attention to the separation of powers implications of such a finding:

> The ostensible difficulty that confronts the appellant here is the general assertion that positive claims against the state for the provision of certain needs are not justiciable because deciding upon such claims would require courts to dictate to the state how it should allocate scarce resources, a role for which they are not institutionally competent . . . the concern raised by this justiciability argument is a valid one. Questions of resource allocation typically involve delicate matters of policy. Legislatures are better suited than courts to addressing such matters, given that they have the express mandate of the taxpayers as well as the benefits of extensive debate and consultation . . . It does not follow, however, that courts are precluded from entertaining a claim such as the present one. While it may be true that courts are ill-equipped to decide policy matters concerning resource allocation – questions of how much the state should spend, and in what manner – this does not support the conclusion that justiciability is a threshold issue barring the consideration of the substantive claim in this case . . . In contrast to the sorts of policy matters expressed in the justiciability concern, this is a question about what kinds of claims individuals can assert against the state. The role of courts as interpreters of the *Charter* and guardians of its fundamental freedoms against legislative or administrative infringements by the state requires them to adjudicate such rights-based claims. One can in principle answer the question of whether a *Charter* right exists – in this case, to a level of welfare sufficient to meet one's basic needs – without addressing how much expenditure by the state is necessary in order to secure that right. It is only the latter question that is, properly speaking, non-justiciable.[104]

Justice Arbour then went on to argue, again in direct contrast to the majority, that the evidence adduced in the case 'overwhelmingly demonstrates that the exclusion of young adults from the full benefits of the social assistance regime substantially interfered with their fundamental right to security of the person and, at the margins, perhaps with their right to life as well'.[105] There had therefore been a breach of the applicants' section 7 rights, and the purported state

---

103 *Gosselin* at paras. 348 and 358; as she put it: 'Freedom from state interference with bodily or psychological integrity is of little consolation to those who, like the claimants in this case, are faced with a daily struggle to meet their most basic bodily and psychological needs. To them, such a purely negative right to security of the person is essentially meaningless: theirs is a world in which the primary threats to security of the person come not from others, but from their own dire circumstances. In such cases, one can reasonably conclude that positive state action is what is required in order to breathe purpose and meaning into their s. 7 guaranteed rights' (at para. 377).
104 *Gosselin* at paras. 331–332.
105 *Gosselin* at para. 377.

objectives – discouraging welfare dependency, etc. – did not justify this infringement.

While the decision in *Gosselin* was a blow to campaigners for socio-economic rights, and crucially to the applicants, the Court, at least, explicitly left open the possibility that an affirmative right to basic subsistence might be protected by section 7. Indeed, a number of commentators argued that while *Gosselin* was a disappointing judgment, it was nonetheless a victory for socio-economic rights, as none of the judges in the case 'denied their justiciability'.[106] Again in an effort to rationalise the Court's judgment, Sharpe and Roach argue that the Court's trepidation in recognising a positive right to subsistence in *Gosselin* is congruent with 'the Court's tendency to defer to legislatures where complex economic and social policy choices are at issue, and reflects a judicial unwillingness to become embroiled in social and welfare policy'.[107]

No such trepidation or deference was evident when the Supreme Court subsequently held that a provincial ban on insurance to provide private health care was in breach of rights protected in the provincial human rights charter and the federal *Charter*, in 'what may well be the most controversial case yet decided under the *Charter*'.[108] In *Chaoulli* v. *Quebec (Attorney General)* the applicants sought to challenge provisions of the Quebec health care code which, in effect, prohibited the provision of private health insurance for procedures or services provided in the public health care system.[109] In particular, the applicants claimed that delays experienced in the public health care system constituted a violation of the security of the person as protected by section 7 of the *Charter* and personal inviolability and security of the person as protected by section 1 of the Quebec *Charter* of Human Rights and Freedoms. Notwithstanding the argument that maintaining the integrity and equity of the public health care system justified the continued prohibition of private health insurance, a majority of the Court found that the legislation was contrary to the protection of the right to personal inviolability and security of the person under section 1 of the Quebec *Charter*.

For the majority Deschamps J. found that, in light of the delays in the public health care system, preventing individuals who could avoid such delays by

---

106 David Matas, '*Gosselin* v. *Quebec (Attorney General)*: Is Starvation Illegal? The Enforceability of the Right to an Adequate Standard of Living' (2003) 4 *Melbourne Journal of International Law* 217 at p. 239; and see Gwen Brodsky, '*Gosselin* v. *Quebec (Attorney General)*: Autonomy With a Vengeance' (2003) *Canadian Journal of Women and the Law* 194 at pp. 199–201.

107 Sharpe and Roach (n. 3) at p. 231.

108 Jeff King, 'Constitutional Rights and Social Welfare: A Comment on the Canadian *Chaoulli* Health Care Decision' (2006) 69 *Modern Law Review* 631 at p. 620. Indeed Sujit Choudhry has gone so far as to say that the Supreme Court's decision in *Chaoulli* may be 'even worse' than the 'thoroughly discredited judgment' of the US Supreme Court in the now infamous *Lochner* case; Sujit Choudhry, 'Worse Than *Lochner*?' in Flood, Roach and Sossin (eds.), *Access to Care, Access to Justice: The Legal Debate Over Private Health Insurance in Canada* (Toronto: University of Toronto Press, 2005) 75 at p. 76.

109 [2005] 1 SCR 791.

relying on private health insurance and services breached section 1 of the Quebec *Charter*. Justice Deschamps rejected the argument, which had been accepted in the lower courts, that opening the door to greater private sector involvement in the provision of health care would jeopardise the public health care system, and therefore held that there was no justification for the continued prohibition.[110] In response to claims that this case involved matters of policy beyond the appropriate purview of the courts, Deschamps J. argued that:

> if a court is satisfied that all the evidence has been presented, there is nothing that would justify it in refusing to perform its role *on the ground that it should merely defer to the government's position*. When the courts are given the tools they need to make a decision, they should not hesitate to assume their responsibilities. Deference cannot lead the judicial branch to abdicate its role in favour of the legislative branch or the executive branch.[111]

Justice Deschamp's finding of a breach of section 1 of the Quebec *Charter* was the only substantial holding in the *Chaoulli* case. However, three of the other judges in the majority also found that the legislative prohibition on private health insurance constituted a breach of section 7 of the *Charter*.

On this point Chief Justice McLachlin, with whom Major and Bastarache JJ concurred, held that while the *Charter* did not confer a freestanding, positive right to health care, where the state does make provision for health care it must do so in a manner which is compatible with the *Charter*.[112] Echoing Deschamps J., the Chief Justice held that the fact that the matter before the Court was 'complex, contentious or laden with social values does not mean that the courts can abdicate the responsibility vested in them by our Constitution to review legislation for *Charter* compliance . . . The mere fact that this question may have policy ramifications does not permit us to avoid answering it'.[113] The Chief Justice went on to find that:

> prohibiting health insurance that would permit ordinary Canadians to access health care, in circumstances where the government is failing to deliver health care in a reasonable manner, thereby increasing the risk of complications and death, interferes with life and security of the person as protected by s. 7 of the *Charter*.[114]

The Chief Justice went on to reject the contention that while the prohibition on private health insurance may represent a prima facie breach of section 7, it could nonetheless be justified under section 1 of the *Charter* as being necessary

---

110 *Chaoulli* at paras. 64 and 74.
111 *Chaoulli* at para. 87 (emphasis added).
112 *Chaoulli* at para. 104.
113 *Chaoulli* at paras. 107–108.
114 *Chaoulli* at para. 124.

to maintain the integrity and equity of the public health system. Therefore, the Chief Justice found the prohibition to be an 'arbitrary' interference with the applicants' section 7 rights, and therefore contrary to the *Charter*.[115]

The decision of the three dissenting judges in this case, Binnie, LeBel and Fish JJ, was delivered by Justices Binnie and LeBel. The dissenting Justices began by stating that the case before them involved a contentious issue of high policy, which should not, or could not, be resolved through the courts,[116] because it was a 'debate about social values . . . not about constitutional law'.[117] The dissenting Justices called their colleagues in the majority to task for embracing 'an overly interventionist view of the role the courts should play in trying to supply a "fix" to . . . major social programs'.[118] In contrast to the majority, the dissenting Justices accepted the findings of fact made by the trial judge, that increased private sector involvement in the provision of health care could operate to the detriment of the single-tier public health care system, and therefore found that while delays might, conceivably, constitute a breach of the rights to personal security and inviolability, the legislative aim pursued justified any such breach.[119] The Supreme Court judgment in *Chaoulli*, or at least the judgment of the majority, was highly controversial because 'it touched on one of the most contentious policy issues in Canada today', namely the privatisation of Canada's public health care system.[120] And while the actual impact of *Chaoulli* may be unclear, in principle at least it seemed to validate a two-tier health system in which the wealthy could access whatever treatment they needed, while the poor were left behind.[121]

It is very difficult to reconcile the Court's stated discomfort with engaging in high policy in cases such as *Auton*, with the majority's headlong dash into highly contentious issues of policy in *Chaoulli*. Indeed, the arch-rationalisers of the Supreme Court's jurisprudence accept that the majority's decision in *Chaoulli* 'represents a striking departure from the Court's consistent deference to legislative judgment on broad policy issues'.[122] Others point to the

---

115 *Chaoulli* at paras. 152–153.
116 *Chaoulli* at paras. 161–164.
117 *Chaoulli* at para. 166.
118 *Chaoulli* at para. 169.
119 *Chaoulli* at para. 256.
120 Peter Russell, '*Chaoulli*: The Political versus the Legal Life of a Decision' in Flood, Roach and Sossin (eds.), *Access to Care, Access to Justice: The Legal Debate Over Private Health Insurance in Canada* (Toronto: University of Toronto Press, 2005) 5 at p. 5.
121 See Lorne Sossin, 'Towards a Two-Tier Constitution? The Poverty of Health Rights' in Flood, Roach and Sossin (eds.), *Access to Care, Access to Justice: The Legal Debate Over Private Health Insurance in Canada* (Toronto: University of Toronto Press, 2005) 161 at pp. 162–163; Martha Jackman, '"The Last Line of Defence for [Which?] Citizens": Accountability, Equality, and the Right to Health in *Chaoulli*' (2006) 44 *Osgoode Hall Law Journal* 349 at p. 364; and Bruce Porter, 'A Right to Health Care in Canada: Only if You Can Pay for It' (2005) 6(4) *ESR Review* 8.
122 Sharpe and Roach (n. 3) at p. 210; see also Macklem (n. 5) at p. 240 and King (n. 108) at p. 643.

separation-of-powers implications of the judgment. For example Peter Russell argues that the approach to section 7 favoured by the McLachlin CJ troika would allow the Supreme Court to 'assume the role of a super-legislature' in the Canadian context and significantly shift the balance of power between the respective branches of government.[123] Christopher Manfredi and Antonia Maioni note that the majority's judgment in *Chaoulli* 'represents a paradigmatic case of judicial policy making',[124] and as such places proponents of judicial review under the *Charter* on the defensive.[125] A clear distinction between *Chaoulli* and cases such as *Auton* is that the latter type of case concerned the rights of marginalised and excluded sections of society seeking positive state action, whereas the former involved the interests of relatively affluent individuals wishing to exit Quebec's single-tier health care system. Thus, Choudhry notes that it 'is impossible to say whether a class bias, unconscious or otherwise, is at work. But, as they say in politics, the optics are bad'.[126] Indeed, many critics of the *Chaoulli* decision argue that it represents a clear expression of judicial privileging of the ideology of liberalism or neo-liberalism, which was latent in the *Charter* from the outset.[127]

There are perhaps two ways of viewing the Supreme Court's decision in *Chaoulli*: the broadly positive and the pessimistic. For example Lorne Sossin argues, much like those who sought out the silver lining in *Gosselin*, that notwithstanding the ostensibly regressive nature of the Court's judgment in *Chaoulli* it may 'nevertheless . . . have a surprisingly progressive influence on *Charter* jurisprudence' by 'establishing the connection between deprivation of the necessities of life and fundamental rights' *Chaoulli* may well open the door for enhanced protection of social rights under the *Charter*.[128] In contrast to this view, Andrew Petter argues that, viewing the Supreme Court judgments in *Chaoulli* and *Gosselin* together, these judgments starkly illustrate the inability of the *Charter* to provide meaningful protection for socio-economic rights. As he, rather caustically, puts it:

---

123 Russell (n. 120) at p. 10.
124 Christopher Manfredi and Antonia Maioni, '"The Last Line of Defence for Citizens": Litigating Private Health Insurance in *Chaoulli* v. *Quebec*' (2006) 44 *Osgoode Hall Law Journal* 249 at p. 270.
125 Ibid.
126 Choudhry (n. 108) at p. 95.
127 See Andrew Petter, 'Wealthcare: The Politics of the *Charter* Revisited' in Flood, Roach and Sossin (eds.), *Access to Care, Access to Justice: The Legal Debate Over Private Health Insurance in Canada* (Toronto: University of Toronto Press, 2005) 116; Allan Hutchinson, 'Condition Critical: The Constitution and Health Care' in Flood, Roach and Sossin (eds.), *Access to Care, Access to Justice: The Legal Debate Over Private Health Insurance in Canada* (Toronto: University of Toronto Press, 2005) 101; and Porter (n. 121) at p. 11, who criticises an 'increasingly neo-liberal Supreme Court', but does not disavow the *Charter* in its totality, as Petter and Hutchinson do.
128 Sossin (n. 121) at p. 178; in a similar vein see King (n. 108); and Martha Jackman, '"The Last Line of Defence for [Which?] Citizens": Accountability, Equality, and the Right to Health in *Chaoulli*' (2006) 44 *Osgoode Hall Law Journal* 349 at p. 373.

The political message and meaning of *Gosselin* and *Chaoulli* become even clearer when these cases are considered together. Despite the *Charter's* fine words, the social rights it confers do not speak to the security of all Canadians, nor to their actual equality. In *Charterland*, persons who lack property enjoy few meaningful social entitlements no matter how much suffering they endure. On the one hand, the *Charter* places no positive obligation on the state to provide them with the basic necessities of life; on the other hand, they have little to gain from the negative rights the *Charter* confers on those with property to prevent the state from restricting that property's use for constitutionally protected ends. Thus while the *Charter* provides Louise Gosselin no right to call upon the state to provide her with food, clothing or shelter, it provides her with the right to purchase private health insurance in the market place – if only she had the money to do so. Like champagne and lobster tails, *Charter* rights are only valuable to those who can afford them.[129]

Consequently, Petter argues, the lesson to be drawn is that 'not only do the disadvantaged have little to gain in the way of social benefits from the *Charter*, they have much to lose'.[130]

Cases such *Gosselin* and *Chaoulli* appear, as Petter and others argue, to have rendered nugatory the promise of *Irwin* that section 7 could be extended to encompass positive state obligations and socio-economic rights, at least for the time being. However, the fact remains that section 7 of the *Charter* is sufficiently indeterminate to allow for a valid interpretation of it which extends to the protection of positive rights. This point is well made by Margot Young when she notes that given 'different politics at large in Canada, a different constitutional culture with respect to notions of judicial competency and institutional appropriateness, as well as different ideas about social and economic justice',[131] a more expansive interpretation of section 7, which encompasses the protection of socio-economic rights, could be a possibility. Indeed, this much is accepted by the majority in *Gosselin*. The problem, however, as Young herself knows, is that to the extent that Canadian politics is changing, it is away from a traditional commitment to the welfare state and social provision, and towards an increasingly neo-liberal state apparatus, which is inherently inimical to the protection of socio-economic rights.[132]

129 Petter (n. 127) at p. 127.
130 *Ibid.* at p. 127
131 Margot Young, 'Section 7 and the Politics of Social Justice' (2005) 38 *University of British Columbia Law Review* 539 at p. 560.
132 See Brodsky (n. 45) at p. 251; Macklem (n. 5) at pp. 118–221; Margot Young, 'Introduction' in Young, Boyd, Brodsky and Day (eds.), *Poverty: Rights, Social Citizenship and Legal Activism* (Vancouver: UBC Press, 2007) 1; and Ed Broadbent, 'Barbarism Lite: Political Assault on Social Rights is Worsening Inequality' available at: www.policyalternatives.ca/publications/monitor/barbarism-lite (last retrieved 14 January 2010).

Nonetheless, an example of the continued hope that the *Charter* can provide some protection for core socio-economic rights is provided by a recent provincial case, in which Ross J. of the Supreme Court of British Columbia found a bylaw which prevented homeless people from erecting temporary shelter when sleeping in public spaces to be unconstitutional as a violation of the applicant's section 7 right to security of the person, by putting them at risk of ill-health and other complications associated with exposure to the elements.[133] Although in this case both Ross J. and the applicants 'effectively sidestepped direct debate over positive versus negative rights', by holding that the case was one of state interference – enactment and enforcement of bylaws – with a section 7 interest, it is nonetheless significant for the acknowledgement that the right to shelter is encompassed, in some form, in section 7 of the *Charter*. It is also significant for Ross J.'s observations, in response to separation of powers arguments raised by the city, that 'it is not the case that choices of the legislature that involve complex issues of policy are immune from review . . . Simply put, the fact that the matter engages complex policy decisions does not immunize the legislation from review by the courts pursuant to the *Charter*'.[134] Of equal significance is that on appeal Ross J.'s judgment was upheld by the British Columbia Court of Appeal,[135] who, echoing the last point, held that 'it is clear that the fact that a legal issue raises political concerns does not render it non-justiciable'.[136]

However, while *Adams* should be greeted, if for no other reason than that it contributed in some small way to improving the lives of the homeless people of Cridge Park, it also serves as a testament to the limitations of advancing socio-economic rights through section 7 of the *Charter*. As Margot Young puts it:

> Of course, one cannot fault either the claimants or their lawyers for arguing what is most likely to succeed in court, but it can be an unfortunate tactic from the perspective of long-term *Charter* development. And that this seems to be how a winning argument in this case must be crafted speaks broadly of the distressing state of constitutional rights jurisprudence . . . If the right that results from this case is the best that the *Charter* can offer in the face of such real and material social injustice as homelessness, then constitutionalized rights are cold and thin comfort indeed for the many individuals sleeping on our streets and in our parks.[137]

---

133 *Victoria (City)* v. *Adams* [2008] BCSC 1363 at para. 155 [hereinafter '*Adams* (SC)']; for a very helpful discussion of this case, and its broader implications, see Margot Young, 'Rights, the Homeless, and Social Change: Reflections on *Victoria (City)* v. *Adams* (BCSC)' (2010) 164 *BC Studies: The British Columbian Quarterly* 101.

134 *Adams* (SC) at paras. 124–125.

135 *Victoria (City)* v. *Adams* [2009] BCCA 563 [hereinafter '*Adams* (CA)'].

136 *Adams* (CA) at para. 67.

137 Young (n. 133) at p. 110.

This assessment of *Adams*, and by implication of section 7, lends weight to the views of Petter and others that the *Charter* cannot, and never could, provide substantive protection for the interests of the most marginalised and excluded. On the other hand, cases such as *Adams* and the continued campaigning of Canadian social justice advocates indicate that the battle field of the *Charter* will not be surrendered lightly.

5.4 Conclusion

Much like the Supreme Court's jurisprudence, any assessment of the Canadian experience must, necessarily, be conflicting and conflicted. On the one hand the Canadian experience in rights protection under the *Charter* has, for the most part, been positive. As Monahan notes 'Canada's first twenty-five years of experience with the *Charter* . . . suggests that, on balance, it has made a significant positive contribution to . . . Canadian law and politics'.[138] Similarly Sharpe and Roach argue that the Canadian experience of rights adjudication under the *Charter* demonstrates that courts can play an active role in enforcing entrenched fundamental rights 'without unduly inhibiting the capacity of the elected representatives to develop social policy'.[139] This was achieved – in large part – through the articulation, if not always the practice,[140] of the concept of constitutional dialogue; which is a creative and promising means through which to understand and reconcile the role of courts of ultimate jurisdiction in enforcing rights, with the democratic prerogatives of elected representatives. By the same token the extent to which the Supreme Court has fully embraced the spirit of dialogue has been inconsistent, oscillating between the extreme deference of *Auton* to the outright usurpation of *Chaoulli*, with *Eldridge* arguably a mid-point along the continuum. It has to be said that the Court's differing approach in each case does not appear to have been based on sound principle, but rather, in many instances, on judicial preference or pre-disposition.

This in many respects feeds into the major shortcoming or difficulty with the Canadian experience, namely the unresolved tension – exacerbated in many ways under Chief Justice McLachlin – between Canada's well-known commitment, at least historically, to the welfare state and social justice, and the Canadian Supreme Court's 'marked reluctance to interpret the *Charter* as protecting social and economic rights'.[141] And while some limited form of

---

138 Monahan (n. 2) at p. 390.
139 Sharpe and Roach (n. 3) at p. 42.
140 Notable 'breaks' with the spirit of dialogue being provided by *Chaoulli*, and the Supreme Court's decision to uphold what Hogg *et al.* (n. 30) at pp. 18–19 call 'a draconian' lower court order requiring the government to build minority language schools within a specified time frame in *DoucetBoudreau* v. *Nova Scotia (Minister of Education)* [2003] 3 SCR 3.
141 Wiseman (n. 5) at p. 186; as Ran Hirschl recently put it: 'An inexplicable gap exists between Canada's long-standing commitment to a relatively generous version of the Keynesian welfare state model and the outright exclusion of subsistence rights from the purview of *Charter* provisions': Ran Hirschl, 'Constitutional Courts and Social Welfare Rights: The

protection for socio-economic rights has been achieved to date, 'this represents only a fraction of the potential' inherent in the *Charter*.[142] Commentators such as Bakan, Petter and Hirschl will argue that this should be no surprise, as the *Charter* was, from its inception, grounded on classical liberal notions of negative liberty and the night-watchman state. However, both the case law to date, and the continued activism of numerous Canadians, lends weight to the observation of Martha Jackman and Bruce Porter that 'the constitutional status of socio-economic rights in Canada remains, to a large extent, an open question – perhaps the most central unresolved issue in Canadian *Charter* jurisprudence'.[143] The resolution of this question, particularly in light of the steady erosion of Canada's welfare state, will be crucial to the future of Canadian society.

In the absence, however, of such resolution, we may say that the Canadian experience, in some ways similarly to the Indian, is a testament to the dangers of an unconstrained judiciary, at least in the realm of socio-economic rights. The absence of express guarantees to socio-economic rights has meant that the Supreme Court could, when it chose to, play the deference card. By the same token the open-textured language used in the *Charter*, in particular in section 7, has allowed the Court to intervene in key policy areas and upset the will of elected representatives. Although episodes such as this certainly fly in the face of the much lauded concept of dialogue, this still represents, arguably, the main contribution of the Canadian experience. Although it has not always been observed in practice, the ideal of constitutional dialogue – of the courts and the elected branches of government engaged in a cooperative exercise to protect and advance the fundamental rights protected in the *Charter* – has much to recommend it, and it is a concept to which we will return. In the final analysis the Canadian experience, so far as vindication of socio-economic rights is concerned, represents an expectation, a hope and a promise unfulfilled, and in truth there are no real signs of this trend being reversed anytime soon.

"Weak Courts, Strong Rights" Argument Re-examined' (2009) 40 *Ottawa Law Review* 173 at p. 180.
142 Wiseman (n. 5) at p. 204; see also Jackman and Porter (n. 5) at p. 228.
143 Jackman and Porter (n. 5) at p. 209.

6   The rejection of socio-economic rights in Ireland

An archetypal example of a constitutional order in which the rejection of judicial enforcement of socio-economic rights is made on the basis of the separation of powers arguments discussed in Chapter 1 is provided by the Irish experience. Notwithstanding the fact that the Irish Constitution contains commitments to civil and political and, to a limited extent, socio-economic rights, in recent years the Irish Supreme Court has, for all intents and purposes, denied any 'adjudicative space' for socio-economic rights claims under the Irish Constitution.[1] Because of this the Irish experience of socio-economic rights adjudication merits consideration as, arguably, a cautionary tale of how not to approach the issue.[2] This chapter begins by setting out an overview of the Irish constitutional system and the constitutional provisions and doctrines relevant to a discussion of socio-economic rights in Ireland. We then go on to look at the experience of the Irish superior courts in adjudicating on socio-economic rights claims in three phases: (i) the first in which a number of High Court judgments appeared to articulate some, limited, scope for the protection of socio-economic rights under various provisions of the Constitution; (ii) the second in which the Irish Supreme Court essentially rejected the notion of meaningful judicial enforcement of justiciable socio-economic rights under the Irish Constitution; and (iii) a third phase in which both the Supreme Court and lower courts have offered differing interpretations of the current place of socio-economic rights in Irish law.

---

1   On the notion of 'adjudicative space' see Bruce Porter, 'Claiming Adjudicative Space: Social Rights, Equality and Citizenship' in Young, Boyd, Brodsky and Day (eds.), *Poverty: Rights, Social Citizenship and Legal Activism* (Vancouver: UBC Press, 2007) 77.

2   For useful introductory discussions of the Irish experience, see Gerard Quinn, 'Rethinking the Nature of Social, Economic and Cultural Rights in the Irish Legal Order' in Costello (ed.), *Fundamental Social Rights: Current European Legal Protection and the Challenge of the EU Charter of Fundamental Rights* (Dublin: Irish Centre for European Law, 2001) 35; Gerry Whyte, *Social Inclusion and the Legal System: Public Interest Law in Ireland* (Dublin: Institute of Public Administration, 2002) at pp. 9–57 and 340–363; and Aoife Nolan, 'Ireland: The Separation of Powers Doctrine vs. Socio-Economic Rights?' in Langford (ed.), *Social Rights Jurisprudence: Emerging Trends in International and Comparative Law* (Cambridge: Cambridge University Press, 2008) 295.

6.1 The Irish Constitutional system

The Irish Constitution was approved by a narrow majority of the people in a referendum in July 1937 and came into force in December 1937. In many ways it was ahead of its time, containing protection of a number of fundamental rights and firmly entrenching the role of the judiciary in defending and vindication these rights more than a decade before the advent of the post-Second World War human rights 'boom'. In this section we will set out certain key provisions of the Constitution and also discuss some of the defining influences on the Constitution and some key doctrines which have emerged under it. The first thing to note about the Irish Constitution is that while it was not a transformative document, in the sense in which the South African and Indian constitutions were, it did involve a substantial break with traditional British-style notions of parliamentary supremacy, and also contained a commitment to a substantive social vision.[3] The defining feature, then, of the Irish Constitution – as enacted – is that it represented 'a self-conscious attempt to combine the liberal democratic tradition . . . with Catholic social teaching';[4] and while this unity of theocratic and liberal democratic traditions may have been an uneasy one,[5] it fundamentally shaped Irish constitutional jurisprudence. In this section we will highlight the provisions of the Constitution which deal with fundamental rights and the separation of powers, as well as noting the central jurisprudential development of Irish constitutional jurisprudence, the doctrine of 'unenumerated personal rights'.

6.1.1 Fundamental rights and the separation of powers

A useful, albeit somewhat rough, way of looking at the Irish Constitution in a way which brings into the relief the dual philosophical and historical influences which shaped it is to say that the liberal democratic influence is clearest in the institutional structure set out in the Constitution (along with some of the rights protected), while the influence of Catholic social teaching is most evident in the Preamble, the fundamental rights provisions and the Directive Principles of Social Policy (DPSP). In terms of the institutional structure it must be said

---

3 On the historical influences which shaped the Constitution and on its drafting see: Dermot Keogh, 'The Irish Constitutional Revolution: An Analysis of the Making of the Constitution' in Litton (ed.), *The Constitution of Ireland 1937–1987* (Dublin: Institute of Public Administration, 1988) 4; Ronan Fanning, 'Mr de Valera Drafts a Constitution' in Farrell (ed.), *De Valera's Constitution and Ours* (Dublin: Gill & Macmillan, 1988) 33; Enda McDonagh, 'Philosophical–Theological Reflections on the Constitution' in Litton (ed.), *The Constitution of Ireland 1937–1987* (Dublin: Institute of Public Administration, 1988) 192; Basil Chubb, *The Government and Politics of Ireland* (3rd edn, London: Longman, 1997); and Dermot Keogh and Andrew McCarthy, *The Making of the Irish Constitution 1937* (Dublin: Mercier Press, 2007).
4 Chubb (n. 3) at pp. 15–16.
5 See Gerard Quinn, 'The Nature and Significance of Critical Legal Studies' (1989) 7 *Irish Law Times* 282 who, at p. 286, criticises the 'essentially unnatural' coexistence of liberal democratic and theocratic visions in the Constitution.

that the drafters of the Constitution chose not to reinvent the wheel, and adopted, in many respects, the inherited British system of parliamentary government. The one major departure from Westminster tradition is that the Irish Constitution entrenched both an extensive catalogue of fundamental rights and a firm assertion of the judicial role in the enforcement and vindication of those rights. And while the Constitution does not explicitly demarcate a separation of powers, various Articles,[6] in particular Article 6(1),[7] do 'point in that direction'.[8] However, while the courts have consistently recognised the separation of powers under the Constitution, the Supreme Court has, on a number of occasions, noted that 'the framers of the Constitution did not adopt a rigid separation between the legislative, executive and judicial powers'.[9]

The adoption of a written constitution, with entrenched rights, a judiciary empowered to enforce them and an – imperfect – separation of powers, was not unrelated to the Irish experience, much like the Indian, of British colonial rule. As O'Dálaigh CJ put it:

> If our Constitution . . . adopted the theory of the tripartite separation of the powers of government with express limitations on the powers alike of the Legislature and Executive over the citizen, the reason is not unconnected with our previous experience under an alien government where parliament was omnipotent and in whose executive lay wide reserves of prerogative power.[10]

Thus, those who drafted the Constitution saw an important role for the courts as guardians of the Constitution and guardians of fundamental rights.[11] Consequently it should come as no surprise that while stressing the equal respect owed from each branch of government to the others, the courts have consistently asserted their central constitutional role in the protection of fundamental rights. For example in *Boland* v. *An Taoiseach* Fitzgerald CJ held that 'in my opinion,

---

6 Such as Article 15.2 (exclusive legislative power vested in the Oireachtas [Parliament]); Article 28.2 (conferring the executive power of the state on the government); and Articles 26 and 34.3.2° (which establish, respectively, the power of the courts to prospectively and retrospectively review legislation for compliance with the Constitution).

7 Which provides that 'All powers of government, legislative, executive and judicial, derive, under God, from the people, whose right it is to designate the rulers of the State and, in final appeal, to decide all questions of national policy, according to the requirements of the common good'.

8 David Gwynn Morgan, *The Separation of Powers in the Irish Constitution* (Dublin: Round Hall Sweet & Maxwell, 1997) at p. 26.

9 *Abbey Films* v. *Attorney General* [1981] IR 158 at p. 171. See also Gerard Hogan and Gerry Whyte, *Kelly's The Irish Constitution* (4th edn, Dublin: Lexis-Nexis, 2003) at pp. 138–139 and Brian McCracken, 'The Irish Constitution: An Overview' in Sarkin and Binchy (eds.), *Human Rights, the Citizen and the State: South African and Irish Perspectives* (Dublin: Round Hall, 2001) 52 at p. 58.

10 *Melling* v. *Ó Mathghamhna* [1962] IR 1 at p. 39.

11 See Gerard Hogan, 'The Constitutional Review Committee of 1934' in Ó Muircheartaigh (ed.), *Ireland in the Coming Times: Essays to Celebrate TK Whitaker's 80 Years* (Dublin: Institute of Public Administration, 1997) 342 at p. 361.

the Courts have no power, either express or implied, to supervise or interfere with the exercise by the Government of its executive functions, unless the circumstances are such as to amount to a clear disregard by the Government of the powers and duties conferred upon it by the Constitution'.[12] And in the subsequent case of *Crotty* v. *An Taoiseach* Finlay CJ stated that the courts had 'a right and a duty to interfere with the activities of the executive in order to protect . . . the constitutional rights of individual litigants'.[13] Similarly in *DG* v. *Eastern Health Board* Hamilton CJ held that 'It is part of the courts' function to vindicate and defend the rights guaranteed by [Article 40.3]. If the courts are under an obligation to defend and vindicate the personal rights of the citizen, it inevitably follows that the courts have the jurisdiction to do all things necessary to vindicate such rights'.[14] An essential part, therefore, of the separation of powers under the Constitution is the role of the courts in reviewing legislative and executive action for compliance with the rights guaranteed in the Constitution.

These include a common catalogue of the rights protected in liberal democracies, such as the right to life,[15] to equality,[16] freedom of expression and assembly,[17] trial in due course of law[18] and freedom of conscience.[19] Alongside these classic liberal rights the Constitution, strongly influenced by Catholic social teaching, gave prominence to the rights of the family, which are described as being 'inalienable and imprescriptible . . . antecedent and superior to all positive law',[20] and to a conception of private property which made it subject to 'the principles of social justice' and the 'exigencies of the common good'.[21] Thus the rights protected in the Constitution – with the exception of the right to education in Article 42 to which we return below – were primarily civil and political. To the extent that socio-economic rights were provided for by the drafters of the Constitution, it was in Article 45 which, again influenced by Catholic social teaching, entrenched the DPSP,[22] committing the state, among other things, to secure 'a social order in which justice and charity' shall prevail,[23]

---

12 [1974] IR 338 at p. 362.
13 [1987] IR 713 at p. 773.
14 [1997] 3 IR 511 at p. 522.
15 Article 40.3.2°.
16 Article 40.1.
17 Article 40.6.
18 Article 38.1.
19 Article 44.2.
20 Article 41.1.
21 Article 43.2; see also the Preamble to the Constitution, which commits the people, through the Constitution, to the pursuit of the 'common good, with due observance of Prudence, Justice and Charity, so that the dignity and freedom of the individual may be assured [and] true social order attained'.
22 For discussion of Article 45, see Hogan and Whyte (n. 9) at pp. 2077–2086; and Gearóid Carey, 'The Constitutional Dilemma of Article 45: An Avenue for Welfare and Social Rights?' (1995) 5 *Irish Student Law Review* 78.
23 Article 45.1.

and to 'safeguard with especial care the economic interests of the weaker sections of the community, and, where necessary, to contribute to the maintenance of the infirm, the widow, the orphan, and the aged'.[24] While these provisions certainly draw on concepts of the deserving poor, they are nonetheless significant for indicating 'a constitutional commitment that public policy should pursue a conception of social justice'.[25] The catch, however, is that these provisions are explicitly made non-cognisable by the courts.

Commenting on Article 45 Gerard Quinn notes that Eamon De Valera – the chief architect in the drafting of the Irish Constitution – 'cleverly genuflected before socio-economic rights but made sure to insert them into a part of the Constitution that is unenforceable by the courts':[26] consequently we are left with 'rhetorical genuflections to egalitarian rights but little more'.[27] Indeed, since the adoption of the Constitution, Article 45 has proved to be little more than a rhetorical flourish, which is somewhat ironic given that Article 45 inspired the Directive Principles of State Policy in the Indian Constitution,[28] and that in the Indian context these principles were central to the Indian Supreme Court's socio-economic rights jurisprudence. In contrast, under the Irish Constitution, aside from occasional use as an interpretive aid in identifying unenumerated rights protected by Article 40.3 of the Constitution,[29] Article 45 has been a veritable dead letter. Consequently claims for socio-economic rights have had to be pursued through other avenues. We will look at the various attempts to ground or advance socio-economic rights under the Constitution in the next substantive section, but first we will mention briefly one of the key developments under the Irish Constitution.

6.1.2 Unenumerated rights

Article 40.3 has given rise to 'an important and beneficial strain of judicial activism' in the form of the doctrine of unenumerated personal rights.[30] The seminal case in the development of this doctrine was the decision of Kenny J. in *Ryan* v. *Attorney General*.[31] In this case the applicant sought to challenge legislation requiring the compulsory fluoridation of public water supplies on the ground, *inter alia*, that the mandatory fluoridation of her water supply violated

---

24 Article 45.4.1°.
25 Rory O'Connell, 'From Equality Before the Law to the Equal Benefit of the Law: Social and Economic Rights in the Irish Constitution' in Doyle and Carolan (eds), *The Irish Constitution: Governance and Values* (Dublin: Thomson Round Hall, 2008) 327 at p. 328.
26 Quinn (n. 2) at p. 49.
27 Quinn (n. 2) at p. 48.
28 See Granville Austin, *Working a Democratic Constitution: The Indian Experience* (New Delhi: Oxford University Press, 1999) at p. 7; and Brij Kishore Sharma, *Introduction to the Constitution of India* (2nd edn, New Delhi: Prentice-Hall of India, 2004) at p. 115.
29 See *Murtagh Properties* v. *Cleary* [1972] IR 330 and *Attorney General* v. *Paperlink* [1984] ILRM 373.
30 Hogan and Whyte (n. 9) at p. 1391.
31 [1965] IR 294. Although one must also acknowledge, as a portent of the doctrine that would

both her and her family's constitutional rights to 'bodily integrity'. On the basis of the scientific evidence presented, and because of the general social good which the fluoridation programme provided to society as a whole, Kenny J. ultimately found against the applicant. However, the more significant aspect of his decision is that he accepted the applicant's claim that she enjoyed a constitutional right to bodily integrity, notwithstanding the fact that no such right was referred to in the text of the Constitution. Kenny J. held that the use of the words 'in particular' in Article 40.3.2 of the Constitution indicated an acknowledgement that there were other rights protected by the Constitution,[32] although not specifically adumbrated therein. He summed up his position thus: 'the personal rights which may be invoked to invalidate legislation are not confined to those specified in Article 40 but include all those rights which result from the Christian and democratic nature of the State'.[33] Having regard to the Papal Encyclical *Pacaem In Terris*, which recognised bodily integrity as one of the natural rights of the individual, Kenny J. satisfied himself that the Irish Constitution protected such a right.

Kenny J's judgment was subsequently approved by a majority of the Supreme Court and once the precedent was established a number of judgments expanded and further entrenched the doctrine. In the case of *McGee* v. *Attorney General*,[34] the plaintiff claimed that legislation, which penalised the importation of contraceptives, was contrary to the Constitution as it violated her right to marital privacy. As was the case in *Ryan*, the right claimed by Mrs McGee was not mentioned in the text of the Constitution. However Walsh J. had this to say:

> Articles 41, 42 and 43 emphatically reject the theory that there are no rights without laws, no rights contrary to the law and no rights anterior to the law. They indicate that justice is placed above the law and acknowledge that natural rights, or human rights, are not created by law but that the Constitution confirms their existence and gives them protection.[35]

The doctrine of unenumerated personal rights, derived from the natural law, once firmly entrenched was of significant benefit to Irish society as a whole, leading to the protection of a number of significant individual rights, including, for example, the right of access to the courts,[36] the right to fair procedures[37] and the right to communicate.[38]

be developed under the 1937 Constitution, the famous dissenting judgment of Kennedy CJ in *The State (Ryan)* v. *Lennon* [1935] IR 170.

32 On this point, even critics of the *Ryan* decision concede that the wording of Article 40.3.1 leads to the interpretation placed on it by Kenny J.; see Gerard Hogan, 'Unenumerated Personal Rights: *Ryan's* Case Re-Evaluated' (1990–2) 25–27 *Irish Jurist (n.s.)* 95 at p. 113.

33 [1965] IR 294 at p. 312.

34 [1974] IR 284.

35 [1974] IR 284 at p. 318.

36 *Macauley* v. *Minister for Posts and Telegraphs* [1966] IR 345.

37 *In Re Haughey* [1971] IR 217.

38 *Attorney General* v. *Paperlink* [1984] ILRM 373.

However, the natural law paradigm, which essentially meant the Catholic conception of natural law,[39] also had its limits. These limits came to the fore in the context of proposed legislation to provide information on abortion services available outside of the state. One prominent proponent of the natural law school, Roderick O'Hanlon, argued that such legislation was unconstitutional, notwithstanding the fact that the Constitution had been amended specifically to facilitate such legislation. The argument advanced by O'Hanlon was that the power of the people to amend the Constitution, contained in Article 46, was limited by the precepts of the natural law, or more specifically the natural right to life of the unborn, which the amendments put in jeopardy. Consequently, any legislation which relied on these amendments for its legitimacy should be deemed unconstitutional as the amendments were themselves invalid.[40] In the *Abortion Information* case this argument was canvassed before the Supreme Court and completely rejected.[41] Along with the rejection of the argument in the instant case, the Supreme Court seemed also to reject the validity of natural law as a method of constitutional interpretation, and with the decline in the influence of natural law came a concomitant contraction of the unenumerated rights doctrine and questioning of its continued viability by senior members of the judiciary.[42]

6.1.3 *The basis for claiming socio-economic rights*

The position, then, is that the Irish Constitution entrenches an extensive catalogue of fundamental rights, supplemented by the doctrine of unenumerated rights, and empowers the judiciary to enforce these rights against the elected branches of government. However, with the exception of the right to education and the right, in exceptional circumstances, for children to be cared for by the state (discussed below), the Constitution does not explicitly provide for the protection of socio-economic rights. In this section we will look at the various ways in which individuals have sought to frame claims for socio-economic rights under the Constitution. First we look at the various options for 'introducing' socio-economic rights into the Constitution, before then looking at the only socio-economic right explicitly protected by the Constitution, education, and how this right has developed over time. According to Tim Murphy recognition of socio-economic rights under the current Constitution could come about in two ways: (i) by amendment to the Constitution; (ii) 'or

---

39 See in this regard Anthony Twomey, 'The Death of the Natural Law?' (1995) 13 *Irish Law Times* 270.

40 See Roderick O'Hanlon, 'Natural Rights and the Irish Constitution' (1993) 11 *Irish Law Times* 8 and by the same author 'The Judiciary and the Moral Law' (1993) 11 *Irish Law Times* 129.

41 *Re Article 26 and the Regulation of Information (Services Outside the State for Termination of Pregnancies) Bill 1995*[1995] 1 IR 1 at p. 43.

42 See the comments of Keane J. in *O'T* v. *B* [1998] 2 IR 321 at pp. 370–375; and his comments in the *TD* case discussed below.

by a decision of the courts to add such rights to the existing range of unenu-merated rights'.[43] We will look at each of these possibilities in turn.

The prospect of amending the Constitution so as to include, in essence, socio-economic rights was considered in the most thorough review of the Constitution to date, the Report of the Constitution Review Group (CRG). In rejecting the arguments in favour of such an amendment the CRG argued that the:

> main reason . . . why the Constitution should not confer personal rights to freedom from poverty, or to other specific economic or social entitlements, is that these are essentially political matters which, in a democracy, it should be the responsibility of the elected representatives of the people to address and determine. It would be a distortion of democracy to transfer decisions on major issues of policy and practicality from the Government and the Oireachtas, elected to represent the people and do their will, to an unelected judiciary.[44]

The CRG further argued that to entrench such rights would mean that the elected branches of government 'would have no discretion as to what amount of revenue could, or should, be raised from the public' to fund the realisation of such rights.[45] However, and somewhat contradictorily, the CRG bolstered its argument by stating that:

> it is obviously important that no one should be allowed to fall below a minimum level of subsistence so as to suffer from a lack of food, shelter or clothing. If this should ever happen, despite the social welfare system, the Constitution appears to offer ultimate protection through judicial vin-dication of fundamental personal rights, such as the right to life and the right to bodily integrity.[46]

So, the CRG ultimately rejected the recognition and entrenchment of socio-economic rights on the basis that it would distort the separation of powers. A similar argument is made somewhat more succinctly by Gerard Hogan who argues that 'if socio-economic rights are made justiciable and are vindicated by the courts, the result will tend to distort the traditional balance of the separation of powers between the judiciary and other branches of government in that more power will flow to the judiciary'.[47]

---

43 Tim Murphy, 'Economic Inequality and the Constitution' in Murphy and Twomey (eds.), *Ireland's Evolving Constitution, 1937–1997: Collected Essays* (Oxford: Hart Publishing, 1998) 163 at p. 165.
44 Constitution Review Group, *Report of the Constitution Review Group* (Dublin: Stationery Office, 1996) at p. 235.
45 *Ibid.*
46 *Ibid.* at p. 236.
47 Gerard Hogan, 'Directive Principles, Socio-Economic Rights and the Constitution' (2001) 36 *Irish Jurist (ns)* 174 at p. 189.

The report of the CRG has been described as 'an extremely disappointing development for proponents of socio-economic rights' in Ireland.[48] It has also been criticised for presenting 'a serious misinterpretation of the nature of socio-economic rights' and for giving the (misleading) impression that 'there is no middle way between stating socio-economic rights in a totally open-ended manner, or excluding them from the Constitution altogether'.[49] Murphy also notes that the 'political issue' argument advanced by the CRG is 'totally undermined when they themselves suggest that judicial vindication of the right to life and the right to bodily integrity under the present Constitution offers the ultimate safeguard against the risk of anyone being allowed to fall below the minimum level of subsistence'.[50] Notwithstanding such criticisms, the view of the CRG has held sway, and there have been no serious initiatives to amend the Constitution to enshrine socio-economic rights.

With the prospect of socio-economic rights being added to the Constitution through amendment unlikely, some proponents of socio-economic rights have argued that such rights can receive protection through the doctrine of unenumerated rights. One of the leading proponents of this view is Gerry Whyte who argues that 'the Constitution, inspired as it is by the Judeo-Christian tradition, can be read as endorsing an understanding of rights which encompass socio-economic rights promoting social justice and participation in society and that those implied rights may be protected by Article 40.3'.[51] Whyte further argues that the Constitution envisages a role for the courts in the protection of such rights. As he puts it, 'one can infer a commitment to social inclusion from the text of the Constitution and . . . the most appropriate agency for policing that constitutional norm is the judiciary, given the failure, indeed at times egregious failure, of our political system to attend to the needs of marginalised minorities'.[52] Indeed following the recognition of the right to bodily integrity in *Ryan* '[a] number of attempts have been made to expand [this] negative right . . . into a positive right to a certain minimum [of] health care'.[53]

The most noteworthy of these was *State (C)* v. *Frawley*, in which a prisoner with severe mental health problems challenged his detention on the basis, *inter alia*, that the mental health treatment provided to him was inadequate for his needs, and thereby constituted a breach of his right to bodily integrity. In this case Finlay CJ was willing to accept in principle that the right to bodily

---

48 Nolan (n. 2) at p. 318.

49 Irish Commission for Justice and Peace, *Re-Righting the Constitution – The Case for New Social and Economic Rights: Housing, Health, Nutrition, Adequate Standard of Living* (Dublin: ICJP, 1998) at p. 11.

50 Murphy (n. 43) at p. 171; and see Gerry Whyte, 'Discerning the Philosophical Premises of the Report of the Constitution Review Group' (1998) 2 *Contemporary Issues in Irish Law and Politics* 216 at pp. 235–237.

51 Whyte (n. 2) at p. 49.

52 *Ibid.* at p. 4.

53 Oran Doyle, *Constitutional Law: Text, Cases and Materials* (Dublin: Clarus Press, 2008) at p. 124.

integrity could, in some circumstances, impose positive obligations on the state, holding that he saw 'no reason why the principle should not also operate to prevent an act or mission of the Executive which, without justification, would expose the health of a person to risk or danger'.[54] However, on the facts the Chief Justice held that the medical and psychiatric treatment, such as it was, provided to the applicant was reasonable in all of the circumstances. Significantly he also held that 'it is not the function of the Court to recommend to the Executive what is desirable or to fix the priorities of its health and welfare policy'.[55] The judgment in *Frawley*, thus, represents both the limited promise of Article 40.3 for the protection of socio-economic rights, and the fundamental limitations of this approach.

And while courts have since indicated, albeit intermittently, a willingness to recognise positive obligations to provide either appropriate accommodation[56] or shelter and care by those with exceptional needs as flowing from the right to bodily integrity,[57] the recent decline in fortunes of the doctrine of unenumerated rights[58] and the Supreme Court's most recent authoritative pronouncements on socio-economic rights (which is discussed below), make the recognition of such rights unlikely. Oran Doyle's characterisation of the decision in *Frawley* as reflecting 'the general reluctance of the courts to become overly involved in the enforcement of positive rights that carry resource implications',[59] would be likely to hold true for any case seeking judicial recognition of unenumerated socio-economic rights.

For the sake of completeness it is also worth mentioning here an argument that has recently been advanced by Rory O'Connell. Cognisant of the general judicial reluctance to recognise and enforce socio-economic rights, O'Connell argues that the guarantee of equality in Article 40.1 of the Constitution may provide a 'fruitful avenue' through which to achieve some form of protection for socio-economic rights, in circumstances where the courts are reluctant to engage directly with socio-economic rights *qua* rights.[60] While O'Connell advances this argument tentatively, it is submitted that given the Irish courts' traditional interpretation of the equality guarantee as a generally limited provision,[61] and the general conservatism of the courts,[62] any such expansive

---

54 [1976] IR 365 at p. 373.

55 *Ibid.*

56 See *O'Brien* v. *Wicklow UDC*, unreported High Court judgment of 10 June 1994.

57 *Re Article 26 and the Health (Amendment) (No. 2) Bill, 2004* [2005] 1 IR 105 at p. 166.

58 See n. 42.

59 Doyle (n. 53) at p. 125.

60 See O'Connell (n. 25) at p. 345.

61 See Hogan and Whyte (n. 9) at p. 1324, who note that the 'jurisprudence on the guarantee of equality in the Irish Constitution is remarkably underdeveloped'; and Oran Doyle's observation that 'Article 40.1 was meant to guarantee civil and political equality, not social equality . . . Although the Constitution did not preclude social equality, it contained no mandate to that effect, leaving the matter to the decision of future legislatures' (*Constitutional Equality Law* (Dublin: Thomson Round Hall, 2004) at p. 65).

62 See Murphy (n. 43) at p. 179.

reading of Article 40.1 is highly unlikely, at least in the short to medium term. Furthermore, even if some headway were to be made along these lines, experiences elsewhere show that it is a very limited form of protection for socio-economic rights, as it concerns only non-discriminatory provision of social benefits when the state chooses to provide them, not where the state omits to provide any such benefits, which is quite often the primary concern of the most vulnerable.[63]

6.1.4 The right to education

It is, then, a rather gloomy story. The various avenues for advancing socio-economic rights claims appear to be foreclosed or exhausted. However, notwith-standing the general exclusion of socio-economic rights from the Constitution, one such right did manage to 'escape into the hard text',[64] namely the right to free primary education contained in Article 42.4, which provides that:

> The State shall provide for free primary education and shall endeavour to supplement and give reasonable aid to private and corporate educational initiative, and, when the public good requires it, provide other educational facilities or institutions with due regard, however, for the rights of parents, especially in the matter of religious and moral formation.

It, thus, confers a substantive socio-economic right on all children and, by implication, a concomitant positive obligation on the state to realise this right. And while, as Quinn notes, recognition of this right in the Constitution has more to do with a desire to copper-fasten the historic agreement between the state and the main religious bodies, whereby the state would fund education but the religious orders would provide it, than with a substantive commitment to the egalitarian right of education for all, it nonetheless provides an explicit basis for claiming a socio-economic right under the Constitution.[65]

The first case of note to address the nature of the right to education was the *Ryan* case, in which O'Dálaigh CJ, disagreeing with the narrower approach of Kenny J. in the High Court, held that 'Education essentially is the teaching and training of a child to make the best possible use of his inherent and potential

---

63 See for example the limitations of the equality guarantee discussed in the Canadian context in Chapter 5, in particular the case of *Auton (Guardian* ad litem *of)* v. *British Columbia (Attorney General)* [2004] 3 SCR 657. It should also be noted that even if an equality-based argument were to succeed in expanding the number of potential beneficiaries for a particular social service or benefit, there is the ever present danger that the state will respond by 'levelling down' and offsetting any additional costs by providing a wider pool of people with substantially reduced benefits, as indeed happened in the case of *Hyland* v. *Minister for Social Welfare* [1989] IR 624; I am grateful to Gerry Whyte for bringing this point to my attention.

64 Quinn (n. 2) at p. 49.

65 *Ibid.*

capacities, physical, mental and moral'.[66] Drawing on this expansive understanding O'Hanlon J., in the subsequent case of *O'Donoghue* v. *Minister for Health*, held that the right to education extended to the needs of severely disabled children, and was thus concerned with allowing children make the most of their inherent and potential capacities 'however limited those capacities may be'.[67] In that case O'Hanlon J. rejected the state's argument that severely disabled children were 'uneducable' and, therefore, did not attract the benefits of Article 42.4. Instead, the learned judge found that the state had failed in its duty to provide adequate educational facilities for children with autism. The significance of the *O'Donoghue* case was that it confirmed, beyond any doubt, that the state's obligation to provide for education extended to severely disabled children, a group which had been systematically neglected by the state for decades. The judgment of O'Hanlon J. thus provided a firm basis for such children and their families to require the state to live up to its positive constitutional obligations.[68]

6.1.5 *Rights of 'at risk' children*

Of equal significance in the context of a discussion of socio-economic rights in Ireland are Articles 42.1 and Article 42.5, which state that:

> 1. The State acknowledges that the primary and natural educator of the child is the Family and guarantees to respect the inalienable right and duty of parents to provide, according to their means, for the religious and moral, intellectual, physical and social education of their children.
> . . .
> 5. In exceptional cases, where the parents for physical or moral reasons fail in their duty towards their children, the State as guardian of the common good, by appropriate means shall endeavour to supply the place of the parents, but always with due regard for the natural and imprescriptible rights of the child.

Read together these provisions have been held to establish a right on behalf of children whose parents, for one reason or another, have failed or are unable to care for them, to require the state to make adequate provision for their needs. The first case of note in this regard is *G* v. *An Bord Uchtala*, where O'Higgins CJ noted that:

> The child . . . has natural rights . . . Having been born, the child has the right to be fed and to live, to be reared and educated, to have the opportunity of working and of realising his/her full personality and dignity as

---

66 *Ryan* v. *Attorney General* [1965] IR 294 at p. 350.
67 [1996] 2 IR 20 at p. 62.
68 See Shivaun Quinlivan and Mary Keys, 'Official Indifference and Persistent Procrastination: An Analysis of *Sinnott*' (2002) 2(2) *Judicial Studies Institute Journal* 163.

a human being. These rights of the child (and others which I have not enumerated) must equally be protected and vindicated by the State. In exceptional cases the State, under the provisions of Article 42.5 of the Constitution, is given the duty, as guardian of the common good, to provide for a child born into a family where the parents fail in their duty towards that child for physical or moral reasons.[69]

Subsequently in *FN* v. *Minister for Education*, Geoghegan J. held that 'where there is a child with very special needs which cannot be provided by the parents or guardian, there is a constitutional obligation on the state under article 42 s.5 of the Constitution to cater for those needs in order to vindicate the constitutional rights of the child'.[70] Rejecting arguments that the costs of such facilities would be prohibitively expensive, Geoghegan J. declared that the state was under an obligation to provide suitable conditions and treatments for the applicant as soon as was reasonably practicable.

In *FN* Geoghegan J., on the basis of undertakings made to him by the respondents, had confined himself to issuing a declaratory order. However, the state failed to adhere to its undertakings and the applicants, and numerous similarly situated children, were left without sufficient facilities or institutions to meet their needs. This subsequently led to the judgment of Kelly J. in *DB* v. *Minister for Justice* ordering the relevant minister to build high-support units for the at risk child in the case.[71] In his judgment Kelly J., drawing on statements of the judicial role in cases such as *State (Quinn)* v. *Ryan* and *Crotty*, held that 'in carrying out its constitutional function of defending and vindicating personal rights, the Court must have available to it any power necessary to do so in an effective way. If that were not the case, this Court could not carry out the obligation imposed upon it to vindicate and defend such rights'.[72] On the basis of the excessive delays on the part of the various state bodies in complying with the judgment in *FN*, Kelly J. found that it was appropriate in the present case to grant a mandatory order requiring the relevant minister to build and maintain facilities to care for the applicant and other similarly situated children. Kelly J. concluded that it was 'regrettable that this course has to be adopted. I am, however, satisfied that the Court could not keep faith, either with its own obligations under the Constitution or with the minors with whose welfare it is concerned, unless intervention is made now'.[73]

While Blathna Ruane argues that in making these orders Kelly J. was 'drawing on longstanding jurisprudence dealing with the wide powers of the courts to enforces constitutional rights',[74] Gerard Quinn argued that, in truth,

69 [1980] IR 32 at pp. 55–56.
70 [1995] 1 IR 409 at p. 416.
71 [1999] 1 IR 29.
72 *DB* at p. 40.
73 *DB* at p. 45.
74 Blathna Ruane, 'The Separation of Powers and the Grant of Mandatory Orders to Enforce Constitutional Rights' (2000) 5 *Bar Review* 416 at p. 418.

the approach adopted by Kelly J. in *DB* was 'a revolutionary step' in terms of the vindication of the rights of marginalised and excluded children.[75] Rather presciently Quinn also noted that if this order, or another such order, were to be appealed to the Supreme Court:

> The main question to be decided there would be the calibration of the separation of powers with the raw jurisdiction claimed by the courts over education. The Supreme Court could either stick to the text (in which case the activism, though it carries the judiciary deeper into territory that is generally the prerogative of the Executive, is fully justified) or carve out some 'political question' exception based on a general theory of the separation of powers.[76]

As we will see in the next section, in two cases in which such orders were appealed a majority of the Supreme Court opted to embrace the latter option.

6.2 The rejection of socio-economic rights in Ireland

In 2001 the Irish Supreme Court delivered two of the most significant recent judgments in Irish constitutional jurisprudence: *Sinnott* v. *Minister for Education* and *TD* v. *Minister for Education*. The cases dealt, respectively, with the state's obligation to provide education for severely disabled people;[77] and the state's obligation to provide for the needs of 'at risk' children, whose parents, for one reason or another, had failed to do so.[78] More broadly, however, these two cases were fundamentally about the extent to which the courts would enforce rights against the elected branches of government, where such enforcement imposed a positive obligation on the state to provide certain services. The two cases were, ultimately, about whether or not the Irish courts would protect socio-economic rights, and if so, in what way. In over-turning the respective High Court orders in both cases, the Irish Supreme Court sent out a clear message: the Irish Constitution was a charter of negative liberties, and socio-economic rights, although laudable aspirations, were not a matter for the courts, but, rather, should be left to the elected branches of government.[79] This section will examine the reasoning of the Supreme Court majorities in both cases, and of the respective High Court judgments, in so far as these judgments relate to: (i) recognition of socio-economic rights *qua* rights; and (ii) the appropriate judicial role under the Constitution. However, before addressing the two leading cases, we digress slightly to look at an earlier case which provided the foundation for the majority judgments in *Sinnott* and *TD*.

75 Quinn (n. 2) at p. 52.
76 *Ibid.* at p. 53.
77 *Sinnott* v. *Minister for Education* [2001] 2 IR 241.
78 *TD* v. *Minister for Education* [2001] 4 IR 545.
79 See Hogan and Whyte (n. 9) at p. 104; and Quinlivan and Keys (n. 68) at p. 183.

6.2.1 *O'Reilly* v. *Limerick Corporation*

Contemporary Irish jurisprudence on socio-economic rights cannot be fully appreciated without prior knowledge of the seminal judgment of Costello J. in the case of *O'Reilly* v. *Limerick Corporation*,[80] which can be considered 'as the origin of the contemporary and dominant approach of the Irish Supreme Court to socio-economic rights'.[81] The plaintiffs in this case were members of the Travelling community residing on an unofficial halting site in Limerick City. In the High Court it was accepted that the applicants had, for a substantial period of time, lived in conditions of considerable deprivation and squalor. The applicants sought: (i) a mandatory order, under the Housing Act 1966, directing the local authority to provide them with adequate, serviced halting sites; and (ii) compensation from the state for suffering, inconvenience and mental distress which they had heretofore endured, on the basis that the conditions which they were required to endure amounted to a breach of their constitutional right to bodily integrity.

The plaintiffs' case failed on both grounds, but it is the second claim that is most significant for the purposes of the current discussion. The learned High Court judge characterised the plaintiffs' second claim in the following terms: 'what is involved in the plaintiffs' case is an assertion that the State has a duty to provide them with the resources and services they lack and the adjudication the court is asked to make is that the State has failed in that duty and to award damages because of it'.[82] Costello J. noted that such a claim raised a question about the Court's jurisdiction, which, essentially, was 'can the courts with constitutional propriety adjudicate on an allegation that the organs of Government responsible for the distribution of the nation's wealth have improperly exercised their powers? Or would such an adjudication be an infringement by the courts of the role which the Constitution has conferred on them?'.[83]

In finding that the courts could not engage in such an exercise Costello J. established an important general principle, which marked the beginning of 'an increased sophistication in the manner by which the judiciary view their relationship with the other branches of government'.[84] Costello J. began by highlighting the traditional Aristotelian distinction between commutative and distributive justice, the former being concerned with the relationships between individuals and what was owed from one person to another, while that latter was concerned with the distribution of a community's shared resources. For Costello J. commutative justice was appropriately the concern of the courts, while the distribution of the nation's wealth was appropriately a matter for the elected branches of government. Furthermore, Costello J. held that this

80 [1989] ILRM 181.
81 Nolan (n. 2) at p. 301.
82 *O'Reilly* at p. 193.
83 *O'Reilly* at p. 193.
84 Raymond Byrne and William Binchy, *Annual Review of Irish Law 1988* (Dublin: Thomson Round Hall, 1989) at p. 115.

distinction correlated with the text and scheme of the Irish Constitution.[85]
Setting off from this Aristotelian premise Costello J. held that:

> It is the Oireachtas or officials acting under the authority of the Oireachtas
> which under the Constitution determine the amount of the community's
> wealth which is to be raised by taxation and used for common purposes and
> the Oireachtas or officials acting on its authority determine how the nation's
> wealth is to be distributed and allotted. The courts' constitutional function
> is to administer justice but I do not think that by exercising the suggested
> supervisory role it could be said that a court was administering justice as
> contemplated in the Constitution. What could be involved in the exercise
> of the suggested jurisdiction would be the imposition by the court of its
> view that there had been an unfair distribution of national resources. To
> arrive at such a conclusion it would have to make an assessment of the
> validity of the many competing claims on those resources, the correct
> priority to be given to them and the financial implications of the plaintiffs'
> claim . . . In exercising this function the court would not be administering
> justice as it does when determining an issue relating to commutative justice
> but it would be engaged in an entirely different exercise, namely, an adju-
> dication on the fairness or otherwise of the manner in which other organs
> of State had administered public resources. Apart from the fact that mem-
> bers of the judiciary have no special qualification to undertake such a
> function, the manner in which justice is administered in the courts, that is
> on a case by case basis, make them a wholly inappropriate institution for
> the fulfilment of the suggested role. I cannot construe the Constitution as
> conferring it on them.[86]

He therefore concluded that for the applicants' claim to succeed it should, to
comply with the Constitution, 'be advanced in Leinster House rather than in
the Four Courts'.[87]

Whyte criticises the judgment of Costello J. on a number of grounds: (i)
first on the basis that the commutative–distributive justice divide articulated
by Costello J. is by no means watertight; (ii) second because based on various
provision of the Constitution, for example Article 42, it is questionable 'whether
the Constitution does erect an impenetrable barrier between the courts and
issues of distributive justice';[88] and (iii) because in Whyte's view 'the Irish

---

85 *O'Reilly* at p. 194.
86 *O'Reilly* at p. 195.
87 *O'Reilly* at p. 195, that is to say 'be advanced in Parliament rather than in the High or Supreme Court'.
88 Whyte (n. 2) at p. 13; similarly Doyle (n. 53) at p. 375, notes: 'The difficulty with mapping the commutative/distributive justice divide onto a rigid separation of powers doctrine is highlighted by the number of enforceable constitutional obligations that have clear resource implications: the duty to provide for free primary education, the duty to provide an Irish translation of statutes, the duty to provide a residence for the President . . . In these

Constitution, partly inspired as it is by the Judeo-Christian tradition, does provide, both explicitly and implicitly, for the protection of socio-economic rights and that such rights are judicially enforceable', albeit that turning to the courts should, ideally, be a last resort.[89] Conor O'Mahony is also critical of the judgment; he argues that the:

> difficulty with *O'Reilly* is not so much that Costello J's analysis is flawed, but that it is unsuitable for application to cases where the State has failed to vindicate a citizen's constitutional right to education. Such cases clearly fall to be classified as commutative/rectificatory justice as they involve a wrong in the form of a breach of a constitutional right of a citizen; any remedy granted is aimed towards rectifying the wrong committed by the State. Of course, such a remedy will usually involve, as a knock on effect, the distribution of public resources; it is, however, merely a secondary symptom of the case, as is the distribution of public resources stemming from an award of damages in a case where a servant of the State commits a tort.[90]

For O'Mahony it is also significant that Costello J. subsequently resiled from the position he adopted in *O'Reilly*, in a later case which also concerned Travellers' rights.[91] For O'Mahony this 'almost complete u-turn',[92] further undermines the judgment of Costello J. in *O'Reilly*. Regardless of these criticisms and Costello J's volte-face, the *O'Reilly* approach was subsequently approved in the Supreme Court,[93] and, as we will now see, was further raised to canonical status by the Supreme Court in the *Sinnott* and *TD* cases.

6.2.2 *Sinnott v. Minister for Education*

The applicant in the *Sinnott* case was a young autistic man who, for the better part of his life, had not received an education sufficient to meet his needs. Relying on the bourgeoning body of education cases discussed above, the applicant claimed that the failure of the state to provide him with educational facilities and support violated his rights under Article 42 of the Constitution. In the High Court Barr J. found in favour of the applicant and made a detailed order requiring the state to, *inter alia*, provide appropriate educational facilities for Mr Sinnott for as long as he might benefit from them. The state appealed

circumstances it is difficult to see why a particular class of social rights should be singled out for special attention (or lack of attention) by the courts'.

89 Whyte (n. 2) at p. 14.
90 Conor O'Mahony, 'Education, Remedies and the Separation of Powers' (2002) 24 *Dublin University Law Journal* 57 at p. 76.
91 See *O'Brien* v. *Wicklow UDC*, unreported High Court judgment of 10 June 1994.
92 O'Mahony (n. 90) at p. 75.
93 See *MhicMathuna* v. *Attorney General* [1995] 1 IR 484.

against the decision of Barr J. In the Supreme Court the state did not dispute that it had failed to vindicate Mr Sinnott's constitutional rights up to the age of 18; however the state was committed to providing Mr Sinnott with the appropriate educational services and facilities for the foreseeable future, albeit on an *ex gratia* basis. Thus, the primary issue on appeal was the extent of the right to free primary education contained in Article 42.2 of the Constitution and whether or not it was a right for life, which was the clear implication of Barr J.'s judgment, or if it only extended to children up to the age of 18.

Should the Supreme Court find against the appellants there would have arisen an ancillary issue as to whether or not the courts had the power to make orders of the sort which Barr J. made in the High Court, although of course if the Court found in favour of the appellants this issue would logically fall moot and thus not require determination by the Court. In any event a majority of the Supreme Court came to the conclusion that on a proper construction of the Constitution, the guarantee of free primary education in Article 42.2 only extended to children up to the age of 18 and not to all citizens regardless of age.[94] Having reached this conclusion the Court was under no obligation to deal with the issue of the courts powers vis-à-vis the elected branches of government.

Nonetheless, a number of members of the majority saw fit to comment on the matter and it is in these comments that we get the first glimpse of the separation-of-powers concerns which the majority of the Court would raise against socio-economic rights claims. In particular Hardiman J., with whom Keane CJ concurred, offered a trenchant account of the separation of powers. After stating the importance of the separation of powers under the Constitution and in particular the independent role of the courts protected by it, Hardiman J. argued that:

> It appears to me that the courts must be equally concerned not to infringe upon the proper prerogatives and area of operations of the other branches of government. The functions of these branches, like those of the courts, are themselves of constitutional origin and constitutionally defined. In my view, the foregoing principles underlie the essential distinction drawn by Costello J. between issues which can be pursued in the Four Courts and issues which, to comply with the Constitution, must be pursued in Leinster House. It is easy to imagine a particular case in which a party might think, and might convince a judge, that a particular act or omission of the legislature or executive was clearly wrong and that another course of action (outlined perhaps in considerable detail in uncontradicted evidence) clearly right or at least preferable . . . But even if a court were quite satisfied that this situation existed, that fact alone would not justify it in purporting to

---

94 For detailed analysis of this aspect of the judgment, see Oran Doyle, 'The Duration of Primary Education: Judicial Constraint in Constitutional Interpretation' (2002) 10 *Irish Student Law Review* 222; and Fergus Ryan, 'Disability and the Right to Education: Defining the Constitutional "Child"' (2002) 24 *Dublin University Law Journal* 96.

take a decision properly within the remit of the legislature or the executive. I reiterate that it is an independent constitutional value, essential to the maintenance of parliamentary democracy, that the legislature and the executive retain their proper independence in their respective spheres of action. In these spheres, the executive is answerable to Dáil Éireann and the members of the legislature are answerable to the electorate.[95]

Hardiman J. held that while the courts retained the power to issue mandatory orders to the executive in the context of a 'constitutional meltdown' – where the state consciously disregarded its constitutional obligations and court orders – the retention of such a power to meet such an extreme example did not justify its exercise in any other circumstances.[96] From this it is clear the some members of the Court were uncomfortable with the notion of the courts enforcing positive obligations against the elected branches of government. However, because of the facts of the case it was not something which was spelled out definitively.

6.2.3 *TD v. Minister for Education*

In the subsequent case of *TD* the majority of the Supreme Court more explicitly conflated the issue of the separation of powers with their opposition to the constitutional protection of socio-economic rights. The applicant in *TD* was a minor with behavioural problems in need of special care and who, due to a combination of factors, was not receiving appropriate support from the relevant state agencies. The applicant claimed that he had a right, derived from Article 42.5 of the Constitution, to be provided with appropriate accommodation, education and maintenance by the state. Kelly J. in the High Court found in favour of the applicant and made a mandatory order requiring the Ministers for Education, Health and Children to take all steps necessary to build and maintain ten high-support units to meet the needs of the applicant and other similarly situated minors.[97] The state appealed on the basis that the order of Kelly J. violated the separation of powers.

A majority of the Supreme Court reversed Kelly J.'s holding and from these majority opinions two key points emerge: (i) the Constitution (with the exception of primary education) does not and should not protect socio-economic rights; and (ii) even where the Constitution explicitly confers a right the courts should only ever seek to enforce those rights through mandatory orders in the most extreme of cases. As to the first of these points Keane CJ expressed his dissatisfaction with the doctrine of unenumerated rights as presently constituted,

---

95 *Sinnott* at pp. 707–708.
96 *Sinnott* at p. 710.
97 Commenting on the High Court judgment, Blathna Ruane (n. 74) at p. 416, notes that 'The cumulative effect of [the High Court orders was] to oblige the State to make heavy expenditure within specific time frames, on specifically targeted projects, in accordance with court orders'.

before going on to note that even if the current practice were to endure he would 'have the gravest doubts as to whether or not the courts *at any stage* should assume the function of declaring what are today frequently described as "socio-economic rights" to be unenumerated rights guaranteed by Article 40',[98] although the Chief Justice refrained from giving a definitive ruling on this matter, as it was not directly at issue in the case. It should be said that Keane CJ was wrong to characterise the applicants' claim in this case as the assertion of a novel right under Article 40.3,[99] as the rights relied on by the applicant were necessarily implied in Articles 42.1 and 42.5.[100]

In a similar vein Murphy J. was not open to the idea of socio-economic rights being recognised in the Constitution. As he put it:

> With the exception of the provisions dealing with education, the personal rights identified in the Constitution all lie in the civil and political rather than the economic sphere. These are indeed important rights which were won for citizens in different societies over a period of centuries often in the face of bitter opposition. Whilst limited poor law relief or workhouse accommodation has existed in this and neighbouring jurisdictions for many years, the demand for a coherent system of socio-economic rights, and more particularly the acceptance of that demand, does not appear to have emerged until the widespread acceptance of socialist doctrines following the Second World War, resulting in the now generally accepted concept of the welfare state. The absence of any express reference to accommodation, medical treatment or social welfare of any description as a constitutional right in the Constitution as enacted, is a matter of significance. The failure to correct that omission in any of the 24 referenda which have taken place since then would suggest a conscious decision to withhold from rights, which are now widely conferred by appropriate legislation, the status of constitutionality in the sense of being rights conferred or recognised by the Constitution.[101]

He noted that while there may well be a number of reasons as to why socio-economic rights were not included in the Constitution, or subsequently added to it, chief among them must have been the apprehension that the entrenchment of such rights would necessarily 'involve . . . a radical departure from the

---

98 [2001] 4 IR 259 at p. 282 (emphasis added).
99 *TD* at p. 279.
100 As Byrne and Binchy note, a criticism of *Sinnott* and *TD* is that in both of the cases the majority failed to distinguish 'between a claim based on a theory of socio-economic rights as opposed to one based on the rights identified expressly or protected and vindicated implicitly by the Constitution . . . the error lies in the notion that the plaintiffs' case sought recognition for some new constitutional right or theory never previously recognised by the courts. On the contrary, in both cases, the plaintiffs argued that the right to education, and not some new, previously unacknowledged, right, required the court to translate fine words into real protection' (Raymond Byrne and William Binchy (eds.), *Annual Review of Irish Law 2001* (Dublin: Thompson Round Hall, 2002) at p. 22).
101 *TD* at pp. 316–317.

principle requiring the separation of the powers of the courts from those of the legislature and the executive'.[102]

In terms of the relief granted in the case Hardiman J. again gave the leading judgment on the separation of powers. He began by stating that:

> If a judge considers that there has been a 'failure of the legislature and the executive' . . . in some particular area of constitutionally significant policy, can he or she on that account 'attempt to fill the vacuum' by ordering either of those bodies to implement a particular policy? If this is possible, it may gratify those who agree with the judge that there has been a failure, and who find the solution which he or she imposes acceptable. But it would represent an enormous increase in the power of an unelected judiciary at the expense of the politically accountable branches of government. It would attribute to the judiciary a paramountcy over the other branches in the form of a residual supervisory governmental power which, once asserted and exercised, would certainly be appealed to again and again. This paramountcy . . . would represent a very significant change in our constitutional order, not easily reversed.[103]

More directly on the question of socio-economic rights and the appropriate role of the courts in enforcing them Hardiman J. held that:

> It would of course be possible by constitutional amendment or by the adoption of an entirely new constitution, to vest the courts with powers and responsibilities in social, economic and other areas which are presently the preserve of the other organs of government. This, perhaps, would give immediate satisfaction to those who thought the courts more likely to adopt their views of the merits of certain social or economic questions than the legislature or executive. But it would vest responsibility in these areas in a body without special qualifications to discharge it which, if its views fell into disfavour, would not easily be replaced by another more congenial. It would also render technical and legalistic discussions, which should properly be conducted in quite a different manner.[104]

It is clear from these comments that Hardiman J's view of the separation of powers is a very rigidly compartmentalised and, in many respects, zero-sum one. Hardiman J. also seems to view the judicial role as being bounded by this restrictive reading of the separation of powers, even where constitutional rights have been breached.

Murray J. agreed that the courts were an 'inappropriate [institution] to make an order directing how national policy should be implemented . . . Adopting

---

102 *TD* at p. 317.
103 *TD* at p. 339.
104 *TD* at p. 358.

a policy or a programme and deciding to implement it is a core function of the Executive. It is not for the courts to decide policy or to implement it'.[105] And he held that if the order made in the High Court were to be upheld it would 'introduce a degree of judicial hegemony in the domain of policy formulation and implementation so as to disturb the balance of powers between the three great organs of state'.[106] He thus held that the order in question breached the separation of powers and was unconstitutional. However, Murray J., with whom Hardiman J. agreed on this point, did not completely rule out the prospect of the courts ever making a mandatory order, although he did hold that it would only be in the most extreme circumstances:

> a mandatory order directing the executive to fulfil a legal obligation (without specifying the means or policy to be used in fulfilling the obligation) *in lieu* of a declaratory order as to the nature of its obligations could only be granted, if at all, in exceptional circumstances where an organ or agency of the State had disregarded its constitutional obligations in an exemplary fashion. In my view the phrase 'clear disregard' can only be understood to mean a conscious and deliberate decision by the organ of state to act in breach of its constitutional obligation to other parties, accompanied by bad faith or recklessness. A court would also have to be satisfied that the absence of good faith or the reckless disregard of rights would impinge on the observance by the State party concerned of any declaratory order made by the court.[107]

The net effect of Murray J's judgment in this respect is to reserve to the courts the power to make mandatory orders where, in essence, the defence of the constitutional order so requires. However, it must be said that the test articulated by Murray J. sets the bar so high for an applicant seeking meaningful judicial enforcement of her constitutional rights that it makes it 'very unlikely that future litigants will be able to obtain affirmative decrees against the organs of state'.[108]

In her dissent from the majority, Denham J. was at pains to stress that, contrary to a number of the judges in the majority, this case did not involve the assertion of a 'novel' right, but one which was well established.[109] On the

---

105 *TD* at p. 333.
106 *TD* at p. 335.
107 *TD* at p. 337.
108 Whyte (n. 2) at p. 359.
109 As Denham J. put it: 'There is a constitutional obligation on the respondents to vindicate the constitutional rights of each of the applicants. The relevant constitutional principles have been established and were not disputed on this appeal. The court in [*FN*] held that a child has a constitutional right to be fed and to live, to be reared and educated and to have the opportunity of working and realising his or her full potential and dignity as a human being and that those rights must be protected and vindicated by the State. In the situation of a child with very special needs, which could not be provided by his or her parents or guardian then there is a constitutional obligation on the State under Article 42.5 to make reasonable

separation of powers Denham J. noted that while the Constitution did establish a separation of powers it was 'not a strict division or distribution of power. It is not a doctrine applied rigidly in the Constitution. A framework for government is established which includes a functional separation of powers to independent organs of State. It is the separation and independence of the institutions which is important'.[110] In an implicit challenge to the rigid reliance on *O'Reilly* by the majority Denham J. also stressed that the 'expense of the case itself and its outcome may have profound and far reaching effects. Simply because a case affects a policy of an institution does not per se render it unconstitutional or bring it into conflict with the principle of the separation of powers'.[111] While accepting that there were both principled and pragmatic reasons as to why the courts should refrain from issuing mandatory orders, Denham J. nonetheless held that:

> It is clear from the case law that in rare and exceptional cases, to protect constitutional rights, a court may have a jurisdiction *and even a duty* to make a mandatory order against another branch of government. The separation of powers in the Constitution of Ireland *is not absolute*. It is a fundamental principle underlying the exercise of the powers of the basic institutions of the State and applied in a *functional manner*. It is a principle relevant to the three great organs of State – the legislature, the executive and the courts – which are independent institutions – and their dynamic relationship one with the other. However, the powers and duties of each organ of State extend across theoretical lines of separation and checks and balances established in the Constitution breach a rigid concept of the separation of powers. The doctrine of the separation of powers has to be balanced with the role given to the courts to guard constitutional rights.[112]

Denham J. concluded that on 'those very rare occasions when such a declaratory approach is not feasible then *the court has the power and indeed the duty and*

efforts to cater for those needs in order to vindicate the constitutional rights of the child. Secure accommodation, services and such arrangements as were necessary to meet the requirements of *FN* were held to be not so impractical or so prohibitively expensive as to come within any notional limitation of the State's constitutional obligations' (*TD* at pp. 295–296).

110 *TD* at pp. 298–299.

111 *TD* at p. 303; in a similar vein Paul Anthony McDermott argues that 'where a citizen's constitutional rights are being breached, be he a prisoner detained in poor conditions or a child living on the streets, the fact that a court order may involve the Government having to spend money to relieve the problem should never dissuade the court from intervening. It is a fact of life that the vindication of some constitutional rights costs money, money that a Government and a proportion of the public might rather see spent elsewhere. However the occasional loss of that choice is the price all citizens must pay for living under the protection of a written Constitution. The implications of non-intervention in such cases are widespread in terms of establishing a culture of effectively protected constitutional rights' ('The Separation of Powers and the Doctrine of Non-Justiciability' (2000) 35 *Irish Jurist (n.s.)* 280 at p. 303).

112 *TD* at p. 306 (emphasis added).

responsibility to uphold the Constitution and to vindicate constitutional rights. This is at the core of the duty and responsibility of the High and Supreme Courts of Ireland.[113] In light of the exceptional character of these cases, Denham J. was prepared to find that the making of a mandatory order was appropriate.

As is the case with any jurisdiction with a written constitution, the Supreme Court had a choice in *Sinnott* and *TD*.[114] As Whyte puts it, the understanding of the separation of powers adopted by the majority 'is not necessarily the only one open under the Constitution';[115] Whyte further argues that an alternative – and equally valid – conception of the separation of powers, which drew on the Christian democratic ethos in the Constitution, would justify both the recognition of socio-economic rights and a judicial role in enforcing them.[116] Similarly Blathna Ruane argues that in granting the mandatory orders in the High Court in *TD* Kelly J. was 'drawing on longstanding jurisprudence dealing with the power of the courts to enforce constitutional rights'.[117] Furthermore, she notes that Kelly J's judgment displayed a 'refusal by the court to be detoured from its constitutional function of the enforcement of constitutional rights on the grounds that an issue of policy might be involved in its decisions'.[118] Unfortunately, the majority of the court opted for a more rigid, formalistic conception of the separation of powers, and, substantively, for a vision of both the Constitution and the judicial role which is fundamentally inimical to the protection of socio-economic rights. Arguably in the view of the separation of powers preferred by the majority in *Sinnott* and *TD* the Court has inverted its proper role under the Constitution, with a rigid, formalistic conception of the separation of powers informing its understanding of the judicial duty to vindicate rights, rather than – as Denham J. would have preferred – the other way around.[119]

The principal implications of the Supreme Court judgments in *Sinnott* and *TD* are that it is 'very unlikely that future litigants will be able to obtain affirmative decrees against the organs of state',[120] and that the Supreme Court is 'extremely unlikely to accede to claims seeking constitutional protection for socio-economic rights'.[121] However, Whyte is highly critical of these

---

113 *TD* at p. 307 (emphasis added).

114 See Richard Fallon, 'How to Choose a Constitutional Theory' (1999) 87 *California Law Review* 535; as Whyte (n. 2) at p. 360 states the vision of the separation of powers adopted by the Supreme Court was by no means 'inevitable'.

115 Gerry Whyte, 'The Role of the Supreme Court in Our Democracy: A Response to Mr Justice Hardiman' (2006) 28 *Dublin University Law Journal* 1 at p. 4. This piece was written in response to the extra-judicial comments of Hardiman J., see Adrian Hardiman, 'The Role of the Supreme Court in Our Democracy' in Mulholland (ed.), *Political Choice and Democratic Freedom in Ireland* (Donegal, 2004) 32.

116 *Ibid.* at p. 7.

117 Ruane (n. 74) at p. 418.

118 *Ibid.* at p. 419.

119 Whyte (n. 2) at p. 22.

120 *Ibid.* at p. 359.

121 *Ibid.* at p. 360.

positions, based, as in his view they are, on an 'ideological' interpretation of the separation of powers which derived solely from 'the liberal democratic tradition of the common law' and ignores 'the fact that the Irish Constitution is not drawn exclusively from that liberal democratic tradition' but is also influenced very strongly by a version of Christian democracy which 'promotes the values of social inclusion and recognises socio-economic rights as indispensible to the common good'.[122] Allowing greater influence for this aspect of the Constitution's philosophical inspiration would, in Whyte's view, provide justification for a strong judicial role in enforcing socio-economic rights. While there is no doubt much merit in this critique, the reality is that the rigid and formalistic conception of the separation of powers by the Supreme Court in *Sinnott* and *TD* has, for all intents and purposes, denied adjudicative space for socio-economic rights claims under the Irish Constitution. Next we will survey the relevant Irish jurisprudence post-*Sinnott* and *TD* to see to what extent, if any, the position has changed.

6.3 Post-*Sinnott* and *TD*

Since *Sinnott* and *TD* the Irish courts have sent out somewhat mixed signals with respect to the protection of socio-economic rights under Irish constitutional law. However, the Supreme Court has yet to definitively rule on the matter again. Nonetheless, a number of *obiter* statements, in both the Supreme Court and High Court, are noteworthy. For example in *Cronin* v. *Minister for Education*,[123] Laffoy J. in the High Court accepted the applicants' argument, drawing on certain *dicta* of Hardiman J. in *Sinnott*,[124] that the constitutional difficulties in granting mandatory orders against the state carried less weight where what was sought was the enforcement of a statutory obligation. In this case, Laffoy J. granted an interlocutory mandatory injunction requiring the minister to provide the applicant, an autistic child whose educational needs were not being met, with specific educational facilities pending the full hearing of the case. For O'Mahony the decision in *Cronin* places a 'new slant' on the Supreme Court judgment in *TD*, and may serve to 'limit much of the damage' caused by this 'highly restrictive' judgment.[125] O'Mahony also argues that the decision in *Cronin* 'would seem to suggest that the true effect of the decision in *TD* is that individual plaintiffs can be awarded mandatory injunctions as long as the facilities which they require are already in place and have simply not been made available to the particular plaintiff'.[126]

---

122 *Ibid.* at p. 361.
123 [2004] 3 IR 205; discussed in Conor O'Mahony, 'A New Slant on Education Rights and Mandatory Injunctions' (2005) 27 *Dublin University Law Journal* 363.
124 *Sinnott* at pp. 711–712.
125 O'Mahony (n. 123) at p. 363.
126 *Ibid.* at p. 365; this view would certainly seem to find support in the judgment of Laffoy J., who held that in her judgment she was 'satisfied that granting a mandatory injunction does

Another hopeful sign was presented in *Re Article 26 and the Health (Amendment) (No. 2) Bill, 2004* – in which the Supreme Court declared repugnant to the Constitution proposed legislation which sought to retrospectively validate charges which had been unlawfully imposed on medical card holders in hospitals and nursing homes – where the Supreme Court per Murray CJ appeared to soften its position on socio-economic rights somewhat when it accepted that:

> In a discrete case, in particular circumstances, an issue may well arise as to the extent to which the normal discretion of the Oireachtas in the distribution or spending of public monies could be constrained by a constitutional obligation to provide shelter and maintenance for those with exceptional needs.[127]

Although the Court subsequently reasserted the primacy of the elected branches of government under the Constitution in relation to decisions concerning the allocation of resources, it held that such would not 'in itself be a justification for the failure of the State to protect or vindicate a constitutional right'.[128] And while in the instant case the Court held that the requirement to pay charges for inpatient care did not constitute a breach of such a subsistence right, it seemed, in principle, to accept the existence of such a right as a right.[129] Eoin O'Dell and Gerry Whyte argue, somewhat tentatively, that this judgment 'suggests that the present Supreme Court may yet see some role for the courts in the protection of implied socio-economic rights'.[130] Also of significance in this case is the fact that it was argued by government sources that paying back those affected by the illegal charging scheme may run to a cost of between €500 million and €1.2 billion, but the Supreme Court gave its judgment regardless of these resource implications.[131] On this point O'Dell and Whyte note that 'Judicial restraint was the dominant catch-cry of the Keane Supreme Court yet in the instant case, the Murray court struck down a proposed Bill dealing with public finances, an area in which the courts are traditionally very deferential towards legislative decisions'.[132]

However, in the subsequent education case of *F* v. *Minister for Education*, Smyth J. in the High Court reaffirmed the view that the allocation of resources,

---

not fall foul of [the Supreme Court decision in *TD*]. The relief granted is limited to the particular needs of the plaintiff and merely extends a programme which the first defendant has already sanctioned' (n. 123) at p. 215.

127 [2005] 1 IR 105 at p. 166.
128 *Health Amendment Case* at p. 167.
129 *Health Amendment Case* at p. 168.
130 Eoin O'Dell and Gerry Whyte, 'Is this a Country for Old Men and Women? – In Re Article 26 and the Health (Amendment) (No.2) Bill 2004' (2005) 27 *Dublin University Law Journal* 368 at p. 371.
131 Nolan (n. 2) at p. 314.
132 O'Dell and Whyte (n. 130) at p. 391.

even where the issue of vindicating constitutional rights was at issue, were 'questions related to distributive justice upon which the courts should refrain from embarking, but if enquiry is undertaken as a necessary last resort, upon which the court should do so with a great deal of self-restraint'.[133] In the subsequent case of *OA* v. *Minister for Justice*, Herbert J. expressed the conventional wisdom, post-*Sinnott* and *TD*, that it was doubtful that the guarantee of personal rights in Article 40.3 of the Constitution encompassed the protection of socio-economic rights.[134] In *Doherty* v. *South Dublin County Council*,[135] a case which involved a claim that the housing conditions of the applicants constituted a breach of their rights, Charleton J. accepted the argument that in certain circumstances the right to life could impose a positive obligation on the state, consistent with its financial and administrative commitments, to provide essential medical services to individuals who could not afford to provide them for themselves.[136] However, the learned judge went on to reaffirm the *Sinnott–TD* orthodoxy, in noting that:

> Whether welfare is provided, and at what level, and in what particular circumstances, is essentially a matter of political decision . . . Like a family, the resources of any nation are limited and it is a matter for political and executive decision as to what resources should be committed to what problems and with what priority. A breach of legislation prescribing such an allocation, as in housing, calls for judicial intervention. Where, however, a plea is made that the court should declare the absence of welfare support to be wrong in a particular situation of itself, the applicant should show a complete inability to exercise a human right from his or her own means and a serious situation that has set the right at nought with the prospect of serious long term harm. Any proposed intervention by the court should take into account that it is the responsibility of the legislature and executive to decide the allocation of resources and the priorities applied by them.[137]

Thus, while the judge in *Doherty* affirms the separation-of-powers concerns which influenced the Supreme Court in *Sinnott* and *TD*, he nonetheless leaves open the possibility of some aspect of socio-economic rights being recognised and enforced.

In the subsequent case of *O'Donnell* v. *South Dublin County Council*,[138] Laffoy J. found that the failure of a local housing authority to provide a Traveller family with an additional, accessible and serviced mobile home so that they could care for their severely disabled children breached their right to private and family

---

133 [2007] IEHC 36.
134 [2007] 1 ILRM 58 at p. 64.
135 [2007] 2 IR 696.
136 [2007] 2 IR 696 at p. 717.
137 [2007] 2 IR 696 at p. 723.
138 [2007] IEHC 204.

life under Article 8 of the European Convention on Human Rights (ECHR) (which had been transposed into Ireland's law by the European Convention on Human Rights Act 2003). However, while this was a significant development, Laffoy J., quoting from the majority in *TD*, accepted that the applicants could not ground a constitutional right to be provided with accommodation of a certain quality on the basis of Article 40.3 of the Constitution. Interestingly in this case Laffoy J. also stressed that:

> This is not a case which is based on an assertion that the State or any of its organs has a positive obligation to make certain provision for every traveller family, for instance, that the State should legislate or have an administrative scheme to provide two de luxe mobile homes for every traveller family. This case is about the particular circumstances of one family, which has three severely disabled members, two of whom were minors when these proceedings started, who to the knowledge of the defendant have been living in unacceptable conditions since 2005 and whose plight is not going to be alleviated until August, 2008 at the earliest, if it will be then.

And while this was not concerned with a constitutionally asserted right, it nonetheless lends some weight to the view of O'Mahony, that the courts may be willing to intervene in cases with socio-economic rights dimensions, where the issues can be individuated.

We should not, however, get too carried away with these judgments, as the Supreme Court – with the exception of the rather exceptional circumstances in the *Health Amendment* case – has, in so far as it has been directly confronted with the issues, reasserted both the view of the limited role of the courts and of the fundamentally negative character of the rights protection by the Constitution. For example in a recent case, dealing with the vicarious liability of the state for abuse which took place at state-funded schools, Hardiman J. trenchantly reasserted the view of the separation of powers being demarcated along a commutative–distributive justice divide, and his view that under the Constitution the courts were firmly confined to the former.[139] Equally significant is the recent Supreme Court decision in *Magee* v. *Farrell*, where Finnegan J. for a unanimous Court reasserted the essentially negative character of the rights protected by the Constitution, when he held that the Constitution did not guarantee a right to civil legal aid:

> The jurisprudence of this court . . . is clear. A right to legal representation does not carry with it a right to State funded legal aid. Where, however, the liberty of the individual is in issue before the Criminal Courts there is an entitlement to State funded legal aid.[140]

139 See *O'Keefe* v. *Hickey* [2009] 2 IR 302 at p. 342.
140 [2009] IESC 60.

This essentially negative vision of the rights protected by the Constitution taken with the fact that a number of judgments have, ostensibly, narrowed the extent of the state's obligation with respect to providing education for children with special educational needs,[141] indicates that the expurgation of socio-economic rights from the Constitution in *Sinnott* and *TD* still very much holds sway.

6.4 Conclusion

Following a survey of the Irish experience Aoife Nolan concludes that a number of recent developments, such as the transposition of the ECHR into Irish law at a sub-constitutional level and the flexibility shown in the *Health Amendment* case 'suggest that the debate on judicial enforceability of socio-economic rights in Ireland has not been foreclosed by the decisions in *TD* and *Sinnott*'.[142] In a similar vein Rory O'Connell argues that 'the decisions in *Sinnott* and *TD* are . . . decisions for a State appealing successfully against an order for the protection of socio-economic rights. They are not unqualified rejections of socio-economic rights'.[143] However, while the debate may not be completely closed, the actual likelihood of socio-economic rights being salvaged from the Constitution is very slim;[144] as Doyle notes following *Sinnott* and *TD*, 'it is almost inconceivable that the courts will enumerate any socio-economic rights'[145] under the Constitution. Furthermore, it may well be doubted that the rigid view of the separation of powers, with concomitant limited role for the courts, preferred by the majority in these cases will be the 'final word' on the matter.[146] It is – at least for the foreseeable future – the dominant view and, as the post-*Sinnott* and *TD* cases show, it is the view preferred by the courts since then.

There therefore appears to be little likelihood of socio-economic rights being further recognised and enforced at a constitutional level in Ireland in the fore-seeable future. It may well be that this was always likely to be the case given the generally negative character of the Constitution and the elite and neo-liberalist leanings of the judiciary. As Tim Murphy puts it:

> The essential reason, why economic rights are not afforded constitutional protection in Ireland is because the state and its institutions (including the

---

141 See, for example, *O'Carolan* v. *Minister for Education* [2005] IEHC 296; *O'C* v. *Minister for Education* [2007] IEHC 170; and *McD* v. *Minister for Education* [2008] IEHC 265. See also the discussion of *O'Carolan* in Conor O'Mahony, 'The Right to Education and "Constitutionally Appropriate" Provision' (2006) 28 *Dublin University Law Journal* 422.

142 Nolan (n. 2) at p. 319.

143 O'Connell (n. 60) at p. 333.

144 As Hogan and Whyte (n. 9) at p. 122 note, the implications of *Sinnott* and *TD* is a clear statement that 'the present Supreme Court does not consider the resolution of socio-economic issues having implications for public spending to fall within the judicial sphere of operations'.

145 Doyle (n. 53) at p. 108.

146 See Byrne and Binchy (n. 100) at p. 109.

judiciary and virtually all of the political parties) are committed to a form of liberal–capitalist economic system which tacitly incorporates [inequality and poverty] . . . Any movement to a situation where substantive economic rights were recognised and protected would have at least the *potential* to undermine, ideologically and perhaps practically as well, that mode of production.[147]

And while Murphy accepts the influence of Christian democracy in the Constitution, he stresses that 'this has never, in the text or through its inter-pretation, extended to the recognition of economic rights'.[148] It seems then that invocation of the 'other' tradition which influenced the drafters of the Irish Constitution, Catholic social teaching, is unlikely to act as a counter to the position adopted by the majority in *Sinnott* and *TD*. It could also be doubted whether such invocation would necessarily be acceptable in modern, secular Ireland,[149] or, as experience to date demonstrates, efficacious from the perspec-tive of socio-economic rights claimants. In the final analysis, then, the Irish experience of adjudicating on socio-economic rights is significant, if for no other reason than that the Supreme Court's categorical rejection of socio-economic rights on the basis of a rigid and formalistic conception of the separation of powers is a salutary lesson in how the judicial enforcement of socio-economic rights should not be approached. In view of this rigid position, we turn in the next chapter to the positive exercise of articulating a framework for judicial enforcement of socio-economic rights which does not run afoul of reasonable conceptions of the separation of powers.

147 Murphy (n. 43) at p. 179.
148 *Ibid.*
149 See Quinn (n. 5) at p. 286.

7 A model adjudicative framework

The foregoing chapters serve to illustrate two core points. The first, and fundamental point, is that '[at] the heart of the . . . debate regarding . . . the constitutional protection of socio-economic rights lies the issue of the proper role of the courts and judicial review'.[1] The core of the argument, then, against the recognition and enforcement of socio-economic rights is framed – in some cases more directly than others – in the language of the separation of powers, which is seen 'as a reason unto itself for not rendering [socio-economic rights] constitutionally justiciable'.[2] However, the second key point which emerges from the foregoing discussions is that while the concerns raised by the separation-of-powers arguments against the constitutional entrenchment and judicial enforcement of socio-economic rights 'are legitimate and cogent, they are not dispositive'.[3] As Paul Craig, writing in a different context, puts it, 'the mere invocation of the "separation of powers" does not in and of itself resolve the relationship between the courts, the legislature and the executive'.[4]

The implication of Craig's observation is that while the separation of powers can provide a frame of reference for discussing the relationship between the courts and the elected branches of government, it cannot, simply by its invocation,

---

1 Gerard Hogan, 'Directive Principles, Socio-Economic Rights and the Constitution' (2001) 36 *Irish Jurist (n.s.)* 174 at p. 187; in a similar vein Yash Ghai argues that in the context of the ongoing debate about the protection of socio-economic rights 'the central question is one of balance, proportion, strategy, and synergy between different institutions and procedures established for the promotion and protection of rights' ('Introduction' in Ghai and Cottrell (eds.), *Economic, Social and Cultural Rights in Practice* (London: INTERIGHTS, 2004) 1 at p. 3).
2 Craig Scott and Patrick Macklem, 'Constitutional Ropes of Sand or Justiciable Guarantees? Social Rights in a New South African Constitution' (1992) 141 *University of Pennsylvania Law Review* 1 at p. 41.
3 Gerard Quinn, 'Rethinking the Nature of Social, Economic and Cultural Rights in the Irish Legal Order' in Costello (ed.), *Fundamental Social Rights: Current European Legal Protection and the Challenge of the EU Charter of Fundamental Rights* (Dublin: Irish Centre for European Law, 2001) 35 at p. 37.
4 Paul Craig, 'Fundamental Principles of Administrative Law in Relation to Basic Principles of Constitutional Law' in Feldman (ed.), *English Public Law* (2nd edn, Oxford: Oxford University Press, 2009) 593 at p. 608.

resolve any perceived tensions or conflicts. This, then, leads on to another point: in response to the concerns raised by opponents of constitutionally protected socio-economic rights, it 'is entirely possible to think of a different kind of [judicial role] – one that informs political choice rather than determines it'.[5] That being so, this penultimate chapter is concerned with articulating a model adjudicative framework, which makes space for the courts to play a role in the vindication of socio-economic rights, while at the same time respecting and maintaining the delicate balance between the respective branches of government.

This chapter begins with a brief 'back to basics' excursion into the historical rationale(s) for the doctrine of the separation of powers, before then showing how this has evolved over time. Understanding that the separation of powers is not static, but rather a fluid and contingent concept, then opens the way to analyse some of the recent comparative constitutional scholarship on alternative forms of judicial review. Finally, then, the bulk of this chapter is devoted to articulating a model (or ideal) adjudicative framework for courts to enforce socio-economic rights, while respecting the primacy of the elected branches of government.[6] This approach pays attention to three critical issues: (i) first it articulates an overarching normative framework through which we should view the relationship between the different branches of government (a reimagining of the separation of powers) in the context of a commitment to socio-economic rights; (ii) then the question of the appropriate standard of review for courts dealing with socio-economic rights claims is addressed; and (iii) finally the crucial issue of remedies in socio-economic rights cases is discussed. Ultimately, it is argued that if we break with the false necessity of the zero-sum separation-of-powers thesis, it is possible to articulate a meaningful and principled role for courts in the vindication of socio-economic rights.

7.1 The separation of powers

The key question, then, in the debate over the constitutional protection of socio-economic rights, at least from the perspective of comparative constitutional law, is the appropriate relationship between the courts and the elected branches of government. A solution to this question is sought in the language of the separation of powers, which is routinely invoked as if its content and contours were self-evident. This, however, is not the case as the concept of the separation of powers is not a static one.[7] It has evolved over time, and takes disparate – if

---

5 Quinn (n. 3) p. 37.
6 As a recent report from the International Commission of Jurists notes, 'responsibility for the design and implementation of measures to comply with [socio-economic] rights ought to lie with the political branches of the State' (*Courts and the Legal Enforcement of Economic, Social and Cultural Rights: Comparative Experiences of Justiciability* (Geneva: ICJ, 2008) at p. 73).
7 On the evolution of the doctrine of the separation of powers see: M. J. C. Vile, *Constitutionalism and the Separation of Powers* (2nd edn, Indianapolis: Liberty Fund Inc, 1998).

also broadly similar – forms in different countries and in different legal orders.[8] Substantively, it is divided along a spectrum of more or less rigid separation between the various branches of government.[9] Historically the rationale for the separation of powers has been concerned less with the formal – even less so efficient – separation of distinct functions, and more so with the ultimate aim of avoiding the concentration of power and the concomitant threat of tyranny.[10] As Montesquieu famously put it, '[when] the legislative and executive powers are united in the same person, or in the same body of magistrates, there can be no liberty; because apprehensions may arise, lest the same monarch or senate should enact tyrannical laws to execute them in a tyrannical manner'.[11]

On the basis of this foundational rationale, and seeking to effectuate it in contemporary society, Eric Barendt argues that a strict, rigid or 'pure' theory of the separation of powers should be eschewed, in favour of a more nuanced 'partial separation'. As he puts it, 'the separation of powers is not in essence concerned with the allocation of functions as such. Its primary purpose . . . is the prevention of the arbitrary government, or tyranny, which may arise from the concentration of power'.[12] Barendt further argues that 'the separation of powers should not be explained in terms of a strict distribution of functions between the three branches of government, but in terms of a network of rules and principles which ensure that power is not concentrated in the hands of one

---

8 See Bruce Ackerman, 'The New Separation of Powers' (2000) 113 *Harvard Law Review* 633. As the South African Constitutional Court held: 'There is, however, no universal model of separation of powers, and in democratic systems of government in which checks and balances result in the imposition of restraints by one branch of government upon another, there is no separation that is absolute . . . Moreover, because of the different systems of checks and balances that exist in [different] countries, the relationship between the different branches of government and the power or influence that one branch of government has over the other, differs from one country to another. The principle of separation of powers, on the one hand, recognises the functional independence of branches of government. On the other hand, the principle of checks and balances focuses on the desirability of ensuring that the constitutional order, as a totality, prevents the branches of government from usurping power from one another. No constitutional scheme can reflect a complete separation of powers: the scheme is always one of partial separation'; *Ex parte Chairperson of the Constitutional Assembly: In re Certification of the Constitution of the Republic of South Africa 1996* 1996 (10) BCLR 1253 (CC) at paras. 108–109.

9 Vile (n. 7) at pp. 14–20, noting the distinction between the 'stark' and 'extreme' 'pure version' of the separation of powers, and the more pragmatic, and workable 'partial' separation of powers theory.

10 See Vile (n. 7) at p. 15; Philip Kurland, 'Structuring the Separation of Powers' (1993) 8 *American University Journal of International Law and Policy* 483 at pp. 489–490; and Ron Merkel, 'Separation of Powers – A Bulwark for Liberty and a Rights Culture' (2006) 69 *Saskatchewan Law Review* 129. For a contrary view, which sees efficiency in government as the *raison d'être* of the separation of powers, see N. W. Barber, 'Prelude to the Separation of Powers' (2001) 60 *Cambridge Law Journal* 59.

11 Baron De Montesquieu, *The Spirit of the Laws* (New York: Hafner Publishing Company, 1949) pp. 151–152.

12 Eric Barendt, 'Separation of Powers and Constitutional Government' (1995) *Public Law* 599 at p. 606.

branch . . . In practice the danger now is that the executive has too much power'.[13] Indeed, in so far as fear of tyranny borne of concentrated power was, at least historically, the driving force behind the separation of powers, the focus should rightly be on the global growth of executive power.[14]

The general point, therefore, is that the separation of powers' allocation of discrete areas of operation is purely a functional choice, to serve particular substantive ends. Historically these ends were the staving off of the spectre that so exercised Lord Acton,[15] but with changes in society must also come a recalibration of the ends of the separation of powers. As Vile notes, an 'idea that finds its roots in ancient constitutionalism . . . has obviously to be reformulated if it is to serve as an instrument of modern political thought'.[16] The crucial point in any reimagining of the separation of powers is to acknowledge from the outset that discussion of separation is unintelligible out of context, that is to say it makes little or no sense until we talk about 'separation on behalf of what?'.[17] In other words: the substantive ends we wish to see our government, and our constitutional order, pursue fundamentally shapes our understanding of how the separation of powers should look;[18] as Bruce Ackerman puts it, 'institutional arrangements serve as concrete expressions of ultimate ideals'.[19]

In the context of our present discussion, therefore, the language of the separation of powers can only be considered dispositive of claims for the justiciability of socio-economic rights, if we start from the prior position that such rights do not deserve protection. If, on the other hand, we accept the validity and legitimacy of socio-economic rights *qua* fundamental rights, we can then rethink the separation of powers so that it still performs its foundational role, preventing the concentration of power in any one branch of government, while also

---

13 *Ibid.* at pp. 608–609.
14 On the growth of executive power see: Paul Craig and Adam Tomkins, 'Introduction' in Craig and Tomkins (eds.), *The Executive and Public Law* (Oxford: Oxford University Press, 2006) 1; Cass Sunstein, 'Beyond *Marbury*: The Executive's Power to Say What the Law Is' (2006) 115 *Yale Law Journal* 2580; Daryl Levinson and Richard Pildes, 'Separation of Parties, Not Powers' (2006) 119 *Harvard Law Review* 2311; Sanford Levinson, 'Constitutional Dictators' (2009) 56(3) *Dissent* 99; and Kurland (n. 10) at p. 494. The tragic irony, then, being that when courts, in the name of upholding the separation of powers, defer to the elected branches of government – which in many respects (with the growth of modern political parties) means to the executive and executive-dominated legislature – they are in fact further undermining the very foundational rationale for the separation of powers: preventing the over-accumulation of power in one body.
15 The famous aphorism attributed to Lord Acton that 'power tends to corrupt, and absolute power corrupts absolutely'; similarly Montesquieu (n. 11) at p. 150, warned that 'constant experience shows us that every man invested with power is apt to abuse it, and to carry his authority as far as it will go . . . To prevent this abuse, it is necessary from the very nature of things that power should be a check to power'.
16 Vile (n. 7) at p. 8.
17 Ackerman (n. 8) at p. 640.
18 As Barber (n. 10) at p. 63, puts it, 'Separation of powers is a theory of the ordering of collective action; it must be prefaced by a political theory if it is to posses any normative force'.
19 Ackerman (n. 8) at p. 639.

allowing for the courts to play some role in protecting socio-economic rights. This point is well made by Jeanne Woods, who notes that the:

> separation of powers as a normative principle is not an end in itself – it is a means of keeping the government in check in order to ensure the protection of preferred rights. In the case of social rights, judicial review serves the function of checking the political branches to ensure they are responsive to the constitutional rights of the least privileged in society, and that policymakers do not lose sight of their suffering in the inevitable political games of compromise and horse-trading.[20]

It is to such a reimagining of the separation of powers that the bulk of this chapter is devoted. The objective is to show that if we are committed to the protection of socio-economic rights, it is eminently possible to articulate a principled separation of powers which allows the courts to play a meaningful role in the protection of socio-economic rights, while respecting the primacy of the elected branches of government. Before articulating this model framework, the next section briefly spells out some of the 'tools' in the constitutional design kit, that provide us with options for articulating an alternative judicial role and separation of powers.

7.2 The smorgasbord of judicial review

Throughout the twentieth century there were, broadly speaking, two options open to states or governments wishing to pursue a democratic, constitutional form of government. As Mark Tushnet puts it:

> One was the so-called Westminster model of parliamentary supremacy, in which democratically elected legislatures had power unconstrained by anything other than the cultural presuppositions embedded in a majority's will. The other was the United States ('U.S.') model of constrained parliamentarianism . . . In this model; the legislature's powers are limited by the terms of a written constitution that courts will enforce. Each model promoted some values of liberal constitutionalism and raised worries about others. The Westminster model maximally advanced democratic self-governance, but made it possible for empowered democratic majorities to violate rights that liberal systems should protect. The U.S. model gave the courts wide-ranging power to invalidate legislation on the ground that the legislation violated those rights, but made it possible for reckless courts to interfere needlessly with policy choices democratic majorities should be allowed to make.[21]

---

20 Jeanne M. Woods, 'Justiciable Social Rights as a Critique of the Liberal Paradigm' (2003) 38 *Texas International Law Journal* 763 at p. 773.

21 Mark Tushnet, 'New Forms of Judicial Review and the Persistence of Rights and Democracy-Based Worries' (2003) 38 *Wake Forest Law Review* 813 at pp. 813–814.

With the expansion of constitutionalism, particularly in the last twenty years, this either/or choice between two homogonous and mutually exclusive systems has been replaced by a veritable smorgasbord of institutional options, encompassing more or less parliamentary or judicial control, depending on the wants and needs of the political community.[22] This section outlines some of the different models and categories which have emerged in this context as a prologue to discussing the appropriate judicial role in enforcing socio-economic rights. The simple point which it is hoped this will illustrate is that there are choices and options available when it comes to calibrating the appropriate relationship between the courts and elected branches of government in the protection of constitutional rights.

7.2.1 Weak-form versus strong-form review

Over the past number of years comparative constitutional scholars have noted the different approaches to judicial review pertaining in different countries, highlighting, in particular, the distinction between 'strong-form' and 'weak-form' judicial review.[23] The dividing line between the two systems, according to Tushnet, is the relative 'normative finality' which each affords to the equally reasonable, albeit differing, interpretations of constitutional provisions proffered by courts and legislatures, respectively.[24] The former system, exemplified by the practice of judicial review in the US, is one which 'insists that the courts reasonable constitutional interpretation prevail over the legislatures', and where the courts' 'interpretive judgments are final and unrevisable'.[25] In contrast, systems of weak-form judicial review are premised on the idea that 'there can be reasonable disagreements about what it is, exactly, that fundamental rights described in abstract terms protect and prohibit'.[26] Consequently, weak-form judicial review, through a variety of institutional arrangements, 'provides mechanisms for the people [i.e. the legislature] to respond to decisions that they reasonably believe mistaken that can be deployed more rapidly than the constitutional or judicial appointments processes'.[27] While there is some common ground between the two forms of judicial review, for Tushnet they are 'different enough in terms of normative finality that we can treat them as binary alternatives'.[28]

---

22 For a discussion of these various models, see Stephen Gardbaum, 'The New Commonwealth Model of Constitutionalism' (2001) 49 *American Journal of Comparative Law* 707.
23 See, generally, Mark Tushnet, *Weak Courts, Strong Rights* (New Jersey: Princeton University Press, 2008) at pp. 18–42; and see the distinction Perry draws between 'judicial ultimacy' on the one hand and 'judicial penultimacy' on the other (Michael Perry, 'Protecting Human Rights in a Democracy: What Role for the Courts?' (2003) 38 *Wake Forest Law Review* 635).
24 Tushnet (n. 24) at p. 34.
25 *Ibid.* at p. 21.
26 *Ibid.* at p. 31.
27 *Ibid.* at p. 23.
28 *Ibid.* at p. 42.

Weak-form judicial review is exemplified by countries such as New Zealand, Canada and the United Kingdom: countries that have adopted, and indeed led the way, with what Stephen Gardbaum calls the 'Commonwealth model' of judicial review. This model rejects the binary opposition between constitutional supremacy and judicial frustrating of majoritarian preferences on the one hand, and parliamentary supremacy with no judicial role in protecting rights on the other, by granting courts a role in the protection of rights while at the same time 'decoupling judicial review from judicial supremacy by empowering legislatures to have the final word' in rights protection.[29] For Gardbaum this model explodes the false necessity of the choice between US-style judicial supremacy – with its counter-majoritarian concerns – and British-style parliamentary supremacy, with the apprehended lack of protection of fundamental rights.

The emergence of these varieties of weak-form review demonstrates that there are more options on the menu than at first may seem to be the case, and at the normative level shows that it is possible to have judicial involvement in the protection of constitutional rights, while retaining the primacy of the elected branches of government in the formulation and implementation of social policy.[30] In this way the new models achieve a more appropriate balance between the need to protect fundamental rights, and to maintain the proper separation of powers in a liberal democracy.[31] There is one important final point to make with respect to these alternative forms of review. Namely, that while Gardbaum's discussion of weak-form review, in the form of the new common-wealth model, deals with 'new' rights protection regimes, which were designed from the outset to provide this sort of weak-form review, Mark Tushnet argues that such an approach can also develop organically in ostensibly strong-form judicial review regimes, and vice-versa.[32]

7.2.2 *The idea of constitutional dialogue*

An important, and recent, addition to the 'toolkit of constitutional design' is the idea of constitutional dialogue, and the concomitant method of dialogic

29 Gardbaum (n. 22) at p. 709.
30 As Gardbaum puts it, the Commonwealth model '[suggests] the possibility that the claims of legislative supremacy and effective fundamental rights protection are not mutually exclusive but rather from a continuum ranging from the most absolute conception of legislative supremacy at one pole, to the American model of a constitutional bill of rights at the other' (*ibid.* at p. 743).
31 See Stephen Gardbaum, 'Reassessing the New Commonwealth Model of Constitutionalism' (2010) 8 *International Journal of Constitutional Law* 167. As Janet Hiebert puts it, this 'new paradigm introduces incentives and obligations for political judgment about rights, but still benefits from exposure to judicial perspectives on the scope of rights and their application to impugned legislation and state action' ('New Constitutional Ideas: Can New Parliamentary Models Resist Judicial Dominance When Interpreting Rights' (2004) 82 *Texas Law Review* 1963 at p. 1964).
32 See Mark Tushnet, 'Alternative Forms of Judicial Review' (2003) 101 *Michigan Law Review* 2781 at p. 2786.

judicial review.[33] The basic idea behind the dialogic model of review is to
encourage cooperative engagement among the different branches of government
in the context of rights protection. For Tushnet, the key advantages of the dialogic model, from the perspective of democratic constitutionalism, are that:

> [dialogic] review capitalizes on the institutional advantages courts have in
> constitutional attentiveness by allowing the courts to bring constitutional
> values, in connection with specific problems, into focus in the legislative
> forum. This advances the constitutionalist value of limitations on democ-
> ratic self-governance. With the issues brought to the legislature's attention,
> we can then advance the value of democratic self-governance by leaving the
> final decision to the legislature.[34]

Although there are numerous forms of dialogue, the key point about the
theory is that, much like weak-form judicial review, the dialogic approach does
'not privilege the contributions of judges' at the expense of the elected branches
of government.[35] Thus the key value of the dialogic model is that within it
'concerns that judicial review necessarily sets judges against the electorally
accountable branches of government are greatly attenuated', because courts and
elected branches are understood to be equal partners in a cooperative enterprise
to protect constitutional rights.[36] In this context, then, courts do not act as
Delphic oracles dispensing constitutional justice from on high, but rather as
facilitators 'fostering society-wide constitutional discussion and debate'.[37]

While on one level the idea of constitutional dialogue might be thought to
be an interesting, but fundamentally Canadian doctrine, Luc Tremblay insists
that the theory of institutional dialogue 'has much broader pertinence and
appeal'.[38] We could even push a little further and argue that the idea of a constitutional, or institutional, dialogue between the courts and the elected
branches of government is not simply a desirable option, but indeed an imperative in a modern, constitutional and democratic state.[39] Indeed, even in the
spiritual home, and heretofore bastion, of parliamentary supremacy attitudes

---

33 Mark Tushnet, 'Dialogic Judicial Review' (2008) 61 *Arkansas Law Review* 205 at p. 206
34 *Ibid.* at p. 212.
35 Christine Bateup, 'The Dialogic Promise: Assessing the Normative Potential of Theories of
    Constitutional Dialogue' (2006) 71 *Brooklyn Law Review* 1109 at p. 1112.
36 *Ibid.* at p. 1118.
37 *Ibid.* at p. 1174.
38 Luc Tremblay, 'The Legitimacy of Judicial Review: The Limits of Dialogue Between Courts
    and Legislatures' (2005) 3 *International Journal of Constitutional Law* 617 at p. 618; although
    arguing for the broader relevance of the concept of constitutional dialogue, Tremblay is
    unconvinced by the argument that dialogue theory can, by itself, serve as a justificatory
    theory for judicial review.
39 See T. R. S. Allan, 'Constitutional Dialogue and the Justification of Judicial Review' (2003)
    23 *Oxford Journal of Legal Studies* 563, who argues, at p. 565, that in 'a common law legal order
    there must be a dialogue between courts and legislatures'.

to the respective roles of the courts and the elected branches of government are evolving, as a leading text on judicial review in Britain recently noted:

> there is a growing appreciation that the courts and Parliament have distinct and complimentary constitutional roles so that the courts will no longer avoid adjudicating on the legality of a decision merely because it has been debated and approved in Parliament, or relates to nationally important policy pursued by a Minister accountable to Parliament. The distinctive roles of judicial review and parliamentary (and other) oversight of executive action create opportunities for synergy, with aspects of a particular decision being scrutinised in different ways by different bodies.[40]

Showing that recognition of the benefits of dialogue – different institutions with distinct perspectives on a given issue engaging in a cooperative and complimentary dialogue about the appropriate solution – is gaining significant headway.

It should however be stressed that the idea of dialogue does not necessarily imply the idle chat of good friends; it can also involve the vigorous exchange of views between equals or – to carry the metaphor of friendship a little further – an 'intervention' by one friend to help to curb the deleterious actions of another. As Lord Steyn argues, it 'is natural and healthy that tensions between the branches of government will sometimes arise. Citizens have reason to worry if such tensions do not arise. For example, a cosy and non-transparent co-operation between the executive and judiciary does not enhance democratic values'.[41] Similarly, Denham J. in her dissenting judgment in the Irish *TD* case, argued that:

> The very nature of the division of power under the Constitution together with its checks and balances, may cause tension between the organs of government. The level of that tension may ebb and flow. However, all institutions of State have a responsibility to the State itself to act in a constitutional manner, which is to the benefit of the State as a whole. Consequently, when an issue arises . . . where the boundaries of the separation of the powers are in issue, both of the relevant institutions should approach the matter constructively.[42]

Thus dialogue can be constructive and beneficial, but does not necessarily imply the subservience of one branch of government to the other. Rather, it respects the relative institutional strengths of each branch, while allowing them to engage in a principled, constructive dialogue. In this way dialogue theory

---

40 Harry Woolf, Jeffrey Jowell and Andrew Le Sueur, *De Smith's Judicial Review* (6th edn, London: Sweet & Maxwell, 2007) at p. 6.
41 Lord Steyn, 'Deference: A Tangled Story' (2005) *Public Law* 346 at p. 348.
42 *TD* v. *Minister for Education* [2001] 4 IR 259 at p. 307.

goes some way towards resolving the tension between the distinct branches of government, and again shows how it is possible to conceive of the relationship between the courts and the elected branches of government in alternative ways.

7.3 Vindicating socio-economic rights: a model framework

Surveying the 'smorgasbord of judicial review' drives home the simple point that there are a number of valid options available in structuring the relationship between the courts and the elected branches of government in the context of constitutional rights protection. Similarly, the various jurisdictions discussed in this study show that courts can, and have, addressed the separation-of-powers implications of enforcing socio-economic rights in a number of different ways, some more commendable than others. With this in view the rest of this chapter aims to draw together some of the more promising threads from the various experiences looked at, as well as drawing from the emergent models of judicial review discussed above, to articulate a model framework for courts – in jurisdictions with written constitutions, entrenched bills of rights and express powers of judicial review – to adjudicate on socio-economic rights claims. It is hoped that this model strikes an optimal balance between allowing the courts to play a meaningful role in the vindication of socio-economic rights, while also respecting the primacy of the elected branches of government in this context.

Before embarking in earnest on the articulation of this model framework, a note of clarification (or indeed caution) is in order. As William Twining recently, and rightly, put it, 'working theories that claim to be of widespread application across jurisdictions and cultures need to be treated with caution'.[43] In view of this, and recalling the cautions in comparative constitutionalism discussed in Chapter 1 of this book, what is articulated here is not a model in the sense of a transplantable, working model – but, rather, an 'ideal type'.[44] That is to say that the model framework elaborated here is of general relevance, if not necessarily general application in the exact same way in every jurisdiction. Instead, the theory articulated here is an ideal, which, in my view, strikes the correct balance between meaningful judicial vindication of socio-economic rights, and respect for the primacy of the elected branches of government in the context of the separation of powers. In any given jurisdiction courts can try to approximate towards the ideal articulated here, but it is not a pre-cut, one-size-fits-all model; more modestly it is an 'ideal practice' model.

While it is undoubtedly true, as Lord Lester and Colm O'Cinneide note, that there 'are limits to what can be achieved by the judicial process in implementing fundamental rights',[45] it is equally true to note, as Jill Cottrell and

43 William Twining, *General Jurisprudence: Understanding Law from a Global Perspective* (Cambridge: Cambridge University Press, 2009) at p. 9.
44 Albeit not necessarily in the strict Weberian sense of that term.
45 Lord Lester of Herne Hill and Colm O'Cinneide, 'The Effective Protection of Socio-Economic

Yash Ghai do, that courts can perform a number of important tasks in adjudicating on socio-economic rights, namely:

> (a) elaborating the contents of rights; (b) indicating the responsibilities of the state; (c) identifying the ways in which the rights have been violated by the state; (d) suggesting the frameworks within which policy has to be made, highlighting the priority of human rights . . . There is a fine balance here, for there is always a risk that the courts may cross the line between indicating failures of policy and priorities and indicating so clearly what those priorities ought to be that they are actually making policy.[46]

Building on this useful catalogue, the pages that follow address a number of key issues in the adjudication of socio-economic rights. First, a commitment to socio-economic rights as fundamental rights is stressed as a key preliminary. Then, an overarching concept of the relationship between the courts and the elected branches of government – drawing on the ideal of institutional dialogue – is framed. Finally, then, drawing both on the idea of a commitment to socio-economic rights and the ideal of a dialogic relationship between the branches of government, the central issues of the level of judicial scrutiny, or standard of review, and appropriate remedies in socio-economic rights cases are addressed. It should be borne in mind that due to their historical neglect, a commitment to socio-economic rights obliges us to rethink many of the 'taken-for-granteds' in constitutional litigation. In the same way in which the 'rights revolution' begun in the 1960s has necessitated a reconceptualisation of litigation and the jettisoning of nineteenth-century notions of the nature of the judicial process and the appropriate judicial role,[47] so, too, the recognition of socio-economic rights requires us to rethink some of the fundamentals of public law litigation.

7.3.1 *The dignity of socio-economic rights*

At present there are, broadly speaking, four different paradigms through which socio-economic rights can be protected in domestic constitutional law, namely: (i) through direct constitutional entrenchment of socio-economic rights; (ii) protection in the form of non-justiciable 'directive principles' of state policy; (iii) protection of socio-economic rights as essential corollaries of civil and political rights – what Ida Elisabeth Koch and others refer to as the 'integrated

---

Rights' in Ghai and Cottrell (eds.), *Economic, Social and Cultural Rights in Practice* (London: INTERIGHTS, 2004) 17 at p. 19.

46 Jill Cottrell and Yash Ghai, 'The Role of the Courts in the Protection of Economic, Social and Cultural Rights' in Ghai and Cottrell (eds.), *Economic, Social and Cultural Rights in Practice* (London: INTERIGHTS, 2004) 58 at p. 86.

47 See Abram Chayes, 'The Role of the Judge in Public Law Litigation' (1976) 89 *Harvard Law Review* 1281 at pp. 1281–1288; cf. Theodore Eisenberg and Stephen Yeazell, 'The Ordinary and the Extraordinary in Institutional Litigation' (1980) 93 *Harvard Law Review* 465, who argue that the 'new' public law litigation of Chayes and others was not that novel at all.

approach';[48] and (iv) protection of socio-economic rights through the expansive application of equality or non-discrimination provisions.[49] While each of these can, and as the jurisdictions examined in this study show have, provide some protection for socio-economic rights, the first point in a model framework is the recognition of socio-economic rights *as fundamental rights*. That is to accord socio-economic rights the same level of protection in the domestic constitutional order as is afforded to civil and political rights. It will be argued here that anything short of explicit recognition of socio-economic rights undermines the level of protection afforded to them. Whereas explicitly recognising and rendering such rights justiciable lends 'greater weight to their underlying values in policymaking and political discourse generally'.[50]

If we begin with the directive principles approach, it is telling that Cass Sunstein notes that while this approach ensures the courts will not become entangled in the realm of political policy, the 'disadvantage is that without judicial enforcement there is a risk that the constitutional guarantees will be mere 'parchment barriers', meaningless or empty in the real world'.[51] Indeed, the Irish experience with the Directive Principles of Social Policy in Article 45 of the Constitution is testament to this apprehension. And while the Indian experience would seem to buck that trend, it must be said that this was a very particular one, borne of a very specific set of historical circumstances. As Scott and Macklem note, by and large '[despite] the best of intentions, this approach serves to marginalize the centrality of [socio-economic] rights, the values they seek to vindicate, and, most significantly, the persons whose chance to be human and whose place in society is most dependent on these rights'.[52] The directive principles approach thus places too much emphasis on the freedom of the elected branches of government on issues of social policy, and pays only scant regard to the interests of those who would receive greatest protection from socio-economic rights.

Likewise, the integrated approach – protecting socio-economic rights as integral aspects of explicitly protected civil and political rights – provides insufficient protection to socio-economic rights. As Ida Elisabeth Koch notes in the context of this paradigm:

> acceptance of social rights as justiciable rights, however, only applies to situations where the social rights appear as necessary fulfilment elements in civil rights, and the Court's criteria for accepting the social fulfilment

---

48 Ida Elisabeth Koch, 'Economic, Social and Cultural Rights as Components in Civil and Political Rights: A Hermeneutic Perspective' (2006) 10 *International Journal of Human Rights* 405 at p. 408.

49 See Jeanne M. Woods, 'Emerging Paradigms of Protection for "Second-Generation" Human Rights' (2005) 6 *Loyola Journal of Public Interest Law* 103.

50 Scott and Macklem (n. 2) at p. 39.

51 Cass Sunstein, *Designing Democracy: What Constitutions Do* (Oxford: Oxford University Press, 2001) at p. 224.

52 Scott and Macklem (n. 2) at pp. 38–39.

elements as part of the civil rights are not very transparent . . . but the acceptance of social rights as justiciable rights cannot be extended to situations where those social rights appear alone – without being closely connected to a civil right. He who is 'only' hungry, homeless or without healthcare cannot count on having the legitimacy of the claim enforced by the judiciary . . . The approach can probably be taken further, but will always have to respect the requirement that the social right is linked to a civil right. This requirement is at the same time the strength and the weakness of the approach.[53]

Again, this approach fails to protect the substantive interests associated with socio-economic rights, and instead leaves the most vulnerable reliant on the inclination and creativity of the judiciary. Such an approach fundamentally undermines the core interests of those who would gain most from socio-economic rights, and provides only partial and incidental protection for such rights.

Finally if we look at the non-discrimination approach we can see that it, too, while retaining the potential to deliver sporadic victories, ultimately fails to provide comprehensive protection for socio-economic rights. As Matthew Craven argues:

> there is the ever-present danger that the concept of non-discrimination might ultimately be used merely as a more ideologically-neutered surrogate for talking about [socio-economic] rights directly. If it is thought to serve the same ends, the temptation may well be there to refuse to speak directly of [socio-economic] rights in their own terms, but only of housing, education and health as domains within which the idea of non-discrimination might play a role . . . [this] would mean giving up on the idea that [socio-economic] rights form some form of substantive entitlement.[54]

Thus, this approach denies the centrality of socio-economic rights as rights. But, more worryingly, this approach also fundamentally limits the reach of any minimal protections that might be developed. As the Canadian and Irish experiences show, relying on this approach means it may be effectively neutered by confining its application to situations when the government has positively acted and not where it has neglected the needs of specific groups,[55] or may even be used as an excuse for 'levelling down' in social provision.[56]

---

53 Ida Elisabeth Koch, 'The Justiciability of Indivisible Human Rights' (2003) 2 *Nordic Journal of International Law* 3 at p. 25.

54 Matthew Craven, 'Assessment of Progress on Adjudication of Economic, Social and Cultural Rights' in Squires, Langford and Thiele (eds.), *The Road to a Remedy: Current Issues in the Litigation of Economic, Social and Cultural Rights* (Sydney: University of New South Wales Press, 2005) 27 at p. 37.

55 See *Auton (Guardian* ad litem *of)* v. *British Columbia (Attorney General)* [2004] 3 SCR 657.

56 See *Hyland* v. *Minister for Social Welfare* [1989] IR 624.

In place of any of these approaches, the ideal is to have socio-economic rights specifically recognised and entrenched at the same level as civil and political rights.[57] This point is well made by Bruce Porter, writing in the Canadian context, who notes that anti-poverty and socio-economic rights campaigners there laboured over whether or not to frame their claims in more limited terms, for example breaches of procedural fairness, so as to make them more 'acceptable' to the courts and legal establishment. However, it was ultimately decided to pursue socio-economic rights as rights so as to gain symbolically significant 'adjudicative space' for the rights and interests of the poor and thereby reaffirm their equal standing and worth in the constitutional order.[58] In a similar vein Abdullahi A. An-Na'im notes the issue of the recognition of socio-economic rights as rights and that their judicial enforcement has:

> serious implications for the acceptance of these rights as human rights. The human rights standing of every right classified [as a socio-economic right] is challenged by implication when this group of rights is deemed to be incapable of meeting a purported criterion of judicial enforcement based on the ideological fiat or prior experience of certain societies with civil and political rights . . . it is critical to challenge the assumption that the implementation of [socio-economic rights] should be confined to the realm of social policy and administrative processes of governments because these rights do not fit the model of judicial enforcement developed for specific civil and political rights . . . to leave the matter to the unfettered discretion of governments, however democratic they may be, without any possibility of judicial guidance and supervision, defeats the whole purpose of recognising [socio-economic rights] as international human rights.[59]

An-Na'im goes on to argue that, in the final analys, is a socio-economic right 'is not a right at all if its provision is entirely left to the political and administrative will of the state, without any possibility of independent judicial supervision and guidance beyond the prohibition of discrimination'.[60]

As well as confirming the equal standing of socio-economic rights as rights, the explicit protection of such rights sends out a strong symbolic message about society's commitment to the interests and needs of the most excluded.[61] And,

---

57 Such an approach, of course, correlates with the insistence at the level of international human rights law that all rights are indivisible, and with the overarching standards developed at the international level: see the discussion in Chapter 2.

58 See Bruce Porter, 'Claiming Adjudicative Space: Social Rights, Equality and Citizenship' in Young, Boyd, Brodsky and Day (eds.), *Poverty: Rights, Social Citizenship and Legal Activism* (Vancouver: UBC Press, 2007) 77 at p. 88.

59 Abdullahi A. An-Na'im, 'To Affirm the Full Human Rights Standing of Economic, Social and Cultural Rights' in Ghai and Cottrell (eds.), *Economic, Social and Cultural Rights in Practice* (London: INTERIGHTS, 2004) 7 at p. 7.

60 *Ibid.* at p. 15.

61 Scott and Macklem (n. 2) at pp. 28–29 note that 'Whereas the constitutionalization of social rights would be a recognition of the fact that adequate nutrition, housing, health, and

on a more pragmatic level, such explicit recognition should mean that these rights also have a greater influence on the shaping of government policy. As Cottrell and Ghai note '[government] policies not grounded in rights are always vulnerable to changes in political philosophy and economic circumstances. And the best legal guarantees of rights are the provisions in national constitutions which cannot be changed, or not without great effort'.[62] The claim, therefore, for the constitutional recognition and protection of socio-economic rights is that, much like freedom of expression and the right to vote, socio-economic rights embody and give protection to fundamental interests which we, as a community, regard as deserving of special protection. Furthermore, the explicit recognition and protection of socio-economic rights would also play the important dual role of empowering the courts to assert themselves when required to do so, and of restraining the courts with reference to explicit textual provisions, thus guarding against the sort of judicial adventurism seen in cases such as *Chaoulli*.[63]

7.3.2 Approaching the separation of powers anew

The fundamental problem with the prevailing discourse on socio-economic rights and the separation of powers is the combative language that is used and the way in which we are presented with false binaries. I refer to this here as the 'zero-sum separation-of-powers thesis'. This approach is exemplified by Hardiman J. in the Irish Supreme Court who argues that judicial enforcement of socio-economic rights will result in the growth of judicial power 'at the expense' of the elected branches of government. As he puts it:

> if the courts (or either of the other organs of government) expand their powers beyond their constitutional remit, *this expansion will necessarily be at the expense of the other organs of government*. It will also be progressive. If citizens are taught to look to the courts for remedies for matters within the legislative or

education are critical components of social existence, the exclusion of social rights from a . . . constitution necessarily would result in the suppression of certain societal voices . . . A constitution containing only civil and political rights projects an image of truncated humanity. Symbolically, but still brutally, it excludes those segments of society for whom autonomy means little without the necessities of life'. Similarly Marius Pieterse argues that 'By awarding enforceable entitlements to goods and services that are essential for human survival and flourishing, socio-economic rights appear capable of effectively reconciling notions of right and need. Moreover, the language of socio-economic rights is empowering in that it depicts claims for subsistence as demands that the state must heed rather than as pleas for state philanthropy. Accordingly, guaranteeing socioeconomic rights contributes to the achievement of an ultimately more just society in which the human dignity of all citizens may be equally respected and affirmed' ('Eating Socioeconomic Rights: The Usefulness of Rights Talk in Alleviating Social Hardship Revisited' (2007) 29 *Human Rights Quarterly* 796 at p. 803).

62   Cottrell and Ghai (n. 46) at p. 66.

63   See *Chaoulli* v. *Quebec (Attorney General)* [2005] 1 SCR 791, discussed in Chapter 5.

executive remit, they will progressively seek further remedies there, and progressively cease to look to the political arms of government. *Such a development would certainly downgrade the political arms of government.*[64]

Ironically, somewhat similar views are expressed by critics of the Supreme Court. For example Conor O'Mahony argues that 'the fundamental question that must be asked is this: which of the two core principles of a liberal constitution is of higher value – fundamental rights or the separation of powers?'.[65]

The fundamental problem, then, is that opposition to socio-economic rights is 'based on an overly rigid assumption that governmental functions must be compartmentalized'.[66] In reconceiving the separation of powers, in a way which contemplates judicial involvement in the vindication of socio-economic rights, we would need to make a conceptual jump from an understanding of the judicial role as concerned with 'policing fixed boundaries' between the branches of government to one in which the focus is 'on the institutions (or combination of institutions) which can be most effective in advancing access to socio-economic rights in the particular context of a case'.[67] Within such a paradigm, rigid demarcation of spheres of influence ceases to be the key dynamic within the separation-of-powers debate; instead, the focus shifts to an acknowledgement that effective protection and implementation of socio-economic rights 'can be carried out only where the proper roles and limits of each branch of government is fully understood' and that '[working] to secure the protection of socio-economic rights across all three branches of [the] constitutional system remains the task of all three branches'.[68]

Setting off from this premise, an approach to the separation of powers that does not pit one branch of the government against the other, but rather sees them as engaged in a cooperative enterprise to ensure the protection of fundamental rights, is particularly suited. Such an approach is advocated by Rosalind Dixon, who argues for a dialogic model of judicial review with respect to socio-economic rights claims. This approach 'allows courts both to define rights in relatively broad terms and to adopt strong remedies, provided they defer to legislative sequels that evidence clear and considered disagreement with their rulings'.[69] For Dixon this dialogic approach is desirable because it allows the courts to 'counter failures of inclusiveness and responsiveness in the political process' or what she refers to as 'blind spots' or 'burdens of inertia', without usurping the role of the

64 *TD* v. *Minister for Education* [2001] 4 IR 259 at pp. 361–362 (emphasis added).
65 Conor O'Mahony, 'Education, Remedies and the Separation of Powers' (2002) 24 *Dublin University Law Journal* 57 at p. 93.
66 Scott and Macklem (n. 2) at p. 147.
67 Sandra Liebenberg, *Socio-Economic Rights: Adjudication Under a Transformative Constitution* (Claremont: Juta, 2010) at p. 484.
68 Lord Lester and O'Cinneide (n. 45) at p. 22.
69 Rosalind Dixon, 'Creating Dialogue About Socio-Economic Rights: Strong-Form Versus Weak-Form Judicial Review Revisited' (2007) 5 *International Journal of Constitutional Law* 391 at p. 393.

elected branches of government in the formulation of social policy.[70] A similar view is advocated by Scott and Macklem, who argue that:

> The inclusion of social rights in a . . . constitution would require rethinking the relationships that would otherwise exist between the executive, legislature, and judiciary. Interpreting constitutional guarantees as requiring positive governmental action, and invoking the constitution to prod the state into better protecting the necessities of life for members of society, would involve some blending of the judicial and legislative functions. The limits of the judicial power in part would be determined by the responsiveness of the judicial, executive, and legislative branches to each other's constitutional stances, and the spheres of each source of governmental authority would be shaped and reshaped by context-specific disputes . . . Ideally, the relationship between the judiciary and the other two branches of government would be cooperative as opposed to antagonistic, interactive as opposed to separate. This is not to deny that, in practice, the relationship will often be shaped by spirited, even bitter, resistance to what one branch perceives as overly intrusive incursions by another. Limits on the spheres of authority of each would emerge from the relationships that they jointly construct through the dialogic encounter, whether cooperative or conflictual, engendered by a judicial role that explicitly blends the legislative with the judicial.[71]

A commitment to socio-economic rights, therefore, requires us to rethink the separation of powers, and to move away from the binaries posited by the zero-sum separation-of-powers thesis. Adopting, instead, a dialogic approach to the separation of powers allows some scope for the courts to vindicate socio-economic rights, while leaving the real 'heavy lifting' to the elected branches of government.

However, the above quote from Scott and Macklem also indicates that such a dialogic approach would not be simple smooth sailing, and would involve some degree of judicial interference in what are considered to be the prerogatives of the elected branches of government and in so-called policy areas. It is, however (or at least should be) axiomatic that the enforcement of all rights, whether civil and political or socio-economic, 'involve matters of policy'; but this alone does not mean that 'these are issues which constitutional principle withdraws from decision by the courts'.[72] Judicial enforcement of any rights will

---

70   *Ibid.* at p. 394. The language used by Dixon in this context, 'blind spots', may be a little overly diplomatic, but it conveys the general idea that courts can, and should, act to protect socio-economic rights where the failure to protect them results from some structural shortcoming in the democratic process.

71   Scott and Macklem (n. 2) at p. 42.

72   Lord Steyn (n. 41) at p. 355. See also Jutta Limbach, 'The Concept of the Supremacy of the Constitution' (2001) 64 *Modern Law Review* 1 at p. 8, noting that adjudication always has a political dimension.

entail some degree of overlap with the activities of the elected branches of government; as Alec Stone Sweet and Jud Mathews observe, 'a political commitment to rights requires massive delegation to judges; and, if the judges do their job properly, they will at times impinge upon policy processes and outcomes'.[73] Similarly Edward Rubin and Malcolm Feeley argue that 'policy making inheres in the basic structure of a modern judiciary. For the foreseeable future, therefore, any discussion of litigation against the government must incorporate the fact that such litigation will regularly induce the judiciary to make public policy'.[74]

Such 'friction' between the different branches of government is thus inevitable in any system of separation of powers; the dialogic approach at least goes some way towards structuring and attenuating such tensions. What is more, as Helen Hershkoff notes, in a regime which values and respects socio-economic rights the constitution:

> not only restrain[s] the government's exercise of power, but also compels its exercise, constraining the government to use its assigned authority to carry out a specified constitutional purpose. Judicial review in such a regime, must serve to ensure that the government is doing its job and moving policy closer to the constitutionally prescribed end. The enforcement of positive rights thus requires [courts] to share explicitly in public governance, engaging in [a] principled dialogue [to resolve social and economic issues].[75]

In such a system, although there would certainly be overlap between the courts and the elected branches of government, as in truth there always is, it would not be a case of one exercising power at the expense of another, or usurping the role of the other; rather it would be a synergistic relationship. Again, as Hershkoff puts it:

> when a . . . constitution commits the state to particular public policies, the role of the . . . court is to ensure that government uses its assigned power to achieve, or at least move closer to achieving, the specified goals. Although the legislature retains discretion over how to implement the state constitutional requirements, its discretion over the various 'manners' and 'means' is constrained by the constitutional mandate. In exercising review,

---

73 Alec Stone Sweet and Jud Mathews, 'Proportionality, Balancing and Global Constitutionalism' (2008) 47 *Columbia Journal of Transnational Law* 72 at p. 93; similarly the ICJ (n. 6) at p. 75, note that the 'boundaries between the "legal" and the "political" are not clear-cut, and judges undeniably make policy choices'.

74 Edward Rubin and Malcolm Feeley, 'Judicial Policy Making and Litigation Against the Government' (2003) 5 *University of Pennsylvania Journal of Constitutional Law* 617 at p. 618. See also Koch (n. 53) at p. 35.

75 Helen Hershkoff, 'Positive Rights and State Constitutions: The Limits of Federal Rationality Review' (1999) 112 *Harvard Law Review* 1131 at p. 1138.

the court would not itself construct welfare policy, but rather would impose a burden on the legislature to show that the chosen 'manner' and 'means' are likely to carry forward the specified constitutional aim.[76]

If, therefore, we adopt or accept a prior commitment to the protection of socio-economic rights, it is possible to conceive of a more nuanced conception of the separation of powers, which sees both the courts and the elected branches of government working cooperatively towards the realisation of such rights. Within such a dialogic system the courts' role could, for example, entail: (i) authoritatively declaring the violation of a right; (ii) notifying the elected branches of this breach; (iii) remitting the matter back to the elected branches to formulate a proportionate response and; (iv) mandating a time-frame within which a response must be both formulated and acted upon (to ensure "teeth" for any judicial declaration). Such an approach would thus allow the courts to insure fundamental socio-economic rights are protected, while at the same time leaving to the elected branches of government the decisions about the best way to realise such rights. With, of course, the key proviso that such rights are in fact being realised. It is to this aspect – how the courts should determine if the state is complying with its obligations with respect to socio-economic rights – that we turn next.

7.3.3 *The standard of review*

Within this overarching framework of a commitment to socio-economic rights and a dialogic understanding of the separation of powers, we now turn to the appropriate standard of review for courts in socio-economic rights cases. In any socio-economic rights case it is essential, as a preliminary, that courts begin to articulate some understanding of what the right in question entails. As a recent report from the International Commission of Jurists notes, the 'content of a right and of the duties that it imposes are a pre-condition for the adjudication of any right'.[77] Indeed, Marius Pieterse has argued that one of the chief obstacles in the realisation of socio-economic rights in South Africa, but also more generally, is the 'abstract and conceptually empty articulation of socio-economic

76 *Ibid.* at p. 1145. In a similar vein Cécile Fabre argues that giving the courts the power to tell the government to do x does not entail giving them the power to tell them how to do it: for the government to be under a duty to do x does not imply that the government is under the duty to do x in a certain way. If the constitution specifies that one has a constitutional right to, say, a reasonable standard of housing given the level of economic development and competing expenditures (and given what other needy people need), the judiciary will have to decide whether the income of the government allows for that level of provision, and whether the government is right to spend x amount of money on certain things. But if they find that the government can afford to provide people with housing, they can simply tell the government that housing provision must be raised, by a certain date' (*Social Rights Under the Constitution* (Oxford: Oxford University Press, 2000) at p. 149).

77 ICJ (n. 6) at p. 5.

rights, which allows for the institutional containment and suppression of the needs they represent'.[78] Pieterse thus argues that if socio-economic rights are to be meaningfully vindicated it is important that we 'increasingly concentrate on clarifying the concrete content of entitlements embodied by socio-economic rights and on explicitly linking such content to the actual satisfaction of material need'.[79] In seeking to articulate the content of socio-economic rights courts can, and should, draw on the standards articulated at the international level, and on comparative jurisprudence. In relying on such international and comparative material the courts should not simply seek to mimic the experiences of others, but should instead use these experiences to enhance and develop their own domestic jurisprudence. As Liebenberg puts it, '[the] purpose of considering international and comparative law sources is not so that they can be slavishly followed, but rather because they broaden the range of options available to courts in developing the interpretation of socio-economic rights'.[80]

Once a court has articulated at least a preliminary understanding of what a given socio-economic right entails or requires in a given context, it can then move on to consider the extent to which the state has complied with the requirements of the right in question. At this stage it would seem that the reasonableness approach of the South African Constitutional Court falls short in terms of providing meaningful protection for socio-economic rights.[81] This does not mean that we must, then, opt for the 'minimum core' approach, which itself has a number of shortcomings.[82] Indeed, the primary insight of the minimum core critique of the South African jurisprudence, that the courts have failed to imbue socio-economic rights with substantive content, is mitigated by the first step advocated above. Sandra Liebenberg, while unpersuaded for a variety of reasons by the argument that the courts should adopt a minimum core approach, is nonetheless aware of the deficiency in the South African courts' failure to engage with the substantive content of a given socio-economic right.[83] Consequently, she argues for a refined, or improved, reasonableness review which will begin with some concept, even if provisional, of the normative character of the right in question, before proceeding to evaluate the reasonableness of state action to achieve this right.[84] This approach, for Liebenberg, will help

---

78 Pieterse (n. 61) at p. 799.
79 *Ibid.*
80 Sandra Liebenberg, 'Socio-Economic Rights: Revisiting the Reasonableness Review/ Minimum Core Debate' in Woolman and Bishop (eds.), *Constitutional Conversations* (Pretoria: Pretoria University Law Press, 2008) 303 at p. 324.
81 Sandra Fredman, for one, is critical of the overly deferential nature of reasonableness review: see 'New Horizons: Incorporating Socio-Economic Rights in a British Bill of Rights' (2010) *Public Law* 297 at p. 317. In a similar vein, Clare Mahon is critical of the 'government friendly' nature of reasonableness review and reasonableness discourse ('Progress at the Front: The Draft Optional Protocol to the International Covenant on Economic, Social and Cultural Rights' (2008) 8 *Human Rights Law Review* 617 at p. 634).
82 Liebenberg (n. 80) at pp. 309–319: and see the discussion in Chapter 3.
83 *Ibid.* at p. 321.
84 *Ibid.* at pp. 322–325.

'guard against reasonableness degenerating into an unprincipled and unduly deferential standard of review'.[85] Unfortunately, recent developments in South African jurisprudence appear to indicate that the Constitutional Court is opting for greater deference instead of greater normative, or indeed principled, clarity.[86]

In place of the reasonableness approach, a more appropriate standard for courts to employ in socio-economic rights cases would be that of proportionality.[87] Over the last fifty years, proportionality has emerged as a veritable Esperanto of constitutional rights adjudication.[88] Proportionality does, of course, have its critics,[89] but generally it is seen, and has been embraced, as an emergent global 'best-practice' standard in constitutional rights adjudication.[90] The contours of proportionality analysis are well known – in general it involves a three/four-part test: (i) in the first instance the courts ask whether the policy and measure pursued by the state is a legitimate one under the terms of the constitution; (ii) the court then assesses whether or not the means chosen to pursue the aim are rationally connected to it; (iii) the inquiry then turns to the core of the proportionality test and asks (a) whether or not the means adopted are the least restrictive and (b) finally the court engages in an assessment of the proportionality of the measure *stricto sensu*, which is essentially a rough calculus of whether the benefit gained from the legitimate state policy outweighs the harm inflicted on the constitutional right.[91]

85 *Ibid.* at p. 325.
86 See *Mazibuko* v. *City of Johannesburg* [2009] ZACC 28 (8 October 2009) and *Nokotyana* v. *Ekurhuleni Metropolitan Municipality* [2009] ZACC 33 (19 November 2009); both discussed in Liebenberg (n. 67) at pp. 465–480.
87 See Fredman (n. 81) at p. 318, arguing that proportionality is superior to reasonableness in providing protection for socio-economic rights.
88 As Stone Sweet and Mathews (n. 73) at pp. 73–74, note: 'Over the past fifty years, proportionality analysis . . . has widely diffused. It is today an overarching principle of constitutional adjudication, the preferred procedure for managing disputes involving an alleged conflict between rights, or between rights provisions and a legitimate state or public interest . . . Although other modes of rights adjudication [are] available . . . [proportionality] has emerged as a multi-purpose, best practice, standard . . . By the end of the 1990s, virtually every effective system of constitutional justice in the world . . . had embraced the main tenets of [proportionality analysis]'. Although some do question the extent to which constitutional orders are converging around a shared conception of proportionality, arguing, instead, that any such convergence is at a very superficial level: see Jacco Bomhoff, 'Genealogies of Balancing Discourse' (2010) 4 *Law and Ethics of Human Rights* 107. For some commentators, such as David Beatty, it is the only approach which can adequately resolve the tension between popular sovereignty and the exercise of judicial power in a system of constitutional supremacy, by providing an objective and impartial method for resolving conflicts between competing constitutional values (*The Ultimate Rule of Law* (Oxford: Oxford University Press, 2004)).
89 See, for example, Stavros Tsakyakis, 'Proportionality: An Assault on Human Rights' (2009) 7 *International Journal of Constitutional Law* 468.
90 Stone Sweet and Mathews (n. 73) at p. 74.
91 *Ibid.* at pp. 75–76; Aharon Barak, 'Proportionality and Principled Balancing' (2010) 4 *Law and Ethics of Human Rights* 1 at pp. 6–7; and Julian Rivers, 'Proportionality and Variable Intensity of Review' (2006) 65 *Cambridge Law Journal* 174.

As traditionally understood, at least in the common law world, proportionality is viewed as a 'state-limiting' device, to prevent encroachment on fundamental rights. This conception is less suitable in the context of socio-economic rights adjudication, at least in terms of the positive obligations imposed by socio-economic rights, where the traditional continental European 'optimisation' conception of proportionality would appear to be more suitable.[92] Within such a framework courts should adopt a 'consequential' approach, which asks whether the 'state action is likely to achieve a mandated policy' and in assessing whether or not the state's arguments ought to be subject to rigorous scrutiny, and the burden of proof should rest firmly on the state.[93] In this context, the key 'judicial question should be whether a challenged law [or policy] achieves, or is at least likely to achieve, the constitutionally prescribed end'.[94]

One of the main advantages of proportionality review is that it is qualitatively different from reasonableness review, in that it imposes a more structured, rigorous and transparent standard of review on government decision making.[95] This, in turn, reduces the extent of judicial subjectivity. Of course it cannot be argued that adopting proportionality over reasonableness completely removes elements of judicial subjectivity,[96] but it certainly makes the process of judicial reasoning more structured and transparent.[97] Of course proportionality, like any adjudicative standard, is an empty vessel;[98] but the more structured and formulaic approach of proportionality review at least forces the courts into more squarely addressing any subjective preferences. A further advantage of proportionality review is that it is seen, generally, to provide a more demanding

---

92 On these two approaches to proportionality, see: Rivers (n. 91) at p. 176.

93 Hershkoff (n. 75) at p. 1184. As Bruce Porter argues that in any claim based on the violation of constitutionally protected socio-economic rights 'the onus must rest on the state to establish that available resources have been allocated in a manner that is consistent with the right of the claimant' ('The Crisis of Economic, Social and Cultural Rights and Strategies for Addressing It' in Squires, Langford and Thiele (eds.), *The Road to a Remedy: Current Issues in the Litigation of Economic, Social and Cultural Rights* (Sydney: University of New South Wales Press, 2005) 43 at p. 54).

94 Hershkoff (n. 75) at p. 1137.

95 As Dyzenhaus, Hunt and Taggart put it: 'The catechetic doctrine of proportionality, with its sequenced series of questions requiring reasoned answers from decision-makers, also underscores the need for justification. Vague assertions of deference or of non-justiciability under the cloak of *Wednesbury* unreasonableness will no longer do' (David Dyzenhaus, Murray Hunt and Michael Taggart, 'The Principle of Legality in Administrative Law: Internationalisation as Constitutionalisation' (2001) 1 *Oxford University Commonwealth Law Journal* 5 at p. 20).

96 Although Alexy may be guilty of trying to do just this: see Robert Alexy, 'The Construction of Constitutional Rights' (2010) 4 *Law and Ethics of Human Rights* 19 at pp. 28–32.

97 Marko Novak, 'Three Models of Balancing (in Constitutional Review)' (2010) 23 *Ratio Juris* 101 at p. 108; and see Stone Sweet and Mathews (n. 73) at p. 77.

98 See Anashri Pillay, 'Courts, Variable Standards of Review and Resource Allocation: Developing a Model for the Enforcement of Social and Economic Rights' (2007) 6 *European Human Rights Law Review* 616 at p. 634 and Rivers (n. 91) at p. 182.

examination of state policy.[99] Indeed in the context of the jurisprudence of the European Court of Human Rights (ECtHR) Julian Rivers notes how the Court rejected reasonableness review on the basis that the effect of adopting it would be 'to proceduralise Convention rights, making them merely mandatory considerations in the process of decision-making, and denying their nature as substantive outcome-related rights'.[100]

Furthermore, if we accept Robert Alexy's understanding of constitutional rights as 'optimization requirements', that is, as imperfectly realised ideals, the full realisation of which can only ever be approximate in light of factual constraints and competing values and principles,[101] it can be argued that proportionality is the ideally suited form of analysis for constitutional rights adjudication.[102] Finally, in the context of any such proportionality analysis, it is essential that the question of resources be addressed, as Liebenberg notes:

> Allowing the state to rely simply on its own budgetary allocations would defeat the purpose of socio-economic rights by allowing the state to determine the extent of its own obligations. Thus courts should examine the resources available in the national budget as a whole as opposed to focusing exclusively on existing allocations. To enable the courts to conduct this assessment, it is imperative that the state be required to place the necessary budgetary and policy information before the court in support of its justificatory arguments.[103]

The courts should, of course, exercise some circumspection, and show a degree of deference to the primary decision maker, but this deference should not amount to abdication and the artificial characterisation of any case with resource implications as a veritable 'no go area'.[104]

Adopting, then, a form of 'positive proportionality' allows the courts to more rigorously scrutinise state policies which impact on socio-economic rights, to determine whether, given the importance of such rights, the state's policies are likely to achieve their realisation and are moving as expeditiously as possible in this respect.[105] However, this approach also requires judicial reasoning to be

---

99 According to Stone Sweet and Mathews (n. 73) at p. 79, proportionality review is 'inarguably, the most invasive form of review found anywhere'.

100 Rivers (n. 91) at p. 191, discussing the ECtHR decision in *Smith and Grady* v. *United Kingdom* (1999) 29 EHRR 493; and see Stone Sweet and Mathews (n. 73) at pp. 145–152.

101 See, generally, Robert Alexy, *A Theory of Constitutional Rights* (Julian Rivers trans.) (Oxford: Oxford University Press, 2002) at pp. 47–49.

102 See Alexy (n. 96) at p. 24.

103 Liebenberg (n. 80) at p. 327.

104 See Eisenberg and Yeazell (n. 47) at p. 507. As Koch (n. 53) at p. 36 argues, respect for the elected branches of government should not 'imply that the judiciary is to abstain totally from judicial control with administrative decisions, even if such decisions are resource demanding'.

105 In this way the proportionality approach also resonates with the international human rights standards requiring states to move as expeditiously as possible towards the realisation of

more transparent and structured, and in this way can facilitate a more active dialogue between the courts and the elected branches of government.

7.3.4 Remedies: the structural interdict

With respect to any constitutional right, the question of remedies is central, as Daryl Levinson notes, 'for most practical purposes, remedies control the value of constitutional rights'.[106] Or as David Rudovsky puts it, 'rights may exist on paper as a matter of court decision or legislation, but their viability, indeed their very essence, depends in large part on the effectiveness of remedial and enforcement measures'.[107] This is particularly the case with respect to socio-economic rights. As Geoff Budlender perceptively notes, the 'problem in litigation involving positive obligations – whether of socio-economic or civil political rights – is not usually in proving the breach of the right. More frequently, it is in establishing an appropriate and effective remedy for the breach of the right'.[108] Similarly from the perspective of constitutional theory, or comparative constitutional scholarship, one of the central fault lines in determining the appropriate role for the courts in vindicating socio-economic rights is the question of remedies. As Fredman puts it:

> On the one hand, the democratic imperative suggests that courts should not impose solutions; but should instead act as a catalyst for democratic initiatives. On the other hand, positive duties would be of no value if they did not make it necessary to take action to fulfil the duty . . . A potential solution is through the declaratory remedy, since it feeds into the political process rather than imposing the will of the court . . . However, this solution leaves too much to the goodwill of the government, both because there is no inbuilt mechanism to prevent the government from reverting to its pre-deliberative stance, and because it pays too little attention to building a deliberative and participative element into the remedial structure.[109]

The task, then, is to articulate an approach to remedies that both provides some meaningful protection for the rights in question, but at the same time does not undermine the separation of powers, and accords with the dialogic approach to the separation of powers articulated above.

socio-economic rights: see Committee on Economic, Social and Cultural Rights (CESCR), General Comment No. 3 – The Nature of State Parties Obligations, UN doc.E/1991/23.
106 Daryl Levinson, 'Rights Essentialism and Remedial Equilibration' (1999) 99 *Columbia Law Review* 857 at p. 914.
107 David Rudovsky, 'Running in Place: The Paradox of Expanding Rights and Restricted Remedies' (2005) *University of Illinois Law Review* 1199 at p. 1200.
108 Geoff Budlender, 'The Role of the Courts in Achieving the Transformative Potential of Socio-Economic Rights' (2007) 8(1) *ESR Review* 9 at p. 10.
109 Sandra Fredman, *Human Rights Transformed: Positive Rights and Positive Duties* (Oxford: Oxford University Press, 2008) at pp. 118–119.

Two preliminary points in relation to the approach to remedies sketched here need to be made before proceeding. The first is that 'it is very important that the traditional principle that rights are not meaningful unless accompanied by remedies' be rethought and adapted for socio-economic rights.[110] This is so because of the inherent tension between 'a received remedial tradition that focuses on the correction of past violations suffered by individuals and a more complex remedial process with distributive and dialogic implications'.[111] The traditional attitude to remedies is born of a hostility to the state and the notion of the courts as guardians of individual liberty; it is thus 'premised on a monologic process in which courts enforce constitutional rights in a coercive manner on governments'.[112] In much the same way as the adoption of the over-arching framework above calls for the rethinking of certain received orthodoxies with respect to the separation of powers generally, so too a commitment to socio-economic rights requires a reconsideration of remedial practice. Rejecting the traditional pattern 'opens up the prospect of domestic courts . . . engaging governments in an ongoing process of continued dialogue and persuasion about the importance and possibility of achieving greater compliance with socio-economic rights'.[113]

The second preliminary point is that while courts always have the entire panoply of remedies at their disposal (declarations, mandatory orders, damages, etc.), the key concern must be whether or not the remedy addresses the violation in issue. Indeed, the granting of weak remedies, or the non-implementation of rare strong remedies, has been one of the fundamental shortcomings of the South African experience.[114] As Christopher Mbazira notes, 'victories at the conclusion of socio-economic rights cases have been hollow, as the lives of successful litigants have not improved dramatically'.[115] The key factor then in articulating remedies for breach of socio-economic rights should be whether the remedy 'meaningfully [vindicates] the rights . . . of the claimants'.[116] As Kent Roach and Geoff Budlender note, while:

> [different] remedial routes may be appropriate in different circumstances, but the ultimate destination that the courts should insist upon is compliance

---

110 Kent Roach, 'Crafting Remedies for Violations of Economic, Social and Cultural Rights' in Squires, Langford and Thiele (eds.), *The Road to a Remedy: Current Issues in the Litigation of Economic, Social and Cultural Rights* (Sydney: University of New South Wales Press, 2005) 111 at p. 111.

111 Kent Roach, 'The Challenge of Crafting Remedies for Violations of Socio-Economic Rights' in Langford (ed.), *Social Rights Jurisprudence: Emerging Trends in International and Comparative Law* (Cambridge: Cambridge University Press, 2008) 46 at p. 46.

112 *Ibid.* at p. 51.

113 *Ibid.* at p. 47.

114 See the discussion in Chapter 3.

115 Christopher Mbazira, 'From Ambivalence to Certainty: Norms and Principles for the Structural Interdict in Socio-Economic Rights Litigation in South Africa' (2008) 24 *South African Journal on Human Rights* 1 at p. 3.

116 *DoucetBoudreau* v. *Nova Scotia (Minister of Education)* [2003] 3 SCR 3 at para. 55.

with the constitution. In the final analysis, the test is one of effectiveness. Court orders that are not effective undermine respect for the courts, for the rule of law, and for the constitution itself.[117]

Similarly Mbazira argues that the 'reason people litigate is to enforce their rights . . . remedies must, therefore, as much as possible, be intended to realise rights'.[118] The objective then is to articulate a remedial practice that will both promote inter-institutional dialogue and, crucially, substantially address the violation of socio-economic rights identified in a given case.

With these two provisos in mind we now move on to articulate the optimum or ideal remedial approach in the context of a dialogic approach to the separation of powers. Craig Scott notes that '[institutional] dialogue operates with partic-ular appropriateness at the level of remedies. When a healthy interaction exists between the courts and other institutions, there is scope for the courts to make decisions and for other institutions to formulate or propose remedies'; he also notes that it 'is important to develop novel and creative remedies for dealing with violations of socio-economic rights'.[119] More expansively Kent Roach argues that:

> Dialogic remedies . . . attempt to persuade governments to internalize the norms they articulate and to make good faith efforts to select from a variety of legitimate options in order to recognize the relevant norm. They . . . anticipate that there are a range of legitimate responses open to government and that much can be gained by allowing governments to select the most appropriate responses. Dialogic remedies . . . contemplate a reiterative process in which governments report on steps to achieve compliance, dia-logic remedies cannot be fashioned in an instant so as to achieve rectification that traces and corrects past wrongs. Dialogic remedies often aim to promote healthy partnerships between courts and governments, and they are often concerned with producing systemic reforms to prevent violations in the future.[120]

This approach then represents a break with the traditional remedial practice of one-off orders, instead within the dialogic framework 'court decisions are not the last word in a political conversation, but rather the first, opening a dialogue

---

117 Kent Roach and Geoff Budlender, 'Mandatory Relief and Supervisory Jurisdiction: When Is it Appropriate, Just and Equitable?' (2005) 122 *South African Law Journal* 325 at p. 351. Similarly Susan Strum argues that in public law litigation the most important factor in determining what remedy to grant is that the remedy 'must be reasonably calculated to produce compliance with the underlying substantive constitutional norm' ('A Normative Theory of Public Law Remedies' (1991) 79 *Georgetown Law Journal* 1355 at p. 1411).
118 Mbazira (n. 115) at p. 26.
119 Craig Scott, 'Towards a Principled, Pragmatic Judicial Role' (1999) 1(4) *ESR Review* 4 at p. 5.
120 Roach (n. 110) at p. 553.

with the legislature and the people and spurring the development of shared solutions to important public problems'.[121]

One approach to achieving such a dialogue would be for the courts, once they have found a violation, to simply issue a declaration, with the expectation that the elected branches will respond accordingly.[122] Declarations, of course, proceed on the assumption that once the elected branches are made aware of their constitutional failing, they will respond in an appropriate manner and that judicial supervision will, therefore, be unnecessary.[123] Such faith, however, is often tested where those whose rights are denied are politically powerless and do not feature in the calculus of re-election.[124] Indeed, writing in the Irish context Conor O'Mahony notes that declaratory orders are 'perhaps the least problematic, but potentially least effective remedy for a breach of constitutional rights'.[125] As O'Mahony notes, such orders are premised on the notion – indeed the belief – that the state will act of its own accord to remedy an unconstitutionality once informed of it, however, as the Irish experience demonstrates, such belief 'is frequently misplaced'.[126]

When the expectation that the elected branches of government will respond appropriately to declaratory orders 'proves false – whether because of legitimate resource constraints or egregious contempt of court – declarations of invalidity fail to remedy the violation in question'.[127] There are, as Dixon argues and the South African experience attests, significant dangers in such a remedial approach, as reliance on declaratory orders can 'substantially undermine [the capacity of courts] to counter legislative inertia'.[128] By the same token, the Indian experience shows that the issuing of one-off mandatory orders can be equally inefficacious.[129] Such an approach also sits uneasily with the dialogic and cooperative approach to the separation of powers advocated here. Instead,

---

121 Hershkoff (n. 75) at p. 1169.
122 Indeed, this is the approach advocated by O'Regan J. in the South African context, who argued that 'A declaratory order is a flexible remedy which can assist in clarifying legal and constitutional obligations in a manner which promotes the protection and enforcement of our Constitution and its values . . . It should also be borne in mind that declaratory relief is of particular value in a constitutional democracy which enables courts to declare the law, on the one hand, but to leave to the other arms of government, the executive and the legislature, the decision as to how best the law, once stated, should be observed' (*Rail Commuters Action Group* v. *Transnet Ltd.* 2005 (4) BCLR 301 (CC) at paras. 108–109).
123 See Roach and Budlender (n. 117) at p. 346.
124 *Ibid.*
125 O'Mahony (n. 65) at p. 62.
126 *Ibid.* at p. 63.
127 Mitra Ebadolahi, 'Using Structural Interdicts and the South African Human Rights Commission to Achieve Judicial Enforcement of Economic and Social Rights in South Africa' (2008) 83 *New York University Law Review* 1565 at p. 1578.
128 Dixon (n. 69) at p. 412.
129 See Shylashri Shankar and Pratap Bhanu Mehta, 'Courts and Socioeconomic Rights in India' in Gauri and Brinks (eds.), *Courting Social Justice: Judicial Enforcement of Social and Economic Rights in the Developing World* (Cambridge: Cambridge University Press, 2008) 146.

then, of either of these approaches, it would seem that the optimum type of remedy in a constitutional system premised on a commitment to socio-economic rights and informed by a dialogic approach to the separation of powers, would be the structural interdict.[130]

The structural interdict finds its origins in the US civil rights movement, where it, or 'the civil rights injunction', was at the very heart of litigation efforts.[131] However, the approach adopted by the courts in the US context arguably involved them far too much in designing the *minutiae* of policies,[132] and would not be suited to the dialogic and cooperative approach to the separation of powers advocated here. Instead, setting off from the premise that within the context of a dialogic approach to the separation of powers, the courts' role at the remedial stage 'is to structure a deliberative process whereby stakeholders in the public dispute develop a consensual remedial solution using reasoned dialogue, and to evaluate the adequacy of this process and the remedy it produces',[133] it is possible to articulate a nuanced approach to structural interdicts, which facilitates dialogue, progresses the realisation of socio-economic rights and retains respect for the separation of powers.

In this context the structural interdict appears to be the most logical and defensible remedy in the context of a dialogic approach to the judicial enforcement of socio-economic rights. For Budlender the value of structural interdicts is that they '[declare] that there has been a breach and require the government to produce a programme on how it is going to remedy the breach. They provide civil society and other participants with an opportunity to comment on the design and implementation of the government programme. They sometimes provide for the court to exercise some supervisory role for a period'.[134] Budlender acknowledges conventional criticisms which deem structural interdicts to be

---

130 As Mia Swart puts it, 'in the context of a constitutional commitment to realising socio-economic rights and in the light of the demonstrated need for [an] ongoing supervisory function by the court because of government inaction employing structural interdicts might make sense. It would also be a remedy that fits the programmatic nature of socio-economic relief' ('Left Out in the Cold? Crafting Constitutional Remedies for the Poorest of the Poor' (2005) 21 *South African Journal on Human Rights* 215 at p. 227). There are five general components of a structural interdict: first the competent court issues a declaration to the effect that the state has breached an individual's or group's constitutional rights, or otherwise failed to comply with its constitutional obligations; secondly the court mandates state compliance with its constitutional obligation; the state is then ordered to submit a plan to the court, within a specified time-frame, setting out the state's proposed course of action to remedy the constitutional violation; when the report is submitted the court is then required to assess whether it in fact will remedy the constitutional violation; following some negotiation, and where appropriate amendment of the plan, the court then makes an order incorporating the state's plan and mandating the state to comply with the implementation of the plan (see Ebadolahi (n. 127) at pp. 1591–1593).
131 Chayes (n. 47) at p. 1298.
132 *Ibid.*; and see Robert Nagel, 'Controlling the Structural Injunction' (1984) 7 *Harvard Journal of Law and Public Policy* 395.
133 Strum (n. 117) at p. 1427.
134 Budlender (n. 108) at p. 11.

undemocratic because of the judiciary's limited democratic pedigree, but argues that they can be 'deeply democratising' because '[they] create spaces for a dialogue between the court, the government and civil society actors. In this way, they strengthen and deepen accountability and participation – the key elements of democracy'.[135] In this way the adoption of structural interdicts serves to structure a dialogue between the courts and the elected branches of government – and ideally to foster a 'polylogue' incorporating the views of society more broadly – without involving the courts in the usurpation of the role of the elected branches of government. As Koch puts it, allowing the courts to '[point] out that a certain matter needs a new solution is not the same as taking over the legislative role'.[136]

While the structural interdict can take a number of forms,[137] the most appropriate form would seem to be that which requires the government to report back to the court with a plan for how it proposes to address the constitutional violation identified by the courts.[138] This has the dual advantages that it allows the courts to defer to the elected branches of government on the most effective way of eliminating the violation, thus shielding the courts from 'accusations that it has usurped functions reserved for the other organs of state'. At the same time, this approach promotes the articulation of a 'self-imposed remedy' by the defendant, which should make its implementation simpler and more likely.[139] Liebenberg argues that such orders should 'strive to preserve the choice of means of the legislative and executive as to the precise manner in which to remedy the situation while not abdicating the court's responsibility to ensure that constitutional objectives are fulfilled'.[140]

This approach, of course, entails a degree of judicial supervision, or ongoing involvement, with the elected branches of government. However, this should not be viewed as the coercive subjugation of one branch of government by another, but rather an instance of the inevitable and continuous interaction between the courts and the elected branches of government in the context of a dialogic separation-of-powers paradigm.[141] A further implication of the dialogic

---

135 *Ibid.*
136 Koch (n. 53) at p. 36.
137 See Mbazira (n. 114) at pp. 6–8.
138 This approach resonates with Cécile Fabre's argument (n. 76) at p. 150, that 'the courts should simply remind the government of what its duties are, should tell them to fulfil these duties by a certain date as deemed reasonable, but should forbear from spelling out in any detail how they should fulfil them . . . Distinguishing in this way between telling the government to fulfil its constitutional duty and telling the government how to fulfil such a duty, and allowing for the first kind of injunction but not the second, enables us to give more scope to democratic decision-making than opponents of bills of social rights think possible'.
139 Mbazira (n. 115) at p. 7.
140 Sandra Liebenberg, 'South Africa: Adjudicating Social Rights Under a Transformative Constitution' in Langford (ed.), *Social Rights Jurisprudence: Emerging Trends in International and Comparative Law* (Cambridge: Cambridge University Press, 2008) 75 at p. 98.
141 As Swart (n. 130) at pp. 227–228 argues, 'redressing systematic violations of socio-economic rights often requires far-reaching institutional and structural reform. Violations of this

approach is that the adoption of remedies such as structural interdicts should come to be seen as the norm, rather than as exception. At present a number of people, including advocates of socio-economic rights, seem to think that what we might term strong remedies, such as the structural interdict, ought only to be granted where there has been some malfeasance on the part of the state.[142] In part, reticence about adopting this form of remedy (viewing it as a 'weapon of last resort') is born of the US experience – in which the federal courts became heavily involved in the detailed planning of programmes and institutional arrangements – which, it was argued, violated the 'spirit and sense of the constitutional principle of separation of powers'.[143]

The US experience, however, is just that – a peculiarly US experience, born of that country's more combative, zero-sum understanding of the relationship between the courts and the elected branches of government.[144] Moving away from the combative, zero-sum approach to the separation of powers characteristic of the US experience, and to a lesser extent the Irish, and viewing the different branches of government as coequal participants in an ongoing and cooperative enterprise, allows us to view remedies such as the structural interdict as positive, dialogue-structuring devices. As Ebadolahi argues, the structural interdict:

> preserves an active role for the judiciary, yet avoids difficult separation of powers problems by requiring appropriate political actors to formulate plans for change. As such, structural interdicts circumvent institutional competency critiques; legislators and/or executive branch officials are required to take action, but are given the necessary flexibility to accommodate complex polycentric decisionmaking.[145]

While the structural interdict may not entirely 'circumvent' institutional competency critiques, and separation-of-powers concerns, it certainly goes a

---

kind cannot be remedied by a single court order made once and for all. If remedies for socioeconomic rights violations are to be effective and meaningful the assumption by a court of a supervisory jurisdiction appears unavoidable'.

142 See for example Roach (n. 111) at pp. 53–54 and Mbazira (n. 115) at p. 20.

143 Nagel (n. 132) at p. 398.

144 See Ackerman (n. 8) at p. 725, who argues that if courts 'lack the remedial capacity to order the big budgetary appropriations necessary to transform "positive rights" into social realities . . . constitutional "guarantees" of social welfare would not be worth the paper on which they were written'; and Gordon Silverstein, *Law's Allure: How Law Shapes, Constrains, Saves and Kills Politics* (New York: Cambridge University Press, 2009) at p. 98 stressing the need for the courts to exercise a 'command function' to be effective in the context of litigation which attempts to address poverty and exclusion. While it is true to say that mere paper guarantees are worthless, the conception of the relationship between the courts and the elected branches of government articulated by these authors is arguably outdated, but certainly inappropriate in the context of socio-economic rights adjudication, albeit not surprising coming, as it does, from commentators schooled in the more 'combative' American system of constitutionalism.

145 Ebadolahi (n. 127) at pp. 1595–1596.

long way to attenuating such concerns in a constitutional order committed to the protection of socio-economic rights, and a dialogic understanding of the separation of powers.

7.4 Conclusion

It is hoped that the model framework sketched here goes some way towards showing that if we are willing to break with the false necessity of the zero-sum separation-of-powers thesis, it is possible to articulate a principled judicial role in the vindication of socio-economic rights, which does not undermine the separation of powers and retains the primacy of the elected branches of government in social policy. In this approach, which sets off from the starting point of a strong commitment to socio-economic rights, the branches of government engage with one another as equals, engaged in the cooperative enterprise of advancing the realisation of socio-economic rights. Through a dialogic process the courts use strong forms of scrutiny, in the form of proportionality, to determine whether or not the state is living up to its commitments in relation to socio-economic rights. This, however, is somewhat tempered at the remedial stage, where the courts, through the use of dialogue-structuring, structural interdicts, remit the matter back to the elected branches of government, to determine the best way in which socio-economic rights can be realised. With the perennial proviso that any proposal must, in substance, be likely to improve the enjoyment and protection of the socio-economic rights of the claimants, and other similarly situated people.

Consequently, the separation-of-powers concerns raised in various jurisdictions and somewhat inconsistently in some of the jurisdictions looked at here, against the constitutional protection of socio-economic rights cannot be considered to settle the matter. But rather must be seen as invitations to articulate a more nuanced conception of the separation of powers. This then brings to the fore Kim Lane Scheppele's observation that '[behind] most critiques of justiciable social rights are two presumptions: (1) that court decisions necessarily come in the form of all-or-nothing mandates to government, and (2) that court decisions giving meaning to social rights must do so by putting effective liens of a particular size on the state budget'.[146] The model framework articulated here, in particular the dialogic approach to the separation of powers, exposes the false necessity of these presumptions. In contrast to the apprehensions underlying these assumptions, it has been shown that it is possible for courts to play a principled, constructive role in vindicating socio-economic rights. Such a role both provides meaningful protection of socio-economic rights through the courts, and respects the separation of powers by ensuring that the elected branches of government retain, as they should, primary responsibility for formulating and implementing social policy.

146 Kim Lane Scheppele, 'A Realpolitik Defense of Social Rights' (2004) 82 *Texas Law Review* 1921 at p. 1931.

8   Conclusions

This study has sought to show that it is possible for domestic superior courts to play a meaningful role in the advancement and vindication of socio-economic rights, while at the same time retaining the integrity of the separation of powers. Based both on the normative ideals of international human rights standards, and the actual experience of a variety of jurisdictions in adjudicating on socio-economic rights, it has been shown that if we depart from rigid conceptions of the separation of powers, a defensible role for the courts can be articulated. Therefore, it can be said, without being flippant, that notwithstanding reasonable concerns about the judicial enforcement of constitutionally entrenched socio-economic rights, it is at least possible for the courts to play a role without undermining the separation of powers. While this addresses one very important point,[1] it is, of course, by no means the whole story. There is a vast world beyond the confines of the courthouse, which has far more influence on the fortunes of socio-economic rights than even the most well-meaning court could have; and it is to some of these wider considerations that we turn in conclusion.

This chapter begins by briefly restating the essential character and broad contours of the model adjudicative framework articulated in Chapter 7. In terms of realpolitik, the next two sections look at some of the key limitations of reliance on juridical 'rights talk' in addressing the poverty and exclusion

---

1   Given the focus in this study on the specific issue of the separation of powers, some might say the focus has been too narrow. Marius Pieterse, for example, argues that 'a disproportionate focus on institutional and procedural aspects of the judicial enforcement of socioeconomic rights, rather than on their content and implications . . . sidelines the content of the rights . . . there needs to be a shift in . . . global socioeconomic rights scholarship, away from its current focus on issues of institutional competence and on the comparative adequacy of different standards of judicial scrutiny or other procedural yardsticks. We need to focus anew on articulating the content and practical implications of socioeconomic rights, the obligations they impose, and the limits inherent in their enforcement' in order to find out how socio-economic rights can, in substance, benefit people ('Eating Socioeconomic Rights: The Usefulness of Rights Talk in Alleviating Social Hardship Revisited' (2007) 29 *Human Rights Quarterly* 796 at p. 822); see also Theodore Eisenberg and Stephen Yeazell, 'The Ordinary and the Extraordinary in Institutional Litigation' (1980) 93 *Harvard Law Review* 465 at p. 467.

experienced by those whose interests would be most closely related with socio-economic rights. In this respect two issues are addressed: first, the inherent limitations in the use of rights and the courts to bring about social change; and secondly a more contingent limitation, namely the marginalisation of socio-economic rights in the context of neo-liberal globalisation. Both of these issues raise serious doubts about the efficacy of reliance on and advocacy for socio-economic rights, and in this respect they raise doubts about the value – if not the strength and coherence – of the argument advanced here; it is therefore appropriate that they are noted at this juncture. Finally, then, this chapter concludes with a tentative assessment of what the future of socio-economic rights may be, in light both of the limitations discussed here and the various issues addressed throughout this study.

8.1 The defensible judicial role

The study undertaken here shows that if we are willing to depart from static notions of the separation of powers and of the roles of various institutions, it is possible to conceive of a legitimate role for domestic courts in adjudicating on socio-economic rights, and thereby contributing to their ultimate vindication, without undermining the entire constitutional edifice. The argument here, of course, is not that the judiciary should play the primary role in the vindication of socio-economic rights, but more modestly that some judicial role be recognised in the protection of socio-economic rights as a valid aid to the political pursuit and protection of such rights.[2] Or, in other words, that socio-economic rights and the claims of those most in need of their protection are afforded some adjudicative space.[3] It is, of course, nonsense to imagine that courts can – or indeed should – take the lead role in vindicating socio-economic rights, but they can play a constructive role; as Gordon Silverstein notes, 'turning to the courts is a powerful tool, but relying on them exclusively is a strategy fraught with risk'.[4]

---

2 A similar approach is advocated by the International Commission of Jurists, see: International Commission of Jurists (ICJ), *Courts and the Legal Enforcement of Economic, Social and Cultural Rights: Comparative Experiences of Justiciability* (Geneva: ICJ, 2008) at p. 3; and see Christian Courtis, 'Standards to Make ESC Rights Justiciable: A Summary Exploration' (2009) 2 *Erasmus Law Review* 379 at p. 380.

3 See Bruce Porter, 'Claiming Adjudicative Space: Social Rights, Equality and Citizenship' in Young, Boyd, Brodsky and Day (eds.), *Poverty: Rights, Social Citizenship and Legal Activism* (Vancouver: UBC Press, 2007) 77. As Scott and Macklem put it, 'in a world increasingly committed to judicial protection of human rights, excluding social rights from the ambit of justiciability will tend to have a negative effect on those rights and ultimately on the people that depend on them' (Craig Scott and Patrick Macklem, 'Constitutional Ropes of Sand or Justiciable Guarantees? Social Rights in a New South African Constitution' (1992) 141 *University of Pennsylvania Law Review* 1 at pp. 40–41).

4 Gordon Silverstein, *Law's Allure: How Law Shapes, Constrains, Saves and Kills Politics* (New York: Cambridge University Press, 2009) at p. 268.

The argument advanced in this study, in a nutshell, is that the separation-of-powers arguments against the constitutional entrenchment of socio-economic rights only really make sense in the context of a rigid, formalistic and arguably outmoded conception of the separation of powers. If, on the other hand, we are genuinely committed to the protection of socio-economic rights (and this is a crucial precondition), it is possible to reimagine the separation of powers as a dynamic and ongoing interaction between the different branches of government, all of which are – or should be – committed to the overall goal of advancing socio-economic rights. Within this paradigm the courts exercise strong-form review, in the form of proportionality analysis, and engage in an exacting examination of state policies with respect to socio-economic rights. At this stage the courts should also consciously engage in the normative development of the content of socio-economic rights, drawing where appropriate on international and comparative standards, and should diligently query resource-based claims advanced by the state.

When it comes to remedies the real benefit of the dialogic approach comes to the fore. If the courts determine that there has been a breach of socio-economic rights, they then remit the matter back to the elected branches of government, for them to articulate an appropriate response. This, however, is not the end of the matter. Through the structural interdict the courts remain involved in the articulation of the state's response, to ensure that it is sufficiently proportionate to realise the important interests at issue, as partners in an ongoing, structured dialogue. Adopting this model approach, or at least approximating towards it, allows us to have both meaningful judicial involvement in the vindication of socio-economic rights, and to retain the integrity of the separation of powers. In this way the defensible judicial role articulated here goes a long way towards negating the zero-sum separation-of-powers thesis routinely invoked against the constitutional protection of socio-economic rights, and shows the false necessity of the binary choice between either the installation of 'philosopher kings', or the complete freedom of the elected branches of government to address socio-economic deprivation and exclusion however they may choose.

8.2 The limits of 'rights talk'

While this study is fundamentally about advocating a role for the courts in the protection of socio-economic rights, and by extension is premised on the value of rights, it should not be overlooked that there are substantial limitations to what can be achieved through the deployment of rights talk. This section briefly highlights two senses in which 'rights talk', in the context of socio-economic deprivation and exclusion, is limited, but then goes on to argue that such limitations do not completely undermine or negate the value of relying on rights in certain specific circumstances. The two limitations to rights talk which will be highlighted here are: (i) the inherent limitations in rights, even in the best-case scenario (with entrenched rights and a committed judiciary), to bring about fundamental social change; and (ii) the limitations of relying on what is, in essence, a conservative social institution, the judiciary, and an arguably conservative medium (rights) to seek to address, and in certain respects transcend, the inequities of the social *status quo*.

There are, of course, inherent limits to what reliance on constitutional rights and courts can actually achieve in terms of concrete social change.[5] In the context of socio-economic rights, Bruce Porter acknowledges that 'the primary locus for claiming [socio-economic] rights is outside of courts, in social movements and historical struggles' and therefore cautions that we should 'have no illusions about the law providing an all-encompassing framework' for socio-economic rights.[6] However, simply remitting the needs and interests of socially and economically excluded groups back to the political process smacks of an irony that Anatole France would appreciate, when the reality is that, for a variety of reasons, 'the official avenues of political representation and participation frequently fail to provide effective protection for the rights of marginalised groups in society'.[7] In such circumstances courts can play a vital role as 'an influential forum where the multifaceted dimensions of poverty and the social responses to it can be evaluated in the light of constitutional rights and values'.[8]

Consequently, accepting that formally entrenched rights are not a panacea for society's ills, does not necessarily require us to completely reject reliance on rights in some circumstances. Acknowledging that progress in vindicating socio-economic rights will, fundamentally, be a matter of substantive politics does not render nugatory the debate over socio-economic rights. As Cécile Fabre puts it:

> I wholeheartedly agree that social rights, and therefore constitutional social rights, are not *the* solution to poverty and deprivation, and that greater structural changes are needed in order to bring about social justice. Let me just say that these changes are unlikely to happen in the near, or indeed not so near, future, however willing some governments might be to make them. There are several reasons for that, not the least of which is that in our interdependent global economy, all governments, or at any rate all the most powerful of them must be so willing in order for social justice to exist; as it happens, they are not. To reject social rights and their constitutionalization on the grounds that one should in fact concentrate on tearing capitalism asunder or at the very least on profoundly reforming it amounts

---

5 See Gerald Rosenberg, *The Hollow Hope: Can Courts Bring About Social Change?* (2nd edn, Chicago: University of Chicago Press, 2008).

6 Bruce Porter, 'The Crisis of Economic, Social and Cultural Rights and Strategies for Addressing It' in Squires, Langford and Thiele (eds.), *The Road to a Remedy: Current Issues in the Litigation of Economic, Social and Cultural Rights* (Sydney: University of New South Wales Press, 2005) 43 at p. 45.

7 Sandra Liebenberg, *Socio-Economic Rights: Adjudication Under a Transformative Constitution* (Claremont: Juta, 2010) at p. 35.

8 *Ibid.* at p. 37.

to holding the poor hostage to these governments' good will, or lack thereof.[9]

We can, therefore, recognise the limitations of rights, while also recognising that rights can deliver some limited protection for excluded and marginalised groups, and that rights in general, and socio-economic rights in particular, can provide 'a tool for mobilisation of societies and social movements', to address the underlying causes of poverty and exclusion.[10]

In terms of the second set of shortcomings with rights talk, the conservative nature of both the judiciary and rights themselves, David Kennedy expresses concern about the potential for entrenched, and hence overly 'legalised', socio-economic rights to make 'people everywhere more passive and isolated'.[11] And the potential for rights talk to blinker social movements, and distract them from more pertinent political and social concerns,[12] he also criticises the 'human rights movement', for fetishising the role of the judiciary and ignoring the political, economic and social forces which influence judicial decision making.[13] Furthermore, he criticises rights talk for marginalising other forms of emancipatory discourse.[14] Similarly, Joel Bakan notes that 'social rights, because of their atomistic form, will not touch the real causes of poverty and other social ills. Social rights that oblige government to provide services, even if they are effective in protecting and improving those services – a big "if" – are unlikely to affect the social and economic relations that produce the need for those services in the first place'.[15]

Certainly there is much force to these combined critiques. To begin, with the judiciary – as J. A. G. Griffiths noted in his monumental study – as a body 'are protectors of what has been, of the relationships and interests on which, in

9 Cécile Fabre, *Social Rights Under the Constitution* (Oxford: Oxford University Press, 2000) at p. 186. In a similar vein Marius Pieterse notes that 'Enforcing socio-economic rights-claims therefore runs the risk of frustrating the progression of structural social and economic reforms, by "individualising" universal social problems and by disrupting or inhibiting established processes aimed at overcoming such problems . . . Yet widespread socio-economic hardship and the need for widescale structural reforms should not mean that legitimate, individual survival interests are sacrificed in favour of a vaguely-defined "common good". Rights terminology is used in relation to social goods precisely to counter the self-defeatism of an "all-or-nothing" communalist approach to social upliftment' ('Resuscitating Socio-Economic Rights: Constitutional Entitlements to Health Care Services' (2006) 22 *South African Journal on Human Rights* 473 at pp. 476–477).
10 Jill Cottrell and Yash Ghai, 'The Role of the Courts in the Protection of Economic, Social and Cultural Rights' in Ghai and Cottrell (eds.), *Economic, Social and Cultural Rights in Practice* (London: INTERIGHTS, 2004) 58 at p. 59.
11 David Kennedy, 'The International Human Rights Movement: Part of the Problem' (2001) 3 *European Human Rights Law Review* 245 at p. 246.
12 *Ibid.* at p. 253.
13 *Ibid.* at p. 259.
14 *Ibid.* at p. 265.
15 Joel Bakan, *Just Words: Constitutional Rights and Social Wrongs* (Toronto: University of Toronto Press, 1997) at p. 139.

their view, our society is founded. They do not regard their role as radical or even reformist, only (on occasion) corrective'.[16] Similarly Marius Pieterse notes that it 'will be difficult to persuade a judiciary, the members of which have been socialized in the liberal democratic tradition and whose class interests are often served by the social and political status quo, to transcend imagined boundaries that inhibit their pro-active participation in the struggle for freedom from material want'.[17] It is also fair to say that the dominant discourse of rights does tend to reflect and privilege existing social relations.[18]

By the same token, however, 'rights ideology' can be 'a powerful transformative force and a potent weapon in the hands of the dispossessed'.[19] And, while the entrenchment of formal constitutional entitlements to socio-economic rights, and the attendant empowerment of the judiciary to play a role in vindicating these rights, is undoubtedly a limited avenue, we should also note that it nonetheless serves valuable and by no means trivial ends. As Matthew Craven puts it, arguments for the recognition and protection of socio-economic rights are:

> responsive to the concern that the rights debate has . . . been captured by an ideology that is content to narrow the possibilities of strategic action in relation to particular types of social claims and, perhaps unconsciously, to naturalise, or legitimate, the forms of deprivation to which they relate. Advancing the possibilities of adjudication, therefore, serves at once to provide a strategic outlet for the advancement of such claims . . . whilst seeking more broadly to reconfigure an existing orthodoxy of rights discourse in which the concerns underlying [socio-economic] rights have been assigned a limited place.[20]

It is therefore possible to acknowledge the limitations of rights talk, while still maintaining that engaging in the debate on rights can be an important dimension in the overall struggle for political change.[21]

16 J. A. G. Griffith, *The Politics of the Judiciary* (5th edn, London: Fontana Press, 1997) at p. 8.
17 Marius Pieterse, 'Possibilities and Pitfalls in the Domestic Enforcement of Social Rights: Contemplating the South African Experience' (2004) 26 *Human Rights Quarterly* 882 at p. 905.
18 See, for example, Duncan Kennedy, *A Critique of Adjudication (fin de siècle)* (Cambridge, MA: Harvard University Press, 1997) and Peter Gabel, 'Phenomenology of Rights-Consciousness and the Pact of the Withdrawn Selves' (1983) 62 *Texas Law Review* 1563.
19 Jeanne M. Woods, 'Justiciable Social Rights as a Critique of the Liberal Paradigm' (2003) 38 *Texas International Law Journal* 763 at p. 793.
20 Matthew Craven, 'Assessment of Progress on Adjudication of Economic, Social and Cultural Rights' in Squires, Langford and Thiele (eds.), *The Road to a Remedy: Current Issues in the Litigation of Economic, Social and Cultural Rights* (Sydney: University of New South Wales Press, 2005) 27 at pp. 27–28.
21 As Scott and Macklem (n. 3) at pp. 6–8 note: 'As with other constitutionalized rights, it is fruitless and even dangerous to look to the courts for the first and last word on any matter concerning the vindication of fundamental societal values. Although the judiciary can spur

8.3 The political economy of human rights

Although this study has been concerned with articulating a role for the courts in vindicating socio-economic rights, the reality is that even entrenched catalogues of rights enforced by a committed judiciary cannot, by themselves, solve society's problems. This general limitation is exacerbated in the area of socio-economic rights, particularly in the current global climate.[22] The point is well made by Ran Hirschl when he notes that:

> Given the stark socioeconomic disparities among and within nations and groups, and given the extrajudicial social and economic conditions that preclude a full realization of substantive equality, it is questionable whether an even more extensive constitutionalization of rights or a more generous judicial interpretation of these rights would significantly improve the real socio-economic status of capitalism's traditional losers.[23]

Hirschl's warning opens up the much bigger issue of one of the most serious threats to truly vindicating socio-economic rights: the real-world political, economic and ideological opposition (or at best indifference) to socio-economic rights, in a global climate which privileges 'market' solutions to all of society's problems.[24]

In the contemporary era of globalisation, the dominant ideology is that of neo-liberalism, which, at least at the level of rhetoric, advocates the 'rolling back' of the state, and the recasting of social provision as of right into consumer choice. As David Schneiderman notes:

> The key actors promoting economic globalization expect national legal orders to undertake measures that will enhance the liberalization of markets. Where appropriate, states are expected to remove themselves from the performance of certain functions, as in the denationalization of public enterprise or privatization of public services . . . domestic legal affairs are restructured to augment norms articulated in the transnational sphere.[25]

---

societal reform, the realization of gains in the area of social justice . . . is more often than not the result of years of grassroots organizing by individuals and social movements committed to social and economic justice'. By the same token they argue that 'it is as unfounded to place one's faith entirely in the realm of constitutional politics as it is to place it entirely in the realm of constitutional adjudication'.

22 See Paul O'Connell, 'The Death of Socio-Economic Rights' (2011) 74 *Modern Law Review* 542.

23 Ran Hirschl, *Towards Juristocracy* (Harvard: Harvard University Press, 2004) at p. 220.

24 See, generally, Paul O'Connell, 'On Reconciling Irreconcilables: Neo-liberal Globalisation and Human Rights' (2007) 7(3) *Human Rights Law Review* 483.

25 David Schneiderman, *Constitutionalizing Economic Globalization* (Cambridge: Cambridge University Press, 2007) at p. 112.

The pursuit of this policy and ideological agenda is inherently inimical to the enjoyment and protection of socio-economic rights. In South Africa,[26] India,[27] Canada[28] and Ireland the adoption and implementation of such neo-liberal economic and social policies has resulted in the continued denial of socio-economic rights.[29] Furthermore, the pervasiveness of neo-liberal ideology has arguably influenced the judiciary in these jurisdictions to engage in a discursive narrowing of the potential of socio-economic rights. Recasting them as negative, market-friendly guarantees.[30]

In this context of neo-liberal globalisation, Asbjorn Eide argues that the 'most dramatic obstacle to the enjoyment of economic, social and cultural rights is the steep increase in income-specific inequality, both among nations and within nations, and the spread of poverty in the midst of plenty'.[31] He further argues that this growing inequality is facilitated and maintained, in large part, by 'the neoliberalist ideology' which 'harnesses a set of assertions and assumptions deployed to justify the priority of market principles over human rights, in particular favouring unrestrained market operations over economic and social human rights'.[32]

---

26 See Patrick Bond, *Talk Left, Walk Right: South Africa's Frustrated Global Reforms* (2nd edn, Pretoria: University of KwaZulu-Natal Press, 2006), John Saul, *The Next Liberation Struggle: Capitalism, Socialism, and Democracy in Southern Africa* (New York: Monthly Review Press, 2005) and John Pilger, *Freedom Next Time* (London: Bantam Press, 2006) ch. 4.

27 On India see Pilger (n. 26) ch. 3 and Prashant Bhushan, 'Misplaced Priorities and Class Bias in the Judiciary' (2009) 44 (14) *Economic and Political Weekly* 32. In the Indian context Muralidhar notes that 'The increasing instances of the State withdrawing from its welfare role and resorting to privatisation of the control and distribution of basic community resources like water and electricity and for providing health care and education are cause for concern for those wishing to assert the obligation of the State in the spheres of economic and social rights' (S. Muralidhar, 'India: The Expectations and Challenges of Judicial Enforcement of Social Rights' in Langford (ed), *Social Rights Jurisprudence: Emerging Trends in International and Comparative Law* (Cambridge: Cambridge University Press, 2008) 102 at p. 123).

28 See, for example, Margot Young, 'Introduction' in Young, Boyd, Brodsky and Day (eds.), *Poverty: Rights, Social Citizenship and Legal Activism* (Vancouver: UBC Press, 2007) 1; and Ed Broadbent, 'Barbarism Lite: Political Assault on Social Rights is Worsening Inequality' available at: www.policyalternatives.ca/publications/monitor/barbarism-lite (last retrieved 14 January 2010).

29 On Ireland see Fintan O'Toole, *After the Ball: Ireland After the Boom* (Dublin: Gill & Macmillan, 2003) and Paul O'Connell, 'The Human Right to Health and the Privatisation of Irish Health Care' (2005) 11(2) *Medico-Legal Journal of Ireland* 76.

30 See, for example, *Auton (Guardian ad litem of) v. British Columbia (Attorney General)* [2004] 3 SCR 657, *Chaoulli v. Quebec (Attorney General)* [2005] 1 SCR 791, *Mazibuko v. City of Johannesburg* [2009] ZACC 28 (8 October 2009), *TMA Pai Foundation v. State of Karnataka* [2002] INSC 455 (31 October 2002) and *TD v. Minister for Education* [2001] 4 IR 259.

31 Asbjorn Eide, 'Obstacles and Goals to Be Pursued' in Eide, Krause and Rosas (eds.), *Economic, Social and Cultural Rights: A Textbook* (2nd edn, The Hague: Martinus Nijhoff, 2001) 553 at p. 555.

32 *Ibid.* at pp. 557–558; and see Paul O'Connell, 'Brave New World?: Human Rights in the Era of Globalisation' in Baderin and Ssenyonjo (eds.), *International Human Rights Law: Six Decades After the UDHR and Beyond* (Hampshire: Ashgate, 2010) 195.

Consequently Eide and Rosas argue that while 'it is fully possible to give concrete legal relevance to [socio-economic] rights, it cannot be overlooked that there are in many quarters ideological aversions to such an approach'.[33] One of the ultimate problems then, as Beetham notes, is that the meaningful vindication of socio-economic rights 'would require a redistribution of power and resources, both within countries and between them',[34] and in the era of neo-liberal globalisation there are powerful and influential vested interests who are opposed to any such redistribution. Similarly Margot Young makes the important point that '[socio-economic] rights, more than the rights more traditional to liberal societies, call for disruption of current balances of power and resources',[35] and for this reason they are actively sidelined in the era of neo-liberal globalisation.[36]

8.4 Prospects for the future

The threats posed to socio-economic rights by the hegemony of neo-liberal ideology are serious ones, and rather than being lessened by the recent financial crisis and persistent economic depression, the incipient age of austerity has heightened these threats. At present social protections throughout the world are being rolled back, and social rights undermined in the name of fiscal discipline, which does not auger well for the advancement of socio-economic rights.[37] However, it is at least possible that in the same way as the Great Depression galvanised the first wave of socio-economic rights assertion and protection,[38] the global economic crisis which came to the fore in 2008 could also be catalytic in claims for the protection of socio-economic rights. As Beetham notes, 'human rights most urgently need asserting and defending, both theoretically and practically, where they are most denied. Indeed the language of rights only makes sense at all in a context where basic requirements are vulnerable to standard threats'.[39]

Precisely what political formations will emerge from the current depression are impossible to gainsay – whether or not support for socio-economic rights

33 Asbjorn Eide and Allan Rosas, 'Economic, Social and Cultural Rights: A Universal Challenge' in Eide, Krause and Rosas (eds.), *Economic, Social and Cultural Rights: A Textbook* (2nd edn, The Hague: Martinus Nijhoff, 2001) 3 at p. 5.

34 David Beetham, 'What Future for Economic and Social Rights?' in Beetham (ed), *Politics and Human Rights* (Oxford: Blackwell Publishers, 1995) 41 at p. 43.

35 Margot Young, 'Rights, the Homeless, and Social Change: Reflections on *Victoria (City)* v. *Adams* (BCSC)' (2010) 164 *BC Studies: British Columbian Quarterly* 101 at pp. 110–111.

36 See O'Connell (n. 32).

37 See Ignacio Saiz, 'Rights in Recession? Challenges for Economic and Social Rights Enforcement in Times of Crisis' (2009) 1 *Journal of Human Rights Practice* 277.

38 See Asbjorn Eide, 'Economic, Social and Cultural Rights as Human Rights' in Eide, Krause and Rosas (eds), *Economic, Social and Cultural Rights: A Textbook* (2nd edn, The Hague: Martinus Nijhoff, 2001) 9 at p. 16; and Cass Sunstein, *The Second Bill of Rights: FDR's Unfinished Revolution and Why We Need It More Than Ever* (New York: Basic Books, 2004).

39 Beetham (n. 34) at p. 44.

will be stronger or weaker is very much an open question. At the very least it is hoped that this study has demonstrated that if the political will exists to provide protection for socio-economic rights on a par with civil and political rights, and in that way to show equal regard to the needs and interests of all members of society, it is entirely possible for the courts to play a positive, principled role in the vindication of such rights, without undermining the separation of powers.

Bibliography

Abramovich, Victor, 'Fostering Dialogue: The Role of the Judiciary and Litigation' in Squires, Langford and Thiele (eds.), *The Road to a Remedy: Current Issues in the Litigation of Economic, Social and Cultural Rights* (Sydney: University of New South Wales Press, 2005) 167.

Ackerman, Bruce, 'The New Separation of Powers' (2000) 113 *Harvard Law Review* 633.

Alam, M. Shah, 'Enforcement of International Human Rights Law by Domestic Courts: A Theoretical and Practical Study' (2006) 53 *Netherlands International Law Review* 399.

Alexy, Robert, *A Theory of Constitutional Rights* (trans. Julian Rivers) (Oxford: Oxford: University Press, 2002).

Alexy, Robert, 'The Construction of Constitutional Rights' (2010) 4 *Law and Ethics of Human Rights* 19.

Allan, T. R. S., 'Human Rights and Judicial Review: A Critique of "Due Deference"' (2006) 65 *Cambridge Law Journal* 671.

Alston, Philip, 'A Framework for the Comparative Analysis of Bills of Rights', in Alston (ed.), *Promoting Human Rights Through Bills of Rights: Comparative Perspectives* (Oxford: Oxford University Press, 1999) 1.

Alston, Philip and Quinn, Gerard, 'The Nature and Scope of States Parties' Obligations under the International Covenant on Economic, Social and Cultural Rights' (1987) 9 *Human Rights Quarterly* 156.

An-Na'im, Abdullahi A., 'To Affirm the Full Human Rights Standing of Economic, Social and Cultural Rights', in Ghai and Cottrell (eds.), *Economic, Social and Cultural Rights in Practice* (London: INTERIGHTS, 2004) 7.

Arambulo, Kitty, *Strengthening the Supervision of the International Covenant on Economic, Social and Cultural Rights: Theoretical and Procedural Aspects* (Oxford: Intersentia/Hart Publishing, 1999).

Austin, Granville, *Working a Democratic Constitution: The Indian Experience* (New Delhi: Oxford University Press, 1999).

Austin, Granville, 'The Supreme Court and the Struggle for Custody of the Constitution' in Kirpal, Desai, Subramanium, Dhavan and Ramachandran (eds.), *Supreme But Not Infallible: Essays in Honour of the Supreme Court of India* (New Delhi: Oxford University Press, 2004) 1.

Austin, Granville, 'The Expected and the Unintended in Working a Democratic Constitution', in Hasan, Sridharan and Sudarshan (eds.), *India's Living Constitution* (London: Anthem Press, 2005) 319.

Bakan, Joel, *Just Words: Constitutional Rights and Social Wrongs* (Toronto: University of Toronto Press, 1997).

Bakan, Joel and Schneiderman, David, 'Introduction', in Bakan and Schneiderman (eds.), *Social Justice and the Constitution: Perspectives on a Social Union for Canada* (Carleton University Press, 1992) 1.

Banner, Charles and Moules, Richard, 'Public Law in the House of Lords: Emerging Trends and Guidance on Petitions for Leave to Appeal' (2007) 12 *Judicial Review* 24.

Barak, Aharon, 'Proportionality and Principled Balancing' (2010) 4 *Law and Ethics of Human Rights* 1.

Barak-Erez, Daphne, 'The International Law of Human Rights and Constitutional Law: A Case Study of an Expanding Dialogue' (2004) 2 *International Journal of Constitutional Law* 611.

Barak-Erez, Daphne and Gross, Aeyal, 'Introduction: Do We Need Social Rights?', in Barak-Erez and Gross (eds.), *Exploring Social Rights* (Oxford: Hart Publishing, 2007) 1.

Barber, N. W., 'Prelude to the Separation of Powers' (2001) 60 *Cambridge Law Journal* 59.

Barendt, Eric, 'Separation of Powers and Constitutional Government' (1995) *Public Law* 599.

Bateup, Christine, 'The Dialogic Promise: Assessing the Normative Potential of Theories of Constitutional Dialogue' (2006) 71 *Brooklyn Law Review* 1109.

Bateup, Christine, 'Expanding the Conversation: American and Canadian Experiences of Constitutional Dialogue in Comparative Perspective' (2007) 21 *Temple International and Comparative Law Journal* 1.

Baxi, Upendra, 'Taking Suffering Seriously: Social Action Litigation in the Supreme Court of India' (1985) *Third World Legal Studies* 107.

Baxi, Upendra, 'The (Im)possibility of Constitutional Justice: Seismographic Notes on Indian Constitutionalism', in Hasan, Sridharan and Sudarshan (eds.), *India's Living Constitution* (London: Anthem Press, 2005) 31.

Bayefsky, Ann, 'The UN Human Rights Treaties: Facing the Implementation Crisis' (1996) *Windsor Yearbook of Access to Justice* 189.

Beatty, David, *The Ultimate Rule of Law* (Oxford: Oxford University Press, 2004).

Beetham, David, 'What Future for Economic and Social Rights?', in Beetham (ed.), *Politics and Human Rights* (Oxford: Blackwell, 1995) 41.

Bhushan, Prashant, 'Misplaced Priorities and Class Bias in the Judiciary' (2009) 44 (14) *Economic and Political Weekly* 32.

Bilchitz, David, 'The Right to Health Care Services and the Minimum Core: Disentangling the Principled and Pragmatic Strands' (2006) 7(2) *ESR Review* 2.

Bilchitz, David, *Poverty and Fundamental Rights: The Justification and Enforcement of Socio-Economic Rights* (Oxford: Oxford University Press, 2007).

Bilchitz, David, 'Judicial Remedies and Socio-Economic Rights' (2008) 9(1) *ESR Review* 9.

Bollyky, Thomas J., 'R If C > P + B: A Paradigm for Judicial Remedies of Socio-Economic Rights Violations' (2002) 18 *South African Journal on Human Rights* 161.

Bomhoff, Jacco, 'Genealogies of Balancing Discourse' (2010) 4 *Law and Ethics of Human Rights* 107.

Bond, Patrick, 'From Racial to Class Apartheid: South Africa's Frustrating Decade of Freedom' (2004) 55(10) *Monthly Review* 45.

Bond, Patrick, *Talk Left, Walk Right: South Africa's Frustrated Global Reforms* (2nd edn, Pretoria: University of KwaZulu-Natal Press, 2006).

Brand, Danie, 'Socio-Economic Rights and the Courts in South Africa: Justiciability on a Sliding Scale', in Coomans (ed.), *Justiciability of Economic and Social Rights* (Antwerp: Intersentia, 2006) 207.

Brodsky, Gwen, 'Social Charter Issues', in Bakan and Schneiderman (eds.), *Social Justice and the Constitution: Perspectives on a Social Union for Canada* (Carleton University Press, 1992) 43.

Brodsky, Gwen, 'Constitutional Equality Rights in Canada' (2001) *Acta Juridica* 241.

Brodsky, Gwen, '*Gosselin* v. *Quebec* (*Attorney General*): Autonomy with a Vengeance' (2003) *Canadian Journal of Women and the Law* 194.

Brodsky, Gwen and Day, Sheath, 'Beyond the Social and Economic Rights Debate: Substantive Equality Speaks to Poverty' (2002) 14 *Canadian Journal of Women and the Law* 185.

Brudner, Alan, *Constitutional Goods* (Oxford: Oxford University Press, 2004).

Budlender, Geoff, 'The Role of the Courts in Achieving the Transformative Potential of Socio-Economic Rights' (2007) 8(1) *ESR Review* 9.

Cassels, Jamie, 'Judicial Activism and Public Interest Litigation in India: Attempting the Impossible?' (1989) 37 *American Journal of Comparative Law* 495.

Chanock, Martin, 'A Post-Calvinist Catechism or a Post-Communist Manifesto? Intersecting Narratives in the South African Bill of Rights Debate', in Alston (ed.), *Promoting Human Rights through Bills of Rights: Comparative Perspectives* (Oxford: Oxford University Press, 1999) 392.

Chaskalson, Arthur, 'The Transition to Democracy in South Africa' (1997) 29 *New York University Journal of International Law and Politics* 285.

Chaskalson, Arthur, 'From Wickedness to Equality: The Moral Transformation of South African Law' (2003) 1 *International Journal of Constitutional Law* 590.

Chaskalson Matthew and Davis Dennis, 'Constitutionalism, the Rule of Law and the *First Certification* Judgment' (1997) 13 *South African Journal on Human Rights* 430

Chayes, Abram, 'The Role of the Judge in Public Law Litigation' (1976) 89 *Harvard Law Review* 1281.

Chenwi, Lilian, 'Towards the Adoption of the International Complaints Mechanism for Enforcing Socio-Economic Rights Under the ICESCR' (2008) 9(2) *ESR Review* 20.

Choudhry, Suit, 'Worse Than *Lochner*?', in Flood, Roach and Sossin (eds.), *Access to Care, Access to Justice: The Legal Debate over Private Health Insurance in Canada* (Toronto: University of Toronto Press, 2005) 75.

Choukroune, Leila, 'Justiciability of Economic, Social and Cultural Rights: The UN Committee on Economic, Social and Cultural Rights' Review of China's First Periodic Report on the Implementation of the International Covenant on Economic, Social and Cultural Rights' (2005) 19 *Columbia Journal of Asian Law* 30.

Clayton, Richard, 'Judicial Deference and "Democratic Dialogue": The Legitimacy of Judicial Intervention under the Human Rights Act 1998' (2004) *Public Law* 33.

Coomans, Fons, 'Some Introductory Remarks on the Justiciability of Economic and Social Rights in a Comparative Constitutional Context', in Coomans (ed.), *Justiciability of Economic and Social Rights* (Antwerp: Intersentia, 2006) 1.

Cooper, Jeremy, 'Poverty and Constitutional Justice: The Indian Experience' (1993) 44 *Mercer Law Review* 611.

Courtis, Christian, 'Standards to Make ESC Rights Justiciable: A Summary Exploration' (2009) 2 *Erasmus Law Review* 379.

Craven, Matthew, *The International Covenant on Economic, Social and Cultural Rights: A Perspective on its Development* (Oxford: Clarendon Press, 1995).

Craven, Matthew, 'Assessment of Progress on Adjudication of Economic, Social and Cultural Rights', in Squires, Langford and Thiele (eds.), *The Road to a Remedy: Current Issues in the Litigation of Economic, Social and Cultural Rights* (Sydney: University of New South Wales Press, 2005) 27.

D'Souza, Radha, 'The "Third World" and Socio-Legal Studies: Neo-Liberalism and Lessons from India's Legal Innovations' (2005) 14 *Social and Legal Studies* 487.

Dankwa, Victor and Flinterman, Cees, 'Commentary by the Reporters on the Nature and Scope of States Parties' Obligations' (1987) 9 *Human Rights Quarterly* 136.

Dankwa, Victor, Flinterman, Cees and Lecky, Scott, 'Commentary to the Maastricht Guidelines on Violations of Economic, Social and Cultural Rights' (1998) 20 *Human Rights Quarterly* 705.

Das, Gobind, 'The Supreme Court: An Overview', in Kirpal, Desai, Subramanium, Dhavan and Ramachandran (eds.), *Supreme But Not Infallible: Essays in Honour of the Supreme Court of India* (New Delhi: Oxford University Press, 2004) 16.

Davis, Dennis, 'The Case Against the Inclusion of Socio-Economic Demands in a Bill of Rights Except as Directive Principles' (1992) 8 *South African Journal on Human Rights* 475.

Davis, Dennis, 'Socio-Economic Rights: The Promise and Limitation – The South African Experience', in Barak-Erez and Gross (eds.), *Exploring Social Rights* (Oxford: Hart Publishing, 2007) 193.

DeCoste, Frederick, 'The Separation of Powers in a Liberal Polity: *Vriend* v. *Alberta*' (1999) 44 *McGill Law Journal* 231.

de Villiers, Berths, 'Directive Principles of State Policy and Fundamental Rights: The Indian Experience' (1992) 8 *South African Journal on Human Rights* 29.

de Vos, Pierre, 'Pious Wishes or Directly Enforceable Human Rights? Social and Economic Rights in South Africa's 1996 Constitution' (1997) 13 *South African Journal on Human Rights* 67.

de Vos, Pierre, 'South Africa's Constitutional Court: Starry-Eyed in the Face of History?' (2002) 26 *Vermont Law Review* 837.

Dennis, Michael and Stewart, David, 'Justiciability of Economic, Social and Cultural Rights: Should There Be an International Complaints Mechanism to Adjudicate the Rights to Food, Water, Housing and Health?' (2004) 98 *American Journal of International Law* 462.

Desai, Ashbin, 'Neoliberalist and Resistance in South Africa' (2003) 54(8) *Monthly Review* 16.

Desai, Ashok and Muralinder, S., 'Public Interest Litigation: Potential and Problems' in Kirpal, Desai, Subramanium, Dhavan and Ramachandran (eds.), *Supreme But Not Infallible: Essays in Honour of the Supreme Court of India* (New Delhi: Oxford University Press, 2004) 159.

Dixon, Rosalind, 'Creating Dialogue about Socio-Economic Rights: Strong-Form versus Weak-Form Judicial Review Revisited' (2007) 5 *International Journal of Constitutional Law* 391.

Doyle, Oran, *Constitutional Equality Law* (Dublin: Thomson Round Hall, 2004).

Doyle, Oran, *Constitutional Law: Text, Cases and Materials* (Dublin: Claus Press, 2008).

Dugger, Cyrus, 'Rights Waiting for Change: Socio-Economic Rights in the New South Africa' (2007) 19 *Florida Journal of International Law* 195.

Dyzenhaus, David, Hunt, Murray and Taggart, Michael, 'The Principle of Legality in Administrative Law: Internationalisation as Constitutionalisation' (2001) 1 *Oxford University Commonwealth Law Journal* 5.

Ebadolahi, Mitra, 'Using Structural Interdicts and the South African Human Rights Commission to Achieve Judicial Enforcement of Economic and Social Rights in South Africa' (2008) 83 *New York University Law Review* 1565.

Eide, Asbjorn, 'Economic, Social and Cultural Rights as Human Rights' in Eide, Krause and Rosas (eds.), *Economic, Social and Cultural Rights: A Textbook* (2nd edn, The Hague: Martinus Nijhoff, 2001) 9.

Eide, Asbjorn, 'Obstacles and Goals to Be Pursued', in Eide, Krause and Rosas (eds.), *Economic, Social and Cultural Rights: A Textbook* (2nd edn, The Hague: Martinus Nijhoff, 2001) 553.

Eide, Asbjorn and Rosas, Allan, 'Economic, Social and Cultural Rights: A Universal Challenge', in Eide, Krause and Rosas (eds.), *Economic, Social and Cultural Rights: A Textbook* (2nd edn, The Hague: Martinus Nijhoff, 2001) 3.

Eisenberg, Theodore and Yeazell, Stephen, 'The Ordinary and the Extraordinary in Institutional Litigation' (1980) 93 *Harvard Law Review* 465.

Erasmus, Gerhard, 'Socio-Economic Rights and Their Implementation: The Impact of Domestic and International Instruments' (2004) 32 *International Journal of Legal Information* 243.

Ewing, K. D., 'Social Rights and Constitutional Law' (1999) *Public Law* 104.

Fabre, Cécile, *Social Rights under the Constitution* (Oxford: Oxford University Press, 2000).

Fallon, Richard, 'The Linkage between Justiciability and Remedies – and Their Connection to Substantive Rights' (2006) 92 *Virginia Law Review* 633.

Fallon, Richard, 'The Core of an Uneasy Case for Judicial Review' (2008) 121 *Harvard Law Review* 1693.

Feldman, David, 'Monism, Dualism and Constitutional Legitimacy' (1999) 20 *Australian Yearbook of International Law* 105.

Finley, Margot, 'Limiting Section 15(1) in the Health Care Context: The Impact of *Auton* v. *British Columbia*' (2005) 63 *University of Toronto Faculty of Law Review* 213.

Fredman, Sandra, *Human Rights Transformed: Positive Rights and Positive Duties* (Oxford: Oxford University Press, 2008).

Fredman, Sandra and Wesson, Murray, 'Economic, Social and Cultural Rights', in Feldman (ed.), *English Public Law* (2nd edn, Oxford: Oxford University Press, 2009) 453.

Fredman, Sandra, 'New Horizons: Incorporating Socio-Economic Rights in a British Bill of Rights' (2010) *Public Law* 297.

Freeman, Mark and Van Ert, Gibran, *International Human Rights Law* (Toronto: Irwin Law Inc., 2004).

Friedman, Barry, 'The Counter-Majoritarian Problem and the Pathology of Constitutional Scholarship' (2001) 95 *North-Western University Law Review* 933.

Fuller, Lon, 'The Forms and Limits of Adjudication' (1978) 92 *Harvard Law Review* 353.

Galanter, Marc and Krishnan, Jayanth, '"Bread for the Poor": Access to Justice and the Rights of the Needy in India' (2004) 55 *Hastings Law Journal* 789.

Galanter, Marc, 'Fifty Years on', in Kirpal, Desai, Subramanium, Dhavan and Ramachandran (eds.), *Supreme But Not Infallible: Essays in Honour of the Supreme Court of India* (New Delhi: Oxford University Press, 2004) 57.

Gardbaum, Stephen, 'The New Commonwealth Model of Constitutionalism' (2001) 49 *American Journal of Comparative Law* 707.

Gardbaum, Stephen, 'Reassessing the New Commonwealth Model of Constitutionalism' (2010) 8(2) *International Journal of Constitutional Law* 167.

Gargarella, Roberto, 'Theories of Democracy, the Judiciary and Social Rights', in

Gargarella, Domingo and Roux (eds.), *Courts and Social Transformation in New Democracies: An Institutional Voice for the Poor?* (Hampshire: Ashgate, 2006) 13.

Ghai, Yash, 'Introduction', in Ghai and Cottrell (eds.), *Economic, Social and Cultural Rights in Practice* (London: INTERIGHTS, 2004) 1.

Ginsburg, Ruth Bader, '"A Decent Respect to the Opinions of [Human]Kind": The Value of a Comparative Perspective in Constitutional Adjudication' (2005) 64 *Cambridge Law Journal* 575.

Glendon, Mary Ann, 'Knowing the Universal Declaration of Human Rights' (1998) 73 *Notre Dame Law Review* 1153.

Glenn, H. Patrick, 'Persuasive Authority' (1987) 32 *McGill Law Journal* 261.

Gonsalves, Colin, 'Reflections on the Indian Experience', in Squires, Langford and Thiele (eds.), *The Road to a Remedy: Current Issues in the Litigation of Economic, Social and Cultural Rights* (Sydney: University of New South Wales Press, 2005) 177.

Harding, Andrew and Leyland, Peter, 'Comparative Law in Constitutional Contexts', in Örücü and Nelken (eds.), *Comparative Law: A Handbook* (Oxford: Hart Publishing, 2007) 313.

Harel, Alon, 'Theories of Rights', in Golding and Edmundson (eds.), *The Blackwell Guide to the Philosophy of Law and Legal Theory* (Oxford: Blackwell, 2005) 191.

Harvey, Philip, 'Human Rights and Economic Policy Discourse: Taking Economic and Social Rights Seriously' (2002) 33 *Columbia Human Rights Law Review* 363.

Haysom, Nicholas, 'Constitutionalism, Majoritarian Democracy and Socio-economic Rights' (1992) 8 *South African Journal on Human Rights* 451.

Hershkoff, Helen, 'Positive Rights and State Constitutions: The Limits of Federal Rationality Review' (1999) 112 *Harvard Law Review* 1131.

Hickman, Tom, 'Constitutional Dialogue, Constitutional Theories and the Human Rights Act 1998' (2005) *Public Law* 306.

Hiebert, Janet, 'New Constitutional Ideas: Can New Parliamentary Models Resist Judicial Dominance When Interpreting Rights' (2004) 82 *Texas Law Review* 1963.

Higgins, Rosalyn, 'The Relationship Between International and Regional Human Rights Norms and Domestic Law' (1992) 18 *Commonwealth Law Bulletin* 1268.

Hirschl, Ran, 'Constitutional Courts and Social Welfare Rights: The "Weak Courts, Strong Rights" Argument Re-examined' (2009) 40 *Ottawa Law Review* 173.

Hirschl, Ran, *Towards Juristocracy* (Harvard: Harvard University Press, 2004).

Hirschl, Ran, 'The Rise of Comparative Constitutional Law: Thoughts on Substance and Method' (2008) 2 *Indian Journal of Constitutional Law* 11.

Hogan, Gerard, 'Directive Principles, Socio-Economic Rights and the Constitution' (2001) 36 *Irish Jurist (n.s.)* 174.

Hogan, Gerard, 'Judicial Review and Socio-Economic Rights', in Sarkin and Binchy (eds.), *Human Rights, the Citizen and the State: South African and Irish Perspectives* (Dublin: Round Hall Sweet & Maxwell, 2001) 1.

Hogan, Gerard and Whyte, Gerry, *Kelly's The Irish Constitution* (4th edn, Dublin: Lexis-Nexis, 2003).

Hogg, Peter, 'Canada's New Charter of Rights' (1984) 32 *American Journal of Comparative Law* 283.

Hogg, Peter and Bushell, Allison, 'The *Charter* Dialogue between Courts and Legislatures (Or Perhaps the *Charter of Rights* Isn't Such a Bad Thing after All)' (1997) 35 *Osgoode Hall Law Journal* 75.

Hogg, Peter, Bushell-Thornton, Allison and Wright, Wade, 'Charter Dialogue Revisited – Or "Much Ado about Metaphors"' (2007) 45 *Osgoode Hall Law Journal* 1.

House of Lords/House of Commons Joint Committee on Human Rights, *The International Covenant on Economic, Social and Cultural Rights* (Twenty-First Report of Session 2003–4, HL Paper 183, HC 1188, Published 2 November 2004).

Hunt, Paul, *Reclaiming Social Rights: International and Comparative Perspectives* (Aldershot: Dartmouth, 1996).

International Commission of Jurists, *Courts and the Legal Enforcement of Economic, Social and Cultural Rights: Comparative Experiences of Justiciability* (Geneva: ICJ, 2008).

Irish Commission for Justice and Peace, *Re-Righting the Constitution – The Case for New Social and Economic Rights: Housing, Health, Nutrition, Adequate Standard of Living* (Dublin: ICJP, 1998).

Jackman, Martha, 'Protecting Rights and Promoting Democracy: Judicial Review under Section 1 of the *Charter*' (1996) 34 *Osgoode Hall Law Journal* 661.

Jackman, Martha, '"Giving Real Effect to Equality": *Eldridge* v. *British Columbia (Attorney General)* and *Vriend* v. *Alberta*' (1998) 4(2) *Review of Constitutional Studies* 352.

Jackman, Martha, 'From National Standards to Justiciable Rights: Enforcing International Social and Economic Guarantees through *Charter of Rights* Review' (1999) 14 *Journal of Law and Social Policy* 69.

Jackman, Martha, '"The Last Line of Defence for [Which?] Citizens": Accountability, Equality, and the Right to Health in *Chaoulli*' (2006) 44 *Osgoode Hall Law Journal* 349.

Jackman, Martha and Porter, Bruce. 'Canada: Socio-Economic Rights Under the Canadian Charter', in Langford (ed.), *Social Rights Jurisprudence: Emerging Trends in International and Comparative Law* (Cambridge: Cambridge University Press, 2008) 209.

Jones, Peris and Stokke, Kristian, 'From Democracy Deficits to Democratising Development: The Politics of Socio-Economic Rights in South Africa' (2005) 6(2) *ESR Review* 2.

Kahn-Freund, Otto, 'On Uses and Misuses of Comparative Law' (1974) 37 *Modern Law Review* 1.

Kelly, James, 'The Charter of Rights and Freedoms and the Rebalancing of Liberal Constitutionalism in Canada, 1982–1997' (1999) 37 *Osgoode Hall Law Journal* 625.

Kende, Mark, 'The South African Constitutional Court's Construction of Socio-Economic Rights: A Response to Critics' (2004) 19 *Connecticut Journal of International Law* 617.

Kennedy, David, 'The International Human Rights Movement: Part of the Problem' (2001) 3 *European Human Rights Law Review* 245.

Keogh, Dermot and McCarthy, Andrew, *The Making of the Irish Constitution 1937* (Dublin: Mercier Press, 2007).

Khilnani, Sunil, 'The Indian Constitution and Democracy', in Hasan, Sridharan and Sudarshan (eds.), *India's Living Constitution* (London: Anthem Press, 2005) 64.

Kim, Natasha and Piper, Tina, '*Gosselin* v. *Quebec*: Back to the Poorhouse . . .' (2003) 48 *McGill Law Journal* 749.

King, Jeff, 'Constitutional Rights and Social Welfare: A Comment on the Canadian *Chaoulli* Health Care Decision' (2006) 69 *Modern Law Review* 631.

King, Jeff, 'Institutional Approaches to Judicial Restraint' (2008) 28 *Oxford Journal of Legal Studies* 409.

King, Jeff, 'The Pervasiveness of Polycentricity' (2008) *Public Law* 101.

Kinsella, Noel, 'Can Canada Afford a Charter of Social and Economic Rights? Toward a Canadian Social Charter' (2008) 71 *Saskatchewan Law Review* 7.

Kirby, Michael, 'International Law – The Impact on Domestic Constitutions' (2006) 21 *American University International Law Review* 327.

Klaaren, Jonathan, 'Structures of Government in the 1996 South African Constitution: Putting Democracy Back into Human Rights' (1997) 13 *South African Journal on Human Rights* 3.

Klaaren, Jonathan, 'A Remedial Interpretation of the *Treatment Action Campaign* Decision' (2003) 19 *South African Journal on Human Rights* 455.

Klare, Karl, 'Legal Culture and Transformative Constitutionalism' (1998) 14 *South African Journal on Human Rights* 146.

Klein, Alana, 'Judging as Nudging: New Governance Approaches for the Enforcement of Constitutional Social and Economic Rights' (2008) 39 *Columbia Human Rights Law Review* 351.

Klug, Heinz, *Constituting Democracy: Law, Globalism and South Africa's Political Reconstruction* (Cambridge: Cambridge University Press, 2000).

Knop, Karen, 'Here and There: International Law in Domestic Courts' (2000) 32 *New York University Journal of International Law and Policy* 501.

Knopff, Rainer, 'Populism and the Politics of Rights: The Dual Attack on Representative Democracy' (1998) 31 *Canadian Journal of Political Science* 683.

Koch, Ida Elisabeth, 'The Justiciability of Indivisible Human Rights' (2003) 2 *Nordic Journal of International Law* 3.

Koch, Ida Elisabeth, 'Economic, Social and Cultural Rights as Components in Civil and Political Rights: A Hermeneutic Perspective' (2006) 10 *International Journal of Human Rights* 405.

Kothari, Jayna, 'Social Rights Litigation in India: Developments of the Last Decade', in Barak-Erez and Gross (eds.), *Exploring Social Rights* (Oxford: Hart Publishing, 2007) 171.

Kratochvil, Jan, 'Realizing a Promise: A Case for Ratification of the Optional Protocol to the Covenant on Economic, Social and Cultural Rights' (2009) 16(3) *Human Rights Brief* 30.

Krotosznski, Ronald, 'Constitutional Flares: On Judges, Legislatures and Dialogue' (1998) 83 *Minnesota Law Review* 1.

Kurland, Philip, 'Structuring the Separation of Powers' (1993) 8 *American University Journal of International Law and Policy* 483.

La Forest, Gerald V., 'The Expanding Role of the Supreme Court of Canada in International Law Issues' (1996) 34 *Canadian Yearbook of International Law* 89.

Langa, Pius, 'Social Justice and Rights: The South African Model' (1998) 16 *Windsor Yearbook of Access to Justice* 149.

Langa, Pius, 'The Vision of the Constitution' (2003) 120 *South African Law Journal* 670.

Langa, Pius, 'Taking Dignity Seriously – Judicial Reflections on the Optional Protocol to the ICESCR' (2009) 27 *Nordisk Tidsskrift For Menneskerettigheter* 29.

Langford, Malcolm, 'Judging Resource Availability', in Squires, Langford and Thiele (eds.), *The Road to a Remedy: Current Issues in the Litigation of Economic, Social and Cultural Rights* (Sydney: University of New South Wales Press, 2005) 89.

Langford, Malcolm, 'The Justiciability of Social Rights', in Langford (ed.), *Social Rights Jurisprudence: Emerging Trends in International and Comparative Law* (Cambridge: Cambridge University Press, 2008) 3.

Langford, Malcolm and King, Jeff, 'Committee on Economic, Social and Cultural Rights: Past, Present at Future', in Langford (ed.), *Social Rights Jurisprudence: Emerging Trends in International and Comparative Law* (Cambridge: Cambridge University Press, 2008) 477.

Lehmann, Karin, 'In Defence of the Constitutional Court: Litigating Socio-Economic Rights and the Myth of the Minimum Core' (2006) 22 *American University International Law Review* 163.

Levinson, Daryl, 'Rights Essentialism and Remedial Equilibration' (1999) 99 *Columbia Law Review* 857.

Liebenberg, Sandra, 'Needs, Rights and Transformation: Adjudicating Social Rights in South Africa' (2005) 6(4) *ESR Review* 3.

Liebenberg, Sandra, 'Socio-Economic Rights: Revisiting the Reasonableness Review/ Minimum Core Debate', in Woolman and Bishop (eds.), *Constitutional Conversations* (Pretoria: Pretoria University Law Press, 2008) 303.

Liebenberg, Sandra, 'South Africa: Adjudicating Social Rights under a Transformative Constitution', in Langford (ed.), *Social Rights Jurisprudence: Emerging Trends in International and Comparative Law* (Cambridge: Cambridge University Press, 2008) 75.

Liebenberg, Sandra, *Socio-Economic Rights: Adjudication under a Transformative Constitution* (Claremont, CA: Juta, 2010).

Limbach, Jutta, 'The Concept of the Supremacy of the Constitution' (2001) 64 *Modern Law Review* 1.

Lord Lester of Herne Hill and O'Cinneide, Colm, 'The Effective Protection of Socio-Economic Rights', in Ghai and Cottrell (eds.), *Economic, Social and Cultural Rights in Practice* (London: INTERIGHTS, 2004) 17.

Lord Steyn, 'Deference: A Tangled Story' (2005) *Public Law* 346.

McCracken, Brian, 'The Irish Constitution: An Overview', in Sarkin and Binchy (eds.), *Human Rights, the Citizen and the State: South African and Irish Perspectives* (Dublin: Round Hall, 2001) 52.

McDermott, Paul Anthony, 'The Separation of Powers and the Doctrine of Non-Justiciability' (2000) 35 *Irish Jurist (n.s.)* 280.

McDonald, Leighton, 'Rights, "Dialogue" and Democratic Objections to Judicial Review' (2004) 32 *Federal Law Review* 1.

Macklem, Patrick, 'Social Rights in Canada', in Barak-Erez and Gross (eds.), *Exploring Social Rights* (Oxford: Hart Publishing, 2007) 213.

Macklem, Timothy, 'Entrenching Bills of Rights' (2006) 26 *Oxford Journal of Legal Studies* 107.

Mahon, Claire, 'Progress at the Front: The Draft Optional Protocol to the International Covenant on Economic, Social and Cultural Rights' (2008) 8 *Human Rights Law Review* 617.

Makinen, Amy, 'Rights, Review and Spending: Policy Outcomes with Judicially Enforceable Rights' (2001) 39 *European Journal of Political Research* 23.

Manfredi, Christopher, '*Déjà Vu* All Over Again: *Chaoulli* and the Limits of Judicial Policymaking', in Flood, Roach and Sossin (eds.), *Access to Care, Access to Justice: The Legal Debate Over Private Health Insurance in Canada* (Toronto: University of Toronto Press, 2005) 140.

Manfredi, Christopher, '"Appropriate and Just in the Circumstances": Public Policy and the Enforcement of Rights under the Canadian Charter of Rights and Freedoms' (1994) 27 *Canadian Journal of Political Science* 425.

Manfredi, Christopher and Kelly, James, 'Six Degrees of Dialogue: A Response to Hogg and Bushell' (1999) 37 *Osgoode Hall Law Journal* 513.

Manfredi, Christopher and Maioni, Antonia, '"The Last Line of Defence for Citizens": Litigating Private Health Insurance in *Chaoulli* v. *Quebec*' (2006) 44 *Osgoode Hall Law Journal* 249.

Matas, David, '*Gosselin* v. *Quebec (Attorney General)*: Is Starvation Illegal? The Enforceability of the Right to an Adequate Standard of Living' (2003) 4 *Melbourne Journal of International Law* 217.

Mbazira, Christopher, 'Enforcing Socio-Economic Rights as Individual Rights' (2008) 9(1) *ESR Review* 4.

Mbazira, Christopher, 'From Ambivalence to Certainty: Norms and Principles for the Structural Interdict in Socio-Economic Rights Litigation in South Africa' (2008) 24 *South African Journal on Human Rights* 1.

Mbazira, Christopher, 'Non-Implementation of Court Orders in Socio-Economic Rights Litigation in South Africa: Is the Cancer Here to Stay?' (2008) 9(4) *ESR Review* 2.

Mehta, Pratap Bhanu, 'The Inner Conflict of Constitutionalism: Judicial Review and the "Basic Structure"', in Hasan, Sridharan and Sudarshan (eds.), *India's Living Constitution* (London: Anthem Press, 2005) 179.

Merkel, Ron, 'Separation of Powers – A Bulwark for Liberty and a Rights Culture' (2006) 69 *Saskatchewan Law Review* 129.

Meyerson, Denise, 'Equality Guarantees and Distributive Inequity' (2008) 19 *Public Law Review* 32.

Michelman, Frank, 'Welfare Rights in a Constitutional Democracy' (1979) *Washington University Law Quarterly* 659.

Michelman, Frank, 'The Constitution, Social Rights and Liberal Political Justification' (2003) 1 *International Journal of Constitutional Law* 13.

Minkler, Lanse, 'Economic Rights and Political Decision Making' (2009) 31 *Human Rights Quarterly* 368.

Moellendorf, Darrel, 'Reasoning About Resources: *Soobramoney* and the Future of Socio-Economic Rights Claims' (1998) 14 *South African Journal on Human Rights* 327.

Moller, Kai, 'Balancing and the Structure of Constitutional Rights' (2007) 5 *International Journal of Constitutional Law* 453.

Monahan, Patrick J., *Constitutional Law* (3rd edn, Toronto: Irwin Law Inc., 2006).

Moreau, Sophia, 'The Promise of *Law* v. *Canada*' (2007) 57 *University of Toronto Law Journal* 415.

Moseneke, Dikgang, 'Transformative Adjudication' (2002) 18 *South African Journal on Human Rights* 309.

Muralidhar, S., 'Implementation of Court Orders in the Area of Economic, Social and Cultural Rights: An Overview of the Experience of the Indian Judiciary' (2002) *IELRC Working Paper 2002–2* (available at: www.ielrc.org/content/w0202.pdf).

Muralidhar, S., 'India: The Expectations and Challenges of Judicial Enforcement of Social Rights', in Langford (ed.), *Social Rights Jurisprudence: Emerging Trends in International and Comparative Law* (Cambridge: Cambridge University Press, 2008) 102.

Mureinik, Etienne, 'Beyond a Charter of Luxuries: Economic Rights in the Constitution' (1992) 8 *South African Journal on Human Rights* 464.

Nagel, Robert, 'Controlling the Structural Injunction' (1984) 7 *Harvard Journal of Law and Public Policy* 395.

Neier, Aryeh, 'Social and Economic Rights: A Critique' (2006) 13(2) *Human Rights Brief* 1.

Neuman, Gerald, 'Human Rights and Constitutional Rights: Harmony and Dissonance' (2003) 55 *Stanford Law Review* 1863.

Neuman, Gerald, 'The Use of International Law in Constitutional Interpretation' (2004) 98 *American Journal of International Law* 82.

Newman, Dwight G., 'Negotiated Rights Enforcement' (2006) 69 *Saskatchewan Law Review* 119.

Nickel, James, 'Poverty and Rights' (2005) 55 *Philosophical Quarterly* 385.

Nolan, Aoife, 'Ireland: The Separation of Powers Doctrine vs. Socio-Economic Rights?', in Langford (ed.), *Social Rights Jurisprudence: Emerging Trends in International and Comparative Law* (Cambridge: Cambridge University Press, 2008) 295.

Nolette, Paul, 'Lessons Learned From the South African Constitutional Court: Toward a Third Way of Judicial Enforcement of Socio-Economic Rights' (2003) 12 *Michigan State Journal of International Law* 91.

Novak, Marko, 'Three Models of Balancing (in Constitutional Review)' (2010) 23 *Ratio Juris* 101.

Nowak, Manfred, 'Indivisibility of Human Rights', in Smith and Van Den Anker (eds.), *The Essentials of Human Rights* (New York: Hodder Arnold, 2005) 178.

O'Connell, Paul, 'The Human Right to Health and the Privatisation of Irish Health Care' (2005) 11(2) *Medico-Legal Journal of Ireland* 76.

O'Connell, Paul, 'On Reconciling Irreconcilables: Neo-liberal Globalisation and Human Rights' (2007) 7(3) *Human Rights Law Review* 483.

O'Connell, Rory, 'From Equality before the Law to the Equal Benefit of the Law: Social and Economic Rights in the Irish Constitution', in Doyle and Carolan (eds.), *The Irish Constitution: Governance and Values* (Dublin: Thomson Round Hall, 2008) 327.

O'Dell, Eoin and Whyte, Gerry, 'Is This a Country for Old Men and Women? – *In Re Article 26 and the Health (Amendment) (No. 2) Bill 2004*' (2005) 27 *Dublin University Law Journal* 368.

O'Flaherty, Michael, 'The Concluding Observations of the United Nations Human Rights Treaty Bodies' (2006) 6(1) *Human Rights Law Review* 27.

O'Mahony, Conor, 'Education, Remedies and the Separation of Powers' (2002) 24 *Dublin University Law Journal* 57.

Office of the United Nations High Commissioner for Human Rights, *Human Rights in the Administration of Justice: A Manual on Human Rights for Judges, Prosecutors and Lawyers* (New York: United Nations, 2003).

Olowu, Dejo, 'Human Rights and the Avoidance of Domestic Implementation: The Phenomenon of Non-Justiciable Constitutional Guarantees' (2006) 69 *Saskatchewan Law Review* 39.

Palmer, Ellie, *Judicial Review, Socio-Economic Rights and the Human Rights Act* (Oxford: Hart Publishing, 2007).

Parkes, Debra, 'Baby Steps on the Way to a Grown-Up *Charter*: Reflections on 20 Years of Social and Economic Rights Claims' (2003) 52 *University of New Brunswick Law Journal* 279.

Pereira-Menaut, Antonio Carlos, 'Against Positive Rights' (1988) 22 *Valparaiso University Law Review* 359.

Perry, Michael, 'Protecting Human Rights in a Democracy: What Role for the Courts?' (2003) 38 *Wake Forest Law Review* 635.

Petter, Andrew, 'Twenty Years of Charter Justification: From Liberal Legalism to Dubious Dialogue' (2003) 52 *University of New Brunswick Law Journal* 187.

Petter, Andrew, 'Wealthcare: The Politics of the *Charter* Revisited', in Flood, Roach and Sossin (eds.), *Access to Care, Access to Justice: The Legal Debate Over Private Health Insurance in Canada* (Toronto: University of Toronto Press, 2005) 116.

Pieterse, Edgar and van Donk, Mirjam, 'The Politics of Socio-Economic Rights in South Africa' (2004) 5(5) *ESR Review* 12.

Pieterse, Marius, 'Beyond the Welfare State: Globalisation of Neo-Liberal Culture and the Constitutional Protection of Social and Economic Rights in South Africa' (2003) 14 *Stellenbosch Law Review* 3.

Pieterse, Marius, 'Coming to Terms with Judicial Enforcement of Socio-Economic Rights' (2004) 20 *South African Journal on Human Rights* 383.

Pieterse, Marius, 'Possibilities and Pitfalls in the Domestic Enforcement of Social Rights: Contemplating the South African Experience' (2004) 26 *Human Rights Quarterly* 882.

Pieterse, Marius, 'Resuscitating Socio-Economic Rights: Constitutional Entitlements to Health Care Services' (2006) 22 *South African Journal on Human Rights* 473.

Pieterse, Marius, 'Eating Socioeconomic Rights: The Usefulness of Rights Talk in Alleviating Social Hardship Revisited' (2007) 29 *Human Rights Quarterly* 796.

Pilger, John, *Freedom Next Time* (London: Bantam Press, 2006).

Pillay, Anashri, 'Courts, Variable Standards of Review and Resource Allocation: Developing a Model for the Enforcement of Social and Economic Rights' (2007) 6 *European Human Rights Law Review* 616.

Porter, Bruce, 'Beyond *Andrews*: Substantive Equality and Positive Obligations After *Eldridge* and *Vriend*' (1998) 9(3) *Constitutional Forum* 71.

Porter, Bruce, 'The Crisis of Economic, Social and Cultural Rights and Strategies for Addressing It', in Squires, Langford and Thiele (eds.), *The Road to a Remedy: Current Issues in the Litigation of Economic, Social and Cultural Rights* (Sydney: University of New South Wales Press, 2005) 43.

Porter, Bruce, 'A Right to Health Care in Canada: Only if You Can Pay for It' (2005) 6(4) *ESR Review* 8.

Porter, Bruce, 'Expectations of Equality' (2006) 33 *Supreme Court Law Review* 23.

Porter, Bruce, 'Claiming Adjudicative Space: Social Rights, Equality and Citizenship', in Young, Boyd, Brodsky and Day (eds.), *Poverty: Rights, Social Citizenship and Legal Activism* (Vancouver: UBC Press, 2007) 77.

Quinlivan, Shivaun and Keys, Mary, 'Official Indifference and Persistent Procrastination: An Analysis of *Sinnott*' (2002) 2(2) *Judicial Studies Institute Journal* 163.

Quinn, Gerard, 'The Nature and Significance of Critical Legal Studies' (1989) 7 *Irish Law Times* 282.

Quinn, Gerard, 'Rethinking the Nature of Social, Economic and Cultural Rights in the Irish Legal Order', in Costello (ed.), *Fundamental Social Rights: Current European Legal Protection and the Challenge of the EU Charter of Fundamental Rights* (Dublin: Irish Centre for European Law, 2001) 35.

Rajagopal, Balakrishnan, 'Limits of Law in Counter-Hegemonic Globalization: The Indian Supreme Court and the Narmada Valley Struggle', in De Sousa Santos and Rodriguez-Garavito (eds.), *Law and Globalization from Below: Towards a Cosmopolitan Legality* (Cambridge: Cambridge University Press, 2005) 183.

Rajagopal, Balakrishnan, 'Pro-Human Rights But Anti-Poor? A Critical Evaluation of the Indian Supreme Court from a Social Movement Perspective' (2007) 8 *Human Rights Review* 157.

Ray, Brian, *'Occupiers of 51 Olivia Road* v. *City of Johannesburg*: Enforcing the Right to Adequate Housing through Engagement' (2008) 8 *Human Rights Law Review* 703.

Rivers, Julian, 'Proportionality and Variable Intensity of Review' (2006) 65 *Cambridge Law Journal* 174.

Roach, Kent, 'Constitutional, Remedial, and International Dialogues about Rights: The Canadian Experience' (2005) 40 *Texas International Law Journal* 537.

Roach, Kent, 'Crafting Remedies for Violations of Economic, Social and Cultural Rights', in Squires, Langford and Thiele (eds.), *The Road to a Remedy: Current Issues in the Litigation of Economic, Social and Cultural Rights* (Sydney: University of New South Wales Press, 2005) 111.

Roach, Kent, 'Sharpening the Dialogue Debate: The Next Decade of Scholarship' (2007) 45 *Osgoode Hall Law Journal* 169.

Roach, Kent, 'The Challenge of Crafting Remedies for Violations of Socio-Economic Rights', in Langford (ed.), *Social Rights Jurisprudence: Emerging Trends in International and Comparative Law* (Cambridge: Cambridge University Press, 2008) 46.

Roach, Kent and Budlender, Geoff, 'Mandatory Relief and Supervisory Jurisdiction: When is it Appropriate, Just and Equitable' (2005) 122 *South African Law Journal* 325.

Rosas, Allan and Scheinin, Martin, 'Implementation Mechanisms and Remedies', in Eide, Krause and Rosas (eds.), *Economic, Social and Cultural Rights: A Textbook* (2nd edn, The Hague: Martinus Nijhoff, 2001) 425.

Rosenberg, Gerald, *The Hollow Hope: Can Courts Bring about Social Change?* (2nd edn, Chicago: University of Chicago Press, 2008).

Ruane, Blathna, 'The Separation of Powers and the Grant of Mandatory Orders to Enforce Constitutional Rights' (2000) 5 *Bar Review* 416.

Rubin, Edward and Feeley, Malcolm, 'Judicial Policy Making and Litigation against the Government' (2003) 5 *University of Pennsylvania Journal of Constitutional Law* 617.

Rudovsky, David, 'Running in Place: The Paradox of Expanding Rights and Restricted Remedies' (2005) *University of Illinois Law Review* 1199.

Russell, Peter, *'Chaoulli*: The Political versus the Legal Life of a Decision', in Flood, Roach and Sossin (eds.), *Access to Care, Access to Justice: The Legal Debate over Private Health Insurance in Canada* (Toronto: University of Toronto Press, 2005) 5.

Ryan, Fergus, 'Disability and the Right to Education: Defining the Constitutional "Child"' (2002) 24 *Dublin University Law Journal* 96.

Sabel, Charles and Simon, William, 'Destabilization Rights: How Public Law Litigation Succeeds' (2004) 117 *Harvard Law Review* 1016.

Saberwal, Satish, 'Introduction: Civilization, Constitution, Democracy', in Hasan, Sridharan and Sudarshan (eds.), *India's Living Constitution* (London: Anthem Press, 2005) 1.

Sathe, S. P., *Judicial Activism in India* (2nd edn, New Delhi: Oxford University Press, 2002).

Scheinin, Martin, 'Economic and Social Rights as Legal Rights', in Eide, Krause and Rosas (eds.), *Economic, Social and Cultural Rights: A Textbook* (2nd edn, The Hague: Martinus Nijhoff, 2001) 9.

Scheinin, Martin, 'Justiciability and the Indivisibility of Human Rights' in Squires, Langford and Thiele (eds.), *The Road to a Remedy: Current Issues in the Litigation of*

Economic, Social and Cultural Rights (Sydney: University of New South Wales Press, 2005) 17.

Scheinin, Martin, 'Human Rights Committee: Not Only a Committee on Civil and Political Rights', in Langford (ed.), *Social Rights Jurisprudence: Emerging Trends in International and Comparative Law* (Cambridge: Cambridge University Press, 2008) 540.

Scheppele, Kim Lane, 'A Realpolitik Defense of Social Rights' (2004) 82 *Texas Law Review* 1921.

Schneiderman, David, *Constitutionalizing Economic Globalization* (Cambridge: Cambridge University Press, 2007).

Schwartz, Herman, 'Do Economic and Social Rights Belong in a Constitution?' (1995) 10 *American University Journal of International Law and Policy* 1233.

Scott, Craig, 'Reaching Beyond (without Abandoning) the Category of "Economic, Social and Cultural Rights"' (1999) 21 *Human Rights Quarterly* 633.

Scott, Craig, 'Towards a Principled, Pragmatic Judicial Role' (1999) 1(4) *ESR Review* 4.

Scott, Craig and Macklem, Patrick, 'Constitutional Ropes of Sand or Justiciable Guarantees? Social Rights in a New South African Constitution' (1992) 141 *University of Pennsylvania Law Review* 1.

Scott, Craig and Alston, Philip, 'Adjudicating Constitutional Priorities in a Transnational Context: A Comment on *Soobramooney*'s Legacy and *Grootboom*'s Promise' (2000) 16 *South African Journal on Human Rights* 206.

Setalvad, Atul, 'The Supreme Court on Human Rights and Social Justice: Changing Perspectives', in Kirpal, Desai, Subramanium, Dhavan and Ramachandran (eds.), *Supreme But Not Infallible: Essays in Honour of the Supreme Court of India* (New Delhi: Oxford University Press, 2004) 232.

Shah, Sheetal, 'Illuminating the Possible in the Developing World: Guaranteeing the Human Right to Health in India' (1999) 32 *Vanderbilt Journal of Transnational Law* 435.

Shankar, Shylashri and Mehta, Pratap Bhanu, 'Courts and Socioeconomic Rights in India', in Gauri and Brinks (eds.), *Courting Social Justice: Judicial Enforcement of Social and Economic Rights in the Developing World* (Cambridge: Cambridge University Press, 2008) 146.

Sharma, Brij Kishore, *Introduction to the Constitution of India* (2nd edn, New Delhi: Prentice-Hall of India, 2004).

Sharpe, Robert and Roach, Kent, *The Charter of Rights and Freedoms* (3rd edn, Toronto: Irwin Law Inc., 2005).

Shaw, Malcolm, *International Law* (6th edn, Cambridge: Cambridge University Press, 2008).

Siegel, Jonathan, 'A Theory of Justiciability' (2007) 86 *Texas Law Review* 73.

Silverstein, Gordon, *Law's Allure: How Law Shapes, Constrains, Saves and Kills Politics* (New York: Cambridge University Press, 2009).

Sloth-Nielsen, Julia, 'Extending Access to Social Assistance to Permanent Residents' (2004) 5(3) *ESR Review* 9.

Sossin, Lorne, 'Towards a Two-Tier Constitution? The Poverty of Health Rights', in Flood, Roach and Sossin (eds.), *Access to Care, Access to Justice: The Legal Debate Over Private Health Insurance in Canada* (Toronto: University of Toronto Press, 2005) 161.

Sripati, Vijayashri, 'Towards Fifty Years of Constitutionalism and Fundamental Rights in India: Looking Back to See Ahead' (1998) 14 *American University International Law Review* 413.

Stark, Barbara, 'Jam Tomorrow: Distributive Justice and the Limits of International Economic Law' (2010) 30 *Boston College Third World Law Journal* 3.

Steiner, Henry, Alston, Philip and Goodman, Ryan, *International Human Rights in Context – Law, Politics and Morals* (3nd edn, Oxford: Oxford University Press, 2008).

Stone Sweet, Alec and Mathews, Jud, 'Proportionality, Balancing and Global Constitutionalism' (2008) 47 *Columbia Journal of Transnational Law* 72.

Sturm, Susan, 'A Normative Theory of Public Law Remedies' (1991) 79 *Georgetown Law Journal* 1355.

Sudarshan, R., '"Stateness" and Democracy in India's Constitution', in Hasan, Sridharan and Sudarshan (eds.), *India's Living Constitution* (London: Anthem Press, 2005) 159.

Sunstein, Cass R., *Designing Democracy: What Constitutions Do* (Oxford: Oxford University Press, 2001).

Sunstein, Cass R., *The Second Bill of Rights: FDR's Unfinished Revolution and Why We Need It More Than Ever* (New York: Basic Books, 2004).

Swart, Mia, 'Left Out in the Cold? Crafting Constitutional Remedies for the Poorest of the Poor' (2005) 21 *South African Journal on Human Rights* 215.

Templeman, Lord, 'The Supreme Court and the Constitution', in Kirpal, Desai, Subramanium, Dhavan and Ramachandran (eds.), *Supreme But Not Infallible: Essays in Honour of the Supreme Court of India* (New Delhi: Oxford University Press, 2004) 48.

Thomas, Katherine Reece, 'The Changing Status of International Law in English Domestic Law' (2006) 53 *Netherlands International Law Review* 371.

Tremblay, Luc, 'The Legitimacy of Judicial Review: The Limits of Dialogue Between Courts and Legislatures' (2005) 3 *International Journal of Constitutional Law* 617.

Tsakyakis, Stavros, 'Proportionality: An Assault on Human Rights' (2009) 7 *International Journal of Constitutional Law* 468.

Tushnet, Mark, 'Civil Rights and Social Rights: The Future of the Reconstruction Amendments' (1992) 25 *Loyola of Los Angeles Law Review* 1207.

Tushnet, Mark, 'Alternative Forms of Judicial Review' (2003) 101 *Michigan Law Review* 2781.

Tushnet, Mark, 'New Forms of Judicial Review and the Persistence of Rights- and Democracy-Based Worries' (2003) 38 *Wake Forest Law Review* 813.

Tushnet, Mark, 'Dialogic Judicial Review' (2008) 61 *Arkansas Law Review* 205.

Tushnet, Mark, *Weak Courts, Strong Rights* (New Jersey: Princeton University Press, 2008).

Vaidyanathan, A, 'The Pursuit of Social Justice', in Hasan, Sridharan and Sudarshan (eds.), *India's Living Constitution* (London: Anthem Press, 2005) 284.

Van Bueren, Geraldine, 'Including the Excluded: The Case for an Economic, Social and Cultural Human Rights Act' (2002) *Public Law* 456.

Vandenhole, Wouter, 'Human Rights Law, Development and Social Action Litigation in India' (2002) 2 *Asia-Pacific Journal on Human Rights and the Law* 136.

VanderMay, Maureen Callahan, 'The Role of the Judiciary in India's Constitutional Democracy' (1996) 20 *Hastings International and Comparative Law Review* 103.

Venhola, Ellie, 'Goliath Arisen: Taking Aim at the Health Care Regime in *Auton*' (2005) 20 *Journal of Law and Social Policy* 67.

Vile, M. J. C., *Constitutionalism and the Separation of Powers* (2nd edn, Indianapolis, IN: Liberty Fund Inc., 1998).

Waldron, Jeremy, 'The Core of the Case against Judicial Review' (2006) 115 *Yale Law Journal* 1346.

Walker, Kirsten, 'International Law as a Tool of Constitutional Interpretation' (2002) 28 *Monash University Law Review* 85.

Weede, Erich, 'Human Rights, Limited Government and Capitalism' (2008) 28 *Cato Journal* 35.

Weir, Stuart, *Unequal Britain: Human Rights as a Route to Social Justice* (London: Politico's, 2006).

Weisburd, A. Mark, 'Using International Law to Interpret Domestic Constitutions – Conceptual Problems: Reflections on Justice Kirby's Advocacy of International Law in Domestic Constitutional Jurisprudence' (2006) 21 *American University International Law Review* 365.

Wesson, Murray, '*Grootboom* and Beyond: Reassessing the Socio-Economic Rights Jurisprudence of the South African Constitutional Court' (2004) 20 *South African Journal on Human Rights* 284.

Whelan, Daniel and Donnelly, Jack, 'The West, Economic and Social Rights, and the Global Human Rights Regime: Setting the Record Straight' (2007) 29 *Human Rights Quarterly* 908.

Whyte, Gerry, *Social Inclusion and the Legal System: Public Interest Law in Ireland* (Dublin: Institute of Public Administration, 2002).

Whyte, Gerry, 'The Role of the Supreme Court in Our Democracy: A Response to Mr Justice Hardiman' (2006) 28 *Dublin University Law Journal* 1.

Willheim, Ernst, 'Globalisation, State Sovereignty and Domestic Law: The Australian High Court Rejects International Law as a Proper Influence on Constitutional Interpretation' (2005) 1/2 *Asia-Pacific Journal on Human Rights and the Law* 1.

Williams, Lucy, 'Welfare and Legal Entitlements: The Social Roots of Poverty', in Kairys (ed.), *The Politics of Law: A Progressive Critique* (3rd edn, New York: Basic Books, 1998) 569.

Wiseman, David, 'Methods of Protection of Social and Economic Rights in Canada', in Coomans (ed.), *Justiciability of Economic and Social Rights* (Antwerp: Intersentia, 2006) 173.

Wiseman, David, 'Taking Competence Seriously', in Young, Boyd, Brodsky and Day (eds.), *Poverty: Rights, Social Citizenship and Legal Activism* (Vancouver: UBC Press, 2007) 263.

Woods, Jeanne M., 'Justiciable Social Rights as a Critique of the Liberal Paradigm' (2003) 38 *Texas International Law Journal* 763.

Woods, Jeanne M., 'Emerging Paradigms of Protection for "Second-Generation" Human Rights' (2005) 6 *Loyola Journal of Public Interest Law* 103.

Woods, Jeanne M. and Lewis, Hope, *Human Rights in the Global Marketplace: Economic, Social and Cultural Dimensions* (New York: Transnational, 2005).

Worden, Nigel, *The Making of Modern South Africa* (2nd edn, Oxford: Blackwell, 1995).

Yeshanew, Sisay, 'Combining the "Minimum Core" and "Reasonableness" Models of Reviewing Socio-Economic Rights' (2008) 9(3) *ESR Review* 8.

Young, Katharine, 'Conceptualising Minimalism in Socio-Economic Rights' (2008) 9(2) *ESR Review* 6.

Young, Margot, 'Change at the Margins: *Eldridge* v. *British Columbia (AG)* and *Vriend* v. *Alberta*' (1998) 10 *Canadian Journal of Women and the Law* 244.

Young, Margot, 'Section 7 and the Politics of Social Justice' (2005) 38 *University of British Columbia Law Review* 539.

Young, Margot, 'Introduction', in Young, Boyd, Brodsky and Day (eds.), *Poverty: Rights, Social Citizenship and Legal Activism* (Vancouver: UBC Press, 2007) 1.

Young, Margot, 'Why Rights Now? Law and Desperation', in Young, Boyd, Brodsky and Day (eds.), *Poverty: Rights, Social Citizenship and Legal Activism* (Vancouver: UBC Press, 2007) 317.

Young, Margot, 'Rights, the Homeless, and Social Change: Reflections on *Victoria (City)* v. *Adams* (BCSC)' (2010) 164 *BC Studies: British Columbian Quarterly* 101.

Index

Schneiderman, David 205
Schwartz, Herman 2, 9
Scott, Craig 28, 54, 57, 110, 168, 179, 181, 183, 184, 193, 200, 204
separation of powers/balance between courts and elected branches of government 3, 11, 21, 168–9; approaching anew 182–6, 199, 201; Canada 109, 111–16, 119, 121, 122–3, 125, 129, 130, 131, 132–3, 135, 136, 137; CESCR: General Comment No. 9 38; constitutional dialogue *see separate entry*; historical rationale(s) for doctrine 169–72; India 85–6, 88–9, 101, 102, 103, 104, 105–6; international law 25, 27; Ireland 138, 139–42, 145, 147, 151, 152–4, 155–6, 157–62, 163, 164, 165, 166, 167, 176, 182–3; 'problem' with socio-economic rights 2, 8, 9, 12, 14, 15, 16–17; smorgasbord of judicial review 172–7; South Africa 50–1, 55, 56–7, 60–1, 68–9, 71, 72, 76
Setalvad, Atul 80
Shah, Sheetal 84
Shankar, Shylashri 194
Sharma, Brij Kishore 79, 80, 81, 84, 87, 89–90, 142
Sharpe, Robert 108, 113, 116, 117, 124, 130, 132, 136
Shaw, Malcolm 23
shelter/housing 3, 4–5, 180; Canada 111, 125, 126, 135; ICESCR 31, 36; India 79n3, 95–6, 98, 102, 104; Ireland 147, 152–4, 157, 163, 164–5; South Africa 52, 57–9, 71; UDHR 29
Shue, Henry 14
Siegel, Jonathon 15, 16
Silverstein, Gordon 197, 200
Sloth-Nielsen, Julia 64
social exclusion 5
social justice 4–5, 17, 202; Canada 124; India 84, 86, 100; Ireland 141–2, 146; South Africa 51, 54
social movements 202, 203
social rights 3
social security/welfare: Canada 111, 126, 127–30, 133–4; ICCPR: non-discrimination (Art 26) 45–6; Ireland 157; minimum level of income 3, 5; South Africa 52, 62–4

socio-economic rights 2–3, 199–200; as constitutional rights 5–7, 20, 178–82; courts' limited institutional capacity 12, 13–14; defensible judicial role *see* model adjudicative framework; definition of 3–6; different paradigms: protection of *see* models for protection of; judicial enforcement of 7–8; limits of 'rights talk' 201–4; non-justiciability/justiciability of *see separate entry*; not real rights 9, 10–11; political economy of human rights 205–7; positive–negative dichotomy 9, 12, 14–15; principled objections to 9, 10–12; 'problem' with 8–17; prospects for future 207–8; undemocratic: judicial enforcement of 9, 11–12, 16
Sossin, Lorne 132, 133
South Africa 20, 48–9, 75–7, 186–7; burden of proof 67; children 52, 57–8; debate over Constitution 50–1; debating jurisprudence of Constitutional Court 66–75; declaratory orders 59, 61, 65, 73–4, 194; health care 52, 55–7, 60–2; housing 52, 57–9, 71; human dignity 63–4, 66; jurisprudence of Constitutional Court 55–66; life, right to (s. 11) 64–5, 66; mandatory orders 61–2, 63–5, 73, 75; minimum core approach 58, 60, 62, 68, 69–72, 187; neo-liberalism 206; non-discrimination 62–4; non-implementation of orders 74–5, 76, 192; post-apartheid and new South African Constitution 49–55; progressive realisation 52, 58; proportionality analysis 63, 67; reasonableness review standard 57–62, 65, 66–72, 187–8; remedies 59, 61–2, 63–5, 73–5, 192, 194; resource scarcity 52, 56, 63, 64, 65; security on train services 64–6; separation of powers 50–1, 55, 56–7, 60–1, 68–9, 71, 72, 76; social security 52, 62–4; supervisory jurisdiction 61, 73, 75; transformative Constitution 53–5, 77
sovereignty 25, 27
Sripati, Vijayashri 87